New Canadian Readings

THE DEPRESSION IN CANADA

Responses to Economic Crisis

New Canadian Readings

THE DEPRESSION
IN CANADA

Responses to Economic Crisis

Edited by
Michiel Horn

Copp Clark Pitman Ltd.
A Longman Company
Toronto

ISBN 0-7730-4761-1

Editing: Camilla Jenkins and Kate Eccles
Design: Kathy Cloutier and Susan Coull
Cover: Illustration by Susan Coull, based on photograph
  Public Archives Canada/C2R94
Typesetting: Compeer Typographic Services Ltd.
Printing and Binding: Alger Press Ltd.

Canadian Cataloguing in Publication Data

Main entry under title:
The Depression in Canada

(New Canadian readings)
Bibliography: p.
ISBN 0-7730-4761-1

1. Depressions — 1929 — Canada. 2. Canada — Politics and government
— 1930–1939.* 3. Canada — Social conditions — 1930–
1939.* I. Horn, Michiel, 1939–
II. Series.

FC577.D46 1988   971.06′2′3   C87-094173-9
HB3717 1929.D46 1988

Copp Clark Pitman Ltd.
2775 Matheson Blvd. East
Mississauga, Ontario
L4W 4P7

Associated Companies:
  Longman Group Ltd., London
  Longman Inc., New York
  Longman Cheshire Pty., Melbourne
  Longman Paul Pty., Auckland

Printed and bound in Canada.

FOREWORD

New Canadian Readings is an on-going series of inexpensive books intended to bring some of the best recent work by this country's scholars to the attention of students in Canada. Each volume consists of ten or more articles or book sections, carefully selected to present a fully-formed thesis about some critical aspect of Canadian development. Where useful, public documents or even private letters and statistical materials may be used as well to convey a different and fresh perspective.

The authors of the readings selected for inclusion in this volume (and all the others in the series) are all first-rank scholars, those who are doing the hard research that is rapidly changing our understanding of this country. Quite deliberately, the references for each selection have been retained, thus making additional research as easy as possible.

Like the authors of the individual articles, the editors of each volume are also scholars of note, completely up-to-date in their areas of specialization and, as the introductions demonstrate, fully aware of the changing nature of the debates within their professions and genres of research. The list of additional readings provided by the editor of each volume will steer readers to materials that could not be included because of space limitations.

This series will continue into the foreseeable future, and the General Editor is pleased to invite suggestions for additional topics.

J.L. Granatstein
General Editor

CONTENTS

INTRODUCTION

A half-century later, the Depression of the 1930s has not yet lost its power to fascinate us. The images of the Dirty Thirties, bread lines, soup kitchens, dust storms, "Bennett buggies" and so on, are still imprinted on the memories of older Canadians. But they are also astonishingly real to younger people who have experienced the 1930s only through stories told by parents or, increasingly, by grandparents. At the same time scholarly interest in the Depression and in Canadian responses to it seems to be increasing. Economic, political, social and intellectual historians have found in the 1930s ample scope for their talents and concerns. The results of their labours include a growing number of detailed studies, books, and especially articles. Any volume of Depression essays is bound to leave out many good articles.

The economic downswing began in the summer of 1929 and ended in the spring of 1933. The uneven recovery that followed excluded large groups of Canadians, including many unemployed and most Prairie farmers. In 1937–1938 a severe recession interrupted the recovery, which was far from complete when war broke out in September 1939. The war brought full recovery at last, as industrial activity increased rapidly and agriculture also improved. By 1942 unemployment had given way to overemployment, and the Depression was becoming a memory.

Of all the western countries, only the United States underwent a greater decline during the downswing from 1929 to 1933 than did Canada. During that period the gross national product in this country fell by 42 percent in current and 29 percent in constant terms. (The difference reflects the deflation of those years.) National income in 1933 was barely more than half of what it had been in 1929. Industrial activity in the first quarter of 1933, the nadir of the Depression, was 57 percent of the average figure for the years 1925–1929. Imports by volume in 1933 were 43.3 percent of the 1929 figure.[1] Canada and the great majority of its people had become significantly poorer.

Business failures, constricted credit, unemployment, deflation: none of these was new. For well over a century the world and Canadian economies had suffered from periodic financial panics and economic slumps. During the first three decades of the twentieth century there had already been two major depressions, one shortly before the 1914–1918 war and one in the early 1920s. Many people suffered severely during these crises, farmers, industrial workers, and small businesspeople in particular. But those economic crises had passed and their major lesson — that in industrialized societies a growing number of people simply could not cope with the results of a depression — had not been learnt or had been forgotten. The 1930s presented economic collapse in its harshest form.

At bottom, depressions were the result of overproduction and underconsumption, compounded by problems in the financial system. Economies in which many people were too poor to purchase more than the necessities of life—and some too poor even for that—but in which new techniques in agriculture and industry were increasing productivity, were ones in which the capacity to produce goods regularly outstripped the ability to consume them. Problems in marketing periodically prompted declining prices and profits, accompanied by business failures and growing unemployment. Banks that were overextended restricted credit, thus intensifying the deflationary pressures that were part of every depression. Declining prices tended to hit farmers particularly hard because they generally reacted to deflation by increasing production, thereby glutting the market even more. Servicing debts incurred during the preceding period of economic growth became more difficult, prompting defaults that brought down some banks as well as some of the people or companies they had lent to.

Economic slumps in the nineteenth century were increasingly devastating as farming became more capital-intensive, and thereby more debt-ridden, and as the urban working class grew in size, there developed an ever larger body of people who simply could not supply themselves with the necessities of life during a slump. Furthermore, the economy had become highly international. Difficulties in one part of the world spread rapidly to other parts. In theory depressions corrected themselves: eventually the world economy would begin to recover after reaching equilibrium at lower levels of prices and activity. In practice this process was unpalatable to almost everyone, not least to businesspeople and politicians. In the half-century before the 1914–1918 war Great Britain, the most powerful national economy in the world, had come to assume responsibility for stabilizing a world economic system that was inherently unstable. From the late 1840s on Britain maintained a relatively open market for distress goods (goods that were in oversupply). After 1874, moreover, Britain provided long-term counter-cyclical lending; that is, lent abroad when domestic investment slackened and vice versa, and discounted in crisis, her bankers acting as lenders of last resort. Thus Britain had mitigated international economic crises that otherwise would have been more serious than they were.

The war gravely weakened Britain and ended her power to stabilize the world economy, though this fact did not become clear to many people until after 1929. The one country that now had the strength to take Britain's prewar position was the United States. Isolationist sentiment was strong in that country, however, and its political and business leaders were unwilling to assume the responsibility that came with strength. This helps to explain the severity of the Depression of the early

1930s. Nobody tried to counteract the effects of the slump. Far from acting as a market for distress goods, the United States joined other countries in actively trying to reduce imports. American long-term lending was cyclical: in the early 1930s investment both at home and abroad declined. American bankers, moreover, increasingly concerned about the weakness of the U.S. banking system, were unwilling or unable to act as discounters in crisis. As a consequence, American trade and financial policies reinforced rather than dampened the shocks that hit the international economic system in the late 1920s: the overproduction of wheat and several other commodities, and the Wall Street stock market crash of October 1929.

Some Canadian leaders in the early 1930s used the argument that the slump was entirely the result of international conditions as a justification for doing nothing. Several of the causes of the devastating declines in Canadian production and income, however, were internal. These included pre-Depression patterns of investment, the heavy burden of debt carried into the 1930s, and government policies with respect to trade, taxation, and expenditures that were too often inappropriate and made matters worse rather than better.

There were major surges in domestic investment before the 1914–1918 war and in the later 1920s. In several industries, among them pulp and paper, railways, automobiles, and construction, as well as base metal mining and agriculture, there was by 1930 significant overinvestment and excess capacity. (There were, no doubt, many Canadians who lacked cars and adequate housing but they lacked the money to buy these goods.) Further opportunities for profitable investment were few. Even after the recovery was underway in the mid-1930s, the existing plant and equipment often sufficed to satisfy the demand. Unemployment stayed high in the construction and capital goods industries.

One legacy of the earlier investment booms was debt. In order to increase productivity, farmers and business corporations had borrowed in the expectation that future growth would make repayment relatively easy. The Depression gave the lie to such optimism. When growth turned into decline, and deflation became the new reality, the debts increased in real terms. They imposed rigid costs: interest had to be paid annually, semi-annually, or monthly, and there were often commitments for the repayment of the principal. The amounts of the payments were fixed while the money available to make them fell. Furthermore, more than four-fifths of the money that farmers and corporations had borrowed had come from abroad. Much of it was ultimately payable in New York, in American currency. This inhibited government-sponsored efforts to reflate the Canadian economy.

Government policies and their contribution to the economic crisis will be discussed later. The components of that crisis affected different areas, groups, and individuals with differing force. But such phenomena as deflation, increased barriers to trade, declining profit and economic activity, growing unemployment, debt, and fiscal crisis that threatened to overwhelm all levels of government, were interrelated. A problem in one industry was apt to spread to other industries and areas, just as a problem in one country was apt to involve others.

One example should suffice to make the point. World prices for wheat were particularly low in the early 1930s. The price per bushel, which had averaged $1.02 during 1925–1929, averaged only 35 cents in 1932. This would have been bad enough for the Prairie economy, but in addition a decade-long drought affected a large part of southern Saskatchewan. Average yield per acre in that province had been 17.8 bushels during 1925–1929; during 1930–1934 the average yield per acre was 10.7 bushels.[2] The effects on farm incomes were devastating. The purchasing power of much of the population of the three Prairie provinces dwindled. Net money income from Prairie agriculture in 1932–1933 was only 6 percent of what it had been in 1928–1929! Total per capita income in the three provinces was only 40 percent in 1933 of what it had been in 1928–1929.[3] When farmers ceased to be able to buy goods and services, there were few Prairie people who did not soon feel the consequences.

The distress on the Prairies spread far beyond that area. Manufacturers of farm equipment, automobiles, radios and hundreds of other things lost a major part of their market. Firms like Eaton's and Simpsons, whose mail order catalogues were a well-established part of farm life, had to do without old and valued customers who no longer had money to buy their goods. Service industries—life insurance and mortgage companies, for example—found it ever more difficult to sell to farmers and even to collect on debts owing to them. Furthermore, when the movement of wheat slowed, the railways earned less. They responded by laying off workers and reducing their purchases of such things as rails and boxcars. This brought declining sales and profits, and growing unemployment, in the railway car and steel industries, chiefly in Ontario and Cape Breton. Lower volumes of freight threw longshoremen out of work in Vancouver, the Lakehead and Montreal. Suppliers to and shareholders of the affected industries felt the effects when purchases declined and dividends were cut or eliminated altogether. Some corporations went into receivership. Thus the impact of low wheat prices reverberated through large parts of the Canadian economy, affecting people who would not have been able to tell wheat from rye if their lives had depended on it.

The consumer price index dropped by almost a quarter from 1929 to 1933. For those on fixed incomes, such as pensioners, this was a boon, but for most Canadians it was the opposite. The deflation hit commodity producers particularly hard. The prices of farm products, fish, metals, paper, and lumber dropped steeply. (Gold was the main exception to this rule, and gold-mining towns became islands of prosperity, particularly after the American government raised the price of gold against the dollar in 1933–1934.) Average export prices for all Canadian goods, most of them primary and processed natural goods, were only 62.6 percent in 1933 of what they had been in 1929. Import prices, however, reflecting somewhat less startling declines in the prices of manufactured goods, were still 71.3 percent of what they had been four years earlier.[4] Canada's terms of trade had deteriorated significantly.

The economic warfare of the period complicated the picture. Its tactics included high protective tariffs, export subsidies, the "dumping" of surpluses in foreign markets, and currency devaluation. An early blow in the international trade war, perhaps the most damaging one for Canada, was the American Smoot-Hawley tariff of 1930. Agricultural exporters in Ontario and Quebec soon felt its effects. Further U.S. duties on lumber and copper in 1932 also hurt Canadian producers, already hard hit by a decline in the American construction industry. The Canadian government joined the mad scramble to protect domestic industries at the expense of foreigners. The economic war, selfish and short-sighted, served no one's long-term interests. As the American economic historian Charles P. Kindleberger has written: "When every country turned to protect its national private interest, the world public interest went down the drain, and with it the private interests of all."[5]

Also of major importance to Canada was the British decision in the fall of 1931 to leave the gold standard. The failure of a major Austrian bank, the *Kreditanstalt*, in May had created serious difficulties for the German and then the British banking systems. Britain's abandonment of the gold standard was one result; the devaluation of the pound sterling against the U.S. dollar followed immediately. The Canadian dollar lost value against the American dollar but rose against the pound sterling. The British government abandoned free trade at the same time, seeking now to protect domestic manufacturers against foreign competition. As a result it became more difficult to export to Britain and to the sterling bloc generally, including Scandinavia as well as most of the British Empire. Furthermore, because the Scandinavian currencies lost value with the pound sterling, forest products exported from northern Europe became cheaper than Canada's competing exports. A matching Canadian devaluation was virtually out of the question. Not only did Canada lack a central bank that might have carried out a carefully planned policy of currency depreciation, but the large proportion of Canadian debt payable in U.S. funds was a powerful incentive to try to maintain the value of our dollar. (Not until 1933–1934, when the United States devalued its currency, did Canadian debtors get some relief.) In the aftermath of Britain's actions, a slight economic rally that had become noticeable in Canada and the United States early in 1931 came to an end.

A loss of confidence in the future was an important feature of the Depression. Having for several years been eager to invest and spend, individuals and corporations became much more cautious. Both international and domestic markets contracted in the early 1930s. Whereas prices of export goods dropped steeply as a result, however, prices of those goods and services that enjoyed either tariff or natural protection tended to be "sticky."[6] (So were wages and salaries in many of the protected industries.) In the absence of genuine competition, and burdened with heavy overhead costs, manufacturers preferred to try to maintain prices at the expense of production. Servicing debts incurred during earlier periods of expansion was bound to seem more urgent than producing goods for an increasingly glutted market. Layoffs hit both the export-oriented and the protected industries, and unemployment soon mounted. Like those farmers and fishermen who saw their incomes dwindle because of low prices, the unemployed had to cut back. There was as yet no unemployment insurance scheme which would have maintained incomes and thus consumption to some extent. Facing destitution, the unemployed were forced to limit their purchases to essentials, thereby adding to the economic decline. Unemployment bred further unemployment.

It also bred problems of providing relief that Canada and Canadians failed to resolve. Coping with unemployment was thought to be primarily the responsibility of workers; they were supposed to save from their wages enough money to tide them over hard times. (Because the wages of labourers were usually so low that most working-class families lived in poverty, few of them actually had savings.) Should that fail, they were expected to get help from family, friends and volunteer charitable agencies. In extreme cases, when these devices failed, they could turn to local government for relief where it was available.

Public poor relief varied from province to province. In Quebec the task of providing relief rested mainly with church-related agencies, which sometimes had access to public funds. In wintertime, when seasonal unemployment was common in the cities, snow clearing was a way in which municipalities could provide for the unemployed. The Atlantic provinces offered relief to the destitute out of taxes paid by local property owners for that purpose; some sort of work was often exacted in exchange. In Ontario and the four western provinces no coherent system existed for dealing with paupers. Traditionally, however, municipalities were supposed to offer assistance, with the provincial governments acting as a sort of backstop, providing funds where local resources were inadequate. Local practices varied, but the principle of "less eligibility" was universal. This meant that poor relief was deliberately ungenerous, providing less income than the wages of the worst-paid employment, thereby guaranteeing that the able-bodied would not seek relief so long as there was any work available. Public relief was a last resort, available only to those who had exhausted all other avenues and who, through illness, disability or plain bad luck, could not survive without it.

All the evidence indicates that people hated to ask for relief. The absence of work, however, forced hundreds of thousands to "go on the pogey." To accept relief was to admit defeat and failure. Reliefers and their families felt themselves to be humiliatingly stigmatized as "dead-beats," people who were unable to make their own way in the world and had to rely on make-work and handouts. Early schemes of relief generally required its recipients to work for what they got on municipal projects designed to relieve unemployment. This was more costly, however, than direct relief, which virtually abandoned the principle that recipients should in some sense earn their incomes. Direct relief could be paid in cash or in vouchers for goods; the latter was experienced as being particularly humiliating. Some work might still be required, but it was infrequent and generally served no purpose other than occupying the reliefer's time.

Immigrants who applied for relief were no longer desired in Canada, and thousands were deported back to their native countries. It is not surprising, therefore, that some of those who qualified for relief found ways to avoid it and the disgrace that attended it. Middle-class people typically tried to rely on near relatives or friends, perhaps moving in with parents until their luck turned. A good many country-dwellers, by denying themselves most or all money purchases, also managed to stay off the relief rolls. This was less common in towns and cities, where unemployed wage-earners had little or no opportunity to grow their own food or cut their own firewood, and rarely had relatives prosperous enough to be able to carry them.

Average annual unemployment in 1929 was 4.2 percent. According to one estimate — no accurate statistics are available for that era — it reached a staggering 26.6 percent in 1933.[7] By the late winter of 1933, hundreds of thousands of people were out of work. On April 1 of that year, more than 1.4 million urban Canadians depended on relief to keep them alive. In addition, several hundred thousand country-dwellers got relief, including more than two hundred thousand people in southern Saskatchewan who were wards of the Saskatchewan Relief Commission and indirectly of the federal government.

These appalling numbers — the total population of Canada was only 10.4 million in 1931 — overwhelmed the country's accustomed ways of dealing with destitution. First local governments and then several of the provinces pleaded to be relieved of the financial burden that had descended on them, a burden that became a crisis. The basic feature of this crisis was that, even as the costs of relief mounted, tax revenues fell at all levels of government. As incomes, imports, and consumption of goods and services declined, so did tax revenues. At the local level, more and more rate payers were in arrears with their property taxes. Governments responded by cutting all expenses that could be cut and by raising taxes in the early 1930s. Total taxes levied by all three levels of government averaged approximately 16.5 percent of national income in the years 1926 to 1930. By 1933 total taxes were 26.5 percent of national income![8] The chief objective was to try to keep government budgets in balance. However, the drastic measures adopted failed to achieve that objective while helping to make the Depression worse. The reduction of governmental spending for goods and services reinforced what was already happening in the private sector. Furthermore, the growing share of national income taken by government was not used for any bold initiatives that might have reversed the downward cycle of the economy. Instead it went chiefly to service growing loads of debt and to keep the destitute barely fed, clothed and warm.

Not only were governments of the day constrained by outworn thinking about budgets—the counter-cyclical ideas of John Maynard Keynes were as yet little known in Canada[9]—but many of them faced the urgent necessity of servicing debts. Like many corporations, most municipal and provincial governments had incurred substantial debt during the investment booms of the Laurier years and the mid- and late 1920s. The federal government had borrowed heavily in order to help finance Canada's contribution to the 1914–1918 war, and in the aftermath of that war had guaranteed the indebtedness of the new Canadian National Railways system. Total government debt, including the debt of the CNR, was almost $6.2 billion in 1930, $3.8 billion owed by Ottawa and the CNR, $1.2 billion by provinces, and $1.2 billion by the municipalities. The size of these amounts is more easily appreciated when they are compared to net revenue and expenses for all governments during that year, $789 million and $836 million respectively. Debt charges took more than 47 percent of Ottawa's current revenue, and approximately 17 percent of the combined revenues of the provinces and municipalities. There were wide variations, however: Alberta's debt charges were 32.4 percent of current revenue in 1930; Quebec's only 4.9 percent. On the other hand, no municipalities were more indebted as a group than those in Quebec.[10]

During a period of deflation these debts weighed ever more heavily. Moreover, persistent budget deficits forced many governments to borrow to the limits of their capacity. Total government debt increased by $1.7 billion from 1930 to 1937. Debt charges constituted a growing proportion of both revenue and expense. In 1933 interest paid on its own and the CNR's debts exacted approximately two-thirds of all federal government revenue, while the debt charges of the provinces and municipalities combined were a third of their revenues! At the same time expenditures for relief sky-rocketed. Totalling $18.4 million for all levels of government in 1930, they were $98 million by 1933 and peaked at $173 million in 1935. The federal share rose during that period, and since much of the provincial share was borrowed from Ottawa, the federal government became the chief supporter of the destitute. All the same, from 1930 to 1936 Ottawa spent more in meeting CNR interest payments than it committed to relief either directly or through its share of provincial expenses, even though by 1936 it spent a combined amount of $81 million on relief.[11]

By the standards of the time that was a huge sum. Even larger were the unavoidable deficits, as high as $277 million for all levels of government in 1932. This represented a crisis in public finance that led many municipalities and eventually one province, Alberta, to default on their debts. Manitoba, Saskatchewan, and British Columbia escaped insolvency only because of loans from Ottawa. The federal government had no trouble borrowing, but it did not add eagerly to the public debt. No level of government felt much incentive to be generous to the unemployed, therefore, and the municipal governments, who were most directly concerned, were quite unable to be generous.

What was done was almost invariably done on the cheap. A striking example of this were the single men's relief camps established by the Dominion government in 1932. Single men presented a special problem to authorities. In order to cut costs, many communities made it very difficult for single young men and women to get relief in their own right. Many of them could in that way be induced to live with their parents. Others, however, reluctant to remain dependent in that way, moved out in search of greener pastures elsewhere in Canada. A good many young men, and some young women, took to the roads and rails in search of work. They joined what had always been a sizable group of transients, usually immigrant men looking for jobs. These transients did not qualify for relief in any municipality because they rarely lived anywhere long enough to meet residency requirements. During the early 1930s their numbers increased greatly.

During 1932 there was growing pressure on the federal government to establish and finance relief camps. R.B. Bennett was reluctant to undertake responsibility for transients and the single unemployed: it was bound to cost money and there was unlikely to be a political payoff. But lack of funds at the municipal and provincial levels in the West, where the large numbers of transients seemed particularly menacing, forced Ottawa to take action. In the autumn of 1932 the federal government authorized the establishment of camps for unemployed single men; by the spring of 1933 they were expanding rapidly. They were under the penny-pinching administration of the Department of National Defence; the men who entered the camps were provided with room, board, work clothes and an "allowance" of twenty cents a day for personal expenses. Those who worked for the camps were little better off: in late 1934 a camp physician got $70 and a camp engineer $60 a month. But General McNaughton's mandate did not allow him to be more generous. He pointed out in June 1934, that in the period from 1 November 1933 to 31 March 1934 "the total cost per man day of relief has been $1.17, and this includes every expenditure made under the Relief Act. . . ."[12] Given that the camps' objectives had been to keep single men away from the cities and out of trouble at minimum expense, the Department of National Defence had obviously done well. But McNaughton said nothing about the despair of the men who inhabited the camps; that was not his responsibility.

A change in government in 1935 brought a change in policy: the following year the Liberals led by William Lyon Mackenzie King closed the camps. This was a campaign promise King had no objection to carrying out. Not only were the camps unpopular, but in King's view the men in them were the responsibility of lower levels of government and an unwarranted drain on the federal treasury. Closing the camps did not solve the problem of transiency, but it did save Ottawa some money!

Throughout much of the 1930s the emphasis, for individuals and business corporations as well for governments and their agencies, was on restraint and belt-tightening. Most Canadians regarded the Depression as a natural disaster that would eventually give way to renewed prosperity. In the meantime they sought to rely on their own efforts and to last through the economic slump. "Toughing it through" was easier for some than for others, however, and for hundreds of thousands of Canadians it was impossible. They could not manage, and they suffered enormous hardships in nevertheless trying to make a go of things. Banding together with others who faced the same problems sometimes helped; at least it gave people a sense of solidarity and sharing. But to a growing number of Canadians the government became the key to survival. At the same time the prestige of businessmen, which had reached a peak in the 1920s, fell. Their inability to solve the problems of the Depression became too starkly evident to be ignored. Although governments really managed to do little better, there was nevertheless hope, embraced by a significant and growing number of voters, that new leaders with new ideas might do the trick.

Many Canadians continued to hope for a return to a past that, rather undeservedly, took on a golden glow in retrospect. Far-sighted people knew that such a return was impossible, and that in any case the 1920s had roared for only a minority. In the Depression, Blair Neatby has written, Canadians "were grappling almost for the first time with many of the problems which are still with us. A study of the 1930s is an introduction to the Canada of today."[13] The Depression laid the basis for later advances towards government intervention in the economy, and towards the modified welfare state that Canada eventually became. In that sense the Depression is still with us. Some of the central features of the positive state are now under attack. It therefore important to read how Canadians half a century ago tried to cope with the problems of an economic slump, unprotected by institutions like unemployment insurance and government medical care that perhaps we take too much for granted.

Notes

1. Data have been obtained from Albert E. Safarian, *The Canadian Economy in the Great Depression* (1959; Toronto 1970). See particularly chapter 3.

2. Seymour Martin Lipset, *Agrarian Socialism*, rev. ed. (Garden City, N.Y., 1968), 46.

3. Canada, Royal Commission on Dominion-Provincial Relations, *Report*, Book 1, *Canada: 1867–1939* (Ottawa, 1940), 150.

4. Safarian, *The Canadian Economy*, 82.

5. Charles P. Kindleberger, *The World in Depression, 1929–1939* (Berkeley and Los Angeles, 1973), 292.

6. Many service industries enjoy "natural" protection, e.g. financial services, transportation, education, and government services, in which competition from abroad is weak or non-existent.

7. James Struthers, *No Fault of Their Own: Unemployment and the Canadian Welfare State 1914–1941* (Toronto, 1983), 215.

8. J. Harvey Perry, *Taxes, Tariffs, & Subsidies* (Toronto, 1955), 1: 275.

9. See Douglas Owram, *The Government Generation* (Toronto, 1986), chap. 8.

10. Canada, Royal Commission on Dominion-Provincial Relations, *Report*, Book 3, *Documentation*, 16, 42-45, 67.

11. Ibid., 18, 97, 120.

12. A.G.L. McNaughton to R.K. Finlayson, 22 June 1934, R.B. Bennett Papers, vol. 805, Harriet Irving Library, University of New Brunswick, reproduced in Michiel Horn's *The Dirty Thirties* (Toronto, 1972), 329-30.

13. H. Blair Neatby, *The Politics of Chaos* (Toronto, 1972), 1.

A RESPONSE TO THE DEPRESSION: THE LOCAL COUNCIL OF WOMEN OF VANCOUVER†

MARY PATRICIA POWELL

The National Council of Women of Canada was founded in 1893 to represent all women in Canada who were interested in organized work in any field. By 1937, it claimed affiliation with sixteen nationally organized societies and forty-nine local councils, including one in Vancouver. It was credited with 500 000 members, making it the largest women's organization in Canada. The Council had been recognized soon after its founding as the most influential group of women in Canada. This recognition was aided by the fact that Lady Aberdeen, wife of the then Governor-General, had founded it and become the first president. In a 1934 address, the Governor-General had acknowledged the primacy of the Council's position, remarking that whenever he spoke to the Council, he felt he was speaking to "the whole great body of Canadian women who are devoting themselves to public service all over this immense country."[1]

The Council considered itself non-partisan, although it aimed to act as a political pressure group for women. Lady Aberdeen had stated that the Council "does not deal with politics, nor ask for the right to vote, nor does it urge the modern dress reform; but nevertheless, the scope of the Council is unlimited, for it includes every branch of moral reform and can take up any question pertaining to women's work and aims in life."[2] The Council aimed to serve as a forum for discussion of topics in

† Barbara Latham and Cathy Kess, eds., *In Her Own Right: Selected Essays on Women's History in B.C.* (Victoria, B.C.: Camosun College, 1980), 255–78. This is an edited version of chapter 3 of Mary Patricia Powell's "Response to The Depression: Three Representative Women's Groups in British Columbia" (M.A. thesis, University of British Columbia, 1977).

which women were interested and to make known to all levels of government the legislation which women wanted, enabling women to speak with one unified voice.

Nevertheless, there were disputes within the Council about its function and nature. As late as 1930, the convenor of the Committee on Child Welfare devoted the majority of her report to a discussion of the nature of the National Council "in order to explain what might otherwise appear to be a rather academic interest, and a lack of practical activity in the Child Welfare program of the Councils."[3] She saw the National Council as primarily a conference and not an operative body:

> The National Council of Women seeks to afford a medium through which the considered opinions and conclusions of the various bodies of Canadian women associated therein may be discussed by a body fully representative of all the participating groups, to the end that judgements, tempered and affected by this interchange of widely differing bodies, may be issued, with the full weight of this corporate authority behind them.[4]

According to this interpretation of the Council's activities, it could act only if, after studying the situation, it found itself better equipped than any other group to initiate action. When questions arose about the efficiency of the Council's use of resolutions and deputations, these methods were defended on the grounds that they had proven very successful in the past. Certainly many reforms which the Council endorsed were enacted by the government.

The Council had campaigned actively for many progressive reforms. From 1910 it had called for women's suffrage, and had supported legislation to improve the legal status and working conditions of women and to provide child and health care, as well as education for the handicapped and for consumers.[5] Even a critic of the Council commented in the 1930s: "Forty or more years ago in its youthful zeal to be the 'voice' through which Canadian women might make themselves heard . . . this Council turned its energies to one crusade after another. It achieved scores of reforms which are now an accepted part of our social, economic, and political life."[6]

The Council of Women was organized on three levels: local, provincial and national. The National Council was actually a federation of many organizations over which its constitution claimed "no power . . . beyond that of suggestion and sympathy." Local councils consisted of at least five societies of women in any locality "federated for the purpose of carrying out the objects of the National Council."[7] Provincial councils, organized after World War One, local councils, and nationally organized societies were known as federated associations.

The real power of the National Council of Women resided in its executive committee, which organized and set the agenda for the annual meetings, and carried on Council business in between such meetings. By its control over the agenda, the executive committee could effectively exclude controversial topics, if it wished, since only a two-thirds majority of those entitled to vote at an annual meeting could suspend the agenda to present an "emergency resolution of national importance."[8] Local councils across Canada were rarely sufficiently unified in purpose to effect a change of the agenda. Yet despite the overriding power of the executive committee, a mere 15 percent of its members constituted a quorum.

In each local council a sub-executive committee composed of the local representatives to the national executive committee wielded the real power. The sub-executive managed day to day business, handled all correspondence from affiliated societies, and drew up the agenda of the national executive committee. However, the sub-executive had no power to withhold resolutions or requests of the national executive committee, and all information from the federated associations had to be forwarded to the executive committee.

Standing committees of the National Council, formed "for the purpose of . . . creating interest in problems relating to the welfare of the country,"[9] included a national convenor elected at the annual meeting and one member from each federated association. The national convenor was responsible for outlining work to be done that year. Thus the work of local committees could be directed firmly from above. However, a resolution of the National Council in 1930 affirmed that no national policy on relief would be set.

The national president, Winnifred Kydd, made a policy comment on the Depression by November 1932: "Practical relief resolves itself today into the study of unemployment and its remedies, and that is receiving the greatest share of the attention of Local Councils throughout the Dominion."[10] As an illustration, Miss Kydd quoted the efforts of various councils: "The canning and preserving of fruits and vegetables, to be donated later to the unemployed; medical work in conjunction with the V.O.N. by assuming responsibility for expensive medical care and providing medical comforts; providing boots and shoes and stockings for children and working people in cooperation with civic authorities in opening clothes depots. . . ."[11] Miss Kydd pointed out that because only the local councils knew community needs, relief programs would have to be handled locally. This was the extent of policy direction given the local councils by their national organization during the 1930s. Therefore, the Vancouver Council was free to shape its own Depression policy.

Unlike many of the other local councils in Canada, the Council of Women in Vancouver noted the effects of the Depression soon after the beginning of the crisis. However, like many others, it did not consider the situation to be an emergency and so its first resolution concerning the Depression simply called for information from the Committee on Trades and Professions for Women. Susan Lane (Mrs. J.A.) Clark, the convenor of the Committee on Trades and Professions for Women in 1930 and representative of the New Era League, had a realistic idea of the grave effects of the Depression on the lives of many business women. When the mayor called a city conference on unemployment, Mrs. Clark attended, representing the Council. In February 1930, she reported to the Council in detail about the discussions held at the conference. Mrs. Clark made the first suggestion for Council reponses to the Depression, recommending that the societies affiliated with the Council "consider the matter of unemployment carefully at their own meetings and invite speakers to explain the subject to them."[12] Then Mrs. Clark moved that the following resolution be passed by the Local Council and forwarded to the National Council: "As unemployment affects women just as much as it does men, any conference, commission or board that may be organized for this matter, official or otherwise, [should] include women as members on the same terms as men."[13] By this resolution, the Local Council in Vancouver had taken action on unemployment, small though it was, and had sent a directive to the National Council. Also, it was the first local council to call the attention of its members to the problem of unemployment. This resolution can be seen in the context of the continuing struggle by the Local Council to secure seats for women on government boards and committees of all kinds, but it was also a genuine response to the Depression. By 1933, the National Council was protesting "the deplorable tendency throughout Canada to entrust the planning, administration and distribution of relief even for families to the administration solely of male officials and the supervision of committees and commissions made up entirely of male members."[14]

By the beginning of 1934, the Vancouver Council still had not been able to place a woman on the local Relief Board, even in an advisory capacity. A new resolution was passed in April, again requesting that women be named to all the committees and boards which were being set up to deal with the situations arising out of the Depression. Because this resolution failed to elicit a response, the Council decided at its May meeting to set up a special committee to consider matters relating to the City Relief Board and to attend its meetings regularly.[15] The women planned that "after showing interest in and sympathy with the work of the Board for some time, the Council will press once more for women representatives on it in an advisory capacity and thus obtain power to bring about desirable improvements in methods of relief distribution."[16] This struggle to have women placed on relief committees continued throughout the Depression.

Although it was interested in many aspects of the Depression, the Local Council of Women devoted most of its attention to the problems of unemployed women. Working women on relief were a relatively new phenomenon during the 1930s. When the crisis began, no provision had been made for them. After many thousands of domestics, secretaries, and clerks were discharged from their positions, it became obvious that some provision for unemployed women had to be made. The Vancouver Local Council of Women was very active in bringing the problems of unemployed women to the attention of the authorities.

The Council's interest in this matter began very early in the decade. In September 1930, a resolution drawn up by Susan Clark, urging relief for women, was endorsed by the Council and forwarded to the City Council, the provincial and Dominion governments:

> Whereas women have always done a great share of the World's Work, and as evolution of the present industrial system has forced women out of the home into a competitive labour market, and Whereas the recent voters census compiled for the recent election, show more women over twenty-one than men in the City of Vancouver, and as all relief and work schemes so far formulated by groups or Government, do not take cognizance of the needs of women. Be it resolved That the Local Council of Women of Greater Vancouver believe that equal consideration and opportunity for work be given to unemployed women, as well as to unemployed men, and further be it resolved That this Council of Women be the medium for conveying this resolution to the various authorities concerned.[17]

In November 1930, Mrs. Clark again proposed an equal opportunity resolution to the Council, asking the City of Vancouver to allow unemployed women to register for relief under a federal government scheme for which the city was already registering unemployed men.

The Local Council during 1930 undertook practical programs for unemployed women. In addition to urging the government to set up registration offices, the Council itself tried to find jobs, housing and meals for unemployed women and girls. In November 1930, the Council began a campaign in the newspapers, urging people to give unemployed women jobs. The "Who will give a woman a job?" campaign was carried on for several months, with the co-operation of the press. The president asked the members to "take this to their associations and treat it very seriously as the conditions existing needed a great deal of help.[18]

Helen (Mrs. Paul) Smith (MLA from 1933 to 1937), a member of Mrs. Clark's committee, in December, 1930, gave a short speech on the housing of unemployed girls. As a consequence, the Council decided to demand of the Million Days Work Fund, a volunteer "make work" organization, that its program for unemployed women included. When the president, Mrs. Kirk, reported back to her sub-executive that the Fund had no provision for unemployed women, she quoted the manager of the campaign who said, "there were very few" unemployed women in any case. Not content with that assessment, the Council was able to persuade the Fund to give unemployed women the same consideration as unemployed men, although married men would continue to be given prior consideration. At the first general meeting in 1931, Mrs. Labsik reported that fifty women had been placed in positions. Most of the jobs had been found either through the individual efforts of members of the unemployment committee or through the co-operation of the Million Days Work Fund.

Although the work of the unemployment committee was commendable, temporary measures could not prove effective in the long run. The committee had found an eating place for women who were completely destitute. It had secured the co-operation of the city relief officer, Colonel Cooper, who had issued meal tickets to a number of women who had applied to the committee. It had also aided the Y.W.C.A. in setting up a workroom for unemployed women, intended particularly to help those women who were not eligible for relief though the regular channels. The committee asked the Council to donate furniture to help set up a hostel for unemployed women. The hostel, "Dunromin", was an important part of the relief program of the Local Council.

In February 1931, the Special Committee on Unemployment of the Local Council presented its report, which was printed in the *Yearbook* of the National Council in 1931, as an outstanding example of what local councils could do to offset the effects of the Depression in their own communities. As yet the National Council had not given the local councils any directions concerning the Depression. Perhaps the Vancouver Local Council acted as it did because of the presence of such knowledgeable and experienced women as Susan Clark, Laura Jamieson, Helen MacGill, Helena Gutteridge, Helen Smith and Dorothy Steeves.[19] Because of them the Local Council as a whole may have been more active than others in Canada. The arrival of transients from all over Canada may also have dramatized the gravity of the crisis, especially since many of the women mentioned had strong ties with labour and the new CCF party.

The Committee on Trades and Professions for Women continued to be active, demanding work for all unemployed women: single, married, divorced, or widowed. In October 1931, this committee presented a resolution identifying work, rather than relief, as the priority:

> Whereas on account of world-wide conditions governments are providing work for their citizens, and the Dominion of Canada in cooperation with its provinces and municipal governments is providing work for men, Whereas there are many wage-earning and dependent women unemployed who do not wish to take direct relief; Be it resolved that we, the Vancouver Local Council of Women ask:
> a) that work be provided for women as well as men

b) that the female earner in a family is just as entitled to relief work as the male members of the family

c) that where a woman becomes the head of the family, through the loss of the natural bread-winner, that she receive the same consideration re: wages, work or relief as men . . .

d) that this Council through its executive and seventy affiliated societies offers cooperation with many suitable schemes initiated by the authorities.[20]

Although the government had set up a registration system for unemployed women and allowed them to apply for direct relief, no government work projects for women had been established. The resolution of the Vancouver Council brought women's need for work to the attention of the civic authorities. However, the Council rejected a proposal by Mrs. Clark that a committee to investigate relief work for women be formed to gather data from as broad an area as possible. The Council was still conservative; it would not commit itself to more positive action. Even so, its influence as the largest and most representative women's organization had an impact.

The Relief Officer in Vancouver offered to follow up any work project for women given to him by those in authority. Mrs. Clark, who was prepared for just such a reaction, presented a work program to the Council immediately: "That a workroom be established along lines similar to that established by clubs last winter. That there be three hour shifts per day for 5 days a week. That the pay be 35¢ to 40¢ an hour. In order to avoid rush and confusion that those women who have already registered be first placed."

The women who registered came practically under three categories:

1) Women who through loss of bread-winner, have become the heads of families.
2) Single women living at home.
3) Single women without home ties.

Class I

Heads of families to be given direct relief same as men heads of families. If family conditions permit, their women might supplement relief with some work.

Class II

Women living in homes where relief is given or who are not the immediate relative, be given 3 shifts per week.

Class III

Women without homes be given shift work five days per week. This should be sufficient to provide room and food. These women might be placed in homes where they could do a certain amount of work for board and room and have, say, three shifts of work per week.[21]

Her report, endorsed by the sub-executive and the general meeting, was sent to the mayor and City Council. The City Relief Committee put some of the program into effect almost at once. However, municipal/provincial jurisdictional problems interfered with the plan being totally accepted and by February 1932, Mrs. Clark was urging the Council to write provincial and federal authorities still pressing for relief work for unemployed women.

A "make-work campaign," which was to occupy the Council's time in 1933 and embodied much of its hope for a workable plan to aid the unemployed, was first mentioned at the November 1932 meeting of the sub-executive. The Vancouver Board of Trade had written to the Local Council, promoting the Employment Service Plan, a voluntary organization of twenty-two associations whose objective was to put people gainfully to work.[22] Every home, apartment block, retail store, and manufacturer was to be asked to pledge a sum of money to be used to hire an unemployed person. The donor of the money could decide how it was to be spent.

Membership was by association and each association was allowed one member on the executive. Mrs. Labsik, the president, would be the L.C.W. delegate. By the end of November, the L.C.W. had agreed unofficially to "take charge of the Women's Division and to be responsible for directing the women's part in the scheme."[23] Margaret (Mrs. Rex) Eaton represented the sub-executive on a committee to make practical arrangements for starting the campaign. Curiously enough the sub-executive requested "that limitation in canvassing be made in certain districts—that the women's part of the campaign be as small as possible, and largely educational, as this is a man's job."[24] This was a remark not often heard in the Local Council of Women. Quite obviously the women found door-to-door canvassing against its mandate and preferred to assist the Plan by contacting its affiliated societies for aid.

The account of the Council's interest in the Employment Service Plan provides an excellent view of the real power within the Council. The sub-executive had carried on negotiations with the members of the Employment Service Plan, sent representatives, and finally agreed to take over the whole women's division — all without mentioning the plan to the general meeting. By the time the majority of members heard about the organization at the February 1933 general meeting, the important decisions had been made and were being carried out. When it was introduced to the Council members they were urged to bring their widespread influence to bear on a project promising great value as a morale builder.[25]

By the summer of 1933, programs for unemployed single women were still minimal. Both the Soroptimist Club and the Y.W.C.A. had failed in their attempts to run hostels for unemployed women.[26] However, through the Council, another group of women, mothers of families on relief, were receiving some aid from a new program organized by one of the Council's members, Mrs. Mildred Cunningham. Mrs. Cunningham reached mothers through the schools in outlying districts, so that they could be organized into groups for work and recreation. The work involved sewing, knitting or quilting, with materials provided by the Local Council. The object of the plan was "the prevention of spiritual tragedies through fear and suffering."[27] Mrs. Cunningham had already started one such group in South Vancouver and it appeared to be quite successful. Gradually "a sort of combined mothers' meeting and work party evolved from which much useful work and social intercourse has resulted."[28] The self-help groups enrolled 103 women. Mrs. Cunningham's idea proved to be very fruitful. According to her: "The greatest tonic in time of trouble was interesting work and it was proving so in this case."[29] Of course, the very reason for the time of trouble was a lack of work, interesting or not. But Mrs. Cunningham's plan worked well within its limited horizons. The philosophy was to help women help themselves. The women in the Local Council endorsed the self-help philosophy, believing that charity, or giving something for nothing, was humiliating to the recipient.

The Board of Trade could readily win the direct support of the Local Council of Women but it was a different story for the Socialist Party, who, like the Council, were also specifically interested in the unemployed women. While the Board of Trade tried to drum up employment, the Socialist Party, observing the continued widespread unemployment, turned its attention to respectable relief payments. In September 1933 the Vancouver District Council of the Socialist Party reported to the sub-executive by letter that the City Council's new relief schedule for single women adopted in August was "one in which it is not possible to keep up standards of decency."[30] It urged the Local Council to protest to the City, believing that a protest "emanating from such a body of women as the Local Council of Women would have a great influence."[31] While the sub-executive did not immediately support the socialist demand the letter was read to the general meeting and a provincial council conference on "Unemployment as it Affects Women" was called for.

At the general meeting in February 1934, the Committee on Trades and Professions for Women proposed a resolution which appears to be a direct result of the letter sent by the Socialist Party months before:

> In consideration of the lengthening period of the Depression and
> the conditions of unemployment, particularly for women, showing
> little or no improvement, your Committee on Trades and Professions for Women submit the following for your consideration:
> Whereas, the Relief Allowance for single unemployed women has
> thus far been set too low for decent living conditions, and Whereas,
> many unemployed single women have been on prolonged relief,
> their resources being at this time much depleted; Be it therefore

resolved that this Local Council of Women does not approve of
the present low scale of relief for single unemployed women and
goes on record as recommending an upward revision in the scale
of relief to these recipients.[32]

It is precisely the protest that the District Council of the Socialist
Party had requested of the Local Council. The Local Council made the
protest only after study by one of its own committees, since it was not
willing to be more directly associated with the Socialist Party of Canada.
One of the Council's most compassionate pleas was on behalf of single
women:

> With 500 single women on Vancouver's relief roll, a major portion
> of the Council's time has been given to the problems connected
> with this situation. It has repeatedly been asked that women be
> placed on all boards dealing with relief but without success as yet.
> It has been asked that the present relief scale of $2.80 per week be
> increased to the point where a woman might hope to live without
> paying too great a physical and spiritual price during the years of
> depression. A room must be found for $1.20 a week and food for
> 20¢ a day. Week after week and month after month of living on
> this scale is intolerable to health and morals and the grave social
> problems which inevitably arise should be the concern, not only
> of the Council, but of every group of right thinking people in
> Vancouver.[33]

Other organizations solicited the lobbying power of the Local Council
of Women. A delegation from the Women's Labour League spoke at
the general meeting of the Local Council in May 1934, and successfully
requested the support of the Council in protesting relief procedures
currently being used. They asked specifically that the relief authorities
supply clothing more readily and at different intervals and that a complete
dental service for the unemployed be supplied. The British Columbia
Joint Committee on Unemployment and the Y.W.C.A. requested the
assistance of the L.C.W. with similar resolutions. The L.C.W. combined
them into one resolution asking relief authorities to create employment
by public works, to raise the relief and food allowance for single women,
to end the practice of sending single men into camps, and to provide
medical attention and hospitalization, maternity and prenatal care for
those unable to pay.

The Vancouver Local Council of Women remained concerned about
the inadequate relief rates. At the general meeting in February 1935, the
special committee on methods of distributing relief suggested a permanent solution. Not surprisingly, the impetus for this committee came
from the New Era League representative, Susan Clark. The committee
had drawn up a resolution calling for the establishment in Victoria of a

Public Welfare Portfolio. It would co-ordinate the various phases of social welfare work, including mothers' pensions, old age pensions, child welfare, health and mental institutions, homes for delinquents, and unemployment relief. Though the resolution had no success at the time, a Portfolio of Health and Welfare was eventually established by the government of British Columbia.

While the Council's work for unemployed women was its major interest during the Depression, a related problem it addressed was that of mothers' allowances. The controversy over the amount and administration of mothers' pensions began in 1932. In February the sub-executive heard Mrs. R.F. Murray of the Civilian Pensioned Mothers' Association speak in favour of a resolution which this organization had sent to the Local Council. The resolution protested the rumoured government interference in the name of economy with certain social legislation, particularly the Mothers' Assistance Act.

The special committee on the Mothers' Pensions Act made its report in August 1933, recommending passage of three resolutions by the Local Council:

1. The restoration of Mothers' Pensions completely according to the Act.
2. The taking over again by the Provincial Government of the full financial responsibility for the Act and of full control of its administration.
3. The clear statement by this Council of Women of its position re the Mothers' Pensions Act at the coming provincial election.[34]

The Council, which was concerned about unemployment generally, had taken an early interest in the relief camps organized for unemployed single men. In June 1933 the Vancouver Council had formed a committee to organize and administer a "Comforts Fund" for the camps nearest to the city, i.e., West Point Grey, Salmon Arm, and Hope. The committee provided magazines, books and games for the men.

By April 1934, the Council was aware that all was not as it should be in the relief camps. A resolution was passed, asking relief authorities "that conditions in relief camps be made as healthful in every sense as possible, with the hope that in the near future the need for these camps may cease and the men be returned to normal life."[35] The Relief Camp Workers' Union began corresponding with the Council in 1934. Although the sub-executive refused union members permission to speak to the general meeting in January 1935, it assured the workers that the Council was closely following their program and working in their interests. At the general meeting in January 1935, the members discussed the grievances of the men in the camps. The Council forwarded to the National Council a resolution petitioning the Department of National

Defence to establish an organized department of physical education in all camps under their administration.[36] The resolution noted that voluntary efforts to provide this service were inadequate. While a physical education program would not have been able to solve all the grievances of the relief campers, it went a step further than merely deploring the conditions in the camps.

At the fortieth annual meeting of the Vancouver Local Council in March 1935, Mr. Shaw and Mr. Cameron were finally allowed to address the Council on behalf of the "Black-listed Men"; that is, those who had some part in organizing the Relief Camp Workers' Union to protest camp conditions and were for this reason prevented from re-entering a relief camp and from receiving city or provincial relief. They spoke for some time on the problems of life in the camps and proposed resolutions asking for relief for all blacklisted men.[37] The Council discussed various plans for immediate action. According to the report of the *Minute Book*: "the inhumanity of this is more than the women can stand."[38]

An emergency resolution, proposed at the same meeting, asked for "immediate remedial action" from George Pearson, Minister of Labour, and the Attorney-General, and stated "that the women cannot tolerate these conditions any longer."[39] The Council sent two representatives to the Cabinet for an interview. They "put the women's stand very firmly before its members."[40] Rarely had the Council taken such quick action or such a firm stand as it did in the relief camp situation.

Throughout 1935, the Council continued to be concerned with the problems of the relief campers. The president reported to the Council at the general meeting in May 1935 that she had represented it at a public meeting in connection with the strike of the relief campers. She had expressed the sympathy of the Council for the situation in which the campers found themselves.

In December 1935, the sub-executive heard from a representative of the relief campers again. Mr. Cumber, speaking for the blacklisted men, urged the Council to help in obtaining immediate relief for them. The Welfare Foundation in Vancouver had set up a Homeless Men Committee and Mr. Carey, the chairman of this committee, also spoke to the Council sub-executive during the reorganization of the whole camp system. The sub-executive referred the matter to the Unemployment Relief Committee, under the chairmanship of Mrs. David Hall, and requested the committee to bring in a report to the general meeting. Mrs. Hall was prepared for this request and the Unemployment Relief Committee brought in a resolution at the general meeting on December 2, 1935 asking for the abolition of relief camps, and that the single unemployed men in the camps be absorbed into normal community life within the coming year. The resolution also expressed concern for the situation of the blacklisted men,[41] although it did not make any more concrete proposals for action to be taken on their behalf. Mrs. Hall was also appointed to meet with the commission which was investigating the relief camps when it met in Vancouver.

At the sub-executive meeting in April 1936, the members heard a representative of the rejected relief campers. He outlined the situation of the men and appealed for the support of the Council "in effecting some form of immediate relief from the City Council since at present their only means of relief is collecting on street corners."[42] The sub-executive wrote to Norman Rogers, [federal] Minister of Labour, deploring the fact that these boys were in Vancouver without means of support. Although the Council was unwilling to go further, at least it heard the complaints of the men and urged that something be done for them, rather than ignoring them as rabble-rousers or "Communists" who should be allowed to starve for the trouble they had caused.

At the annual meeting in March 1937, the Council endorsed a resolution "that the special Committee set up for providing comforts for the boys at Relief Camps be now dismissed."[43] The Council had little idea of the conditions that continued to prevail at the relief camps, nor could it foresee the trouble to come during June of 1938 when the men from the provincial forestry projects and some from the camps would stage a sitdown strike in the Vancouver Post Office and Art Gallery.

In October 1937 the sub-executive again heard speakers from the single unemployed men, and also from the ex-service veterans. Mr. Harvey, of the ex-service veterans organization, spoke first, and asked that the Local Council request the British Columbia government to institute a works program or relief. He complained that all ex-service men had been cut off relief if they were under the age of fifty. Then Mr. March, representing the Relief Projects Workers' Union for single unemployed men, spoke, explaining that these men, including the ex-service men, had co-operated to the best of their ability but wanted some work scheme to support themselves. The sub-executive listened and turned the issue over to a special committee for study. The situation was addressed at the general meeting in October 1937. Helena Gutteridge, Vancouver's first alderwoman and a member of the CCF, had studied the position of the single unemployed men in the city and urged haste in dealing with it. The New Era League had also sent in a resolution in favour of a works scheme, which was read by the president. Dorothy Steeves, a prominent CCF MLA, moved that the Local Council appeal to the provincial government to take immediate steps to provide food for the single unemployed men.[44] The general meeting also decided to send a delegation to Victoria, to relay to the minister of labour the gravity of the situation in Vancouver, where more unemployed men were drifting into the city daily, and many were being sent to jail.

In January 1938 the Council endorsed yet another resolution from Susan Clark: "Resolved that any works scheme, either now existing or arranged in the future, by civic or legislative bodies shall provide for the payment of wages, sufficient to maintain a standard of living based upon the government figures as contained and published in the *Labour Gazette*."[45]

Since the Council had continued to press for higher relief scales, the resolution was not a new policy, but it was an indication that the Council continued to be aware of the Depression and its problems.

TABLE 1

Affiliated Societies of the Council of Women of Vancouver, 1935

Altar Society of Our Lady of Perpetual Help	King's Daughters Van. Mizpah Circle
Altar Society of Holy Rosary Cathedral	Kitsilano W.C.T.U.
Alexandra Orphanage	Ladies' Guild British Sailors Society
Business and Professional Women's Club	League of Women Voters
Canadian Daughters' League No. 1	L.O.B.A. No Surrender Lodge No. 90
Canadian Daughters' League No. 4	Mary Forbes W.C.T.U.
Canadian Daughters' League No. 8	New Era League
Canadian Daughters' League No. 9	Ryerson United Church Women's
Canadian Daughters' League No. 16	Association
Canadian Daughters' League No. 22	St. Andrews-Wesley United Church
Canadian Federation for the Blind	Women's Association
Canadian Memorial United Church	St. John's United Church Women's Guild
Ladies' Aid	St. Paul's Anglican Church Women's Guild
Catholic Women's League	St. Paul's Hospital Auxiliary
Chalmers United Church Women's Guild	Soldiers, Sailors, Mothers and Wives
Chown United Church Ladies' Aid	Association
Civilian Widows and Orphans	Soroptimist Club
Association	Vancouver Graduate Nurses' Association
Crippled Children's Hospital	Vancouver Horticultural Society
Daughters of England Queen of the West	Vancouver Women's Liberal Association
Lodge No. 33	Victorian Order of Nurses
Daughters of England Glazier Lodge No. 96	West End W.C.T.U.
Daughters of Scotia Heather Lodge No. 84	Women's Alliance Unitarian Church
District King's Daughters	Women's Auxiliary to the Hellenic
District W.C.T.U.	Community
Dunbar Heights United Church Women's	Women's Building Limited
Association	Women's Educational Auxiliary to
Fairview W.C.T.U.	United Church
First Baptist Women's Society	Women's Institute, Point Grey
First United Church Ladies' Aid	Women's Institute, The Delta, Ladner
Girl Guides of Greater Vancouver	Women's International League of Peace
Kerrisdale Baptist Women's Auxiliary	and Freedom
Kerrisdale W.C.T.U.	Women's Missionary Auxiliary to Church
King's Daughters Inasmuch Circle	of England

The Depression was brought home again to the Council by the sitdown strike in the Vancouver Post Office and Art Gallery by unemployed men from the relief camps and the provincial government forestry projects. The Council castigated both the provincial and city governments for doing nothing to relieve the situation. An emergency resolution was brought forward, at the general meeting in June, asking federal authorities yet again to provide a works scheme for single unemployed men, and to give them food and housing at once to try to alleviate their plight.[46] This quick and drastic action by the Council is not the last mention made of the situation or the fate of the men involved in the strike. In September 1938, a letter from the Mothers' Council was received asking that the Local Council of Women "consider the boys who were convicted during the Post Office trouble, by attending the Assizes."[47] The Council decided "that we as a Council cannot be represented but we go on record as reiterating our stand for a works program."[48] There must have been some dispute about this resolution because another was drawn up and read to the general meeting: "As a Council we have every sympathy with the young men but cannot represent the Council as a whole, but in the matter of attending the trials we suggest any Council woman can attend and get information."[49] Some members of the Council probably believed that the men were getting just what they deserved, but the Socialist women, like Clark, Gutteridge, Jamieson and Steeves, would have been adamant in their support of the strikers. The resolution, which was a compromise between the two, did not commit the Council to any action or principle.

The attitude of the Council towards the underlying causes of the Depression was demonstrated by the measures it advocated as possible cures for the economic crisis. In August 1930, the Council sub-executive had endorsed a project which was to become one of its most important campaigns during the Depression. The group issued "Where From" slogan cards to their members. Shoppers were to buy B.C., Canadian, or Empire goods only. Half of the card was to be kept as a pledge, and the other half was to be deposited in a box during the Pacific National Exhibition. This was not a new idea for the Council, which had always supported such campaigns to buy only provincial, Canadian, or Empire products, but the reasoning behind its endorsement of the campaign had changed. The "Where From" project would help unemployment in Canada and in the Empire. This fitted in very well with the emphasis being placed by the National Council of Women on the recommendations of the Imperial Conference. The Council continued to endorse such plans as the "Where From" campaign throughout the Depression.

The fact that the Council continued to hear speakers dealing with the economic crisis in its various manifestations demonstrates that it was sincere in its fear that it did not know enough to take action. It is impossible to estimate how much influence these speakers had on the Council and its policies. The continued emphasis on buying B.C., Canadian, and Empire products was encouraged by any number of speakers, particularly by those from the B.C. Board of Trade. In thanking one of these speakers, Margaret Eaton said that "if every country's resources were pooled internationally, the greatest era of prosperity the world has ever seen would result," and "it is up to the women of the world to see that the principles of separatism, racialism, and nationalism be over-come."[50] This sentiment directly opposed the idea that buying local products would end the Depression. Certainly, vague and nebulous as it was, Eaton's statement was as liberal as any of the Council's progressive pronouncements, but it does not seem to have had any lasting effect.

The Council was exposed to radical proposals for dealing with the Depression. At the general meeting in November 1933, the president of the Local Council read a manifesto for the use of any affiliated society from the International Women's Congress. The manifesto asked women to undertake a crusade "directed towards the winning of security and opportunity for all mankind,"[51] stating:

> We recognize that, beneath the perplexities and dislocations of the present period, there has occurred a shift from the problems of production and of the mastery of the material forces to the problems of social control. To build a social order providing security and opportunity for all we accept as the task of our time. In it there is no place for complacent reliance upon fixed concepts and specific measures of reform.[52]

It called for a comprehensive government public welfare plan, and regulation of industry and agriculture. The manifesto struck a responsive chord in the Vancouver Local Council, although it was much more radical than any of the Council's resolutions or actions had been. The Vancouver Local Council was more liberal than the National Council, which did not discuss the manifesto. Given the fact that the *Minute Book* for these years reads like a "Who's Who" in provincial socialist circles, it is likely that the Vancouver Council was more radical than most other local councils.

The Council was not hostile to radical solutions for the Depression, but it did not initiate any such solutions, nor did it ever fully endorse one. That would be unlikely, in view of the majority of the Council members. Its official view of the crisis was basically conservative. The plans initiated by the Council were temporary measures and were designed only to alleviate some of the worst results of the Depression.

During 1938 and 1939, the Council became more and more con-cerned with the international situation, and correspondingly, less and less concerned with the Depression and unemployment. Domestic prob-lems paled before the possibility of a World War, although a special Committee on Unemployment Relief still existed. Pleas to help the unemployed elicited a stock response from the Council: "That we the Vancouver Local Council of Women reiterate our stand taken on several occasions that a works program with fair wages be provided for unemployed men, and until such work is provided, that relief be given with no discrimination."[53] This resolution was passed again on June 5, 1939, at the general meeting. Predictably, from this time on, all the attention of the Council was caught up by the war effort which brought the Depression to a halt as the unemployed were absorbed into the armed forces, the war industries, or forgotten.

The Vancouver Local Council of Women was recognized as the outstanding local council in its efforts to deal with the results of the Depression. The Council attempted to understand the Depression which neither it nor others affected by it could totally explain. Yet, it did not fail in its attempts to help those most affected by the crisis. The Council worked successfully in its attempt to get relief for single unemployed women, a group totally unrecognized by the authorities at the beginning of the Depression.

The Council also worked to alleviate the plight of unemployed men in British Columbia's relief camps, not only by providing funds for recreation, but also by pressing for an end to the camps, and for provision for alternative forms of assistance for the single unemployed men.

The women of the Vancouver Local Council may not have been able to understand why the Depression occurred, but they gave practical help to those most affected by it, and consistently represented those whom others preferred to forget.

Notes

1. Rosa Shaw, *Proud Heritage* (Toronto: Ryerson Press, 1957), 185.
2. National Council of Women of Canada, *Yearbook*, 1933, 29.
3. National Council of Women of Canada, *Yearbook*, 1930, 63.
4. Ibid.
5. Shaw, *Proud Heritage*, 109.
6. "A National Waste—Leaderless Women," *The Financial Post* 32 (10 December 1938): 1.
7. National Council of Women of Canada, *Yearbook*, 1933, 244.
8. Ibid., 247.
9. Ibid., 252.
10. Local Council of Women of Vancouver, *Minute Book*, 1932–1933, 112.
11. Ibid.
12. *Minute Book*, 1929–1930, 121.
13. Ibid.
14. *Minute Book*, 1933–1934, 11.
15. Ibid., 1934–1935, 17.
16. Ibid.
17. *Minute Book*, 1930–1931, 58.
18. Ibid., 73.
19. See the biographies in *In Her Own Right: Selected Essays on Women's History in B.C.*, ed. Barbara Latham and Cathy Kess (Victoria, B.C., 1980).

20. Local Council of Women of Vancouver, *Minute Book*, 1931–1932, 84.
21. Ibid., 96.
22. *Minute Book*, 1932–1933, 91.
23. Ibid., 106.
24. Ibid., 115.
25. Ibid., 155.
26. *Minute Book*, 1933–1934, 67-70.
27. Ibid., 73.
28. Ibid., 74.
29. Ibid., 98.
30. Ibid., 78.
31. Ibid., 79.
32. Ibid., 181.
33. Ibid., 200.
34. Ibid., 97.
35. Ibid., 200.
36. *Minute Book*, 1934–1935, 102.
37. Ibid., 135.
38. Ibid.
39. Ibid., 136.
40. Ibid.
41. *Minute Book*, 1935–1937, 69.
42. Ibid., 110.
43. *Minute Book*, 1937–1938, 14.
44. Ibid., 58.
45. Ibid., 89.
46. *Minute Book*, 1938–1939, 27.
47. Ibid., 35.
48. Ibid.
49. Ibid., 36.
50. *Minute Book*, 1932–1933, 13.
51. National Council of Women of Canada, *Yearbook*, 1934, 140-41.
52. Ibid.
53. Local Council of Women of Vancouver, *Minute Book*, 1939–1940, 8.

WORKERS, GROWERS AND MONOPOLISTS: THE "LABOUR PROBLEM" IN THE ALBERTA BEET SUGAR INDUSTRY DURING THE 1930s†

JOHN HERD THOMPSON and ALLEN SEAGER

Unions of agricultural workers have been rare in Canada. Although the agricultural sector was the largest single component of the Canadian labour force until the 1940s, a majority of this group was always made up of farm operators whose ownership of land set them apart from traditional definitions of a working class, however miserable their lives and working conditions and however low their cash incomes. But even those agricultural workers who sold their labour to earn their living remained largely untouched by labour unions. Isolated on farms, they were written off as unorganizable by the trade union movement and with the exception of the Industrial Workers of the World no labour union made a serious attempt to enroll farm hands. An exception to this rule was provided by those unusual situations in which agricultural work closely paralleled an industrial occupation. One of the best examples of this was the sugar beet growing area of Southern Alberta, where farmers hired workers to thin, cultivate and harvest beets planted on small acreages of irrigated land. Faced with a situation more like factory work than work on a prairie farm, beet workers formed a radical industrial union during the 1930s and struck against their employers. The 1935 and 1936 strikes of the Beet Workers' Industrial Union were a phenomenon for Western Canada, a class struggle *within* agriculture, unlike the "agrarian protest" against the National Policy which has been such an enduring theme in Canadian historiography.

The sugar beet industry in Alberta began in 1902 when Jesse Knight of Provo, Utah built a factory for processing beets into sugar at Raymond,

† *Labour/Le Travailleur* 3 (1978) : 153–74.

twenty miles south of Lethbridge. Knight was a devout Latter Day Saint, as were many of the settlers in the area, and his motivation in creating the Knight Sugar Company was not to create "a commercial enterprise so much as a benefit for the settlers of the surrounding countryside."[1] A further spur to this philanthropy was a promise of a twelve-year exemption from taxation and a bonus of 50 cents for each hundredweight of sugar his factory produced. But despite the tax holiday and the subsidy provided by the provincial and Dominion governments, the company was not a financial success. Many reasons were advanced for the factory's closing in 1914, but all could be reduced to one common denominator, the "labour problem." When the sugar beet was introduced to Canada, the labour-intensive nature of beet growing was held to be one of its benefits, a way to keep boys and girls on the farm and prevent rural depopulation. As the editor of one Western paper rhapsodized, "children working but a few hours a day participate with pleasure in a task which helps themselves, helps father, and upbuilds health by free outdoor life. . . . Neighbourhood and community are better altogether."[2]

The less pleasant realities of sugar beet husbandry soon became well known to those farmers who tried to grow them. Beet cultivation was tedious, back-aching stoop labour, and a farmer and his family had to sweat long hours under the summer sun for every acre of beets they produced. Until the 1950s sugar beets were grown from a multigerm seed which produced a bunch rather than a single beet plant. Once the seed germinated the bunch had to be hand thinned until only one plant remained. To perform this task properly a worker had to crawl along the rows on his knees. Then the tiny seedlings had to be weeded — sometimes as many as three times during the growing season — for the beets never grow tall enough to kill the weeds by cutting off their sunshine. Finally in the autumn the crop had to be harvested by hand, knocked together to remove excess dirt and "topped" — the leaves and crown cut away — to be ready for shipment to the sugar factory. These operations could not be done mechanically. Beets could be planted with a seed drill but all subsequent work had to be done with hand tools. About 115 hours of hand labour was required to produce an acre of beets, more than ten times the labour required for an acre of grain. Most farmers who tried beets gave them up after a season or two. Those who tried to hire workers to thin, hoe and harvest their beets found that most farm hands would do almost anything else before they would accept beet work.[3]

Thus the Knight Sugar Company was never able to obtain enough beets to operate at an efficient level, even with an attractive price of five dollars a ton. Beet acreage in Alberta reached a maximum of 5 200 in 1908 and then decreased annually.[4] The company tried to provide its own beets by planting as many as 2 000 acres on its own and hiring labour to work them, but it had no more success than the local farmers.

Few whites wanted to hoe sugar beets. Japanese and Chinese labour could not be obtained in sufficient quantities without arousing community opposition to the importation of Orientals. Indians were less productive, sometimes damaged plants at the critical thinning stage and could not be counted upon to remain on the job throughout the season.[5] When the twelve-year tax exemption ended in 1914, the Knight Sugar Company's Board of Directors voted to cease operations, and the factory was dismantled and moved to the United States.[6]

A decade passed before the industry could be revived. The agricultural depression which followed the Great War convinced Southern Alberta farmers that they needed a cash crop which would be less soil exhaustive and which could make weed control easier. In addition more irrigated land was available to make possible greater tonnage of beets per acre. Boards of Trade in Raymond and Cardston initiated beet-growing projects to convince prospective investors that farmers would grow enough beets to support a new factory. The *Lethbridge Herald* promised editorially that a new sugar factory would have "beets shooting in from all over the horizon," and a group of farmers who promised to devote land to beet growing lent support to this pledge.[7] The stumbling block to the creation of a factory was the question of an adequate supply of cheap labour. When the Utah-Idaho Sugar Company agreed to begin operating in Raymond for the 1925 season it did so on the understanding that not only would there be sufficient beet production but that the prospective beet growers would assume full responsibility for providing their own labour.[8]

The growers could give this assurance because the Canadian Pacific Railway had suggested what they hoped would be the solution to the "labour problem." Under an agreement with the Dominion Government, the railway was given the privilege of importing immigrants of the "non-preferred nationalities" — those from Eastern Central and Southern Europe—if farm work could be guaranteed for them on arrival in Canada.[9] When the idea of importing Europeans to do beet work had been first proposed by James Colley, the C.P.R.'s Assistant Superintendent of Colonization, not all farmers accepted it. At a meeting of the United Farmers of Alberta in Coaldale, Colley was "sharply challenged" by those who felt that "it would be detrimental . . . to the country to import a class of settlers whose standards of living are so much lower than our own."[10] But the alternatives—Japanese labour or no sugar beet factory — were even less palatable. The "little yellow fellows" were specifically rejected and the C.P.R.'s Colonist's Service Association at Lethbridge began to transport Eastern Europeans to Alberta for the beet "campaign" of 1925.[11] Arrivals continued throughout the 1920s until over twelve hundred European immigrants were employed as beet labour by 1929, and beet acreage underwent a parallel expansion given a reliable supply of workers.

Just as it differed from the rest of prairie agriculture, the beet industry differed from the simple worker-capitalist dichotomy of Marxist class struggle. Like the nineteenth-century British agriculture described in Hobsbawm and Rudé's study of rural class relationships, *Captain Swing*, there were three classes in the sugar beet system.[12] At the top was the "aristocracy," Canadian Sugar Factories — as the Utah-Idaho Company called its Alberta subsidiary. With an absolute monopoly over all beet sugar production in the province the company owned the indispensable means of making and marketing the finished product. Next in line came the growers, who signed contracts to deliver the total tonnage of beets produced on a certain acreage of land at a price stipulated by the company. At the bottom were the beet workers, who signed contracts with the growers to cultivate and harvest an acreage of beets. Contracts provided for a fixed fee for each stage of the cultivation, with a "hold back" of about 30 percent which was not paid until all operations had been completed. A bonus system was incorporated into the contract based on the tonnage of beets grown per acre to encourage workers to strive for maximum production.[13]

During the 1925 to 1930 period it was possible for a beet worker to earn a good living at his trade. His work was unpleasant but if he could handle the average contract of ten acres a year he could earn more than two hundred dollars for his efforts. Beet thinning and weeding was finished in late July, and since harvest did not begin until early October, a beet worker could add another hundred dollars to his annual income by working in the grain harvest in August and September. A beet contract also stipulated that a worker be provided with a "habitable house" for himself and his family. Unlike other farm workers, beet labourers provided their own food. It was customary, however, for growers to allow their contract workers an area for a vegetable garden and space to raise a cow, a hog or a few chickens.[14]

The depression of the 1930s upset the relationships among sugar company, growers, and workers. Its first effect was to force out the Utah-Idaho Sugar Company and in 1931 control of Canadian Sugar Factories passed to E.T. Rogers' B.C. Sugar. Rogers had a monopoly of cane sugar production in Western Canada, and his initial intention seems to have been to shut the factory in Raymond and eliminate beet sugar competition. The Utah-Idaho Sugar Company, however, was "more or less controlled by the Latter Day Saint Church," which did not want to see its members in Southern Alberta without a place to sell their beets. When Utah-Idaho insisted as a condition of the sale that the factory operate for another ten years, Rogers determined to make a profit on his new Alberta operation.[15] The price his factory paid for beets was not determined on an open market as the beet growers had no alternative purchaser for their crop, and as the operator of the only game in town

Rogers could make his own rules. By reducing the price he paid for his raw material—sugar beets—he was able to put Canadian Sugar Factories into the black with 20 percent profit in the first year after the takeover.[16]

Despite the reductions, beet growers had no alternative to growing beets. The prices of grains and animal products had declined even more precipitously and growers actually increased the acreage they devoted to beets in 1932, the year following the takeover. Their response to the price cut was a traditional agrarian protest which took the form of pressure group action by the Growers' Association to obtain government help to establish a competitive beet sugar factory in Southern Alberta. The Growers' Association tried to convince the Dominion Government to rebate half of the two-cent sugar tax to beet sugar producers, while leaving the tax on cane sugar untouched.[17] This advantage, it was argued, would attract a second factory and the resulting competition would increase beet prices. When their attempts to have the tax removed were unsuccessful, the beet growers responded in the outraged tones typical of Western farmers, denouncing the "big-interests" — the cane sugar producers—which had "too much influence" in Ottawa.[18] W.F. Russell, secretary of the Growers' Association Development Committee, described the situation as "war" and promised that the beet growers would "keep on fighting until we root out the evil."[19]

One Albertan even warned R.B. Bennett of the danger that the growers, although "not fundamentally red," would become easy converts for the radical Farmers Unity League.[20] The F.U.L., organized in 1930, was the Communist Party of Canada's "mass organization" devoted to the Western farmer. The League was never made a priority of the party, which concentrated on the urban industrial worker, but it was an active and vocal critic of the established farm organizations as well as of capitalist agriculture. The League found most of its members among non-Anglo-Saxon farmers in the northern park belt, where it was responsible for organizing several farm delivery strikes and for preventing evictions with large demonstrations. With the price of beets declining, the F.U.L. moved to establish a foothold in Southern Alberta.

But it was not the petit bourgeois growers who provided receptive audiences for the Communist organizers, it was their beet workers. Squeezed by Rogers Sugar the growers squeezed the final link in the chain, the beet worker. Between 1931 and 1934 the contract rate for beet labour declined from twenty-one dollars an acre to seventeen dollars, despite the fact that the productivity of each worker, as measured by the number of tons of beets produced on each acre, increased. The worker's share of the farmer's return from the beet crop was reduced from an average of 38.6 percent in the 1925–1930 period to 28.3 percent between 1931 and 1934, and during the autumn of 1934 rumours spread that the Growers' Association intended to make further wage cuts in 1935.[21] This reduction in wages would have been bad enough in normal

times, but because of the glut of farm workers available and the masses
of urban unemployed, it was impossible for beet workers to supplement
their incomes with harvest work. It is not surprising that the initial
impetus for organization came from the Communist Party. Communists
had been active in the coal fields of the Lethbridge and Drumheller areas
and as early as 1928 there were complaints about "agitators" trying to
"discourage men from accepting [sugar beet] work on the regular contract
basis."[22] The F.U.L. conducted a series of rallies in the beet-growing areas
over the winter of 1934–1935, rallies directed by George Palmer, an
English war veteran who had been active in the One Big Union and was
now the Party's chief propagandist in the frustrating debate against Social
Credit fantasies in the Alberta countryside.[23] Palmer found the going
slow with the growers at whom his work was aimed, and as wage
labourers, beet workers were constitutionally excluded from membership
in the F.U.L. Instead, the workers were organized into the Beet Workers'
Industrial Union which affiliated with the Workers' Unity League.

The president of the new B.W.I.U. was Peter Meronik, a Ukrainian
coal miner from Lethbridge, a Communist and former organizer for the
Mine Workers' Union of Canada. Blacklisted in coal, Meronik made a
living teaching music, and helping out on his father's beet farm near
Coaldale. According to Meronik, when the beet worker "found out I
had a little bit of union history they asked me if I'd be their President
to present their demands." Meronik brought to the job the firm conviction that only through higher productivity and better co-operation
between worker and farmer could a higher standard of living for the
beet labourers be obtained. As he admitted, this approach sometimes
came into conflict with the "gut" reaction of the labourers against their
immediate oppressors:

> [with] the beet workers [it] was always "Fight the farmer! Fight the
> farmer!", and I was trying to teach them to educate the farmer. . . .
> Well, having a background as a grower on our farm . . . I seen that
> the fight wasn't between the growers and the beet workers, it was
> a fight with the sugar company that was getting excessive profits.[24]

The strategy of the B.W.I.U. was predicated upon this basic assumption of a unity of interest between farmer and worker. While withhold-
ing, or threatening to withhold the labour of its members from the
farmers, the union nevertheless appealed to the latter to join with it in
a joint struggle with the sugar company, the "real" enemy which the
union could not confront directly. These tactics reflected the prevailing
ideological conceptions of the Communist Party in the 1930s, which
considered the bulk of the farming population to be a potentially revolutionary class. This was the rationale behind the formation of the
Farmer's Unity League. As the Party moved into the Popular Front era

in the mid-thirties, even the "middle class" came to be included among the progressive forces in society, an ideological twist which could not help but reinforce the idea of farmer/labour unity against monopoly.

The decision to appeal to the growers for unity against the sugar company perhaps doomed the B.W.I.U. to failure from the moment of its creation, for there is little to suggest that the Communist Party's assessment of the potential militancy of the growers was realistic. The only beet growers who sympathized with the Communist-led F.U.L., and thus with the B.W.I.U., were small operators, some of whom were tenants, who did their beet labour themselves.[25] The only articulate radical among the more successful growers was W.H. Childress of Iron Springs, whose name is to be found in the ranks of the most efficient beet producers, Class One of the "Fifteen Ton Club."[26] An article by Childress appeared in the Communist Party's newspaper *The Worker* in early 1935. Childress described the beet industry in Alberta as a "sugar swindle" in which farmers, beet workers and sugar factory workers were annually fleeced by the C.P.R. and the Rogers Sugar Company.[27] But only a tiny minority of his fellow growers could have been prepared to accept Childress' analysis or to share his views on co-operation with the workers. Nor was the Rogers Sugar Company — not the most popular of institutions in Southern Alberta — about to sit idle while a working-class organization led by the Communist Party challenged its hegemony by appealing to the grievances of the beet growers. The Company actively worked to divide grower and beet worker to enable itself to emerge ultimately with its control of the industry intact.

The B.W.I.U. presented its demands for twenty-two dollars an acre for beet labour and improved living quarters to the Growers' Association at its February Convention. The Growers' original tactic was to deny that the B.W.I.U. existed and to offer beet workers, on an individual basis, a continuation of the seventeen-dollar rate that had been in effect in 1934.[28] Peter Meronik's claim that the Union had the support of the "vast majority" of the 2 500 beet workers is substantiated by what happened next. Unwilling to work any longer at starvation wages, hundreds of beet workers refused to sign their individual contracts for the 1935 season. Reports of roving mobs of trade unionists tramping through the countryside enlisting or intimidating other workers into their ranks spread throughout the area. Even more alarming were stories of striking workmen making threats against persons and property. One Taber man wrote the Premier that rebellious "Roumanians, Bulgarians, Slaves [sic]and some others" were "threatening to do away with anyone who attempts to go to work . . . and to burn any farmer's home who hires any other labour." Bleakly he predicted that "From the present outlook it is doubtful if the beets will be planted at all this year!"[29] Another "concerned citizen" fearfully noted the fact that "there is no doubt that some of our police are in full sympathy with the strikers."[30]

Both correspondents urged that punitive action be taken, at least against the ring leaders of the operation. Although the local daily, the *Lethbridge Herald*, thought it wisest not to report the strike in its columns, it constituted in fact a social crisis in the countryside.[31] On May Day, the Royal Canadian Mounted Police was dispatched to Iron Springs to supervise a "monster demonstration" of the beet strikers, and the Growers' Association instructed its members to evict all recalcitrant labourers from their shacks by 4 May.[32]

The power of eviction was one of the most effective weapons in the hands of the growers. Being thrown out of shelter, regardless of how humble, was a hard blow indeed for a family, and most of the beet workers had wives and children. Individual farmers, however, seem to have been reluctant to carry out the order to evict their labourers. Many growers, no doubt, had satisfactory personal relations with their workers, while others feared the future consequences of poisoning their labour relations by taking draconian measures. According to Meronik, those who did "had a hell of a time getting beet workers" after they had dispossessed their staff, and for this reason the power of eviction does not seem to have been widely used. Nevertheless, 4 May 1935 did not pass without incident. According to the account in *The Worker*, several evictions and numerous acts of vandalism were carried out by "fascist gangs of 150, made up of storekeepers, school teachers, preachers, elevator men, reactionary, exploiting farmers, and two R.C.M.P. men." It is unfortunate that we have no means to corroborate this interesting description of the class nature of the opponents of the beet workers in the community.[33]

Once it became obvious that the B.W.I.U. could not be simply ignored the tactics of the Growers' Association changed. Shouting "Communism," they "dragged the red herring over the whole situation" and appealed to the Provincial Government to protect them.[34] Ted Sundal, representing the Growers, wrote piously to the Alberta Minister of Agriculture that "we do not deny the rights to organize on fundamental lines, but most of our growers believe the affiliation is a branch of the Communist Party," and so were reluctant to enter into any contractual agreement with it.[35] Similarly, a spokesman for the Lethbridge Northern Irrigation District argued that the "main point at issue" was not the workers' demands for twenty-two dollars an acre, but recognition of the Workers' Unity League.[36] In reply, the B.W.I.U. accused the growers' leadership of taking a "Kulak stand of aligning themselves with the sugar company" and reiterated its "standing invitation" to all growers to "unite with the workers . . . in their own interest."[37]

The two sides did ultimately come to terms before the onset of the thinning season. The B.W.I.U. was not formally recognized, nor did it sign a collective agreement with the Growers' Association or gain check-off privileges. Nevertheless, the strike had wrenched important concessions from the growers. In the Taber-Barnwell district strikers signed individual contracts which provided for a basic pay rate of nineteen dollars an acre, a two-dollar increase, with extra work such as irrigation to be paid for by the farmer on a daily basis. In the Raymond area, the workers signed for nineteen dollars an acre, with no special payment for extra work. The strike was at an end by 20 May. *The Worker* admitted that "had they [the strikers] been successful in uniting the growers with them . . . much more could have been achieved," but claimed that "many growers are saying that the strike has been an example which can be copied."[38]

The strike had most certainly put the fledgling beet workers' union on the map. During the summer the B.W.I.U. called a "Harvesters' Conference," attended by representatives from the miners, farmers, and unemployed, who pledged themselves to initiate the ambitious task of organizing labour in the wheat fields.[39] The Communist Party itself scored direct gains from the beet strike. *The Worker* reported the founding of a new branch in Iron Springs in August, attributing the growth of Party influence in the area to its "good work" of the previous spring. Although no Communist candidate ran in the provincial election of that summer in the Lethbridge area, beet workers from Turin were reported to have attended a fund raising picnic for Pat Lenihan, candidate in Calgary.[40]

The beet workers lost no time in preparing for 1936, calling on the Growers' Association for talks even before Christmas. The local at Picture Butte wrote to the sugar company itself requesting direct negotiations. One wonders how many farmers would have agreed with the reply of company spokesman George Wood, who denied any interest in the matter, saying that "the growers themselves have full control of the rates which they will pay."[41] The B.W.I.U. had no intention of simply withering away, as its opponents hoped it would. The new union, of course, suffered from many organizational problems, compounded by the agricultural context in which it functioned and the fact that its membership was scattered over an area of hundreds of square miles. During the first year of its existence, the union was said to have "functioned in a very loose manner, and many members failed to pay their dues . . . [and] the centre had to carry on under very difficult conditions." Meeting in convention on 16 February, B.W.I.U. delegates resolved to strengthen and consolidate their organization, to open an office in Lethbridge, and to raise annual dues to $4.20 in order to "bring the union out of financial difficulties and to build the union on a sound basis." During the next two months, a "100% improvement" in the union's affairs was reported, along with an increase in membership.[42] According to Meronik, the B.W.I.U. enrolled 1 800 beet workers of a total labour force of approximately 2 500. In a circular entitled "Beet Growers,

Protect Your Crop," the B.W.I.U. laid down its position towards the farmers in 1936. The tract concluded:

> Last year we won an increase in wages because we organized and fought for our demands, while you were left holding the bag. You lost out . . . while the sugar company was able to sit back and feel that they had pulled a fast one over the growers.
>
> This year we propose that all growers unite with us. Our demand is $22 per acre for labour and $7 per ton for beets. We ask you to . . . present a united fight against those who have in the past so politely robbed you of your beet crops, while the producers were left with a meagre existence.
>
> Let our slogan be: FOR UNITY OF GROWERS AND LABOURERS TO MAKE THE SUGAR COMPANY PAY![43]

Initially, there were signs of a more positive relationship between workers and farmers. A workers' committee composed of Meronik, John Beluch of Barnwell, Secretary of the B.W.I.U., and two other workers, Andy Konti and Joe Semoly, met with Ted Sundal and Phil Baker of the Growers' Association on 22-24 February 1936. The agreement which they reached, presented in the form of recommendations to the upcoming annual convention of the Growers' Association, represented real gains for the workers. The representatives agreed on a wage rate of $21.50 an acre for the ten ton yield, and a scale ranging from $1.95 to $2.70 a ton for those who chose to work on a tonnage basis. Irrigation and extra work were to be paid for at a daily wage, although rates were not laid down. Ten percent extra would be paid if the beets were planted in narrow rows. The proposed agreement also provided for improvements in working and living conditions, and a grievance procedure which would bring representatives from both sides together in case of local or individual disputes. The contract, however, was still to be signed by workers on an individual, and not a collective basis.[44]

The draft agreement was a model of the sort of farmer/labour co-operation which had been the original objective of the Union. The workers' hopes were dashed, however, by the attitude of the members of the Growers' Association. Their convention "absolutely rejected" the contract proposal in a "lengthy and sometimes stormy discussion." Although a faction led by W.H. Childress held out for ratification of the original proposal, it was defeated and the rate reduced to twenty dollars an acre. Even this reduced rate was accepted with difficulty. The convention also elected Phil Baker to the presidency after he supported an attack on a contract which he himself had helped negotiate. The new executive seemed to be more anti-labour than its predecessor. Denunciations of the sugar company, standard rhetoric at previous conventions, were replaced with platitudes about the "straightforward" and "friendly" relationship between the Growers' Association and Canadian Sugar Factories. The new villain was the B.W.I.U.[45]

The decision to renege on the agreement with the beet workers demonstrated the stiff-necked resistance of many farmers to collective bargaining with a labour union, but it also reflected the work of the sugar company to prevent any rapprochement between growers and labourers which could be catastrophic to its interests. During 1935–1936 E.T. Rogers made two significant concessions which won the support, if not the affection, of the growers for the sugar company. Although the company did not formally grant a higher price for beets, it agreed to the introduction of the "50-50 split," a form of profit sharing in which beet growers were guaranteed half of the value of the white sugar produced by Canadian Sugar Factories.[46] Under the new system, to take effect on the 1935 crop, growers received an initial payment which was almost as high as the old price for beets and a bonus payment later in the winter when the sugar had been marketed. This arrangement would probably have been enough to detach the growers geographically close to the factory in Raymond from any possible alliance with labour. But to sweeten the pot Rogers agreed—after tax concessions from the Alberta Government — to establish a new factory at Picture Butte, north of Lethbridge.[47] Any chance of a worker-grower common front against the sugar monopoly was now dead.

Despite the drastically different situation, the leaders of the B.W.I.U. did not give up hope for a peaceful settlement. They warned the Board of Directors of the Association that the growers' stand "will only lead to deadlock which will . . . impair co-operation," and suggested that "if the beet growers do not consider they can pay a higher wage . . . because of low prices for beets, our union is prepared to back the just demands of the growers to the limit."[48] The Association was not interested in any such offer, yet by capitulating to the growers on the wage issue, the B.W.I.U. was able to come to yet another tentative agreement by late March. It included clauses concerning working conditions satisfactory to the union, and provided for a basic rate of twenty dollars per acre, with similar tonnage increases for those on volume contracts.[49] If ever a union was prepared to sacrifice its immediate demands in the interests of "co-operation," it was the Communist-dominated Beet Workers Industrial Union of 1936.

Yet even this did not appear to be enough for the growers. Sure of the support of the company, they were determined to provoke a fight in the course of which the B.W.I.U. could be destroyed, and the previous status quo restored. The second contract agreement had not been final-ized, and in further discussions the growers' representatives dragged their heels over a contentious clause permitting scrutiny of individual contracts by union officers to prevent deviation from general norms. On 7 April, Baker made a speech in which he decried "agitation" in the beet fields, and "impossible demands" on the part of the workers.[50] That same week the sugar company distributed twenty-eight thousand dollars to eight hundred beet growers, as an extra bonus for the 1935 crop.[51] On 14 April, B.W.I.U. representatives were turned away from Baker's office, with the weak explanation from Russell that the two sides had met as often as was necessary.[52] It was obvious that the leadership of the Association had set its face against coming to any formal agreement with the B.W.I.U. which would be binding on its members. To the union leaders there was "no doubt that this policy has been instigated by the sugar company, working through their henchmen in the Beet Growers' Association." The company, they maintained, "recognizes the dangers which lie in the co-operation . . . between beet growers and labourers." To prevent this, Peter Meronik concluded, "the sugar company would like to see a fight between labourers and growers."[53]

That fight now became unavoidable. Raising demands that the original offer of $21.50 be honoured, priority for work be given to local labour, no discrimination be shown against union members, and the B.W.I.U. be given the right to scrutinize all contracts, union leaders prepared for another strike.[54] At the May Day celebration at Lethbridge, Meronik called for solidarity amongst the beet workers, who were to be put to the test in the next few days, when contracts for the 1936 season were supposed to be signed. Encouraged by the success of 1935, the majority refused "until such time as a settlement is reached between your Association and ours." Although announcing that the union intended "to retain the sympathy and good feeling" of the growers, Meronik declared to Growers' Association Secretary W.F. Russell that "we have tried hard to develop co-operation . . . but it seems to us that you would like the co-operation to be a one sided affair."[55]

The first priority from the growers' point of view was the procurement of enough "scab" labour to smash the strike before the beet crop could be damaged. In early April, Russell had requested the aid of the Provincial Department of Labour in recruiting non-union beet workers, cynically explaining that the B.W.I.U. had been responsible for sabotaging the negotiations.[56] Any labour that would be forthcoming from Alberta, however, would most likely be drawn from the ragged ranks of the urban unemployed, and would not have included "specialists," skilled beet workers. An official of the sugar company, Frank Taylor, tried to line up a group of experienced Belgians who were living on relief in St. Boniface, Manitoba. Taylor advised Russell to take 100 to 200 of this group, "as a possible source [of] . . . additional labourers, as these Belgians would make a very good break up in the general [ethnic] type."[57] Publicly the Canadian Sugar Factories threatened the union with the prospect of 400 Belgians coming into the beet fields. Most of the 450 scabs who arrived, however, were not experienced beet workers but unemployed city dwellers.

The strike breakers were recruited by the Alberta Department of Labour in Calgary and Edmonton and transported to the beet fields in buses chartered by the Growers' Association, protected by the R.C.M.P.[58] Although Communists in the cities printed handbills warning of the situation in the Lethbridge area and urged the unemployed not to serve the "interests of the rich," most of the strike breakers did not know that they were being sent Southern Alberta to work as scabs.[59] Many would not have cared if they had known. One eager scab wrote to Frank Taylor that he and his son "were not concerned with the so-called strike, but with the opportunity to fill whatever the agreement calls for."[60] Although some of the imported workers protested that they had been deceived, most went to work and although they were "slow, not being used to that labour" the growers were able to increase beet acreage to a record level.[61]

This successful importation of relief recipients could not be countered by the B.W.I.U. Picketing the beet fields was an impossible task, although the strikers demonstrated at the bus depots where the imported workers arrived.[62] While the growers had automobiles, the workers had to rely on bicycles for transportation and communication.[63] The R.C.M.P. patrolled what the *Lethbridge Herald* called the "strike front," work which earned the force a letter of thanks from the Growers' Association to commend its "excellent service" and "cooperation in handling the labour situation in the sugar beet fields."[64] This "cooperation" took the form of telling strikers to "move on" if they attempted to demonstrate at the farms of prominent growers. Only one arrest was made, that of Steve Koleszar who was charged with "intimidation" of scabs working the beets of Growers' Association President Phil Baker.[65]

The Growers supplemented their use of strike breakers and police with a policy of evicting strikers from their beet shacks. The evictions were carried out in a more aggressive manner than in 1935. The most tense moments of the strike occurred in connection with the evictions and threatened evictions of beet workers in the Taber area, the strikers' strongest base. While hundreds of angry strikers demonstrated outside, hearings to determine the legality of the evictions took place in the Taber Courthouse. The arguments soon turned away from the subtleties of the case to the merits of the beet workers' struggle. Speaking for the growers, lawyer B.L. Cooke claimed that "fear of communism or foreign influence, call it what you will" was the main motivation of his clients. On behalf of the strikers, L.C. Hendry, counsel for the B.W.I.U., charged that the labourers had been ready to sign the agreement, "but had got no chance," and added "whether Communist or Hindu did not affect contract matters." In the end the presiding judge approved the eviction orders, but urged delay in implementing them pending further negotiations between the opposing parties. The next day half a dozen families were thrown out of their homes in the Taber area.[66]

The strike had turned into a disaster for the Union, and it made a tactical retreat by announcing its intention to disaffiliate from the Workers' Unity League, in response to employer claims that the W.U.L. lay at the heart of the dispute. The B.W.I.U. announcement stated that the union was expecting to receive a charter from the Trades and Labour Congress, and that communications to that effect had already been sent to Paddy Draper, the President of the T.L.C. This, of course, was no great concession, since the W.U.L. was in the process of dissolving itself at that very moment, yet the union was hopeful that the move would deprive the Growers' Association of an effective rhetorical weapon which had been "poisoning public opinion against the B.W.I.U."[67] The Growers' Association had maintained from the beginning that its objection was to Communism, not to labour unions, and had promised to negotiate if the workers were represented by a "legitimate" union.

But the officers of the Growers' Association were not impressed by the disaffiliation. Sensing that they had their adversary on the run, they refused further negotiations as suggested by the judge, and handed down a simple ultimatum. This demanded that both the union and individual workmen formally renounce any connection "directly or indirectly," with the "Communistic Party of Canada." Further, rates for those workers who contracted on a share rather than a straight cash basis were to be negotiated individually. The grower was to "retain the privilege of . . . hiring or dismissing any unsatisfactory employee." Union officers were to sign immediately, while the strikers were given twenty-four hours to "negotiate" their contracts with the farmers.[68] Although the leaders of the union disregarded the ultimatum — probably because the growers' threat "to secure other labour" if they did not sign must have seemed rather ludicrous in the light of the scabbing of previous weeks — the end was drawing near. On Wednesday, 27 May, the day after the ultimatum was handed down, Meronik chaired a meeting in Taber at which the strikers voted with but one dissenting voice, to return to the fields. The next day, the second and last strike of the beet labourers of Southern Alberta came to an end. In a final statement the B.W.I.U. declared that the strikers had gone back to work in order to preserve the basis of "co-operation between growers and workers" necessary to "overcome the problems connected with the raising of beets."[69] Rather than see the crop destroyed and the future of the industry damaged, the Union would "temporarily call off the fight" against the sugar company.[70] Despite the face-saving posture, it was obvious to all parties that the B.W.I.U. had been soundly defeated. Workers went back to the fields, and though over three hundred of the scabs stayed on the job, the large acreage of 1936—planted in response to the "50-50" agreement with the sugar company—provided work for most of the now humble strikers. There is little evidence of any large scale blacklisting of beet workers for their union activities, although there was certainly some discrimination.[71] The man who suffered most from the strike was rebel grower W.H. Childress, who had tried to unify his fellow growers with their workers against the sugar company. Childress was expelled from the Growers' Association and the Rogers Sugar Company refused to contract with him for his beets. He was left with no choice but to give up beet culture.[72]

The Growers were determined to consolidate their victory of 1936 and to crush the last vestiges of trade unionism among their workers. President Baker told the 1937 Growers' convention that "the grower is the one to determine what he can pay labour." "Negotiations with the present organization," he continued, "cannot be carried on."[73] The Growers' Association resumed a policy of ignoring the Union, pretending that it simply did not exist. Steve Varju, Union Secretary, had written to request that the Union Executive be allowed to appear before the convention.[74] The request was rejected on the ground that "the amount of business" made this impossible.[75] This letter of refusal was the last written communication between growers' and workers' representatives. The Union persisted in a one-way dialogue with the Growers' Association until 1942, pathetically clinging to this line of "worker-grower cooperation" to produce "increased yields and incomes." But requests, never demands, for negotiations and discussions of grievances continued to go unanswered. A name change to the Alberta Beet Workers' Union, to demonstrate further independence from the Communist Party, had no effect on the growers' determination to treat the Union as if it were not there. In 1937 and again in 1938 the Union tried to invoke Alberta's labour legislation to force the creation of a Board of Conciliation, and appealed to the Alberta Board of Industrial Relations for its support. After correspondence with the Growers' Association, however, the Board accepted the growers' argument that "beet workers should come under the heading of farm labour" and thus be ineligible for any legal protection.[76] With the outbreak of war the Union suffered a blow with the internment of its only full-time organizer, Bill Repka, a member of the Communist Party who was arrested in the general roundup of Communists after Canada declared war. Repka, who describes himself as having been "a small fry in the party organization" feels his arrest was designed more to intimidate the immigrant beet workers than to remove a serious threat to national security.[77]

The Second World War, however, provided the Union with more favourable circumstances in which to operate. Wartime sugar shortages increased beet sugar's share of the domestic market, but the necessary increase in beet production had to be carried out with labour in short supply because of mobilization and the revival of the rest of the prairie agricultural economy. Armed with a charter as local 103 of United Cannery, Agricultural, Packing and Allied Workers, a Canadian Congress of Labour affiliate, the Alberta Beet Workers' Union reappeared in 1941 to request, "in a spirit of co-operation and good will," negotiations on wages and working conditions.[78] The Growers' Association maintained its "no negotiations" stance and appealed to federal and provincial governments to "protect us from unfair labour demands."[79] The A.B.W.U. refused to disappear. On 14 February 1942, it once again requested negotiations, promising that its members were "prepared to do our utmost towards the war effort by producing vast quantities of sugar beets" if assured of "a decent living wage."[80] Less than a week later, over the vociferous protests of those Southern Albertans who were not associated with the beet industry, the Growers' Association, with the support and encouragement of P.T. Rogers of Canadian Sugar Factories, began to negotiate with the B.C. Security Commission to import more than a thousand Japanese from internment camps to the beet fields.[81] These indentured Japanese workers unwittingly and unwillingly drove the last nails into the coffin of attempts to unionize Alberta's beet workers.

The outcome of the struggles of the mid 1930s calls into question the viability of the radicals' model of the farmer/labour coalition against monopoly. Was it in fact soundly based? The farmers manifestly had failed to take their place shoulder to shoulder with their workers. What had caused their failure to do so — subjective factors which might not have inevitably determined the outcome, or "objective" ones, of conflicting class interest between themselves and the working class? In the former category might be placed the effectiveness of anti-radical propaganda, and its underlying ethnic context. After all, as Frank Taylor of the Canadian Sugar Factories noted, "the Unity League . . . comprises [sic] mostly of the Hungarian and South European workers."[82] The farmers, on the other hand, were, by and large, "true" Canadians, Anglo-Saxons, immune to "communism." In a pattern familiar to students of Western Canadian society class lines tended to be strongly reinforced by ethnicity. If this facilitated, in many cases, the organization of the working class by the radicals, it made the prospect of the kind of class alliance which the Beet Workers' Union sought with the farmers all the more difficult to cement.[83] There was, of course, a certain impetus towards the "united front" amongst some of the more discontented and "progressive" farmers, but if the rank and file could be convinced that the workers' aim was to "bolshevize" them, to drag them down into the ranks of the proletariat, this could be nipped in the bud. The "natural" antipathy of the farmers towards organized labour generally did not hurt the campaign against the beet workers' programme of action. Perhaps this programme was presented in a manner too crude, too dogmatic by the beet workers and their left-wing friends to be effective in reaching the farmer-grower.

On the other hand, although it could be argued that both groups were being "fleeced" by the sugar monopolists, there were objective factors standing in the way of farmer/labour unity. The beet growers belonged to a fortunate group of prairie agriculturalists that was not ruined economically by the Depression. If their relative prosperity was rather precariously balanced on the backs of the labouring class, it is not to be expected that they would be among the first to want to upset this arrangement. Despite the overall hegemony of the sugar monopolists, it was the farmers who were the actual employers of labour. It was *their* profits that were most directly threatened by demands for higher wages. The union answered that both groups should join hands against the company. Yet where did the path of struggle outlined by the workers lead? To risky, perhaps ruinous confrontations with corporate power or even to the closure of Canadian Sugar Factories? Rogers Sugar by no means depended upon Alberta sugar beets alone for profits. By means of small but significant concessions, the sugar interests were able to keep the farmers in line. The growers' leadership was shrewd enough to turn the labour situation to account, as a bargaining lever, to improve their Association's position in relation to the sugar company. The "50-50" split and the construction of a new plant at Picture Butte provide two important examples of this. Ironically , the agitation by the beet workers, designed ostensibly to unite grower and worker, drew the company and the growers closer together. C.C. Spencer, president of the Growers' Association during the 1935 strike, later commented that "we got closer to *our* company" [emphasis added] during the strike and that the Executive decided from then onward "not to buck them on large issues."[84] The most symbolic demonstration of this new grower-company relationship came during the growers' convention of 1940. After the members unanimously re-elected Phil Baker to a fifth consecutive term as president of the Association, they rose, bowed their heads and remained silent to commemorate the memory of the recently-departed president of the sugar monopoly, the late E.T. Rogers![85]

Notes

1. O.S. Longman, "The Beet Sugar Industry in Alberta" (unpublished mss., Archives of the Glenbow-Alberta Institute [hereinafter Glenbow], 1960), 10.
2. *Strathmore and Bow Valley Standard*, 3 December 1910. For similar enthusiastic comments see the testimony given before the House of Commons Tariff Commission, 1905, published as *The Beet Sugar Industry* (Ottawa, 1909), 45-54.
3. For descriptions of the effort necessary to cultivate sugar beets see Franklin A. Harris, *The Sugar Beet in America* (New York, 1925), 44-48, 117-25, 149-57; Heather Robertson, *Sugar Farmers of Manitoba* (Altona, 1968), 127-50; L.S. Arnington, *Beet Sugar in the West: A History of the Utah-Idaho Sugar Company* (Seattle, 1966), 23-37. The estimate of the number of hours of labour per acre is from F.R. Taylor, "Twenty-

five Years Show Many Improvements," in Alberta Sugar Beet Growers, *Twenty-fifth Annual Report* (Lethbridge, 1949), 11-12. Mechanization came slowly to the beet industry. Machines that could handle the beets without damage at all stages of the growing cycle were slowly developed, but until complete mechanization could be achieved there were always "bottlenecks" at which large concentrations of labour were required. To be available when needed, workers usually demanded a season's employment.

4. Alberta Department of Agriculture, *A Historical Series of Agricultural Statistics for Alberta* (Edmonton, 1971), 22-23. Complaints about the inability to obtain beets can be found in the Minutes of the Knight Sugar Company, Glenbow. See especially the annual report of E.P. Ellison, manager for 1907. For an editorial comment see *Canadian Farm Implements*, April 1911, 38.

5. Glenbow, Papers of the Knight Sugar Company, E.P. Ellison to John Hallstead, 22 February 1908 and J.E. Ellison to Joseph Friedl, 28 January 1913; *Beet Sugar Industry*, 71.

6. Glenbow, Canadian Pacific Railway Collection, *Alberta's Sweetest Industry*, pamphlet, f.876.

7. *Lethbridge Herald*, 29 January 1923. This Association became the basis of the Alberta Cooperative Beet Growers' Association, which represented the growers in their dealings with labour, the sugar company and with governments. Since the Association was not a true co-operative and did not pool production for sale the "Cooperative" was later deleted.

8. In its American operations the Utah-Idaho Company, like most other American Beet Sugar Companies, was responsible for providing workers to their growers at a pre-arranged cost.

9. See J.B. Hedges, *Building the Canadian West* (New York, 1939), chap. 12, for a discussion of this agreement.

10. *Lethbridge Herald*, 13 February 1925.

11. *Lethbridge Herald*, "No Need for Japs," 22 May 1925; interview with Mr. A.E. Palmer, Lethbridge, 1958, quoted in Longman, "Beet Sugar Industry in Alberta," 464. Nationalities most represented among the newcomers were Hungarians, followed by Yugoslavs and Czechs. The C.P.R. also brought Mennonite settlers into the area although the Mennonites usually worked as share-croppers on rented land or were assisted to make small land purchases by the Mennonite Colonization Board, established by the C.P.R.'s Department of Colonization.

12. E.J. Hobsbawm and George Rudé, *Captain Swing* (London, 1969).

13. Sample labour contracts can be found in Glenbow, C.P.R. Collection, f.685 and in Glenbow, Beet Sugar Papers [hereinafter BSP], through various files. The "hold back" system was introduced in 1928, after high wages in the grain harvest made workers reluctant to return to dig beets. There were eventually three types of contract: straight cash contract, as described above; a tonnage contract which paid for each ton of beets produced; and a crop share contract which gave the worker a share of the value of the beets produced. The first examples of crop share contracts do not appear in BSP until 1939. Most workers could not afford to wait for the sale of the crop to receive their pay and chose the cash option.

14. See Glenbow, C.P.R. Collection, Art Dahl to J.E. Brownlee, 13 February 1929, f.1017. Beetworkers, like most agricultural workers, lived in quarters that are better described as shacks than houses. Growers provided them with whatever was available —an abandoned chicken coop, an unused granary, or what was left of the house once occupied by the grower and his family.

15. Longman, "Beet Sugar Industry in Alberta," 432, 463-65.

16. Glenbow, BSP, J.S. Stewart, MP, to J.M. Macdonnell, MP, 20 June 1933, f.2. The weighted average beet price for 1925 to 1930, when Utah-Idaho operated the factory, was $6.88 a ton. From 1931 to 1934 the weighted average price was $6.01 a ton. Authors' calculations using data from the Alberta Department of Agriculture, *Agricultural Statistics for Alberta*, 22-23.

17. Glenbow, BSP, W.F. Russell to R.B. Bennett and H.H. Stevens, 28 November 1932, f.1.

18. Glenbow, BSP, Russell to J.S. Stewart, 27 March 1933, f.2.

19. Ibid.

20. Glenbow, BSP, J. Sutton to R.B. Bennett, 8 March 1934, f.10. On the F.U.L. see Ivan Avakumovic. "The Communist Party of Canada and the Prairie Farmer: the Interwar Years" in *Western Perspectives*, ed. David J. Bercuson (Toronto, 1974), 1: 78-87.

21. This is a weighted average, calculated from contract rates in Glenbow, BSP, f.1-4. Rumours of further cuts are reported in The Beet Worker, 11 May 1936. Various copies of this paper may be found in Glenbow, BSP.

22. Glenbow, C.P.R. Collection, James Colley to C.A. Van Scoy, 30 June 1928, f.727.

23. *The Worker*, 11 May 1935. Palmer ran as a Communist in Drumheller in the provincial election of 1935.

24. Interview with Peter Meronik by the authors, 19 June 1977, at Coleman, Alberta. A transcript of this interview is available in the Glenbow Archives.

25. Details of radical activity among the growers are sketchy. From press reports of F.U.L. meetings it appears that the workers got their greatest degree of grower support from those areas north and west of Lethbridge which were furthest from the factory in Raymond. These were the areas that had the largest percentages of growers with less than fifteen acres of beets and the smallest percentages of growers with three acres of beets and more. Authors' calculations based on Glenbow, BSP, "Division of Growers By Acreage Classes," f.9.

26. *Lethbridge Herald*, 18 March 1936. Membership in the "Fifteen Ton Club" was an honour bestowed by the Growers' Association and the *Herald* upon those farmers who raised more than fifteen tons of beets to an acre.

27. W.H. Childress, "Rich Spoils in Alberta Handed to Big Capital," *The Worker*, 20 April 1935.

28. Glenbow, BSP, J. Sutton to Hon. F.S. Grisdale, 29 April 1935, f.10.

29. Glenbow, BSP, T.H. Harris to Premier Reid, 27 April 1935, f.10.

30. Glenbow, BSP, J. Gragan to Attorney General, 13 April 1935, f.10.

31. W.A Buchanan, editor and publisher of the *Herald*, was a member of the Board of Directors of Canadian Sugar Factories.

32. *The Worker*, 4 May 1935. There is a copy of the eviction announcement in Glenbow, BSP, f.10.

33. *The Worker*, 7 May 1935.

34. The quotation is from the interview with Peter Meronik, see n. 24, above.

35. Glenbow, BSP, Ted Sundal to Hon. J.S. Grisdale, 3 May 1936, f.10.

36. Glenbow, BSP, L.C. Charlesworth to Grisdale, 9 May 1935, f.10.

37. Glenbow, BSP, B.W.I.U. Circular, "To All Workers," f.10. This was the position taken by the Agricultural and Cannery Workers Union, W.U.L., which conducted a small scale attempt to organize Ontario beet labour at the same time.

38. *The Worker*, 21 May 1935.

39. Ibid., 8 August 1935.

40. Ibid., 20-22 August 1935.

41. Glenbow, BSP, Nick Wilwerth to T.G. Wood, 16 January 1936 and reply, 21 January 1936, f.4.

42. *The Beet Worker*, 11 May 1936.

43. Glenbow, BSP, B.W.I.U. Circular, "Beet Growers Protect Your Crop," f.4.

44. Glenbow, BSP, "Recommendations for 1936 Labour Contracts," 24 February 1936, f.4.

45. *Lethbridge Herald*, 28-29 February 1936.

46. For a discussion of the operation of this contract, see Canada, Restrictive Trade Practices Commission, *Report Concerning the Sugar Industry in Western Canada* (Ottawa, 1957), 48.

47. Glenbow, BSP, f.3.

48. Glenbow, BSP, Peter Meronik and John Beluch to Growers' Association, 17 March 1936, f.3.

49. Glenbow, BSP, "Recommendations for 1936 Labour Contracts," 21 March 1936, f.3.

50. *Lethbridge Herald*, 7 April 1936.

51. Ibid., 11 April 1936.

52. Glenbow, BSP, B.W.I.U. Circular, "To All Sugar Beet Growers," f.4.

53. *The Worker*, 1 May 1936; *The Beet Worker*, 11 May 1936.

54. *The Worker*, 5 May 1936.

55. Glenbow, BSP, Meronik to Russell, 5 May 1936, f.4.

56. Glenbow, BSP, Russell to Walter Smitten, Provincial Labour Commissioner, 7 April 1936, f.4.

57. Glenbow, BSP, Frank Taylor to Russell, 28 March 1936, f.4. Manitoba farmers experimented with beets in 1933 but did not succeed in obtaining a factory until 1941. This created unemployment among skilled beetworkers in 1936. See J.H. Ellis, *The Ministry of Agriculture in Manitoba* (Winnipeg, 1971), 331ff.

58. Glenbow, BSP, Ernest Bennion to Russell, 18 June 1936; Russell to Smitten, 29 June 1936; Russell to Greyhound Bus Lines, 17 June 1936, f.4.

59. Glenbow, BSP, W.U.L. Circular, "Workers on Strike on Lethbridge Northern," f.4.

60. Glenbow, BSP, S.C. Cain to Taylor, 26 May 1936, f.4.

61. Alberta Department of Agriculture, *Agricultural Statistics for Alberta*, 22-23. Since beets were planted by machine this stage of the operation was carried out without reliance on hired labour.

62. Interview with Peter Meronik, 19 June 1977.

63. Ibid.

64. Glenbow, BSP, Russell to H.M. Newsome, Assistant Commissioner R.C.M.P., 30 June 1936, f.4.

65. *Lethbridge Herald*, 20 May 1936.

66. Ibid., 23-26 May 1936.

67. Glenbow, BSP, "Statement of the Central Executive Board of the B.W.I.U. of C. on National Affiliation to the W.U.L. and Relation to Political Parties," f.4.

68. Glenbow, BSP, Phillip Baker and W.F. Russell to Peter Meronik, 28 May 1936, f.4.

69. *Lethbridge Herald*, 28 May 1936.

70. *The Worker*, 6 June 1936.

71. Glenbow, BSP, f.5 contains a report of a grower named C.M. Quam refusing to re-employ a Union beetworker, Andy Saly.

72. Glenbow, BSP, George Babint to T.G. Wood and Phillip Baker, 1937, f.5.

73. *Lethbridge Herald*, 26 February 1937.
74. Glenbow, BSP, Steve Varju to W.F. Russell, 25 February 1937, f.5.
75. Glenbow, BSP, Russell to Varju, 27 February 1937, f.5.
76. Glenbow, BSP, Clayton Adams to Russell, 23 May 1938, f.5. This decision also had the effect of denying beetworkers coverage by the Workmen's Compensation and Minimum Wage Acts.
77. Bill Repka, Interview by Allen Seager, Toronto, March 1978.
78. Glenbow, BSP, John Beluch to W.F. Russell, 26 February 1941, f.8.
79. Glenbow, BSP, Phillip Baker to Hon. J.A. MacKinnon, 22 July 1941, f.8.
80. Glenbow, BSP, William Tarasoff to W.F. Russell, 12 February 1942, f.9.
81. Glenbow, BSP, A. MacNamara, Assistant Deputy Minister of Labour to Russell, 17 February 1942, f.9. For examples of local opposition see Phil Baker to Humphrey Mitchell, 16 March 1942. Mayor David Elton of Lethbridge led the opposition to the use of Japanese labour, calling the Japanese "ourang-outangs" who would cause problems which outweighed their advantages to the beet growers. *Lethbridge Herald*, 27 June 1942. See also David B. Iwaasa "The Japanese in Southern Alberta 1941–45," *Alberta History* 24 (Summer 1976): 5-19.
82. Glenbow, BSP, Frank Taylor to S.C. Cain, 23 May 1936, f.4.
83. Officers and directors of Alberta Cooperative Sugar Beet Growers were without exception of British Isles, American or Scandinavian descent, as far as one may judge from their names, despite the fact that many small growers were Mennonite or Eastern European. It is interesting to compare a list of A.C.S.B.G. officers with the names of members of the "Fifteen Ton Club." Since the smaller farmers, the Europeans, did most of their own work, they qualified for this honour more often than the members of the executive of the Growers' Association!
84. Glenbow, BSP, C.C. Spencer to Russell, 10 December 1936, f.4.
85. *Lethbridge Herald*, 21 February 1940.

NORTHERN SETTLEMENT, 1929–1935†

T.J.D. POWELL

During the thirties thousands of people living on farms and residing in urban centres across Canada were forced by severe drought conditions or unemployment to seek a livelihood elsewhere. Some farmers moved to other provinces, others to urban centres and still others sought refuge in northern districts of their own provinces. Many of the unemployed travelled throughout the country in an attempt to find work, others returned to the land in order to provide food and shelter for their families.

In Saskatchewan, many of these farmers and the unemployed, either through their own initiative or under government-sponsored settlement schemes, migrated to the northern part of the province in order to establish new homes. At first, this "back-to-the-land" movement appeared promising to the countless families who trekked northward. They had received assurance through the media, government officials and word-of-mouth that the northern lands would certainly provide the necessities of life if not improve their standard of living. Some families, in fact, did improve their economic status, but others experienced poverty or even worse conditions. Pioneering experiences were found to be quite unlike those recorded by prairie farmers as the challenges confronting the northern settler were greater and the risks much higher.

The development of this northern region was also quite different from the history of prairie settlement. Since the 1870s, the colonization of Western Canada has constituted part of the National Policy, whereby the northern half of the continent would be linked together from coast to coast by railroads and settlements. By the late 1920s this period of

† *Saskatchewan History* 30, no. 3 (Autumn 1977): 81–98.

prairie expansion had definitely concluded, with the better agricultural areas of the park belt occupied by homesteaders. Settlers in ever increasing numbers turned to the forested areas of the province in order to seek new agricultural land. Settlement and development of northern lands, however, was not a national objective or an economic end. As a result, rapid development as experienced in the southern parts of the province did not materialize in northern Saskatchewan. Colonization companies and railroad companies could not realize profits from activities in the northern region. Even the government was slow to react to the needs and problems of the northern settlers. When the government did act, its methods and actions often showed a lack of forethought and knowledge about the conditions and the way of life in the northern region. According to Denis Fitzgerald,

> Canada's great "Dream of the North" flickers uncertainly on the horizon. . . . In the Legislature the northern flea has little hope of counter-balancing the political weight of the southern elephant. In the Prairies, legislative barriers to the location and direction of settlement were few, but in northern Saskatchewan they have exerted a paramount influence.[1]

If any measure has helped to populate the northern areas of Saskatchewan Fitzgerald feels that it has been the development of natural resources.[2] Most pioneers who travelled to and settled in the northern areas depended on non-agricultural sources in order to survive. Reliance on these sources for income would depend on how long a pioneer had been in a certain district and the locality in which he homesteaded. If a settler possessed fertile land, his dependence on forest resources might decline. On the other hand, if he owned poor soil he might be encouraged or forced to seek other forms of income during the long winter months. A fortunate settler might be able to work " . . . as a lumberjack, planer, millman, trapper or fisherman. He may find temporary employment on a railway or road construction gang; sometimes he is hired as a carpenter, plumber or odd job man. . . ."[3]

Until the transfer of natural resources to the provinces in 1930, the northbound settler had to contact Dominion authorities about settlement on Crown lands. During the 1920s provincial control of natural resources and Crown lands had become a popular demand on the Prairies, receiving much coverage in the provincial press. Organizations such as the Ku Klux Klan and the United Farmers of Canada constantly referred to the natural resources issue at their meetings.[4] As early as 1926 the Anglican clergy of the Diocese of Saskatchewan passed a resolution regarding the matter.[5] Both the Progressive and the Conservative parties of Saskatchewan demanded the transfer of natural resources in their respective platforms.[6] For instance, the Saskatchewan Conservative party listed the natural resource issue as a second priority in its platform for the 1929 election. The Conservatives advocated

> that in the best interests of Confederation and the economic development of Saskatchewan, the Province of Saskatchewan should be granted its natural resources free from restrictions, within the legislative competence of the Parliament of Canada but in compliance with the letter and spirit of the constitution and that the claims of this Province to compensation for loss of funds and resources alienated should be granted. . . .[7]

If the natural resources were returned to the provinces, both political parties wished to see a rational policy of land settlement undertaken by the party in power. By means of an aggressive, yet selective immigration policy a Conservative-elected government would "take the fullest advantage of all assistance tendered by the British Government to promote Empire Settlement" and would see "special concessions granted to Canadians to enable them to settle our vacant lands."[8] After the turnover of power to an amalgam of Conservatives, Progressives and Independents in 1929, it was naturally expected that the newly-created Co-operative government headed by Premier J.T.M. Anderson could move forward with the transfer of natural resources and the return of Crown lands.

Given the prevailing opinion in the province that immigration and land settlement policies required some re-adjustment to meet the changing conditions of the time, the Anderson administration decided to establish a Royal Commission to study the matter and make recommendations to the government. Moreover, by this time the Dominion government had already declared not only its intention to return natural resources to the provinces, but also to draft all policies on immigration to meet with the expressed wishes of the various provinces involved. To meet these new challenges in an informed manner, the Saskatchewan government created a Royal Commission by Order-in-Council on January 4, 1930.[9] Persons appointed Commissioners included Dr. William W. Swanson, Professor of Economics, from Saskatoon, as Chairman; Thomas Johnson, farmer, from Govan; Percy Shelton, Chief Court Reporter, from Regina; Garnet C. Neff, barrister, from Grenfell; and Alfred R. Reusch, insurance agent, from Yorkton.[10] After conducting public hearings in thirty-seven Saskatchewan points and at Winnipeg, Manitoba, the Commission transmitted its report to the Government on September 10, 1930.[11]

Recommendations in the *Report* of the Royal Commission concerned all aspects of immigration and settlement with the hope that such principles and policies suggested might "encourage the complete development of the land and other natural resources of the province; while at the same time correcting the conditions complained of in the past and making provision for changes in administration necessary to meet the return of the natural resources to the province."[12] Briefly, the Commissioners recommended greater control of immigration and settlement policies and activities by Dominion and Provincial authorities through administrative machinery and legislation; more selective policy regarding the entry and settlement of immigrants on land or in communities; and a supervised programme of land classification, settlement and possible land re-adjustment.[13]

With regard to northern settlement the Report suggested several procedures which should be followed by the Provincial government once natural resources were turned over by Dominion authorities. First of all, the government should see

> that a complete soil and economic survey of the province be made, and that the conclusions arising from it be used as a basis for future settlement policies, and that all existing cases of location of settlers on unsuitable lands be brought to the attention of the Provincial Council of Immigration and Settlement and to land-owning corporations in cases concerning them.[14]

With drought-stricken farmers already moving to the northern forested areas, the Commissioners asked that this survey should be implemented with the remaining Crown lands first. Other noteworthy recommendations included the discontinuance of homesteading,

> and that the remaining Crown Lands where immediately available for agriculture be sold (a) to residents of the province, (b) to other Canadians, (c) to British settlers, (d) to other immigrants. Also that the Government investigate the "use lease" method of disposing of Crown lands with a view to testing it. And ... that Crown lands found suitable for settlement but which require clearing, be cleared under Government auspices, and the cost of this [be] included in the sale or lease price or such lands.[15]

Generally the recommendations of the Royal Commission suggest an orderly and systematic approach to land settlement in northern Saskatchewan. Doubt may be cast upon the optimism of the Commissioners, however, in declaring that the eventual limits of settlement might go as far north as a line drawn northwest from Amisk Lake and running just north of Ile à la Crosse.[16] The line far exceeded the areas of black and transitional (degraded black and wood calcareous) soil coverage. Furthermore, this conclusion did not take into account the wide variations in climatic conditions which prevail across the pioneer region. Although few records were kept, settlers' experiences reveal important regional variations in climate across the north, both from place to place and at different time periods. A district might possess fertile soil, but it would still be classed as sub-marginal land if it did not have adequate rainfall or average temperature.[17] Pockets of fluvial soils such as in the Meadow Lake, Goodsoil and Big River districts were found to be limited indeed. Fitzgerald feels that the thinking of Commission members in this case was based on the agricultural success of early missionaries.[18]

Optimism about the existence and productivity of agricultural lands in northern Saskatchewan had been created over the years by surveyors, newspapers, settlers' guides, word-of-mouth, and government officials. Reports of an abundant hay supply, plenty of fish, animal and timber resources and good pastures were numerous. During the period 1900–1910 surveyors such as F.J.P. Crean and other Department of Interior personnel presented favourable reports about the Green Lake, Big River and Beaver Plain districts.[19] Unfavourable reports of other regions made by Federal investigators were minimized or omitted in the *Settlers' Guide*.[20] The *Western Producer* printed the following glowing account from Arthur Dumais, district agricultural representative, who visited the Indian Boarding School Farm at Beauval (west of Lac La Plonge) which had recently escaped the frost damage that had affected crops in the more settled parts of the province.

> Sixty-five acres were sown in grain this year 1928, wheat (Marquis) was cut on August 20. Grain has been raised for the past 20 years on this farm. Injuries by frost occurred in these instances and losses were partial only.
>
> A field of five or six acres of potatoes is one of the best I have seen in Saskatchewan this year, vegetables of all kinds and description seem to do well also.

Mr. Dumais concluded, "This means to say that at a distance of 150 miles north of Prince Albert, the climatic conditions are not yet a real handicap to agriculture. What is being done at Beauval is the best proof of it."[21] Such assessments of soils and climate attracted many pioneers, but at the same time proved costly to the many farmers who did not investigate the local situation closely before taking up a homestead.

Advancement of settlers into the pioneer region did not really begin until after the First World War. Prior to that time most farmers settled on land west of the Saskatoon-Prince Albert railway and along the southern fringes of the pioneer region. During the war both the Dominion and Provincial governments conducted surveys and made new assessments of the agricultural potential of unsettled lands across the whole of Western Canada. Optimism ran high. At this juncture many government authorities seemed to believe that the failure of early settlers was due to their own inexperience and misjudgement. Although there was a greater awareness of the difficulties facing northern settlers than a decade earlier,

The Pioneer Region of Saskatchewan

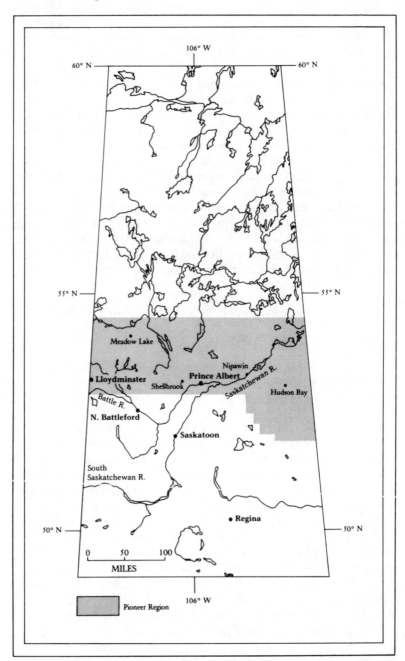

Pioneer Region

confidence abounded that these problems could be remedied. As a result, the settlement frontier advanced considerably during the post-war period, particularly with the movement of returned soldiers to the land under the auspices of the Soldier Settlement Board.[22] At this time the prospective settler was able to choose his homestead or buy land in a leisurely manner. Should the farmer make a mistake in his choice of land, he could easily rectify the matter the following year by moving to another section of land. The construction of railway branch lines to Nipawin, Fairholme and St. Walburg helped the process of settlement to some extent. By 1928 new outposts of settlement were established right across the pioneer region. Fitzgerald describes this movement in the following manner:

> The advancing frontier was stopped, or sometimes slowed by the legally established boundaries of the forest or Indian Reserves. Settlement pushed to the reserve boundaries and then often swung in the direction of least resistance. Examples are to be found in the population tongues extending northward along the Whitefox River, into the Saskatchewan Lowland northwards along the valley of the Garden River and its tributaries, west of Paddockwood and eastwards from Hudson Bay. However, the number of squatters, those with no legal rights settled within the forest reserves, increased during the 1920's. . . . The movement, at least in part, ignored differences in agricultural potential across northern Saskatchewan. It represented the first major movement on to the grey podzolic soils.[23]

The advancement of the frontier continued unabated despite some questioning of this extension. Land classification surveys made in the mid-twenties showed settlement in the following areas to have a marked dependence on agricultural income; namely, parts of the Upper-Swan-Upper-Assiniboine Plain, southern sections of the Debden-Big River Plain, the Turtleford Plain and to a lesser degree the Saskatchewan Lowlands.[24] Outside these areas increasing reliance was placed on income from a variety of non-agricultural sources. Other factors caused disappointment for many settlers. The clearing and breaking of land proceeded at a slower pace than was expected. Occasional poor weather, forest fires, inadequate equipment and swamp fever all confronted the pioneer. While discouragement and disaster fell upon some northern enthusiasts, the majority of northern settlers in the late twenties made some progress. Improvements in transportation, abundant forest, animal and fish resources prevented many pioneers from experiencing severe difficulties. In fact, by the end of the decade many northern settlers shared some hope that the good times where just around the corner.

Of course, such expectations were not to be realized in the thirties. As early as 1929 many drought-stricken farmers abandoned their lands in southern and central Saskatchewan to seek agricultural land in northern Saskatchewan.[25] The greatest migration of these people to private or public lands in the north was to take place in the years 1931 and 1932.[26] The drift of population from farm lands and urban centres to northern lands was termed a "back-to-the-land" movement. Robert England felt this land settlement movement to be a unique process in Western Canada as it was " ... perhaps the first time in the history of land settlement of the West that internal colonization has become active within the borders of the provinces."[27] The *Leader-Post* correspondent who toured the Meadow Lake district in 1931 recalled a similar, but much smaller movement of farmers from the drought-stricken southeastern part of the Assiniboia District to the park belt in the 1880s and 1890s.[28]

Many reasons have been given by scholars for the "back-to-the-land" movement. L.M. Grayson and Michael Bliss feel that the movement was a reflexive response to difficult economic times.[29] People with farming experience who had lost hope in urban life believed that agriculture would take up the slack when the industrial society broke down. A return to the farmland would at least provide a family with a modest livelihood. George Hoffman stated further that

> the large amount of support for such migration indicated that the myth that all economic problems could be solved by moving "west" onto the available frontier land was not completely dead. An original motivation behind western immigration in the early part of the century was the desire of rural and urban poor in Canada and other parts of the world to raise their standard of living. The people who left the drought area and the cities in the 1930's for the north had similar hopes.[30]

An earlier experience recorded by Robert England was the migration of people from Ontario cities to Western Canada during the economic recession of 1907–1908.[31] Numerous settlers moved northward on their own initiative and means. Others received encouragement and financial assistance from governments in order to do so. Before the transfer of natural resources in October 1930, the Saskatchewan government had made arrangements to move sheep, cattle and swine from the drought areas to other parts of the province where supplies of feed were more readily available.[32] Under this plan, the railway companies paid one-quarter of the transportation costs and the Saskatchewan government another quarter, so that the farmer was required to pay just one-half the regular freight tariff. If the farmer involved planned to move to northern Saskatchewan, the government undertook to facilitate this move by refunding one-third of the transportation charges of his farm machinery, livestock and household effects to two carloads.

While the Saskatchewan government was active in encouraging and moving settlers to the pioneer region, at the same time it was anxious to prepare and administer the remaining Crown, now Provincial, lands for homesteading purposes. In order to do this, the Anderson administration had created the Department of Natural Resources by Order-in-Council on the 29th May, 1930.[33] Under legislation passed the following spring, the Department of Natural Resources was to administer the Provincial Lands Act, the Mineral Resources Act, the Forest Act, the Water Rights Act, the Water Power Act, and other legislation assigned to it.[34] As recommended by the Royal Commission on Immigration and Settlement, the free homestead policy of the Dominion Government was discontinued. The old regulations, whereby a homesteader could settle on 160 acres of Crown land, pre-empt another quarter section, and after completing a three-year period of duties obtain a patent, were abolished. Instead the Conservative government enacted the Provincial Lands Act which allowed for the classification and disposal of all Crown lands thought suitable for settlement.[35] The Department of Natural Resources were ordered to sell this land in parcels of 160 acres. More specifically, it was decided that valuable settlement land would be sold at the minimum or upset price of three dollars per acre, and ordinary settlement land would be sold at the minimum price of one dollar per acre.[36] An initial downpayment of 10 percent of the upset price was required by the terms of the sale, with the balance owing to be spread over a period of twelve years with interest at 6 percent.[37] The reason given for this change in homestead policy was estimated cost. According to Britnell,

> an early review was made of the cost of survey and administration of homestead lands, and it was estimated by Department officials that every homestead entry and disposition involved an administrative cost of from $100 to $200 per homestead unit. This included cost of survey, inspection, general correspondence and issuing of patent. It was felt that the general public and general revenues of the Province should not be called upon to subsidize entrants on homestead lands by bearing all the cost of administration . . . the necessary order-in-council amending the existing Dominion regulations was passed within a few weeks of the transfer of administration from federal to Provincial control.[38]

In December 1930, Premier Anderson announced a new plan of assisted land settlement by his government for those Saskatchewan citizens who were experienced in and conversant with local methods of farming, yet could not afford to settle on Provincial lands.[39] The Saskatchewan leader added further that both senior governments would contribute to this settlement plan which would give preference to Canadian citizens by birth or naturalization. Several months later, the Land

Settlement Act was passed by the Legislative Assembly and scheduled to come into effect on May 1, 1931.[40] The Act stipulated that advances made to settlers were to be used "for the purpose of providing housing material and fuel, and for land clearing, ploughing and fencing, in order to relieve the immediate necessities of the settler and his family and to place him in a position to provide for himself and them."[41] Prior to application for a loan, a person must have resided in Saskatchewan for five years and possessed livestock or other farm equipment to the value of two hundred dollars. The debt incurred by the prospective home-steader was repayable to the Crown at a rate of interest at 6½ percent per annum with the instalments not to extend beyond a twenty-year period. Once the individual had passed these qualifications he was entitled to an advance of not more than five hundred dollars in any one case. Later in 1934, an amendment to the Act allowed a further sum of not more than one hundred dollars to be advanced to a settler ". . . by way of credit for the purchase price of such farm equipment as may be necessary to enable the settler to carry on operations."[42] In order to qualify for this advance, a settler had to have not less than ten acres under cultivation and to have increased the commercial value of his property through permanent improvements.

Through the Land Settlement Scheme and relief expenditures, the senior governments attempted to alleviate distress, not only in the rural areas, but also in the urban centres. Initial reaction to the Land Settlement Scheme by local city governments was one of caution. When approached by the British Workers' Association to provide monetary assistance in placing some of the unemployed on northern lands, the city councils of Saskatoon and Regina were reluctant at first to endorse the scheme.[43] According to a newspaper account, several councillors in both centres approved of the settlement scheme, but the municipal bodies as a whole were hesitant to approve of the principle of extending financial assistance to such settlers. The City of Saskatoon did show interest and co-operation in the "back-to-the-land" movement under the government assisted scheme.

In late spring of 1931, forty-two families with farming experience left from that city by covered wagon, automobile and truck to settle in the Loon Lake district. Saskatoon assisted this endeavour by providing trans-portation to their destination, paying the sixteen-dollar filing fee and distributing a sum of forty dollars to each family. Until their departure, the families were kept on city relief while an advance party constructed dwellings on their homesteads.[44] C.G. Hoffman of Turtleford, one of the first settlers to take advantage of the land settlement programme, reported in March of the following year that the inhabitants of "Little Saskatoon"

> were comfortably established in warm log houses which they them-
> selves had built. Clothing and groceries were being supplied by the

Saskatchewan Relief Commission, assisted by the Red Cross Society. Game was plentiful and none wanted for the necessities of life.

During the winter months members of the community occupied themselves with their various duties, improving their farms and buildings, tending to the comfort of their stock and preparing for the spring work. In the evenings the fathers and mothers gathered at various homes for social intercourse and every Friday evening a dance was held in one or another of the houses. . . .[45]

An editorial in the Regina *Leader-Post* suggested that the "back-to-the-land" movement might eventually take on the form of a province-wide enterprise and be extended to those without farming experience.

It might be in order to consider an enlargement of this scheme as an experimental proposition. Regina, for instance, where [un]employment has been serious, might be prepared to join with the Provincial Government in seeking to place some of its unemployed on the land, provided, of course, any risk involved were not too great. It may be doubted if the scheme should be confined to those who have had farm experience or to those having assets in the form of farm equipment. Western Canada has had some arresting examples of people from England and other countries conspicuously succeeding on the land here while they have no previous farming experience. The man without farming experience has not infrequently been found to have "it" to succeed at agriculture.[46]

This response to some extent reflects the problem of unemployment in Regina, but it also shows a lack of knowledge and understanding about agricultural conditions and the situation of newly arrived farmers in the north.

Reports by newspaper correspondents, government officials, and others indicate that while there were some farmers achieving success, others were not so fortunate. Even before the Land Settlement Scheme was activated, reports had been received from northern areas about poor crop conditions. Charles A. Ayre, Liberal M.L.A. for Turtleford, had indicated that farmers in his constituency and elsewhere across the north were in serious difficulty and that many of them might need relief to tide them over the winter months. According to Mr. Ayre,

approximately 60 per cent of the wheat crop was at present in the stook, and that between 85 per cent of the oat crop was still standing in the field. He pointed out that it will be almost impossible to thresh this crop, and also that where farmers do not put the crop through the machines it will grade tough.[47]

In October 1931 Wilfrid Eggleston, Toronto *Star* representative, reported the need for government relief to be swiftly distributed to many people in the northern districts.[48]

About the same time a correspondent for the Regina *Leader-Post* toured the Meadow Lake district and reported on the condition of the settlers there.[49] His findings varied considerably. Some of the people he talked to were making a comfortable living off the land or from other non-agricultural sources, but others were not. There were other problems as well. For example, many farmers moved to the Meadow Lake area fully equipped with furniture, livestock and implements. Before they could use their equipment and furniture, however, the land had to be cleared and a home had to be constructed. Both tasks required time and effort, and if a family did not have enough money for food, then their work was seriously curtailed.[50] House construction was not considered a problem by many as the only expense would be glass for windows and lumber for the door. But the *Leader-Post* correspondent added the fact that if the construction and plastering were not done properly, headaches would continue for the inhabitants.

> The log building work seen was good, but none of the settlers seemed to have mastered the art of mud plastering as practiced by the Ukrainians. They were using straight mud which always cracks and falls out. The Ukrainians tramp together mud and slough grass with just enough mud to hold the fibres together. A double handful of this thrown with force into the crack between the logs would "key" and stay there for ten or twenty years if the roof has enough overhang to keep most of the rain off.[51]

Inexperience and little supervision seemed to be the major problem confronting newly arrived settlers.

The Anderson government seemed quite sensitive to any criticism of its Land Settlement Scheme and the movement in general. It was also anxious to fulfil the demands for more agricultural land. Premier Anderson and Howard McConnell, minister-in-charge, toured northern districts to get a first-hand look at the condition of settlers, progress made and problems confronting them. Both men expressed concern about farmers not establishing themselves in time to prepare gardens, or build houses before the cold winter.[52] When reports of destitution among new farmers in the Meadow Lake and Big River districts were received, the Premier announced that relief officers had immediately been sent by the Government to ascertain their needs.[53]

On the other hand, the Saskatchewan government, caught up in the idealism of the time, was perhaps too quick in responding to demands for more agricultural land. For instance, in July 1931 the Department of Natural Resources threw open for settlement 434 quarter-sections of land formerly in forest reserves created by the Federal government.[54]

Again on October 30th seven townships of land from the proposed Candle Lake Indian Reserve were made available to settlers.[55] Later, sections of the Pasquia and Porcupine Forest reserves had to be allotted for homesteads. In some cases, squatters pushed by the forest boundaries going so far as to invade the southern fringes of Prince Albert National Park. The pressure for land could also be shown in the movement of settlers onto the southern Missouri Coteau and the northern sections of Shellbrook-Meath Park Plain, areas hitherto avoided. Many of these moves seem to have been made in desperation with people willing to settle almost anywhere. Perhaps the conditions they left behind them influenced their decisions on the choice of a homestead. Although the soil was poor, many thought the ample moisture of the north would make up for that deficiency. As Fitzgerald points out:

> According to longer established pioneers most crops could be grown. Livestock fattened on rich natural pastures would find a good market. There was little doubt that any difficulties would eventually be overcome. Any suggestion that the new home might, under certain circumstances, provide as precarious and as low a standard of living as the prairie farm was not to be entertained, even briefly.[56]

For its part, the Anderson government seems to have been caught off-guard by this invasion of the north. In order to catch up, the Government did not take the time to carry out detailed investigations of the soil, climate and topography, as recommended by the Royal Commission. As a result, many pioneers were allowed to settle on marginal land apparently oblivious to any drawbacks and disadvantages of the locality. In order to make up for these mistakes, the Provincial government in late 1932 began to decrease the number of farm titles registered in each successive month. Only those with sufficient equipment and capital could make a successful entry. Forest reserves were once again increased in size, Bronson and Meadow Lake Forest Reserves were established, and an extension of Pasquia Forest Reserve into the Saskatchewan and Manitoba Lowlands was contemplated.[57]

Before the Anderson administration started cutting back on entries, Saskatchewan, along with seven other provinces, entered into another land settlement scheme with the Dominion government and the respective municipal governments of each province. The 1932 Relief Settlement Plan stipulated that the Federal government would make a non-recoverable expenditure of one-third of an amount not to exceed six hundred dollars per family. The other two-thirds of the financial aid was to be contributed by the municipality and province concerned. Under this agreement the contribution of the Dominion would

> be payable to the province progressively as expenditures were made by the province and municipalities and the total expenditure on

behalf of any one family during the first year should not exceed
$500 for all purposes inclusive of subsistence and establishment, a
minimum amount of $100 to be withheld to provide subsistence
if necessary during the second year.[58]

The details of Saskatchewan's relief settlement scheme were formu-
lated at a conference of urban and provincial government representatives
held in Regina on May 9, 1932. Contrary to Federal wishes the delegates
decided that the amount to be given to each family would be a non-
recoverable grant not to exceed three hundred dollars.[59] According to
William Redhead of the Regina civic relief board, this money was to be
expended in the following manner: reserved for twelve months' maintenance, $120; for building material, $50; reserved until three acres of
land were broken, $15; reserved for land inspection if necessary, $25;
and the balance available for farm equipment, $90.[60]
In order to qualify for this assistance, applicants had to be either on
relief or otherwise be in receipt of relief. All applications for assistance
were to be sent to the local municipal authorities. In urban municipalities
usually a committee of the local relief board handled the applications.
For those residing in a rural municipality, the procedure was more
complicated. First of all,

a certificate must be issued by the proper officers that should
persons now farming apply for assistance in moving to a new
location, such applicants must abandon their equities in their present lands, and that so far as practicable the municipality will undertake that the lands abandoned will be withdrawn from settlement.
A certificate may also be required to the effect that there is no
unoccupied location available within the municipality for the settler.
This latter provision is to guard against moving settlers great dis-
tances to doubtful locations when equally good farms are available
within the municipality.[61]

Once a family was nominated by the local committee, its application
was then forwarded to the Provincial Advisory Committee for final
approval. Before that was received, however, candidates desirous of
settling in northern Saskatchewan had to satisfy the officials that they
had inspected the actual land to be settled upon by the family. Applicants
had to submit either a copy of the agreement under which they were
buying land, or proof that they had acquired or owned land.[62] Finally,
the wife of the household was interviewed in the matter.[63]
The Relief Settlement Plan was in effect until March 31, 1934, at
which time the agreement was renewed by the parties involved. Despite
urgings from Thomas M. Molloy, deputy-minister of the Department
of Railways, Labour and Industries, the Regina City Council at first

refused to have the three-hundred-dollar per family grant increased to six hundred. According to Mayor McAra, members of City Council feared that if the grant were raised to six hundred dollars, those who participated in the Relief Settlement Plan the previous year on a three-hundred- dollar advance, would seek the extra amount.[64] After much debate, details of a new financial agreement were released which allowed a four-hundred-dollar advance.[65] Not only did the cost per family rise, but also the municipality participating in the plan had " . . . to assume one third of any excess expenditure over $400, but limited to an additional $200."[66]

Another programme under the "back-to-the-land" movement was the transfer of groups such as the Mennonites to more northerly regions. As early as 1931 the Anderson government had aided approximately fifty Mennonite families from the Warman district in settling on lands west of Prince Albert.[67] Two years later, a delegation headed by the Hon. W.W. Smith, minister without portfolio, and R.C. Lane, secretary of Warman municipality, and Mennonite representative, approached the Provincial government about financial assistance for another transfer of Mennonite people to northern Saskatchewan.[68] According to members of the delegation, many landless Mennonite farmers were "squatting" on road allowances and in villages. Their presence thus created a financial burden for the local municipalities. This plea was given consideration by cabinet and in the following spring of 1934, sixty Mennonite families were moved northwards by means of government assistance to lands north-west of North Battleford.[69]

It is extremely difficult to make a detailed assessment of the "back-to-the-land" movement in the Province of Saskatchewan. First of all, figures as to the number of people who participated in the trek prior to 1935 are not available. According to secondary sources, 35 000 to 45 000 persons located in northern Saskatchewan during the years 1930–1935.[70] Just how many people packed up their belongings on hay racks or Bennett buggies and travelled to the north lands can not be determined. A family upon arrival might homestead in a certain locality for one year and then after disappointment with a crop, move to a more suitable site. Even government records offer little help. Financial statements and audit reports of various government departments provide little information about government-assisted settlement schemes. Figures reported in newspapers about the number of people and estimated costs of a scheme are often misleading or vary considerably. Because of the variety of relief projects the reader of a newspaper cannot always determine exactly what scheme is being reported. The Provincial Land Settlement Scheme of 1931 provides a good example of dubious statistics.

Fortunately, Provincial Auditor's statements are available for the Relief Settlement Plans of 1932 and 1934.[71] Under the two Plans a total of $510 620.67 was spent by the three levels of government on moving

920 settlers as of April 30, 1937. The Federal government expended $167 644.53, the urban and rural municipalities $110 111.00 and the Provincial government the highest amount, $232 865.14. For its part the City of Saskatoon sent 319 settlers to the land at a cost of $188 811.78, the City of Regina, 165 at $93 094.95 and the City of Moose Jaw, 60 at $32 755.43. A sum of $131 263.14 was spent on 220 homesteaders from other urban and rural municipalities and $64 451.38 on 156 Mennonite settlers. According to newspaper accounts not all of these settlers migrated to the pioneer region of northern Saskatchewan.[72] Some were moved to better agricultural lands in the southern part of the province and in the park belt.

Criticism from non-government sources can partially determine the accuracy of the statements made by government officials that, with very few exceptions, those already settled were making progress. Newspaper accounts record few instances, however, where the "back-to-the-land" movement received any bitter or prolonged criticism. For the most part, people favoured the land settlement schemes and the Saskatchewan government reflected such feeling by encouraging further settlement in the northern parts of the province. If the Anderson administration did receive criticism it was for its lack of preparation and supervision in the "back-to-the-land" movement. Its land classification surveys at best were superficial, and as soon as a settler had fulfilled the necessary requirements for an advance, he and his family were left alone to fend for themselves in their new "home."

The Opposition Liberals occasionally attacked the government-assisted settlement schemes, not because they opposed the movement, but for the way they were being conducted and the conditions that resulted. As early as 1931, Charles McIntosh, Liberal M.L.A. for Kinistino, attacked the Anderson administration for its inconsideration in charging a homesteading fee, particularly when so many settlers had been forced from their homes to seek a livelihood elsewhere. In the opinion of the Kinistino member, the government should either revert to the old homestead policy or adopt another scheme. When pressed in the Legislature to suggest an alternative measure, Mr. McIntosh proposed the adoption of the use-lease system whereby title to the land would always remain in the hands of the Crown and not pass to the occupant of the land. Mr. McIntosh tempered his remarks by adding

> that there should be no attempt made to reduce or handicap those who are settling along in a legitimate way, but we should give a lift to those who through misfortune or economic circumstances are lagging behind. Democracy has the right to make its own experiments and my recommendation is to try out the use lease proposal in the north part of the province under proper safeguards and under the best regulations.[73]

In the Legislative Assembly, J.G. Gardiner stated that he had received complaints from pioneers of the Porcupine Plain district which would indicate that there was urgent need for relief through the Saskatchewan Relief Commission.[74] In an address to the Regina Rotary Club at the Hotel Saskatchewan, Charles Dunn, Liberal M.L.A. for Pleasant Hills, called for a fully supervised land settlement scheme involving five hundred families. Mr. Dunn stressed in his speech that ". . . each family . . . be given one quarter section, with a farm expert for supervision purposes provided for each 50 families for three years."[75] A practical scheme was being worked out by the Anderson government, but there was no guidance for the settlers, Mr. Dunn charged.

Alderman M.J. Coldwell had expressed similar sentiments about the lack of supervision and the deplorable conditions facing many settlers, at a city council meeting in November 1932.[76] His warnings went unheeded.

The only constant source of criticism about northern resettlement came from the United Farmers of Canada who were in charge of relief distribution in the northern half of the province. Officials of the farmers' organization sympathized with the desire of authorities to solve the unemployment problem, but at the same time, protested against further settlement of the unemployed in the northern district until an impartial yet thorough investigation of the suitability of the soil was conducted. As early as 1931 A.J. Macauley, U.F.C. president, had warned about the difficulties some north-bound settlers would encounter upon reaching their destination.[77] For his warnings against indiscriminate settlement of families Mr. Macauley was roundly attacked by Premier Anderson. A *Western Producer* article attempted to justify Macauley's statements in light of comments made by a United Church missionary, the Reverend A.R. Taylor, who visited the Loon Lake district in the early spring of 1932. Mr. Taylor reported that, " . . . he found many of the women in a highly nervous state due to the loneliness of the life shut in the bush. We cannot wonder, therefore, that many of the men are unwilling to leave their homes to work in the relief camps." Of conditions in general, the clergyman added,

> that about one-third of the population are receiving relief, although they were sent up there to make them self-supporting. Few of the city men . . . have accomplished much in the way of farm work, and he therefore . . . does not consider the placing of such men on the land an unqualified success. Also, the horses are in poor shape, many of them being too weak to haul the feed from St. Walburg, which emphasizes the lack of sufficient sustenance for stock.[78]

As time wore on, charges and counter-charges mounted between the United Farmers of Canada and government officials over the operation of land settlement schemes. By 1933, the situation seems to have deteriorated to the point where claims of inadequate relief and possible malnutrition in the Porcupine Plain district by one side were treated as "political propaganda" by the other.[79] Persons living in the district were unfortunately caught in the middle of this verbal barrage.

Reaction by those people already established in the northern districts to the influx of prospective homesteaders has been difficult to document. As early as 1929 farmers living in the Kenville district had protested the drainage of a large area of swamp land lying between the Carrot and Saskatchewan Rivers in order to bring that land under cultivation for grain production.[80] However, their reasons for opposition to the drainage project were purely economic in that more production would lower grain prices further and thus create a lower standard of living for the farmer.

The *Leader-Post* correspondent who toured the Meadow Lake district in the autumn of 1931 reported that he was told by local inhabitants that it would be a mistake to give all relief to newcomers in the form of road work. Instead, they felt payments could be made to men for clearing their own homesteads and then added to the purchase price of the land, a recommendation made by the Royal Commission on Immigration and Settlement. Initial reaction to these pioneers would seem to be surprise at the number of them, and then sympathy towards their plight.[81]

Later reports indicate a feeling of frustration and anger towards the continuing influx of relief settlers. As an example, ratepayers of Medstead municipality at a mass meeting in Belbutte objected to the municipality having to assume responsibility for the provision of feed, fodder and seed. "In a resolution passed without dissension the meeting protested against the provincial government's action in thus fixing responsibility and endorsed the action of the municipal council in refusing to meet relief demands."[82] From such meagre evidence, it is difficult to assess if this reaction to the newcomers was widespread.

Nevertheless, H. Clifford Dunfield, in a serialized story appearing in the *Western Producer*, claimed that some of the land seekers encroached on the hunting grounds of the native people and thus caused undue hardship.[83] Not only did these newcomers kill large quantities of game for commercial gain, but also they depleted the number of fur-bearing animals. Those natives who earned a livelihood by commercial fishing on the northern lakes were forced to retire from that industry. Mr. Dunfield concluded that as a result of this plunder native people as far north as Ile à la Crosse had to subsist increasingly on a diet of roots and fish supplemented by the occasional relief package.

By the time the Liberal Party under J.G. Gardiner was returned to power in 1934, the situation in northern Saskatchewan had become intolerable. Refusals to pay taxes, illegal entries on homesteads and school and grazing lands, and evictions being met by force, were increasing. In order to provide a quick solution to these immediate problems, the Liberal government amended the Provincial Lands regulations. As a result of these changes,

> land could be acquired without a thorough survey as long as the potential settler was satisfied that he could make a living. Cultivation duties and other obligations were relaxed. Credit of up to 6 dollars per acre was promised, to be used principally for breaking and clearing of land and buying seed.[84]

Under these relaxed regulations, homesteaders proceeded to occupy land in other parts of the Big River Country, the Pierceland district and the Shand Creek area. Suitable land in the Porcupine and Big River Forest Reserves was also released.

Further amendments to the Provincial Lands Act of 1931, which bore some resemblance to the former Dominion legislation, were passed by the Saskatchewan Legislature in February 1935.[85] Regulations under the Act authorized all surveyed lands classified as suitable for homestead entry to be made available to the first eligible applicant upon payment of a ten-dollar fee. At the end of three full years the entrant would make application for patent if he had completed the required homestead duties.[86] Furthermore, "most squatting under this Act became legal. Sale contracts were cancelled and all, except the initial payments, were refunded. Any future payments were cancelled. Most loans were also liquidated."[87] With this initial flurry of activity by the Gardiner administration one cannot but wonder how many more people moved onto marginal land.

Not only was the new Saskatchewan government concerned with putting people on the land, but also in seeing that those already settled were on suitable agricultural land. In order to do this, more supervision had to be applied to the process of settlement and re-location. The Land Utilization Act and the Northern Settlers' Re-establishment Branch were created by the statute[88] and Order-in-Council[89] respectively. Under the provisions of the Land Utilization Act, a Board had the Power through the Lieutenant Governor-in-Council to declare any specified part of the province under the jurisdiction of the Act. Furthermore, the Board could decree that any land found unsuitable for agriculture within this specified area might be converted to public land. During its first year of operation the Land Utilization Board collected data on lands unfit for grain growing within each municipality. Municipal councils were requested to forward this information to the Board, and to halt financial assistance in the way of seed grain or other supplies to occupants of any inferior lands.

The Northern Settlers' Re-establishment Branch was created to perform several major tasks in the pioneer region of northern Saskatchewan. First of all, the Branch was to provide assistance to those settlers in economic trouble so that they could eventually become independent. Often this meant finding new land for those homesteaders whose first selection of land was a costly mistake. Secondly, the agency was to initiate drainage projects in order to provide more arable land, and by the same token create employment for northern residents. Operations began immediately in the Shand Creek district and in the Carrot River valley.[90] In order to see mixed farming established in northern Saskatchewan, the Northern Settlers' Re-establishment Branch initiated an educational programme. Government officials hoped that closer supervision and economic assistance would help those families in dire need overcome their problems, and improve the standard of living of those people already established. By these initial measures the Saskatchewan government attempted to bring about the recovery of the northern part of the province.

During the period 1929–1935, the settlement frontier advanced everywhere across northern Saskatchewan, often without regard to the drawbacks of terrain, climate and soil. People who immigrated under the "back-to-the-land" movement came on their own initiative or were assisted through government-sponsored land settlement schemes. Pressure for agricultural land was high, and in its haste to get people settled, the Saskatchewan government unwillingly relaxed its control and allowed families to move onto sub-marginal lands. For this indiscriminate placement of settlers and lack of supervision, the Anderson administration was taken to task, particularly by the United Farmers of Canada. On the whole, however, people supported the "back-to-the-land" movement despite its limited effect in getting families to become self-supporting. The northern districts did not prove to be a mecca for many who moved from the urban centres and drought-stricken farms of the south. Direct relief still had to be expended by the municipal and provincial governments when the unemployed and farmers reached their destination. Perhaps the movement lightened the burden of southern urban and rural municipalities, but this was no consolation for those who moved to worse conditions. Eventually, some control was brought to the "back-to-the-land" movement through the Land Utilization Board and the Northern Settlers' Re-establishment Branch. Under their supervision, inferior lands were taken out of cultivation, settlers re-located and other economic measures initiated. Northern Saskatchewan gradually entered a period of settlement consolidation and recovery, but for many of the settlers the process would be slow and difficult.

Notes

1. Denis Patrick Fitzgerald, "Pioneer Settlement in Northern Saskatchewan" (Ph.D. diss., University of Minnesota, 1965), 9.

2. Ibid., 10.

3. Ibid.

4. For a more detailed discussion of the natural resources controversy see C. Martin, *"Dominion Lands" Policy* (Toronto, 1938), 204-26; *S.S.P.*, 1928-1929, 120-36; Proceedings of U.F.C. Conventions 1927-1929; W. Calderwood, "Pulpit, Press and Political Reactions to the Ku Klux Klan in Saskatchewan," *The Twenties in Western Canada* (Ottawa: National Museum of Man, 1972), 192.

5. Calderwood, "Pulpit, Press and Political Reactions," 192.

6. Progressive party (Saskatchewan), *Saskatchewan Progressive Principles and Policies* (Regina: Saskatchewan Progressive Association, n.d.), n.p.; and Liberal party (Saskatchewan), *Manifesto and platform — Saskatchewan Conservative Party* (1929; reprint Regina: Saskatchewan Liberal Association, 1934), 2, Archives of Saskatchewan (hereafter cited as A.S.).

7. Liberal Party (Saskatchewan), *Manifesto and platform — Saskatchewan Conservative Party*, 2, A.S.

8. Ibid.

9. Saskatchewan, Executive Council, O.C. 21/30, A.S.

10. Saskatchewan, Royal Commission on Immigration and Settlement, *Report* (Regina: Printed by R.S. Garrett, King's Printer, 1930), A.S.

11. Ibid., 9.

12. Ibid., 12.

13. Ibid., 13-17.

14. Ibid., 15.

15. Ibid., 15.

16. Ibid., 146.

17. F.H. Auld papers, File 9(2), "Some Problems relating to the use of submarginal lands" (c. 1934), 2, A.S.

18. Fitzgerald, "Pioneer Settlement," 297.

19. Ibid., 116.

20. Ibid., 121.

21. Saskatoon, *The Western Producer*, 13 September 1928, 27.

22. For a more detailed discussion see E.C. Morgan, Soldier Settlement in the Prairie Provinces," *Saskatchewan History* 21, no. 2 (Spring 1968): 41-55.

23. Fitzgerald, "Pioneer Settlement," 205.

24. Ibid., 237.

25. Ibid., 280; *The Western Producer*, 26 December 1929, 6.

26. G.E. Britnell, *The Wheat Economy* (Toronto: University of Toronto Press, 1939), 203.

27. Robert England, *The Colonization of Western Canada: A Study of Contemporary Land Settlement (1896-1934)* (London: P.S. King and Son Ltd., 1936), 116.

28. Regina *Leader-Post*, 17 October 1931, 13.

29. L.M. Grayson and M. Bliss, eds., *The Wretched of Canada* (Toronto: University of Toronto Press, 1973), xv-xvi.

30. George Joseph Hoffman, "The Saskatchewan Provincial Election of 1934: Its Political, Economic and Social Background" (M.A. thesis, University of Saskatchewan, 1973), 40-41.

31. England, *Colonization of Western Canada*, 116.

32. *The Western Producer*, 4 September 1930, 2.

33. Saskatchewan, Executive Council, O.C. 965/30, A.S.

34. Legislative Assembly, *Statutes of Saskatchewan*, 1931, c. 11, s. 6.

35. Ibid., 1931, c. 34.

36. Britnell, *The Wheat Economy*, 204.

37. Ibid., 204n.

38. Ibid., 203n-204n.

39. *The Western Producer*, 11 December 1930, 3.

40. *Statutes of Saskatchewan*, 1931, c. 22.

41. Ibid., 1931, c. 22, s. 8.

42. Ibid., 1934, c. 9.

43. Regina *Leader-Post*, 14 May 1931, 3.

44. Saskatoon *Star-Phoenix*, 5 March 1932, 3.

45. Turtleford *Sun*, 24 March 1932, 2.

46. Ibid., 8 March 1932, 4, 3d.

47. *The Western Producer*, 23 October 1930, 3.

48. Ibid., 8 October 1931, 3.

49. Regina *Leader-Post*, 17 October 1931, 31; 19 October 1931, 18; and 20 October 1931, 12.

50. Ibid., 17 October 1931, 13.

51. Ibid., 19 October 1931, 18.

52. *The Western Producer*, 15 October 1931, 1; 14 July 1932, 3; Regina *Leader-Post*, 17 September 1932, 3.

53. *The Western Producer*, 15 October 1931, 1.

54. Ibid., 9 July 1931, 1.

55. Regina *Leader-Post*, 21 October 1931, 2.

56. Fitzgerald, "Pioneer Settlement," 317.

57. Ibid., 321.

58. Canada, Department of Labour, *Annual Report*, 1932–1933 (Ottawa: J.O. Patenaude, Printer, 1933), 66.

59. Saskatoon *Star-Phoenix*, 10 May 1932, 3.

60. Regina *Leader-Post*, 28 May 1932, 5.

61. Saskatchewan, Department of Railways, Labour and Industries, Circular C.L. No. 41 re Relief Settlement Plan, n.d., A.S.

62. Ibid.

63. Regina *Leader-Post*, 2 July 1932, 2.

64. Ibid., 8 March 1933, 3.

65. Ibid., 28 April 1933, 3.

66. Ibid.

67. Ibid., 14 May 1931, 3.

68. Ibid., 28 September 1933, 1.

69. Ibid., 9 May 1934, 19.

70. From statistics provided by the Department of Natural Resources, G.E. Britnell calculated that 6 539 families or 35 552 persons moved from drought areas to northern Crown land in the period 1930–1936 (*The Wheat Economy*, 203). D.P. Fitzgerald estimated that 45 000 people moved into northern Saskatchewan during the same period ("Pioneer Settlement in Northern Saskatchewan," 314).

71. Saskatchewan, Provincial Auditor, "Statement of Relief Settlement Account under the Dominion-Provincial-Municipal Agreements of 1932 and 1934 as at April 30, 1937," A.S.

72. Regina *Leader-Post*, 28 May 1932, 5.

73. Ibid., 12 February, 11.
74. Ibid., 28 March 1933, 5.
75. Ibid., 26 March 1934, 1.
76. Ibid., 18 November 1932, 3.
77. Hoffman, "Saskatchewan Provincial Election," 39.
78. *The Western Producer*, 31 March 1932, 5.
79. Ibid., 20 April 1933, 5.
80. Ibid., 2 January 1930, 32.
81. Regina *Leader-Post*, 20 October 1931, 12.
82. *The Western Producer*, 28 February 1935, 2.
83. Ibid., 7 October 1971, 36.
84. Fitzgerald, "Pioneer Settlement," 325.
85. *Statutes of Saskatchewan*, 1934–1935, c. 17.
86. Saskatchewan, Executive Council, O.C. 704/35, A.S.
87. Fitzgerald, "Pioneer Settlement," 327-28.
88. *Statutes of Saskatchewan*, 1934–1935, c. 62.
89. Saskatchewan, Executive Council, O.C. 1038/35, A.S.
90. Fitzgerald, "Pioneer Settlement," 328.

Unemployment Relief Camps in Saskatchewan, 1933–1936†

LORNE A. BROWN

The efforts of the federal government to deal with the problem of the single, homeless unemployed in Saskatchewan from 1933 to 1936 were based on federal policies which were applied on a nation-wide basis. The methods chosen to deal with the problem, in Saskatchewan as elsewhere, were meant to minimize the possibility of violent upheavals in the urban centres. An examination of the state of the single unemployed during these years reveals that the fear of violence and even insurrection, though greatly exaggerated by the authorities for political and economic reasons, was not entirely unfounded.

The people who, as a group, suffered perhaps more than any others from the economic depression were the unskilled workers in primary industries such as mining, forestry, and agriculture and the unskilled workers who depended upon the many facets of the construction industry. The severe decline in the price of primary products dealt a stunning blow to what had always been an unstable part of the economy. In Saskatchewan the disastrously low prices for agricultural products combined with repeated crop failures destroyed the livelihood not only of farmers but of thousands of transient labourers who depended upon seasonal agricultural work. The same factors spurred on the near collapse of the construction industry in the private sector and federal and provincial public works came nowhere near taking up the slack. The people deprived of their livelihood comprised a class which had played an indispensable role in building Canada. They had been the mainstay of the forestry industries, railway and road construction and maintenance

† *Saskatchewan History* 23, no. 3 (Autumn 1970): 81–104.

and were absolutely essential for seasonal agricultural work. Many were recent immigrants who had been lured to Canada by the propaganda of the Canadian Pacific Railway and the Canadian government. During prosperous years they did much of the most undesirable work at lower than average wages and during the Depression they were the first to be sacrificed.[1]

As the economic situation worsened the federal government was pressed strongly by the provinces to assume responsibility for the transient unemployed and particularly the unmarried transients. Municipalities, hard pressed to look after their permanent residents, were reluctant to assume responsibility on the grounds that if any province provided adequate food and shelter or provided work on relief projects for the single unemployed they would be inundated by an influx from across the country. This was particularly true of British Columbia where unemployed from other provinces gathered in large numbers because of the moderate climate during the winter months and in the hope of employment in the forestry and other primary industries. The same was true to a lesser extent of the Prairie provinces during the summer months when thousands would migrate from other provinces in the hope of obtaining work in the agricultural sector and failing this, would congregate in the cities and require relief. The practice of "riding the rods" across the country had become a common pastime of the single unemployed. It was this mobility, mainly an enforced mobility, which made the problem of the single unemployed even more a federal issue than unemployment in general and caused the provinces to demand federal action.

By 1932 the radical political potential of the single unemployed was becoming increasingly apparent to the federal government. Workers in primary industries such as mining and lumbering and the unemployed in the urban centres were given little assistance by the established unions in the Trades and Labour Congress (T.L.C.) and the All Canadian Congress of Labour (A.C.C.L.) who were busy trying to hold themselves together in the face of the Depression and were, at any rate, too conservative to take the militant action that the times required. The result was that new unions were built by left-wing militants under the auspices of the Workers' Unity League (W.U.L.), which was dominated by the Communist Party. Unions and associations of the unemployed sprang up in most of the major cities and many of the larger towns throughout Canada. Many such associations grew up spontaneously but the largest and most effective were built by supporters of the Workers' Unity League. Demonstrations, hunger marches, strikes, and disturbances became more widespread than at any other time since 1919. All of this was going on at a time when the country was gripped in an orgy of anti-Communism unequalled before or since in Canadian history.[2] The federal and most provincial governments were applying R.B. Bennett's "iron heel of ruthlessness" against radical political and labour unrest in a wholesale fashion. Political deportations, raids on the headquarters of the Communist Party and affiliated organizations, arrests under Section 98 of the Criminal Code, and the use of police to suppress strikes, demonstrations and even public meetings were widespread.[3]

The people feared most of all by the political authorities at all levels of government were the single transient unemployed. Having no families to provide for and often no firm roots in any one locality they were the most difficult to intimidate by threats of the cutting off relief or even imprisonment and the latter was hardly feasible given the large numbers involved. By 1932 it was estimated that there was a minimum of seventy thousand single homeless unemployed transients who congregated in the cities when they were not travelling between cities. These unfortunates, along with hundreds of thousands of other unemployed, were becoming frustrated and militant to the point where the federal government believed that disorder could become general. Reports from welfare authorities and the police indicated that trouble might soon escalate to the point where the armed forces would have to be used on a large scale.[4] Many businessmen and newspapers were urging that more be done to get the single jobless out of the cities before major trouble erupted. Others were recommending for humanitarian reasons that a "peacetime army" of the unemployed be organized to construct great public works as a means of alleviating economic suffering and raising the morale of the populace.

During a tour of the country in the summer of 1932 General A.G.L. McNaughton, Chief of the General Staff, observed the deteriorating situation and conceived the idea, which he sold to Bennett's cabinet, of establishing, under the auspices of the Department of National Defence, relief camps throughout the country for the accommodation of physically fit single homeless males. The scheme was begun by Order-in-Council on October 8, 1932, and was to be carried on by successive Orders-in-Council until the spring of 1936. It got underway on a major scale during the spring and summer of 1932 when, by agreement with the provinces, the Dominion assumed responsibility for all physically fit single homeless unemployed men. It was during May and June of 1933 that Dundurn relief camp became the major centre for accommodating the single unemployed in Saskatchewan.

From the very beginning, in Saskatchewan and elsewhere, the primary purpose of the camps was to keep young men out of the cities and the camps were compulsory for thousands of the single unemployed who were cut off relief and left with a choice between the camps or facing arrest for vagrancy.[5] Even "riding the rods" became more difficult as the RCMP and railway police reversed their earlier policy of leniency in this regard. The camps were not meant to accommodate all the physically fit single homeless unemployed but merely to relieve congestion in those cities where trouble was most likely to break out and camps were located, where possible, with this purpose in mind.[6] The camps also made it possible to step up the intimidation of those single unemployed who obtained relief jobs on farms or remained in the cities. The threat of being sent to a camp could be and was used to discourage would-be critics among relief recipients.[7] From the beginning to the bitter end R.B. Bennett and his government insisted publicly that residence in the camps was purely voluntary though it was clear to anyone familiar with relief policies in the cities, and this included a significant proportion of the population, that many of the single unemployed had no choice in the matter. It was this type of credibility gap which helped to discredit the Bennett government and assure broad public sympathy for the camp inmates when they rebelled against the authorities as they occasionally did.

Unrest among the unemployed in Saskatchewan cities prior to the establishment of Dundurn relief camp in 1933 appears to have been fairly widespread though in magnitude, and probably intensity, it had not reached the proportions of the situation in the larger urban centres like Winnipeg and Vancouver. Saskatchewan, lacking any large urban centre, was generally less troubled by demonstrations and disorder (excepting the Estevan-Bienfait coal miners' strike of 1931) than any of the other provinces outside of the Maritimes. There were, however, organizations of the unemployed in Saskatchewan's four major cities and many of the smaller urban centres by the summer of 1932.[8] From 1931 much of the organizing in Saskatchewan had been done by the Workers' Unity League. As the agricultural and employment situations deteriorated and the grievances of the unemployed mounted their organizations used increasingly militant tactics.

In Saskatchewan as elsewhere the married unemployed were provided with relief by the municipalities with financial assistance by the provincial and federal governments. The provincial government, and this was also true in other provinces, played a more direct role in providing for single transients. Until the autumn of 1932 the two main methods used by the provincial government were to try to place as many single unemployed as possible in farm labour jobs and to provide relief employment for some in work camps which the province began setting up in the autumn of 1930. At one time the province had twenty-three such camps with the larger ones being in the vicinity of Prince Albert National Park.

In the autumn of 1932 when the federal government began to take a more active interest in the single unemployed the province, in co-oper-ation with the federal authorities, commenced with a three-pronged attack upon the problem. By federal-provincial agreement an allowance of five dollars monthly would be paid to "destitute unemployed homeless single men or women now resident in any urban centre of the Province who will accept work on the farms in the Province."[9] The five dollars monthly plus room and board would, in most cases, constitute the total wages received by these workers. The farm labour plan was supplemented by federal work camps operated by the Department of the Interior in Prince Albert National Park, where the pay would also be five dollars monthly, and a few provincial work camps, though these were being phased out in anticipation of an expanded federal program. By federal-provincial agreement the Saskatchewan Relief Commission would also operate concentration camps in Saskatoon, Regina, and Moose Jaw where the single unemployed would be provided with food and shelter until they could be placed on farms or in work camps.[10] The camp in Moose Jaw was for single unemployed ex-servicemen and was begun largely by the efforts of the Canadian Legion. The program of the Department of National Defence began too late in the year for them to establish work camps in Saskatchewan until the spring of 1933 at the earliest.

Before the Saskatchewan and federal governments launched their expanded programs in late October and early November 1932, the unemployed, single and married, had alarmed the provincial authorities on several occasions. The RCMP in Regina were sufficiently alarmed that they requested and received from the Department of National Defence an issue of three hundred bayonets and thirty thousand rounds of .303 ammunition in October 1931.[11] Demonstrations were numerous with perhaps the largest being a May Day parade in Regina in 1932 which involved ten thousand participants and spectators and resulted in scattered violence and nine arrests. On October 27, 1932, several hundred relief workers employed on city relief projects in Regina went on strike under the leadership of the Regina Unemployed Workers' Council. Mayor McAra blamed the strike on five or six leaders who allegedly forced the majority to strike against their wishes though news reports indicate that the strike had widespread support with the support of a large majority on at least some work projects.[12]

At the same time as the strike of the married relief workers in Regina, federal officials were conferring with the provincial cabinet and both governments were issuing announcements about their plans for the farm labour scheme and the relief camps. The associations of the single unemployed complained loudly against working for five dollars monthly and being segregated into relief camps which unemployed leaders in Regina referred to as "slave camps." Delegates of the unemployed from Saskatoon and Regina waited on Hon. J.A. Merkley, provincial Minister of Railways, Labour and Industry and demanded twenty-five dollars monthly or one dollar daily for farm or camp work. In Saskatoon the provincial government had authorized the city to provide the single unemployed with meal tickets pending their removal to farms or work camps. On October 27 Mayor J.E. Underwood exacerbated an already tense situation by announcing that before obtaining meal tickets men would have to register at the government employment office and signify their willingness to take farm work. "Throughout the day unemployed thronged around the relief office, many of them in an ugly mood and threats of disturbance were noised abroad although no disorder occurred."[13] On November 2 a proposed protest march of the unemployed was cancelled after being banned by the Mayor. That the authorities expected trouble was evidenced from the fact that RCMP were ready to assist city police, special constables had been sworn in and tear gas bombs were in the hands of police. Instead of a march the unemployed held a meeting on Market Square and declared that, though it was banned in advance by the Chief of Police, they would hold a mass rally in front of the relief offices on November 7 to protest, among other things, establishment of the relief camp at the Exhibition grounds. On November 7 about eighty RCMP and city police dispersed the rally and the result was what the Canadian Press called "the bloodiest riot ever seen in this city."[14] Dozens of unemployed and policemen were injured but apparently only one policeman was hospitalized. Several people were arrested for unlawful assembly. Further outdoor meetings were temporarily banned and the resistance of the unemployed against the new government plans appears to have waned for the time being.

With the approach of winter the single unemployed registered in large numbers and were absorbed into the various sections of the federal-provincial relief program. About eight thousand were placed on farms with the numbers in work camps at Prince Albert National Park and the concentration camps in the three major cities fluctuating from month to month. There appear to have been about six hundred accommodated in the National Park and about twelve to fifteen thousand in the three city camps during the early spring of 1933.

During this time the Department of National Defence (DND) was making plans for opening a number of projects across the county as soon as weather permitted. The decision as to where projects would be located and on what scale depended upon where useful work could be done, the state of unrest in the various localities and the demands of provinces and municipalities for particular public works. From the standpoint of the DND enlargement of existing facilities and construction of additional permanent facilities at the militia camp near Dundurn would be a useful project and one which the Department was well equipped to undertake. Plans were made for opening a relief camp for these purposes if and when the situation warranted one. Events in the Saskatoon relief camp during April and May were to move the provincial government to demand urgently that the federal government expand its camp program with all possible speed.

That there would probably be some trouble in the Saskatoon relief camp was evident from the fact that the establishment of the camp had been one of the factors contributing to the increased unrest in Saskatoon during November 1932. Many of the people who had raised objections in November would be inmates of the relief camp. Added to this would be the environment of the camp, which was designed as a temporary holding centre pending transfer of the men to farms or work camps and not as a work camp itself. The men were given food, shelter, medical care and some necessities such as clothing and were required to perform minor fatigue duties such as washing dishes and cleaning the camp. They were not, excepting a minority who were hired to perform cooking and other more specialized camp duties, required to do much work and hence they had time on their hands to dwell on their grievances and could be easily organized. The author has not been able to locate copies of the specific regulations which the supervisors attempted to enforce at the Saskatoon relief camp. However, it was reported in the press that the camp was to be "of a military character" and it was under the supervision of a former military officer, Captain P.J. Philpott, M.C., then president of the local branch of the Canadian Legion and vice-president of the provincial command.[15] There were attempts to introduce some military routine into the camp and it is likely that, given the rules commonly in force in camps of this nature at that time and the attitude of the authorities towards the single unemployed, there would be little agreement between the supervisors and the men on how the camps should be operated. The environment appears to have been eminently suitable for the development of radicalism and militant protest.

Militant agitators, many of them supporters of the Workers' Unity League, lost no time in organizing the inmates of the Saskatoon camp. Superintendent Philpott was faced with trouble two months after the camp opened.

> As early as January, 1933, I encountered and reported, organized opposition and propaganda, to the Relief Commission's policy of drafting men to Prince Albert National Park Work Camp. I received a ruling from the Commission under date of February 4 that inmates refusing to proceed to Prince Albert camp when drafted should be dismissed from my camp and reported to local police as vagrants.[16]

Philpott attempted to carry out this policy but was unable to do so and attributed this to insufficient co-operation from the Saskatoon City Police and the militancy of the camp inmates. He cited an instance when, with police assistance, he evicted five people but they were only kept over night in the police station and returned to camp the next day. "By this time inmates had rallied to the cause of the malingerers, until I was powerless to evict and keep out the troublemakers."[17] Philpott reported on numerous occasions during January and February that he was unable to fill drafts for the National Park work camps "due to the fact that a radical organization within the camp had gained sufficient influence over the men generally that there was a total disregard of constituted authority."[18] He also reported instances of men refusing to do camp fatigue and destroying camp property.

That the radicals had the support of the general camp population is evident from the report of an official of the Saskatchewan Relief Commission (SRC) who visited the camp on April 5.[19] He found the morale of the camp entirely broken down and the inmates under the influence of an unnamed radical organization which he claimed was led by about twenty men. "I found the Superintendent and his assistants in a state of nervous excitement due to the continued demonstrations which had been conducted within the confines of the Camp during the past months."[20] The SRC official reported that delegations were hourly making demands upon the superintendent and his assistant and that as many as eight or ten meetings were held daily where a crowd of from three to six hundred men "were addressed in violent language and advised to make further demands for better food, clothing and tobacco, and at the same time refusing to perform any kind of work, including the necessary fatigues."[21] The Chief Constable of Saskatoon and the officer in charge of the local RCMP recommended that action be taken to avoid more serious trouble but not until more police were available to cope with the situation. The SRC insisted that the grievances of the men were unfounded except the one concerning sanitary conditions and that this was the fault of the men themselves. The Commission embarked upon a program to restore order and institute a cleanup "putting the premises in a sanitary and healthy condition."[22]

Captain P.J. Philpott resigned as superintendent on April 7 and was replaced by Captain L.G. Woodward, who had been recommended by the Mayor of Saskatoon and members of the Civic Relief Department. New regulations were passed which included a ban on speeches and demonstrations and there were greater efforts to enforce them. RCMP officials had previously been posted at the camp and on April 11 a full troop of mounted RCMP arrived in Saskatoon to be on hand in the event of trouble. At least one police spy was placed among the men.[23] The authorities appear to have been preparing for a showdown with the radicals not only in the Saskatoon relief camp but throughout the province. May Day parades were banned in Regina and Saskatoon. In the latter city two troops of mounted police were posted near the Market Square during the rally of about five hundred persons. In Moose Jaw RCMP and city police were stationed at the relief camp where one alleged Communist agitator was arrested and charged with creating a disturbance. Both parades and meetings were banned for May Day in Moose Jaw and a labour hall was raided by RCMP and city police who seized banners, lapel buttons and a list of names of about one hundred single unemployed whom they claimed had refused to go to work camps at the pay offered.[24]

There were some indications that the radicals were concentrating their forces for a potential showdown at Saskatoon relief camp. The population of the camp greatly increased in late April and early May and the superintendent claimed that the "Reds" had sent out word to their supporters in Prince Albert and Moose Jaw to congregate in Saskatoon.[25] The author has seen no documentary proof of this but, whatever the reason, the camp population at Saskatoon swelled from 391 in February to about 1 000 in early May, by which time there were only a couple of hundred in each of the Regina and Moose Jaw camps. The Saskatchewan Relief Commission decided to transfer some of the Saskatoon inmates to the Regina camp and to include the most militant men in the first draft of fifty in an effort to deprive the men of their leadership and make it easier to reassert the authority of the camp supervisors. The camp inmates demanded, to no avail, that the Commission call for volunteers to go to Regina since overcrowding was the ostensible reason for the transfers. On May 7 the fifty men chosen by the Commission were given notice that they must board the train at noon, May 8, for transportation to Regina and, failing this, they would be evicted from the Saskatoon camp and denied further assistance at any relief camp in Saskatchewan.[26] Their names were posted around the camp. This brought the crisis to a head and led to a violent clash with the police the next day.

The fifty men refused to accept transfer to Regina and they and their supporters protested that the single unemployed should be allowed to go to or remain in the camp of their choosing. A resolution to the same effect was passed by the executives of seven Saskatoon labour and unemployed organizations including the Trades and Labour Council, and sent to Superintendent Woodward on the night of May 7.[27] Neither side would back down and on May 8 the fifty men did not report for transportation to Regina but announced that they intended to remain in the Saskatoon camp and would be at the dining hall for supper as usual at 5:30 p.m. Meetings were held at the camp during the day to solidify support for their position. The superintendent called in the police and at 5:30, city police and RCMP, mounted and on foot, arrived at the camp. Saskatoon Police Chief G.M. Donald announced that the fifty men scheduled for transfer would be allowed to eat supper at the camp only if they agreed to board the train for Regina immediately afterwards. This they refused to do and a fight broke out between inmates and police in the waiting room of the dining hall. Simultaneously with this mounted police attempted to disperse a crowd of from two to three hundred men in front of the dining hall and a riot ensued. "Wheeling their horses again and again, the policemen chased the fugitives all over the grounds, striking right and left."[28] During the riot Inspector L.J.

Sampson of the RCMP was struck by a flying rock and fell from his horse; he was killed when the horse dragged him about one hundred yards and his head struck a telephone pole. About thirty people were arrested during and after the riot. Of twenty-six people eventually brought to trial eleven were convicted of rioting, eleven of unlawful assembly and four were acquitted. Four of the twenty-two were also convicted of one or more charges of assaulting a police officer. A man charged with manslaughter in connection with Sampson's death was acquitted. The twenty-two convicted were sentenced to prison terms ranging from five to twenty-one months.

The reaction of the provincial government to the May 8 disturbance was to demand that the federal government provide more accommodation for the single unemployed in work camps and to attempt to whip up anti-Communist hysteria in the province. Premier Anderson wired to Hon. Wesley Gordon, federal Minister of Labour, the night of the riot relating the seriousness of the situation and stressing the urgency of getting at least two hundred additional men into National Park camps.[29] The Deputy Minister of Labour telephoned General McNaughton the next day "to say he was in receipt of a rather hysterical telegram from Premier Anderson of Saskatchewan" and asked McNaughton if it would be possible to construct a relief camp at Dundurn without delay.[30] The DND agreed to this and arrangements were forthwith made with the provincial government for the transfer of men from the provincial camps as quickly as facilities could be made available at Dundurn. When Premier Anderson publicly announced the establishment of Dundurn relief camp he used the occasion to describe Saskatoon as the headquarters of Communism in the province and to rededicate himself to the destruction of Communism and all its works. "As long as I live in public life I shall do all in my power to drive those disciples of the 'Red Flag' out of Saskatoon and out of the province."[31] The Premier announced that initial accommodation at Dundurn would be for about six hundred men and about two-thirds of these would be transferred from the Saskatoon camp. "If the men from this camp refused to go (and he thought the majority would go) the city would be advised to furnish no relief and the police would be ordered to deal severely with begging and vagrancy."[32]

Dundurn relief camp, known to the Department of National Defence as Project 44, was originally planned for a twelve-month period with the intention that it would employ up to a thousand of the physically fit single unemployed. The plans were later extended by successive orders-in-council and Dundurn developed into one of the half dozen largest relief camps in the country and was not closed down until July 1936, when the entire relief camp system was abandoned by the federal government. Dundurn was used to service most of Saskatchewan and to accommodate most of the single unemployed who were not taken care of by the farm labour scheme and the National Park camps, which continued to be operated by the Department of the Interior. Only two other small projects, each accommodating fifty to sixty people, were operated by the DND in Saskatchewan. One was a project at White Fox where men were employed at Forestry conservation and cutting ties for a railway spur at Dundurn. The other involved building a provincial airport at Ladder Lake. Dundurn was made capable of accommodating about two thousand people and there were seldom fewer than fifteen hundred during the peak winter months.

Much of what presently constitutes Dundurn military training camp was built by relief labour between May 1933 and July 1936. The construction done in this period included forty-five permanent buildings of a residential or service nature, several miles of road and railway spur, a landing field and a rifle range, power and telephone lines, sewer and water lines and bridges. The total expenditure, including the cost of machinery and building materials, came to $1 287 215.11. The number of man-days of relief provided was 1 043 984 which meant an average expenditure per man-day of $1.23. It must be remembered that the $1.23 per man-day included the cost of materials and machinery used, board and room, medical care, clothing and personal essentials and twenty cents per diem for labourers as well as salaries and expenses for supervisory staff and some specialized labour. Captain N.I. Fraser of the Royal Canadian Engineers, Officer in Charge of Dundurn Camp in September 1936, estimated that the total cost of the construction and improvements, if they had been carried out by contract, at $556 391.00[33] That the government expenditure was over twice this amount (assuming Fraser's estimate to be reasonably accurate) is probably due partly to the fact that the work was done with the use of as little machinery as possible. It was DND policy to do as much work as possible by the most primitive methods to avoid heavy expenditures on machinery and maximize the number of man-days relief which could be provided.[34] The excavation of earth and gravel, clearing of brush and many other jobs which would ordinarily be done by machines were done largely by hand. The actual extra cost to the government of building things the primitive way, at least in the short run, was much less than might appear at first glance given that the government would have to provide relief in any case regardless of whether the men were working. The relief camp scheme was, in fact, used by the Department of National Defence to construct military facilities which the government would probably not have financed otherwise.[35] It did not add to the morale of the men to be doing make-work jobs at twenty cents a day, which they knew could be done more efficiently by machines and this was reflected in their work efficiency. There are no figures specifically for Dundurn camp but the labour efficiency of the relief camp workers across the country was found to be 48.7 percent that of ordinary labour employed at prevailing rates and it was found that overall efficiency dropped as time passed.[36]

In Dundurn, as in camps across the country, the single unemployed were provided with food and lodging, medical care, necessary clothing when they had none of their own, and an issue of tobacco. They were required to work eight hours per day five and one-half days per week. The pay of twenty cents per diem became one of the chief grievances of camp inmates and one of the major criticisms levelled at the camp system by the opposition political parties, the press and the public. Where it was possible skilled tradesmen among the inmates were encouraged to work at their trade to maintain their proficiency but would be paid at the same rate as if they worked at common labour. In some instances skilled tradesmen from the locality who were married were employed at regular union rates. This was the case in Dundurn where a few skilled tradesmen from Saskatoon were employed. Where horses were needed nearby farmers might be hired as teamsters who would supply their own horses and this was also the case at Dundurn. Civilian engineers at Dundurn as elsewhere were hired from among unemployed engineers who were recommended by the Engineering Institute of Canada. Likewise, the College of Physicians and Surgeons were consulted about the hiring of medical personnel.

The senior supervisory staff at Dundurn consisted of both civilians and regular army personnel and the camp was run as a civilian operation with no military drill and no uniforms worn by members of the military. The junior supervisory personnel, under which category was included specialized workers like cooks, were chosen where possible from the inmates of the camp. They were paid a monthly salary which was somewhat more than twenty cents per diem but much less than would have been received in regular employment. Some idea of the proportion of staff to labourers can be seen from the plans proposed for Dundurn camp for the period April 1 to September 30, 1935.[37] These plans called for 1 711 labourers, 45 teamsters, and 129 supervisory personnel for a total of 1 885 men. Included among the supervisory personnel were 4 foremen, 18 sub-foremen, 51 gang bosses and 19 cooks. Also included in this category were 4 truck drivers, a machinist and a tractor operator. Examples of monthly salaries paid to junior supervisory staff were: cookee, $10; gang boss, class 1, $25; cook, class 4, $25; clerk, class 3, $20; gang boss, class 2, $10; first aid man, $10.

The fact that the relief camp system was operated under the Department of National Defence meant that the camps were probably run more efficiently and at less cost to the government than might have been the case otherwise. The use of army officers at regular army pay as administrators (and they would have been paid anyway if there had been no relief camp scheme) meant a financial saving. The experience of DND in handling large numbers of men under circumstances similar to relief camps was also a factor adding to efficiency. There was also generally less crude political patronage in terms of hiring personnel and granting

contracts largely because the system was administered under the supervision of the Chief of the General Staff and National Defence Headquarters (N.D.H.Q.) which minimized interference from party
politicians. Career army officers had a vested interest in not unduly
favouring either of the two major political parties. There was, however,
some patronage in letting contracts for supplies and services. Lists of
businesses eligible to bid for contracts were supplied by F.R. MacMillan,
M.P. for Saskatoon, who occasionally made suggestions on the hiring of
personnel as well.[38] After the change of government in 1935 the same
privileges were extended to A. MacG. Young and D.A. McNiven, M.P.'s
for Saskatoon and Regina respectively.[39]

There were also many administrative problems encountered at Dundurn camp including the incompetence of some members of the senior
supervisory staff and corrupt practices on the part of others. An investigation by the DND and RCMP in April and May 1934, indicated that
rations had been stolen and that the sergeant in charge of fuel, light,
rations, and mechanical transport at the camp had defrauded the government of $1 001.10 by arranging, in conjunction with the employees of
a Saskatoon produce company, payment for 100 110 pounds of potatoes
which were never delivered.[40] The sergeant was discharged and convicted
in civilian court of defrauding the public. The investigation also revealed
inadequate accounting procedures by camp officials. On January 4, 1935,
a court of inquiry composed of the Quartermaster General and the
District Accountant of Military District 12 (headquarters at Regina)
conducted an inquiry at Dundurn camp into irregularities concerning
the preparation of allowance (wage) sheets for the project.[41] It was
discovered that the officer in charge of administration who was also the
camp accountant had, in collaboration with a clerk, been collecting pay
in the name of labourers who were no longer at the camp. The amount
involved was only thirty-nine dollars and the guilty parties had not kept
the money personally but had used it to cover up for funds which had
been stolen from the petty cash fund because of the carelessness of the
accountant. The court of inquiry found the accountant and the clerk
responsible for the irregularities and the camp superintendent, Captain
E.J. FitzHenry, negligent in his duties because he had known of previous
irregularities but had not reported them.

What was important about the court of inquiry and follow-up investigations was not the minor irregularities uncovered but the evidence of
much more widespread incompetence. A report from Brigadier H.E.
Boak, District Officer Commanding of M.D. 12, to the Adjutant-General
on January 17, 1935, was extremely critical of the administration of the
camp.[42] Boak claimed that FitzHenry was incompetent and that the
discipline and administration of the supervisory staff was greatly inferior
to what it should be. He recommended that FitzHenry be relieved of
his duties and that other administrative personnel, excepting the medical

assistant, be retained pending a test of how they operated under a new superintendent. FitzHenry was replaced as superintendent and some other positions were changed by demotion of the occupants and matters seemed to improve somewhat, at least temporarily.

One of the serious problems of Dundurn, and a cause of much dissatisfaction among the inmates, was the quality of medical care provided. There was a twenty-four bed hospital at the camp designed to be used for minor illness, minor surgery and convalescence, with the more serious cases being handled by Saskatoon hospitals and doctors who then billed the DND for their services. It was intended that there would be a full-time doctor at the camp but the DND had great difficulty obtaining one at the salary they were prepared to pay. The Saskatchewan College of Physicians and Surgeons were of little assistance in this regard and appeared more interested in assuring that any doctor hired must, even if fully qualified elsewhere, be registered with the College and pay the hundred-dollar registration fee.[43] The result was that for most of the time until February 1935, the camp was serviced by a part-time doctor who had a full-time practice elsewhere. Between visits by this part-time doctor the camp hospital was left in charge of a non-qualified medical assistant whom DND officials knew to be incompetent.[44] "The hospital [before March 1, 1935] was not clean and was badly run; there was excessive consumption of drugs and rubbing alcohol, and I received numerous complaints affecting the interior economy of the hospital."[45] The DND might have resolved the situation in July 1934, when they had a chance to hire Dr. Phyllis L. Steele but she was rejected by the Director General of Medical Services on the grounds that a woman would be inappropriate.[46] The medical assistant was not fired until January 1935, and then the grounds given were not medical incompetence but "using obscene and threatening language to the Camp Superintendent."[47] The situation improved on February 1, 1935, with the appointment of Dr. W.K. Blair who became the full-time doctor until he resigned to accept another position on December 7, 1935. After some difficulty and delay another full-time doctor was appointed and remained until May 20, 1936, by which time the relief camps were in the process of being closed down.

Unrest among inmates in the DND relief camps was general across the country from the spring of 1933. A chart compiled by General McNaughton indicated that between June 27, 1933, and March 31, 1934, there were fifty-seven disturbances in relief camps, which were large enough to be reported to N.D.H.Q. in Ottawa.[48] One large camp, Long Branch in Ontario, had to be closed and the nearly seven hundred inmates discharged because they refused to work and the supervisory staff could not maintain control. In the same period at least twenty-one inmates received prison sentences resulting from their involvement in the disturbances. Another of McNaughton's charts reveals that up to

December 31, 1935, a total of 3 379 men (including the whole Long Branch camp) had been expelled from the camps for disciplinary reasons.[49]

As people were expelled from the camps they went back to the cities where they would often demand relief from the municipal authorities and if this was refused would sometimes be maintained through the efforts of the unemployed associations. They could be imprisoned for up to six months for vagrancy but as their numbers increased the provincial authorities discouraged the courts from imposing long sentences because this would mean more expense to the province and virtually turn the gaols into relief camps. General McNaughton complained of what he considered to be the undue leniency of the courts and argued that they should impose maximum penalties as a deterrent but this policy was seldom followed.[50] The federal government even prepared legislation and plans for special prison camps known as "Camps of Discipline" for the incarceration of agitators and people who did not co-operate with relief officials.[51] The intention was that these prison camps would be established in any province where they were requested by provincial Order-in-Council.[52] This request was never made and the country was spared establishment of camps of discipline. What the situation revealed, however, was the length to which the federal government was prepared to go and the fact that the DND relief camps were far from successful as a stabilizing political influence. The struggle of the single unemployed for a better deal had merely been transferred from the cities to the relief camps.

An analysis of why the DND relief camps were unpopular among a large segment of the single unemployed should begin with an examination of the rules and regulations which N.D.H.Q. insisted be strictly enforced in all camps. These rules were extremely authoritarian and, in effect, deprived camp residents of their most elementary civil rights. Section 353 of the Policy and Instructions for the administration of Unemployment Relief Camps for Single Homeless and Unemployed Men reads as follows:

> The following rules regarding complaints will be observed:
> (a) One of the fundamental and most necessary rules for the administration of Unemployment Relief Camps is to forbid anything bearing the appearance of combination to obtain redress of alleged grievances. Appeals for redress by means of any document bearing the signature of more than one complainant, or by organized committees combining to make a complaint, are strictly forbidden.
> (b) If any man has a complaint or accusation to bring against a member of the supervisory or administrative staff, such complaint should be laid before the Camp Foreman, who, if necess-

ary, will transmit it to District Headquarters or Camp Superintendent.

(c) If the Camp Foreman neglects or refuses to attend to a complaint, the complainant may bring the matter to the notice of the District Headquarters or Camp Superintendent.

(d) The Department will not countenance any steps to bring accusations before the tribunal of public opinion, either by speeches, or letters inserted in the newspapers, by men actively employed on Relief Work. Such a proceeding is a glaring violation of the rules and shows a contempt for properly constituted authority.

(e) It is the duty of the Camp Foreman to investigate all complaints, and, when receiving complaints for transmission to superior authority, to point out to the parties concerned any irregularity in the means they employ in seeking redress. In hearing complaints or statements, etc., Camp Foremen are advised to invariably have another member of the Supervisory Staff present as a witness to all proceedings. The complaint, when forwarded to District Headquarters or Camp Superintendent, is to be accompanied by a statement and recommendation if any, of the Camp Foreman.

(f) No application or complaint should ever be made to the Civil Power, except through the Camp Foreman or with his sanction.[53]

The above-quoted rules were strictly enforced and supervisory personnel who disregarded them were promptly dismissed. Anyone refusing to work, disobeying the rules or deemed an agitator could be "discharged for cause" whereupon he would be blacklisted from all government camps and often denied relief in the cities as well. Men expelled from the camps were given no transportation back to the city and this was an added incentive for good behaviour, especially during the winter months. The rules were invariably defended by R.B. Bennett and his ministers on the grounds that they were not stricter than those which would apply in "any well conducted lumber camp" which perhaps reveals something about their concepts of the proper relationship between capital and labour. The other argument used constantly by government leaders, and which they knew to be true only in the most legalistic sense, was that the camps were not compulsory and men who were dissatisfied could leave at any time.

The actual physical conditions in the camps, and this was particularly true of Dundurn, compared favourably with privately operated work camps of the time and were frequently better in terms of sanitary conditions. The same was true of the food (based on the standard army ration) which was sufficient to maintain the men in a healthy condition though good food was sometimes ruined by poor cooks and there were many complaints about both the quality and the quantity of the food.

The food costs per man-day were exceptionally low, ranging from nineteen to twenty-two cents and for a small additional cost the DND could have improved upon the army ration. Many of the men were familiar with camps run by the Department of the Interior where the food was generally greater in quantity and of better quality and it was a frequent demand of inmates that the DND camps be brought up to these standards. General McNaughton, obsessed with the need for economy, attempted to solve the problem by complaining of the "unnecessary extravagance" of the Department of the Interior camps and requesting that they reduce their rations to conform with DND standards.[54] It was also the policy of N.D.H.Q. that, if extras were to be provided for special occasions such as Christmas, it would have to be done either by donations from the public or by cutting regular rations so as to accumulate some surplus.

The primary cause of dissatisfaction in the camps was not, however, the petty stinginess of the DND or the condition of the physical facilities though these were often the type of specific grievances which would provoke a strike or a demonstration. The fundamental reason for unrest and militant action, plain to anyone except the federal government by 1935, was the sense of indignation felt by the men at the denial of their rights and the waste of their lives.[55] A large percentage of camp residents were men in their early twenties who, under normal circumstances, would have looked forward to obtaining jobs, marrying and raising families. At a time when they were just getting started in adult life there were no jobs available and the government of the day, unable or unwilling to provide them with work and wages, pushed them aside and decreed that they should be satisfied to live in work camps at twenty cents a day and with few rights and little hope. This might have been tolerated for at time but as the "temporary" camps continued for months and then years (provincial camps had been established in 1930) and it appeared they might become permanent, the indignation of the single unemployed increased — directed by the more politically sophisticated among them and spurred on by the arrogance of the authorities. The relief camps became fertile areas for militant organizers and perhaps the most dedicated organizers in the country were the supporters of the Relief Camp Workers' Union, one of the many branches of the Workers' Unity League.

The amount and intensity of unrest in Dundurn relief camp appears to have been, until the prolonged strike of December 1935, on a lesser scale than in most Alberta and British Columbia camps. One of the reasons for this was because Dundurn was a permanent militia camp and as facilities were constructed they could be used by the relief workers. The accommodation, dining, recreational and other facilities were designed as permanent structures and were greatly superior to those in most camps where the buildings were temporary and of a more rudimentary kind. The recreational program was, for instance, one of the best in the relief camp system and athletic teams from the camp often competed in Saskatoon and surrounding towns. This kind of program helped to maintain the morale of the men. Another factor was that many of the men could find employment on farms for perhaps a month in the spring and another month in the autumn and then return to the camp. This helped to relieve the tedium and to provide the men with some extra pocket money. Dundurn, unlike many DND camps, was not in an isolated wilderness area and had some social intercourse with the surrounding communities. At the same time it was far enough from Saskatoon that collaboration with radical unemployed associations in the city was difficult. Dundurn was also easy to police because of it being the only major DND camp in the province. In British Columbia agitators sometimes entered camp under assumed names after they had been blacklisted. Once an agitator was expelled from Dundurn he was neutralized in Saskatchewan outside of the cities.

The authorities kept a watchful eye on Dundurn with the help of the RCMP from Hanley and Saskatoon and by means of camp constables appointed to patrol the area and police spies who were placed among the men. Most militants and potential militants were spotted and expelled before trouble could erupt. On August 14, 1933, the regular report from M.D. 12 to the Adjutant-General noted that discipline was good, and "all cases of insubordination, refusal to work, etc., have met with instant dismissal from the camp."[56] The report of November 20, 1933, stated that a Communist organization had attempted to introduce agitators into the camp but the situation had been dealt with by police authorities. This report also mentioned a rumour that there was a plot to burn down the entire camp so that it could not be resurrected before the winter and men could go into Saskatoon but concluded that there was no organization within the camp capable of such a feat. Dismissal for cause appears to have been used frequently during the initial period of the camp. From May to December 31, 1933, there were 115 inmates expelled for disciplinary reasons.[57] Insubordination could take many forms. One man was dismissed when the supervisors found a socialist book among his belongings. The vigilance of the authorities combined with other factors seems to have kept the camp free of major disturbances for the first two years of its existence and the inmates appear to have had some antipathy to radicals. A letter from Attorney-General M.A. MacPherson to R.B. Bennett on February 12, 1934, mentions the latest group of alleged agitators who were put out of the camp a few weeks previously and relates to a story told to him by Assistant Commissioner Wood of the RCMP about a police spy who posed as a Communist and was told by the inmates that if he did not keep quiet they would put him out of the camp themselves. MacPherson concludes in a burst of optimism. "I understand there is some opposition to the camps in Ontario, but certainly this story, which is absolutely true, indicates that we are not having any difficulty at Dundurn and that the men there are most appreciative."[58]

As time went on dissatisfaction increased at Dundurn as it did almost everywhere and during the On-to-Ottawa Trek of June 1935 about two hundred inmates left Dundurn camp to join the trekkers in Regina. The walkout from Dundurn was organized mainly by members of the Trek, indicating the lack of organization within the camp itself. A delegation from Regina addressed a meeting of Dundurn inmates adjacent to the camp on June 15. The two hundred men left the camp on June 18 in an exceptionally quiet manner by legally discharging themselves as was their right under the regulations.[59] They proceeded to Saskatoon and were transported to Regina in trucks hired by their supporters. The Dundurn recruits played no prominent part in the events surrounding the Trek in Regina. They did not comprise a unit by themselves but were dispersed among the existing units to allow them to learn the tight discipline, which was a notable feature of the Trek, from the seasoned veterans from British Columbia. The Dundurn trekkers of 1935 do not appear to have had a list of grievances specific to Dundurn to add to the grievances common to all camps which were included in the list of demands publicized by the On-to-Ottawa Trekkers. These demands included:

1. Work and wages at a minimum rate of 50¢ per hour for unskilled workers and trade union rates for all skilled work.
2. That all camp workers be covered by the Workmen's Compensation Act and adequate first aid supplies be carried on the job at all times.
3. That the camps be removed from the control of the DND and all blacklisting be abolished.
4. That democratically elected committees be recognized in every camp.
5. That there be instituted a system of non-contributory unemployment insurance.[60]

When the Trek was disbanded in Regina after the riot of July 1, the Dundurn recruits returned to their homes or to the camp according to the agreement worked out with the provincial and federal governments.

During the months from July to December 1935, unrest among the unemployed in Saskatchewan, inside and outside of Dundurn camp, appears to have been building up. The organized unemployed in the cities objected to attempts to force them to accept lower than standard wages for farm harvesting work or be cut off relief and the struggle against this helped to develop contacts between unemployed in the cities and the single unemployed in Dundurn camp and on farms. Many of the single men who took part in protests over this issue in August would be back in the Dundurn camp in late autumn and more inclined to be militant than previously. There was, during the summer and fall of 1935, considerable public discussion of conditions in Dundurn camp and criticism by organizations like the United Farmers of Canada.[61]

One of the grievances of the men in Dundurn, or in most camps, was the procedure for voting in federal elections. Under existing electoral procedures a majority of inmates in relief camps were, in effect, disfranchised because they had not lived in the camps for a long enough consecutive period to meet residential qualifications (most men leaving camps for varying periods during the summer months) and the government refused, despite repeated attempts by the Opposition and demands by the Relief Camp Workers' Union, to extend the right of absentee voting to relief camp inmates so that they could cast ballots for candidates in their home constituencies.[62] The right to vote had been one of the chief demands of the On-to-Ottawa Trekkers in June and was an issue which was of particular interest to Dundurn inmates because of the federal election campaign and the fact that they had been allowed to vote in the 1934 provincial election. This and other issues added to the resentment against the authoritarianism of the camp system and made it possible for the Relief Camp Workers' Union (R.C.W.U.) to become organized in a really effective manner for the first time in Dundurn camp.

Growing unrest among Dundurn inmates and the resulting increase in strength of the R.C.W.U. was reflected in a major strike which began on December 12, 1935, and was not completely terminated until January 23, 1936. For at least four days the strike was actively supported by about 800 of the 1 526 men on strength and the authorities lost effective control of the camp for about ten days.[63] The strike was set off spontaneously when the camp authorities attempted to evict two young men, aged eighteen and nineteen, on grounds of insubordination and refusal to obey camp regulations. They resisted eviction and about seventy men congregated to prevent their removal. On December 13 warrants were issued for the arrest of the two men for allegedly assaulting members of the supervisory staff while resisting eviction. They took refuge in one of the huts where their supporters refused to give them up and eight hundred of the camp inmates came out on strike in their support and began picketing so that the work of the entire camp ground to a halt.

What had begun as a spontaneous protest quickly became a well organized strike with the R.C.W.U. playing a prominent role. Camp authorities claimed that about 50 percent of the men could be persuaded to work but were prevented from doing so by pickets and that at least a hundred police would be needed to protect any of the men who went back to their jobs. As it turned out some of the men did go back to work on December 14 with no violence reported but over half of the men stayed out until December 17 and there were still 596 reported on strike on December 20 with many of those who were working employed at the hospital or on camp fatigue by consent of the strikers. The authorities were faced with a situation where they either had to make concessions or resort to the use of police force which would have almost certainly resulted in bloodshed.

There was a similarity between the situation in Dundurn camp in December and the situation in Regina which preceded the riot of July 1 in that the provincial government authorities took a conciliatory attitude towards the strikers. The difference was that the government at Ottawa had changed hands and was more willing to listen to the advice of the provincial government. Had the situation been left to the discretion of DND officials there would almost certainly have been bloodshed at Dundurn in December. On December 13 the strikers decided that they would not return to work until the two men in question had been reinstated and the Superintendent agreed to negotiate grievances concerning the food, the tobacco issue and the twenty cents per diem allowance. The strike leaders also requested a telephone conversation with Saskatchewan Attorney-General Davis, who was at that time in Ottawa, indicating that they had more faith in the provincial than in the federal and particularly the DND authorities. Davis played a key role in how the strike was handled because of his authority over the police. On December 13 Davis ordered the RCMP not to attempt to forcibly arrest the two men or to take any other action until they had fully investigated the situation.

After a meeting between Davis and the Minister of Defence it was decided to send the Rigg Committee, previously appointed by the federal government to investigate and report upon the relief camp system, to Dundurn to attempt to negotiate a settlement with the men.[64] The committee returned from Alberta where they had been investigating camps and began negotiations with strike leaders at Dundurn camp on December 15. The strike committee stood firm on its demands that the two men be reinstated and the Rigg Committee, over the objections of the superintendent, suggested that this might be a suitable compromise. A mass meeting of a hundred men was addressed on the night of December 15 by Rigg and by John Young of Saskatoon on behalf of the R.C.W.U. and the Workers' Unity League but no decision was made on the Rigg proposals. On December 16 General Ashton, C.G.S., urged the Minister of Defence not to reinstate the men or make any other concession even it if meant using force to restore order.[65] On the same day Brigadier Boak, D.O.C. 12, suggested swearing in 150 special constables from the men within the camp who opposed the strike and using them to restore order or, as an alternative, bringing in a large force of RCMP on the railway spur by night. On the morning of December 16, the Rigg Committee had presented proposals for ending the strike to a mass meeting of seven hundred strikers. These proposals included the reinstatement of the two men and the promise that the committee would include the men's complaints in their report to the government on the camp system as a whole. This was rejected by the mass meeting and a new list of demands were presented, which included:

1. Investigation of the canteens and the monthly reports signed by a chartered accountant;
2. Allowances on days when work could not be done;
3. Retaining of sufficient clothing when leaving camp;
4. Demotion of straw bosses and foreman when there was just cause;
5. A man on trial (presumably for dismissal with cause) should be notified and allowed to bring witnesses;
6. No man over 55 to go to work unless he wants to;
7. Better food facilities and investigation of cooks;
8. New clothing instead of second-hand;
9. Free cigarette papers with tobacco issue;
10. Camps pay fare of individuals with just reasons to leave camps.

The Rigg Committee left the camp failing to reach a settlement and recommended that no further concessions be granted on the grounds that it would undermine the authorities of the camp supervisors and encourage organized resistance elsewhere.

The DND officials proceeded with preparations to use force. On December 18, Brigadier Boak informed Attorney-General Davis that he had been instructed to restore order and requested that the necessary police be provided by dawn on December 19. The Attorney-General declined to send police and on December 19 Boak began applying pressure by referring to the Federal-Provincial Agreement under the Relief Act, under which the province had agreed to supply police in the event of disturbances. Boak also argued that the regular pre-Christmas allowances should be paid on December 20 and it was unsafe to bring the cash to the camp without a large police guard. Simultaneously with this, the C.G.S. was bringing pressure on his Minister in Ottawa. The Attorney-General still refused to send police and argued that the extent of the strike was gradually declining anyway. The Chairman of the Strike Committee had, in fact, deserted the strike and gone back to work after the Rigg proposals were rejected and all necessary work around the camp was being done. Only the non-essential work such as construction was still included in the strike which now involved about 675 men. The rejections of the Rigg Committee proposals had caused a split in the strikers. It was pointed out that the strike had been free of violence and the Acting Attorney-General cautioned the DND against provoking violence. "May I recall to you the riots experienced at Estevan, Saskatoon, and Regina and urge upon you that you seriously reconsider the necessity of immediate police action before a move is made which may result in similar consequences."[66]

The DND, having ruled out further significant concessions to the men, proceeded to exert further pressure on both the men and the Attorney-General. On December 20 the men who were still on strike were informed that those who returned to work immediately would not suffer the deductions from pay commonly used in relief camps to compel men to work. Under this system men who refused to work were charged sixty cents per diem for board and room for each day they spent in camp and this was deducted from their pay. While offering to free the men from this penalty the DND refused to pay the twenty cents per diem to men who had been on strike. The Attorney-General was informed that this might cause a disturbance and police would be needed. A mass meeting of 800 men rejected the new proposal but more men did return to work and on December 21 there remained only 474 actually on strike. In keeping with the policy of the strike committee an undetermined number of strike supporters were working at camp fatigue duties. The project was still out of the control of the authorities in that a large proportion of the men refused to work and yet had to be fed and could not be ejected until the provincial government agreed to send the necessary police. The DND authorities kept up pressure on the federal Ministers and the provincial government for forcible action. Boak again demanded that police be supplied under the federal-provincial agreement and this time set the latest possible date for police action at December 23.

The provincial government still refused to send police and began working on plans to transfer men to Prince Albert National Park where they could be accommodated in Department of Interior facilities. By December 23, the strike was beginning to lose much of its strength anyway. Men who had relatives nearby were taking Christmas leave, a few were returning to work and on some days it was too cold for anyone to work so that a strike became less relevant. By December 27 only 140 men were listed as being on strike and by then the DND officials had decided to wait until the number declined more and then pressure the Attorney-General into sending police when the number of strikers had reached an irreducible minimum. By now arrangements had also been made to transfer up to 500 men to National Park camps on a voluntary basis. It was thought that some men who objected to Dundurn camp would not object to a National Park camp where conditions were generally somewhat better and discipline less rigid. The transfer to the National Park camps began in early January 1936. Only men in particularly good physical condition or with some bush experience were chosen for these camps and of 260 who volunteered on January 7 the Superintendent of National Parks, who was at the camps to choose them personally, rejected 100. By now only 102 men were on strike and more pressure was applied to the Attorney-General to use force. He still refused and worked out an agreement whereby about 60 of the remaining 100 agreed to go to Prince Albert National Park. Part of the agreement was that the accrued board and room of sixty cents per diem would be dropped and that those men who had gone to work at Dundurn after the deadline for abrogation of accrued charges (December 21) would also have their charges dropped and would not have to work them off. The only other concession from DND was that strikers refusing to go back and who would leave camp voluntarily would be given transportation back to the point from which they were admitted to Dundurn. A few left camp under this agreement. By January 16 the Attorney-General had agreed to use force if necessary to get the remaining strikers evicted if they did not return to work or leave voluntarily. Police arrived in the camp on January 22 and of forty men still on strike thirty-nine returned to work and one was evicted. On January 23 sixteen of those who returned to work the previous day were evicted for refusing to perform the normal amount of work.

The long December-January strike revealed a number of things about the way the DND chose to operate relief camps and about how the single unemployed viewed life in the camp. The DND made no concessions of significance other than agreeing to reinstate the two men whose dismissal had provoked the strike and agreed to this only under pressure from the Rigg Committee and the provincial government. Later they made the other minor concessions under pressure from the provincial authorities and perhaps federal Ministers. They made no concessions on the list of demands of the camp workers mainly on the grounds that the men should never gain anything by organization and militancy. The relief camp inmates, as the regulations clearly stated, had no rights except those decreed by the Department of National Defence. The other notable thing about the DND handling of the strike was the insistence upon the use of force when it was plain that the strike could be settled and even defeated, as it eventually was, by other means.

The fundamental causes of the strike are equally revealing. The Rigg Committee report looked mainly at the superficial causes, citing such things as Communist agitation and too many people in one camp, though their report on the camps as a whole saw them as less than desirable institutions which should be closed down as soon as possible. Nor were the primary causes individual grievances of a minor nature such as inadequate dining facilities, a lack of cigarette papers and other annoyances. These things merely added to frustrations and were not important enough in themselves to spark a strike. An examination of the contents of *The Agitator*, official organ of the R.C.W.U., which was illicitly distributed fairly regularly in Dundurn camp in the winter of 1935–1936 and was designed for use in the Dundurn camp, only shows that very little attention was paid to grievances about food, clothing, cigarette papers, etc., though they were mentioned. Most of the space was devoted to attacks on the indignity of working for twenty cents a day, demands for work and wages and attacks on the entire camp system.[67] When the strike was provoked by the attempted eviction of two men the strikers had no list of demands. The list was produced later when the authorities agreed to reinstate the two men and it appeared the strike might be settled. A *Star-Phoenix* reporter who covered the strike and interviewed many of the men found that their grievances were more general than specific. "But whether an acquiescence to all their demands would settle the trouble is doubtful. They are rebelling against the condition of society in and out of the camps."[68] By 1935 men in the camps did not need specific reasons for rebelling. The fact that they were in the camps was enough in itself.

After the end of the strike in January 1936, there were no more major disturbances at Dundurn camp though men continued to be "dismissed for cause" at frequent intervals. The new Liberal government instituted a policy of bringing the camps more directly under the Department of Labour. Previously the Labour Minister had been nominally in charge of the camps but the N.D.H.Q. had been given a blank cheque for their administration and all the major decisions were made by order-in-council on the advice of the Chief of the General Staff. Few significant changes were made under the new regime. One change was that the pay for laborers was raised to fifty cents per diem on March 1, 1936. Two months later the camps were in the process of closing down altogether as had been suggested in the Rigg report. Nearly all the camps including Dundurn were closed down by June 30, 1936. Most of the Dundurn inmates found jobs, though often only temporarily, on farms or with extra gangs on the railways as part of a plan worked out by the federal and provincial governments. In the autumn of 1936 the struggle was continued in the cities.

Notes

1. H.M. Cassidy, "Relief and Other Social Services for Transients," in *Canada's Unemployment Problem*, ed. L. Richter (Toronto: MacMillan, 1939).

2. Stuart Jamieson, *Times of Trouble: Labor Unrest and Industrial Conflict in Canada 1900–1966*. Prepared for and received by the Federal Task Force on Labour Relations, 15 October 1968, 227-28.

3. Cassidy, "Relief and Other Social Services," 38, 197, and Jamieson, *Times of Trouble*, 227-28.

4. Public Archives of Canada (hereinafter PAC), McNaughton Papers, vol. 10, file 46. Memorandum by Chief of the General Staff, 13 June 1931, on a meeting of C.G.S., the Adjutant-General (Secty. of Militia Service) and the Quartermaster General, in which plans were made for calling out the Non-Permanent Active Militia and the Permanent Force should it become necessary. McNaughton thought that about twenty thousand of the N.P.A.M. might have to be mobilized in the autumn and "might probably be on duty for some considerable time."

5. PAC, Bennett Papers, microfilm pp. 494713-23, Hugh G. Farthing to A.E.

Millar (PM's secretary), 7 and 8 September 1933; also Mayor Andrew Davison of Calgary to A.E. Millar, 6 October 1933. See also microfilm p. 494237, R.K. Finalyson (PM's assistant) to A.E. Millar, 6 October 1933: "It would be a great mistake to lose sight of the main objective that the government has in this work, namely to keep urban centres clear from such single men as more readily become amenable to the designs of agitators." See Regina *Leader-Post*, 11 May 1933, for a statement by Premier Anderson about Saskatoon single unemployed being forced to go to Dundurn.

6. PAC, McNaughton Papers, vol. 58, C.G.S. to D.O.C. 13, 14 December 1934.

7. PAC, McNaugton Papers, vol. 58.

8. By 1933 there were six such organizations in Saskatoon alone with three of them affiliated to the Workers' Unity League.

9. Archives of Saskatchewan, Saskatchewan Relief Commission (S.R.C.), Thomas Molloy (Deputy Minister of Railways, Labour and Industry) to Municipal Councillors, 27 October 1932.

10. Archives of Saskatchewan, S.R.C., roll B, memo on Saskatoon Relief Camp. Unsigned and undated but probably written by A. Kendall, Manager, Field Service Branch, Unemployment Division of the Sask. Relief Commission, shortly after 8 May 1933.

11. PAC, McNaughton Papers, vol. 10, no. 46, C.G.S. memo of 16 October 1931.

12. Regina *Leader-Post*, 28 October 1932.

13. Ibid., 27 October 1932.

14. Ibid., 8 November 1932.

15. Ibid., 3 November 1932.

16. Archives of Saskatchewan, S.R.C., roll B, undated memo on Saskatoon Relief Camp.

17. Ibid.

18. Ibid.

19. Ibid.

20. Ibid.

21. Ibid.

22. Ibid.

23. *Saskatoon Star-Phoenix*, 21 September 1933. It came out at the trial of the arrested men that Constable H.M. Wilson of the RCMP had been in the camp as an undercover man from April 18 to May 8.

24. Ibid., 1 May 1933.

25. Superintendent Woodward to A. Kendall, 6 May 1933.

26. Archives of Saskatchewan, S.R.C., roll B, undated memo.

27. Archives of Saskatchewan, S.R.C., letter (illegible signature) to Superintendent Woodward, 7 May, 1933.

28. *Saskatoon Star-Phoenix*, 9 May 1933.

29. PAC, Department of National Defence (DND) Papers, Unemployment Relief, vol. 23, file no. 44, Anderson to Gordon, 8 May 1933.

30. PAC, McNaughton Papers, vol. 48, 331A, McNaughton memorandum, 9 May 1933.

31. Regina *Leader-Post*, 11 May 1933.

32. Ibid.

33. PAC, DND Papers, Captain N.I. Fraser to N.D.H.Q., 4 September 1936.

34. John Swettenham, *McNaughton* (Toronto: Ryerson, 1968), I: 271.

35. Ibid.

36. G.M. LeFresne, "The Royal Twenty Centers: The Department of National Defence and Federal Unemployment Relief 1932–1936" (B.A. thesis, Royal Military College, Kingston, 1962), 179.

37. PAC, DND Papers, Unemployment Relief, H.Q. file 1376-11-10-1, undated.

38. PAC, DND Papers, Unemployment Relief, vol. 155, F.R. MacMillan, MP to Col. D.M. Sutherland (Minister of Defence), 7 May 1934.

39. PAC, DND Papers, Unemployment Relief, vol. 158, Quartermaster General to D.O.C. 12, 16 November 1935.

40. PAC, DND Papers, Unemployment Relief, vol. 168.

41. PAC, DND Papers, Unemployment Relief, project 44, proceedings of court of inquiry.

42. PAC, DND Papers, Unemployment Relief, Project 44, Brig. H.E. Boak, D.O.C. of M.D. 12, to Adjutant-General, 17 January 1935.

43. PAC, DND Papers, Unemployment Relief, vol. 167, Young to Blair, 1 March 1935, and Young to D.O.C. 12, 2 June 1933. See also file H.Q. 1376-11-10-2, vol. 1 on medical arrangements in vol. 167.

44. PAC, DND Papers, Unemployment Relief, Project 44, H.E. Boak to Adjutant-General, 14 February 1935.

45. PAC, DND Papers, Unemployment Relief, vol. 167, D.O.C. 12 to Adjutant-General, 4 December 1935.

46. Ibid., District Medical Officer of M.D. 12 to Director General of Medical Services N.D.H.Q., 24 July 1934, and the reply of D.G.M.S. to D.M.O. 12, 31 July 1934.

47. Ibid., D.O.C. 12 to A.G., 4 December 1935.

48. PAC, McNaughton Papers, file 359 (vol. 1).

49. Ibid.

50. PAC, McNaughton Papers, 2d ser., vol. 57, McNaughton to A.E. Millar, 2 March 1934.

51. PAC, McNaughton Papers, vol. 41, file 314 (vol. 1).

52. Ibid., and file 359 (vol. 1).

53. PAC, DND Papers, Unemployment Relief, Policy and Instructions for the Administration of Unemployment Relief Camps for Single Homeless and Unemployed Men.

54. PAC, McNaughton Papers, file 377.

55. PAC, Bennett Papers, microfilm pp. 495782-88. By 1935 Bennett was receiving dozens of submissions and letters from the most respectable sources on what the men and the public thought of the camps.

56. PAC, DND Papers, Unemployment Relief, Project 44, D.O.C. to A.G., 14 August 1933.

57. Ibid., vol. 47, file 328.

58. PAC, Bennett Papers, microfilm pp. 495029-30, M.A. MacPherson to R.B. Bennett, 12 February 1934.

59. PAC, McNaughton Papers, vol. 61, file 380B, An outline of the events of the On-to-Ottawa Trek.

60. PAC, Manion Papers, Minutes of meeting of Manion and Weir with Evans.

61. Regina *Leader-Post*, 15 August 1935.

62. House of Commons, *Debates*, 11 February 1935, vol. 2, pp. 1124-25, 672, 980-88.

63. The account of this strike is based on a diary of the strike kept by the C.G.S. as well as memos and correspondence in PAC, DND Papers, Unemployment Relief, vol. 168.

CANADA'S FIRST DOCTORS' STRIKE: MEDICAL RELIEF IN WINNIPEG, 1932–4†

C. DAVID NAYLOR

From the time of Confederation to the end of the First World War the emergence and occupational success of Canada's medical profession was critically dependent on government. It was the provincial legislatures, after all, that enacted the licensing laws requested by medical lobbyists in the nineteenth century and also allowed doctors to incorporate self-governing provincial Colleges of Physicians and Surgeons. At the same time, various levels of government offered increasingly generous support for medical education, construction and maintenance of hospitals, and the development of public health programs. State intervention therefore gave doctors a legalized monopoly on provision of medical services, strengthened medicine's occupational autonomy, and improved the status, education, and working conditions of medical practitioners.[1]

Government intervention in the medical-care market was maintained during the twentieth century, and eventually increased substantially with the gradual implementation of a national health insurance program. Of interest is the fact that Canadian doctors at times took a very positive view of the government's role. Even before the First World War medical spokesmen had pointed out that state-sponsored health insurance might improve the profession's economic position by increasing the payments doctors received for work with low-income patients; and during the war

† *Canadian Historical Review* 67, no. 2 (1986): 151–80. The author wishes to acknowledge the assistance of the Social Sciences and Humanities Research Council (Grant 410-83 1162). Thanks also to Ms. Jane Stewart, information officer for the Manitoba Medical Association; helpful librarians in the Manitoba Legislative Library and at the University of Western Ontario; the staff of the Public Archives of Canada in Ottawa; and Dr. Isle Treurnicht.

64. The Committee was chaired by R.E. Rigg, senior civil servant with the Department of Labour.

65. PAC, DND Papers, vol. 168, General Ashton to Minister of Defence, 16 December 1935.

66. PAC, DND Papers, vol. 168, J.W. Estey (Acting Attorney General) to Brig.-General H.E. Boak, 19 December 1935.

67. PAC, DND Papers, vol. 168.

68. *Saskatoon Star-Phoenix*, 27 December 1935.

many prominent doctors publicly endorsed a national sickness insurance plan on the grounds that the profession and public alike would benefit.[2]

Medical interest in health insurance faded in the 1920s, a period of unprecedented prosperity for the Canadian medical profession.[3] But when the economic collapse of the 1930s sharply cut doctors' incomes, the profession again looked to government for help in the form of health insurance or medical relief.[4]

This positive view of state intervention persisted into the early years of the Second World War,[5] and then was supplanted by ever-greater anxiety about the role of government. Private medical insurance plans sponsored by organized medicine itself were seen as a better alternative to any government-administered programs, and, from 1949 on, the Canadian Medical Association officially rejected the concept of universal coverage by the state.[6] Since most provinces already provided coverage for those unable to afford private medical insurance, the economic benefits to doctors of a universal state-sponsored plan were uncertain; while at the same time, organized medicine clearly and accurately perceived that coverage by a single state-controlled carrier could bring both hard bargaining over medical fees and an erosion of the profession's autonomy.[7] The debate about state medical-care insurance escalated into a bitter conflict in Saskatchewan during 1962, when the province's Co-operative Commonwealth Federation government introduced Canada's first universal medicare scheme.[8] In July the majority of Saskatchewan doctors withdrew all but emergency services in a strike[9] aimed at forcing withdrawal or modification of the medicare legislation.

Though the Saskatchewan dispute is well-known, it was not Canada's first doctors' strike. Pressure group activities involving the withdrawal of services were a feature of Depression medical politics in Winnipeg, and harassing tactics that limited the availability of medical care were used by doctors elsewhere in western Canada. All of these actions had a similar goal: to augment doctors' incomes by ensuring that some level of government paid at least partial fees for medical services given free of charge to patients in receipt of municipal relief. Indeed, the Winnipeg doctors' strike denied all except urgent services to any recipient of municipal relief payments, and therefore affected about fifty thousand Canadians over several months.

The Winnipeg work-action was simply an extreme response to a problem that existed from coast to coast during the Depression. A tradition rooted in the Elizabethan Poor Laws and maintained in Canada placed the responsibility for food, shelter, and medical services for so-called "indigents" onto municipal authorities. With the economic collapse of the early 1930s, a large number of Canadian municipalities found themselves with lower tax revenues, even as demands for municipal relief increased sharply. Larger cities in particular were saddled with a sizeable debt, and the financing of all aspects of relief became a source

of friction among municipalities, their respective provincial governments, and Ottawa.

The position of the medical profession was akin in some ways to that of the municipalities. Doctors were ethically bound to provide free services for those unable to pay, and, as the Depression wore on, cash flows fell while the demand for charitable services mounted steadily higher. Between 1928 and 1933 average per capita money income of small businessmen and professionals in general registered a 36 percent decline,[10] and the available evidence suggests doctors lost at least that much ground. In most rural areas, for example, practitioners who had hitherto prospered found their clients paying them in kind if at all. As for urban centres, a survey of doctors in Hamilton, Ontario, revealed that the amount of unremunerative work had risen from an average of 22.5 percent of all services rendered to 50 percent. The Hamilton practitioners estimated that their total volume of practice had fallen by 36.5 percent between 1929 and 1932, and almost half of the respondents to the same survey claimed that they were no longer able to meet overheads and "bare living expenses."[11] Suburban doctors were supposedly hit hardest of all. Whereas those in the older and well-established parts of a city served more affluent families, and those in rural areas might at least receive payment in kind, the suburban doctor's income was claimed by Dr. J.H. MacDermot of Vancouver to be "gone to the vanishing point, because the people in his district are mainly out of work and on relief. But they used to be his patients and still call him in. He has to use his car and his time and his supplies, with no chance or hope of payment. . . ."[12]

The attitude of doctors varied somewhat from province to province, but there was, in fact, only a limited range of options to deal with the profession's economic malaise. Organized medicine could press for direct payment to cover free services given to those in receipt of municipal relief; or it could actively seek the implementation of some broader reform such as provincial health insurance. The first option, promotion of medical relief schemes, was actively pursued by organized medicine in every province of the dominion. The second option — sweeping measures such as state health insurance or a state medical service with doctors on salary — was more controversial. A salaried system was strongly rejected by all organized medical groups, but a large number of doctors favoured state health insurance if it would pay them for their work among low- and no-income groups. Endorsements of a state health insurance plan to cover all low-income groups on a compulsory basis were given in 1932–1933 by organized medicine in Alberta, Saskatchewan, and British Columbia. And in 1934 the Economics Committee of the Canadian Medical Association (CMA) produced a blueprint for national health insurance along the same lines; the CMA plan specified that families with a household income above $2 400 per annum were

not to be eligible for medical coverage under a government scheme, although they could purchase state hospital insurance on a voluntary basis. This emphasis on income ceilings for medical insurance was obviously designed to maintain an optimum price discrimination position for private practitoners, since patients with moderate to high incomes were believed capable of paying higher fees than would be provided by public insurance.[13]

Apart from T.D. Pattullo's Liberal government in British Columbia, no province actually attempted to implement a state health insurance plan, and thus the solution to the profession's economic woes, almost by default, came to rest in municipal medical relief.[14] Indeed, most provinces not only failed to emulate British Columbia in attempting to implement a health insurance scheme, but also avoided, so far as possible, assuming responsibility for helping the municipalities with medical relief payments. The major exception was Ontario, where, as of October 1932, the province agreed to subsidize two-thirds of the costs of any municipally organized medical relief plan so long as it conformed to certain operating conditions: doctors were not to be paid more than 50 percent of the Ontario Medical Association minimum tariff for any given service; in-hospital services could not be covered; and no doctor was to receive more than one hundred dollars per month for medical relief work. Not all municipalities took advantage of these conditional grants, and the OMA was later successful in pressing the provincial government for an altered program that encouraged wider civic participation.[15] Eventually, most large cities in Canada set up medical relief programs; however, contemporary commentaries by doctors make it clear that smaller centres frequently refused any payments and other cities paid only token amounts.[16]

A variety of tactics were used by civic and provincial medical groups to press for implementation of medical relief payment plans. In Moose Jaw, for example, the local medical society had made no progress in negotiations with the city council. Even an offer to take payment for medical relief services as credit on property or business taxes was refused. Finally, to underscore the city's responsibility, the doctor advised that while they would continue treating relief patients, the civic officials must give every such patient a letter requesting treatment unless the situation was an emergency.[17] Excepting Winnipeg, which will be discussed below, Vancouver saw the most militant medical activity. The Vancouver Medical Association recommended in the early spring of 1933 that the out-patient department of the city's general hospital should be closed because of the excessive load of free ambulatory care imposed on doctors working there.[18] Negotiations with municipal authorities concerning payment for these and other medical relief services continued for months, and on 1 August 1933 every doctor in the city signed an undertaking to refuse further work in the out-patient department except in case of emergency or on referral for specialist consultation.[19] The city responded in the autumn by agreeing to pay partial fees for maternity cases.[20] Although the Vancouver medical profession contemplated extending their limited work-action so as to institute a full-scale strike against relief recipients, discussions in December 1933 led to the amicable implementation of a medical relief plan.[21] These developments are noteworthy, but the Vancouver doctors patterned their work-action on a wider-ranging withdrawal of services organized by the Winnipeg Medical Society. In fact, Winnipeg doctors were both first to use the strike weapon, and first to withdraw services from relief recipients in all sectors — in-patient, outpatient, and office alike. This work-action was maintained for several months until the city finally capitulated and instituted a payment plan for medical relief work.

Even before the full impact of the Depression was felt, Manitoba doctors had evinced interest in health services reform. During 1930 and 1931 virtually every issue of the monthly *Bulletin of the Manitoba Medical Association* carried articles on health insurance and other aspects of health services reorganization.[22] A particular impetus for medical attention to these matters came from the provincial legislature where, in late 1930, a resolution had been unanimously passed supporting the creation of a Special Select House Committee to evaluate all aspects of public and medical services. The medical profession responded by creating its own committee with a similar mandate.[23]

The chairman of the profession's medical services committee was Dr. Ernest Samuel Moorhead, a graduate of Trinity College, Dublin, former chairman of the provincial Welfare Supervision Board, and a consultant physician to the Winnipeg General Hospital.[24] Moorhead was an appropriate choice to head the doctors' study group, for in October 1930 he had written a concise report on the feasibility of provincial health insurance at the request of the Manitoba government. Since Moorhead also became the chief organizer of the Winnipeg doctors' strike, it is important to note that his view of health insurance was cautionary: some system of contributory health insurance might be instituted in cities, but the low population density and seasonal work patterns of rural Manitobans were, in Moorhead's opinion, severe impediments to implementation of a complete provincial scheme.[25] On these grounds, then, Moorhead might be expected to view medical relief payments as the most practical immediate response to the profession's economic difficulties, with state-administered or private insurance reserved for later experimentation.

The Special Select House Committee did not even begin deliberations on health services reform until March 1931.[26] By this juncture the doctors' own committee had already drafted a report and recommendations on public medical services. This report, submitted on 30 March 1931, eschewed the formulation of any specific plans, and instead set out certain cardinal principles that should be respected in any health services reorganization.[27] As the months passed, the Special Select Committee frequently consulted organized medicine,[28] but mere consultations did nothing to alleviate the decline in professional incomes caused by the increase in non-paying clientele. Dr. W. Harvey Smith, a prominent Winnipeg surgeon, estimated that prior to the Depression the profession across the province made a combined annual contribution of $1.3 million worth of free services, and the total could well have doubled since 1930. Some form of government subsidy was needed.[29]

Smith's claims raise an issue of no small importance: just what was the income position of Winnipeg doctors before and during the Depression? In the first place, his estimate of the amount of unpaid service was probably accurate, for it leads to an average of about $2 150 unpaid work per practitioner prior to the Depression — a figure that corresponds almost exactly with independent estimates and survey data from elsewhere in Canada.[30] However, this free service was not provided simply as a result of professional altruism: a survey of five hundred Ontario doctors shows a pre-Depression annual average of $815 worth of work actually done without charge, with an additional $1 247 per year billed but not collectable from patients. In Winnipeg itself, a 1930 survey revealed that general practitioners had a pre-Depression average gross income of $6 523 per year, while specialists earned $11 368. These incomes, which were not atypical for Canadian doctors between 1925 and 1930, compare favourably with the 1928 national average earnings for men paid by salary or by hourly wage: $1 915 and $1 024, respectively. At the same time, the Winnipeg doctors noted average annual expenses of $2 080 for general practice and $3 332 for specialist work. Winnipeg general practitioners further claimed that they provided an average of $2 544 in unpaid services to office and hospital patients, with specialists claiming $5 501 on the same basis.[31] Predictably, most of the unpaid specialist services were in hospitals, since specialists were expected both to arrange free out-patient clinics and to treat the general ward in-patients without charge; this was seen as a form of recompense for the income earned by specialists when they dealt with wealthier patients in operating theatres and private wards of the hospitals.

By reference to 1933 figures from Hamilton, Ontario,[32] it can be estimated that Winnipeg doctors' incomes on average would have fallen by from 40 to 60 percent between 1929 and 1932, leaving some general practitioners with net incomes of less than $1 000 per year. The majority of doctors must have remained at or above the Winnipeg average household earnings for 1931; $1 472[33]; and even allowing for a 50 percent drop in cash flow, the average specialist income after expenses remains comparable with Winnipeg teachers who were paid an average of $2 675 in 1931.[34] However, the absolute level of medical earnings was probably less important in shaping doctors' attitudes than the magnitude of the

decline in the face of previously high income expectations,[35] along with
the ongoing irritant of an unprecedented volume of demands for unpaid
services.

These financial concerns were given publicity in the autumn of 1931
by Dr. C.W. MacCharles, the editor of the provincial medical *Bulletin*,
who observed in his October number that doctors were being forced to
make "a sacrifice of time and money which no other citizens as a group
are asked to do. Even the social workers are paid."[36] By December
MacCharles had changed emphasis, pointing out how unfair it was that
"thousands of good citizens temporarily on relief" now found themselves
"forced to attend the already crowded outdoor clinics of the various
hospitals." If the family doctor was paid the "fair and modest return
which everyone else who deals with the unemployed is receiving," these
patients would again feel comfortable calling him in, and would "be
released from the stigma of charity insofar as medical care is concerned."[37]

That same month a group of activists persuaded the Winnipeg Medical
Society to take up the matter and seek "payment of minimum fees to
doctors who attend sick people who are on City relief."[38] A special
meeting of the society on 21 December 1931 authorized the executive
to negotiate the matter with the city council, but no further action was
taken. Even the doctors' *Bulletin* published nothing more about medical
relief payments for several months. It may well have been that the
profession's leaders deliberately set the matter aside until the report of
the Special Select Committee was tabled in the Manitoba legislature.

No economic panaceas for the doctors appeared in that document
when it was presented to the legislature during April 1932. The Special
Select Committee did offer a wide-ranging endorsement of modifications
in the organization of a variety of public medical services; however, the
plans were sketchy and no agenda for implementation was given. It was
instead suggested that a royal commission be established to deal further
with these issues.[39] In fact, no such royal commission was ever appointed.

The profession's growing resentment was starkly evident in an anonymous comment on medical relief published by the *Bulletin of the Manitoba
Medical Association* a few months later. Written as a conversation between
three practitioners, this essay decried free services at the out-patient
departments of Winnipeg's hospitals as a waste of public funds and an
exploitation of the medical profession. Reference was made to the pre-
ponderance of immigrants in the clinics, the supposedly unjustifiable
need for interpreters, and "the peculiar aroma of a well known vegetable
long a favourite in certain European countries." One doctor, "the Strong
Silent One," proposed that all those seeking free care should be subjected
to a means test at a central office. However, "the Cynic" objected:
"people of the social worker type" would control the office and "use
their position as an outlet for their inhibited sympathies by being generous at the expense of the taxpayer and the medical practitioner." He

proposed that the clinics should operate only for emergencies and refer-rals from general practitioners. The article concluded that it would be better financially for the profession and ultimately cheaper for the tax-payer if some variation on these proposals were implemented.[40]

There is no record of any action stemming from this call to arms. In September, when the Manitoba Medical Association met at Winnipeg's Royal Alexandra Hotel for their annual convention, the MMA president, Dr. Ross Mitchell, urged consideration of government health insurance as a way of improving the profession's economic position,[41] but medical relief itself was not formally debated.

Meanwhile, the number of relief patients continued to mount.[42] It was later calculated that the volume of out-patient visits at the Winnipeg General Hospital rose from 50 441 in 1930 to 64 131 in 1931, and again to 83 969 in 1932. Finally, in November 1932 the eye, ear, nose and throat section of the Winnipeg Medical Society set in motion an initiative that was eventually to be carried out to the point of strike action. A series of resolutions was framed that noted the willingness of the civic authorities to pay for rent, fuel, and clothing expenses of those on relief and demanded payment on a similar basis for doctors. Dr. W.E. Campbell of the otolaryngology group presented the resolutions to a meeting of about a hundred Winnipeg practitioners at the physiology lecture theatre of the medical school, introducing them with a humorous but biting speech on the worsening financial situation of the average doctor.[43] These resolutions were adopted, and a Special Relief Commit-tee was then appointed with sixteen members to seek political action on the issue. The committee membership read like a 'Who's Who' of the Manitoba medical profession. Dr. E.S. Moorhead served as chairman, and among the others were A.T. Mathers, the provincial psychiatrist and dean of the medical school; W. Harvey Smith, the 1930 president of the Canadian and British medical associations; Ross Mitchell, former editor of the doctors' *Bulletin* and MMA president; F.W. Jackson, the deputy minister of health who was also on salary as secretary of the Manitoba Medical Association;[44] and George F. Stephens, the superin-tendent of the Winnipeg General Hospital.[45]

Over the next four weeks the Special Relief Committee (SRC) co-opted extra representatives from the provincial medical association and the younger doctors in the city, and sprang into action. Several general and executive meetings of the committee were held to plot strategy. The executive of the SRC interviewed relief authorities of the city, the prov-ince, and the federal government, and mailed a questionnaire to all practitioners in the municipality seeking additional data on the actual amount of free work done. In addition, press releases were prepared and mailed to the local daily newspapers.[46]

On the evening of 16 December 1932 the campaign received a boost when the *Tribune* editorialized favourably on the doctors' plea for payment:

> The province of Ontario has recently conceded the point raised by the Winnipeg physicians, and has adopted a scheme whereby the province assists the municipalities in meeting the cost of medical care for the unemployed. All that is being asked is that the extra demands on physicians arising out of unemployment be paid for on a basis of service at cost, the arrangement to be temporary and to be adequately safeguarded. In the circumstances it is a modest and reasonable request from a body of men who have the best possible claim upon public consideration.[47]

The following day, the *Free Press* addressed the issue, accepting without dispute that the doctors had "substantial ground for their contention that they are required to carry more of the load than it is fair to ask of them." The editors, however, were concerned that the proposal to pay doctors half fees for services to relief patients would leave too much opportunity for abuse by both patients and doctors, with the result that costs would spiral up unnecessarily: "The alternative, if the City is to administer medical relief, is the direct taking on to the City staff of a panel of physicians for the caring of the City's wards, the work to be either on a whole or part time basis."[48] However, Dr. C.W. MacCharles, who had offered strong editorial support for the doctors' new political militancy,[49] rejected the *Free Press* suggestion of a panel system with doctors on salary in his December editorial. As MacCharles saw it, if citizens were given relief funds to purchase groceries wherever they wished, they should surely retain the privilege of consulting a doctor of their choice on intimate health matters.[50]

Preliminary discussions with the minister of the interior, T.G. Murphy, in late December brought only a promise that the matter would be raised in cabinet. Hence, the Special Relief Committee pressed successfully for a meeting with Premier John Bracken and other officials of the Liberal-Progressive government. On 12 January 1933 the premier and R.A. Hoey, minister of health and welfare, held discussions with the entire Special Relief Committee, twenty doctors in all. The premier underlined the difficult financial position of his government, but did request the written submission of a plan from the doctors and also promised to raise the matter at an upcoming federal-provincial conference in Ottawa.[51]

On his return from Ottawa, Bracken wrote the doctors' committee to report on a resolution passed by the premiers: the provinces had agreed in principle that a limited expenditure for medical services should be permitted as acceptable use of federal transfer payments earmarked for direct relief.[52] No further developments on the federal or provincial front took place, however, and the doctors turned back to the municipality.

In February the executive of the SRC met with Mayor Ralph Webb and two members of the city council's own special committee on unemployment relief, Aldermen C. Rice-Jones and J.A. McKerchar.[53] No agreement was reached on medical relief; indeed, the meeting was prompted in part because the councillors wished the doctors' advice about financial problems in the local hospitals. The trustees of the Winnipeg General Hospital had notified the city that they could no longer bear the costs of maintaining the out-patient department, and requested additional subsidies. In a subsequent report to council, Rice-Jones and McKerchar noted that whereas in 1929 the total gross cost of indigent hospital care to the city was $238 931, in 1932 the cost was $378 970. Admissions increased by more than 50 percent in the same period, and the actual net amount collected from public ward patients towards their hospital costs fell by 65 percent. The two aldermen agreed that doctors were "bearing an uneven share of the burden" and suggested that the demands of the profession might well repay consideration, since the lack of payment for office and home attendance on relief patients invited doctors to refer charity cases along to the hospitals where the city would bear part of the costs anyway. They remarked, however, that a definite plan had not been drawn up by the profession.[54]

On 16 February the executive of the doctors' relief group met and outlined a formal proposal as requested. Their plan was simple and virtually identical to that used across Ontario. The relief recipients must register with a central office, to which the doctor would report within twenty-four hours after seeing any patient on relief. The relief office would then act as a clearing house for follow-up visits, thereby assisting in ensuring that abuses of the guaranteed payment system would be minimized. Doctors were to be paid monthly at 50 percent of the MMA fee schedule to a maximum of one hundred dollars per practitioner, and patients who did not have a regular family physician could choose one from a rotating roster to be posted in the relief office. This plan was discussed and approved the very next night at a regular monthly meeting of the Winnipeg Medical Society,[55] and presented to the city council a few days later by Dr. Alex J. Swan, the secretary of the Special Relief Committee.[56] The prompt action of the doctors was not rewarded: negotiations with the city council continued over the next several weeks, but little progress was made.

At this time, Vancouver doctors were taking the first steps to limit free out-patient services in their civic general hospital. An editorial from the *Bulletin of the Vancouver Medical Association* reviewing the situation was reprinted by the Manitoba *Bulletin* in March, and perhaps fuelled the determination of the Winnipeg group.[57] But whereas Vancouver doctors effectively closed the out-patient department of the Vancouver

General Hospital in August 1933, this being the full extent of their work-action, Winnipeg doctors found the largest out-patient clinic closed even before their pressure-group strategies went into effect. The Winnipeg General Hospital, like the doctors, had waited in vain for financial assistance from the city council, and now advised that $36 000 must be provided to keep the out-patient department open. On 13 March the council recommended against such a payment,[58] prompting the hospital trustees to warn that without the subsidy the out-patient department would have to be closed by 15 April.

The doctors meanwhile were in the process of making their own decisions about charitable services for those on relief. The chairman of the Civic Relief Commission had fanned resentment by claiming repeatedly in radio broadcasts that a full medical service was being provided, even though the Commission itself had only one full-time medical health officer and a few nurses to care for relief patients then believed to number over fifty thousand. Now, in Moorhead's words, "It was necessary to find out to what extent the doctors were behind the movement, and how much real authority they were prepared to give their committee." A meeting of the honorary medical staff members of all civic hospitals was convened on 31 March, and the following form was circulated:

> I hereby authorize Dr. E.S. Moorhead, Dr. A.H. Swan, or _____ to notify the Board of Director of _____ Hospital that, on and after a date to be decided by the above, I shall no longer attend any patients in the Out-Door Department or Wards of the above Hospital who are officially in receipt of unemployment relief from City, Province or Dominion. I reserve to myself the right to attend all indigent patients other than those on relief, and cases referred to me by another doctor, and all emergency cases.

Within three days, 129 of 132 hospital staff doctors had signed this document.[59] The first step towards strike action had been taken.

Two weeks later a mass meeting of medical practitioners in Greater Winnipeg was convened. An estimated 320 doctors attended, representing the overwhelming majority of the city's medical community.[60] A vote of support for the actions taken thus far was passed unanimously. But the most important development came when about 90 percent of those in attendance signed a resolution empowering the Special Relief Committee "to carry out such negotiations as they may deem expedient for the furtherance of its objects." It was also decided that any offers to individual doctors should be referred to the executive of the SRC before acceptance. This would prevent the city council from hiring additional full-time or part-time doctors on salary and force the acceptance of a fee-for-service plan as demanded by organized medicine.[61]

At about this time the trustees announced the closing of the Winnipeg

General Hospital out-patient department; thus, one of the main arenas for high volumes of free services was no longer to be a problem. The *Bulletin of the Manitoba Medical Association* underscored this point in May with an editorial laying out the profession's many objections to the ambulatory-care clinics. According to *Bulletin editor* C.W. MacCharles, "a large section of the medical profession of Winnipeg" believed "that all out-patient departments should be closed and kept closed."[62]

On 1 June 1933 the Special Relief Committee sent a letter to every doctor in Greater Winnipeg that reviewed the negotiations thus far, and accurately remarked: "at the end of several months, we are no nearer to a free discussion of problems, let alone a settlement of them." The letter alluded to medical relief plans elsewhere in Canada, and went on to state:

> At a mass meeting recently, you authorized your committee to take whatever steps were considered necessary. You are therefore requested to refuse to supply medical service, in the home or office, to cases on relief who ask that your services should be given for nothing. . . . This step is being taken now so that, when the usual increased illness and consequent demand for medical attention develop in the fall and next winter, those in authority will not be able to state that the medical profession embarrassed them and created a dangerous situation by suddenly refusing their services.

The two exceptions were in cases of emergency, or if patients on relief were formerly part of the doctor's paying practice so that there was "a moral or personal obligation" to attend them. All other relief recipients in hospital clinics, hospital wards, or doctors' offices should be turned away. The strike plan was to be implemented on 1 July 1933, twenty-nine years to the day before a very different doctors' strike began in Saskatchewan.[63]

On 12 June 1933 a notice was also sent over Moorhead's signature to the chairmen of the boards of trustees of every hospital in the municipality. This advised that as of 1 July, the honorary attending staff would no longer treat patients in either the out-patient departments or the wards of the hospital, if those patients were "officially in receipt of unemployment relief from Municipality, Province or Dominion . . . Your Honorary Staff will be quite willing to attend indigent patients other than those on relief, indigent or relief patients when referred by a private practitioner for consultation, and emergency cases."[64] Copies of this letter were forwarded to the press, and both the Winnipeg daily papers reproduced it promptly.[65]

The *Free Press* initially offered no editorial comment but, on 16 June, the *Tribune* — as had been the case in the winter when the issue first surfaced — gave the profession strong support in an editorial suggestively entitled "Doctors Must Live." As the *Tribune* saw it, "Many a doctor today is little better off than the unemployed families to whom he has been giving so unselfishly of his services."

The press approached Alderman Herbert A. Andrews, chairman of the Civic Unemployment Relief Committee, for comment. Andrews was sanguine: "I am inclined to sit back and see what happens. I believe the situation will smooth over in time. The hospitals had no particular rush of patients when the out-door clinics of the General Hospital closed, and the refusal of the doctors to treat the unemployed may not be as serious as first anticipated." He suggested the city council might well respond by simply hiring additional salaried medical staff.[66]

But this option was again rejected by the *Bulletin of the Manitoba Medical Association* in an editorial that also warned against any breach of solidarity:

> It is possible, of course, that the municipal authorities may decide to appoint a few full-time physicians to care for relief cases, and make no attempt to adopt the comprehensive scheme suggested by the profession. Any member of the profession who is approached with a proposition such as this will naturally refer the matter to the Central Committee. If it should so happen that a member of the profession were considering accepting such an appointment without first discussing it with the representatives of the general body of the profession, he would be considering the matter purely from the point of view of what was to his own advantage, and therefore would naturally weigh carefully the balance between any temporary financial advantage that might come to him as a result of accepting the appointment, as against any unfortunate repercussion in his relations with his professional colleagues in later years.[67]

The appointed day came and the doctor's strike plan went into effect. Perhaps because the group being denied services was a low-profile minority,[68] there was no immediate outcry or media reaction. As well, earlier in the spring the doctors' Special Relief Committee had taken the canny step of arranging for a liaison with the various representatives of unemployed workers' unions and associations. Moorhead commented later that the relief recipients' group "felt that their aims and requests were similar to those of the doctors, *viz.*, adequate medical service and free choice of doctor. . . . Once given the assurance that emergencies would not be neglected, they approved of the withdrawal of indiscriminate free service, even though it would entail some hardship for them."[69] Thus the victims of the work action were more likely to condemn the city than the doctors.

Alone among the hospitals, Victoria—a private corporation—refused to bow to the profession's pressure tactics, and announced early in July that it would continue taking any relief patients, including those turned away by the other hospitals. The Winnipeg General, St. Boniface, St.

Joseph's, Misericordia, Grace, and even the Mount Carmel Clinic fell into line, allowing a casualty officer to screen every patient on relief and turn away those deemed not in need of emergency services. Dr. George F. Stephens, the medical superintendent of the Winnipeg General and, as noted above, an organizer of the strike, played down the matter when approached by the press. He stressed that the doctors were being "very generous in their interpretation of what constitutes an emergency."[70] But as the *Canadian Medical Association Journal* remarked, "There is no record in Canadian medicine of a situation similar to that which has developed in Winnipeg":[71] fifty thousand citizens on relief were being denied basic services by doctors whose national code of ethics explicitly promised that care would "always be cheerfully and freely accorded" to indigents.[72]

The Winnipeg *Free Press*, which had not commented since the doctors' June strike threat, apparently obtained a copy of the June medical *Bulletin* and, on 6 July, sternly chastized organized medicine for the call to solidarity. The editors accurately characterized this communication as "virtually an ultimatum to the members of the profession, and indirectly to the city, that there must be no countenancing or attempt to carry out, any other plan than that proposed by the Medical Association." As in December 1932 the *Free Press* editors suggested the city might save money by hiring additional doctors on salary; they were clearly angered that the organized profession was trying to close off this possibility.[73]

During the summer the value of the doctors' alliance with the unemployed associations became clear. Parades were organized where the relief recipients demonstrated in favour of a medical services plan. On one occasion the police intervened and dispersed the demonstration with tear gas.[74] Concern on the part of the city councillors was clearly manifest in a motion tabled on 17 July, calling for the civic unemployment relief committee to make provision for medical services "as soon as possible." This motion was narrowly defeated on a nine to seven vote, with the split on a left-right basis. Independent Labour aldermen favoured prompt settlement; the more conservative majority supported a harder line.[75]

Initially, venereal disease cases were to be exempted from the general strike action. However, in late July additional pressure was applied on the council when the Special Relief Committee decided that many sexually transmitted conditions "could not be classified as emergencies from a curative point of view." The provincial government at once entered the fray in light of the legal and public health implications of allowing these contagious diseases to go untreated; and a call was put out for tenders from the hospitals for operation of a venereal disease clinic. Only the St. Boniface Hospital came forward with a bid. After protracted negotiations that continued into September, the doctors agreed to permit the operation of this clinic as a concession to public health considerations. Since, however, the medical director of the clinic was to be on salary, the SRC stressed that its agreement to such an arrangement "shall not be construed a precedent."[76]

Meanwhile, the deadlock continued. The victims of the strike supposedly had few complaints, but it was noted that "One source of distress to the unemployed was the way in which the officials of the relief authorities passed them from one place to another." Patients could spend all day seeking medical services, "each health or municipal official being anxious to get them off his hands by referring them elsewhere, though without any assurance of assistance."[77]

In the autumn the Special Relief Committee focused its attention on Victoria Hospital, the only institution operating in defiance of the profession's work-action. On 30 September Moorhead wrote to the Board of Trustees of the hospital, requesting that the board meet with representatives of the SRC and the attending medical staff on 2 October. The board agreed at once and suggested a time for the meeting. No further word was heard from the doctors, however, and on the appointed day the board waited in vain for the medical delegation to appear. Two weeks later a letter arrived from Moorhead advising that the majority of the honorary staff were resigning effective 1 November.[78] Board chairman E.L. Taylor later complained that "Dr. Moorhead's letter was immediately handed to the press. . . . The apparent purpose was, if possible, to coerce our board into putting relief patients out of the hospital."[79] In his own press release Taylor announced that those consultants — four of fifteen — who had not resigned would try to provide service as usual: "We shall have had the satisfaction of knowing that we continued to carry on with the work for which our hospital was organized, and that we did not involve it in a method of political propaganda which we consider cannot be justified on any grounds."[80]

Although the executive of the SRC decided it would be strategically unwise to enter into a newspaper debate,[81] MacCharles of the provincial medical *Bulletin* offered his own succinct rejoinder: "The doctors are not prepared to be onlookers while the Victoria Hospital is used to pull the civic chestnuts out of the fire."[82] At a meeting of the Winnipeg Medical Society on 30 October the assembly passed a motion expressing approval of the Victoria consultants' resignations.[83] Two days later eleven doctors left the hospital indefinitely.

While the Victoria Hospital dispute was unfolding, two other important developments had also taken place. On 6 October a delegation representing organized medicine from across Canada met with Prime Minister R.B. Bennett in Ottawa to request federal assistance in the medical relief situation; Ernest Moorhead was the Manitoba representative. The doctors' brief stated that the profession, "adhering to its ideals and traditions, and having in mind that its first duty is the protection of the public health," was willing to accept payment at half the usual provincial tariff, and "would respectfully suggest that the other half of the cost of their professional services be assumed by the State." Bennett expressed sympathy for the doctors in their one-hour meeting but was immovable on the question of responsibility, stating, "you really have no contact with me; the matters you have presented are strictly the business of the provinces."[84] He indicated, however, that if a province initiated a medical relief scheme and requested financial help from Ottawa for this purpose, "sympathetic consideration" would be given to a federal subsidy "according to the merits of the case." The general impression of the delegation was that this meeting cleared the air for once and for all. The provinces and municipalities should be the first line of attack.[85]

The other development in October was at the Winnipeg General Hospital. Medical faculty members needed an out-patient clinic in the city's major hospital so that students could be given instruction in ambulatory care. The clinic accordingly reopened but took only patients who presented a letter of referral from a general practitioner, thereby ensuring that there was no real break in the boycott of relief patients.

November brought the Winnipeg civic elections. One of the aldermanic candidates was Dr. Ellen Douglass, a general practitioner who campaigned primarily for institution of a civic medical relief plan; her proposal was identical to that of the organized profession.[86] During and immediately after the election the *Tribune* called for action on the issue of medical services for the unemployed.[87] However, Douglass was unsuccessful in her candidacy; and, despite the *Tribune* editorials, the entire question of medical relief never really featured prominently in a campaign that saw the majority of the incumbents easily re-elected.[88]

Moorhead, writing in the *Canadian Medical Association Journal* for December, understandably stressed the support that the profession had received from the press, and added that there was very little other public commentary on the ongoing doctors' boycott. He emphasized, too, that all practitioners were "prepared to play the game, and are giving the movement loyal support": "Finally, the last move in the contest has not yet been made. More drastic action on the part of the profession is conceivable, but it must be justified before it can be taken. It is probable that the normal increase of illnesses during the Winter will force the issue."[89]

The Victoria Hospital controversy was resolved in early December when the Board of Trustees accepted all of the profession's demands. This victory notwithstanding, the civic officials had still shown no intention of instituting the desired medical relief payment plan.[90] Soon after, R.B. Bennett followed up belatedly on his October meeting with the doctors' delegation by writing to every premier. Dated 12 December, his letter reviewed the delegation's brief and sharply rejected the argument, attributed to certain provincial governments by doctors, that Ottawa had somehow prevented the provinces from providing medical services for those on relief. Bennett also reaffirmed his previous conditional offer of federal assistance to provinces that needed additional funds for medical relief.[91] Copies of this letter were sent to CMA headquarters and it was subsequently reproduced in the *Tribune* and the *Bulletin of the Manitoba Medical Association*.[92]

Backing from the two Winnipeg newspapers continued. On 21 December the *Free Press* reviewed the situation as it had developed thus far, and alluded to the success of the Ontario plan as proof that a workable scheme of medical relief could be developed. The *Free Press* made its sympathy for the profession clear: "The Doctors have had to give up their time, skill and gasoline—with sometimes the addition of medicine and the right kind of food—to those unable to pay, while as they state the grocer and the landlord have been protected."[93]

The *Tribune* added its voice on the doctors' behalf on Christmas Day 1933. Its editors pointed out that matters had been "at a standstill for six months — ever since the physicians decided they could not go on providing free medical attention." Even if the strike was not damaging to public health, psychological factors must be considered: "The feeling of fear and of helplessness with an ailment in the family is no less a hardship because it is mental or because in most cases a physician could dispel it in five minutes." Hence, "a good deal more decisive action" on the part of the city was needed in the question of medical care for those on relief.[94]

There continued, however, to be ample evidence of continued indecision over which level of government was to blame for problems not just with medical services, but all aspects of unemployment relief. At the year's end, Mayor Webb and Aldermen Rice-Jones and Flye made statements to the press claiming that the major obstacle to better funding and administration of all phases of the relief situation was the provincial government. Webb, a Conservative, insisted that the federal government would have taken over the relief problem long ago "if the provincial governments hadn't prevented it by standing on their rights." Premier Bracken retorted that these charges were "all poppycock and the mayor knows it." He pointed out that the province had asked "time and again" that Ottawa "assume a larger share of the cost of relief in order to relieve the heavy burden now being borne by the municipalities," and had been rebuffed, as had Webb himself on his several trips to seek aid for Winnipeg specifically.[95]

On 5 January 1934 a delegation of doctors met again with Premier John Bracken. The delegation reviewed the October meeting with R.B. Bennett and quoted from his letter of 12 December, stressing that Bennett had indicated a willingness to consider payments for medical relief on an individualized basis, so long as the province agreed that it required financial help.[96] However, Bracken was unimpressed by the federal offer, and his only concession was to agree that the matter would be discussed at a federal–provincial conference on 17 January.[97] Press reports do not indicate Bracken's precise reasons for rejecting the offer, but these are not difficult to surmise: Bennett was actually promising nothing except a hearing if the provinces over-extended themselves with medical relief schemes and came cap-in-hand for federal handouts. It was not an attractive deal.

Initially, however, there was no report from the premier's office on the federal–provincial conference, and negotiations continued at the municipal level. In a letter to Moorhead dated 6 January, Alderman Herbert Andrews suggested that the city be divided into ten zones with each zone served either by a physician on salary or by a panel of physicians who would take duty individually for a month and be paid a retainer. Moorhead replied, upholding two tenets: free choice of doctor by patients, which meant no panel or salary arrangement; and payment for services actually rendered, or, in other words, no departure from the fee-for-service system.[98] By this time medical relief schemes on a prorated fee-for-service basis were already in operation in several major western municipalities, not to mention across the province of Ontario. And as the doctors later explained to the press, while the costs could not be as well defined as if the city hired doctors on salary, estimates could nonetheless be made for budgetary purposes. After all, "there are many services the cost of which the city council can only estimate, e.g. the removal of snow from the streets."[99]

On 19 January 1934, with no word from Premier Bracken's office and little progress on the civic front, Moorhead spoke at a regular meeting of the Winnipeg Medical Society, calling for a special meeting in one week's time to decide on further action. One day before this special meeting Bracken advised the executive of the society that "the problem now rests in its original position, namely, one in which the immediate responsibility lies where it has always been, that is, with the municipalities affected." Bracken, having rejected the vague federal offer of assistance, now used exactly the same indefinite terminology to describe the province's view of municipal expenditures on medical relief: each municipality would "receive the sympathetic consideration of the Provincial Government" in the matter of subsidies.[100] In short, the cycle of one level of government passing responsibility to another was continuing. Faced with this fresh setback, the 150 doctors who met on Friday, 26 January in the physiology lecture theatre of the medical school unanimously agreed to an escalation in the work-action. All those present signed a pledge refusing free medical service in office, hospital, or home, unless "life is in imminent danger and for which immediate action is required." Not even ordinary labour and delivery would be considered an emergency. As Moorhead commented to the newspapers, "In the past we have been working on a very liberal definition of emergency, which has allowed anyone to get attention whether emergent or not." The new definition was to be much more stringent, and would go into effect on 15 February.[101]

First to comment of the two daily newspapers was the *Tribune*, which editorialized on Saturday, 27 January in complete support of the profession's position. The *Tribune* assessed the doctors' proposed fees as "a reasonable and moderate scale," and remarked:

> The physicians have all along done more and made greater sacrifices than the community has any right to demand of them. They have been patient and reasonable in advocacy of their interest. If the other interests involved had been as ready to serve the unemployed, this problem would have been satisfactorily settled long ago. . . . It is up to the city to act promptly, and to act on the assumption that the provincial and Dominion governments will participate in the cost.

The *Free Press* published an editorial that Monday, trying to walk a middle ground in the dispute. The medical profession was "quite within its rights in declining to give medical care, without compensation, to people on relief. The doctors cannot be blamed for their decision to discontinue such care after Feb. 14, except in cases where there is a serious danger to life." However, the city council was also "within its rights in deciding just how it will provide medical care for those on relief — through an arrangement with the medical profession as a whole, or through the employment of a number of doctors for this specific purpose." In any event, the council was duty-bound to adopt some plan: "If it declines the offer of the medical association, it must make immediate arrangements for engaging more physicians for this work."[102]

The council met that same day, Monday, 29 January. Spokesmen for five of the unemployed associations in the city appeared at the council meeting to urge "most serious consideration of the ultimatum of the doctors," reminding the councillors that the situation was already unacceptable and could not be allowed to deteriorate further. Alderman Herbert Andrews, in his capacity as chairman of the Unemployment Relief Committee, confirmed that a meeting with the doctors had been arranged.[103] Two days later, on the afternoon of Wednesday, 31 January, Aldermen Andrews and Simpson met with Moorhead, Swan, and other executive members of the doctors' Special Relief Committee. A settlement was reached on a plan exactly as proposed by the medical society, including appointment of a medical referee to audit accounts and prevent abuses of any kind. The medical referee would be a general practitioner on part-time salary with the Civic Relief Department; he would be advised in turn by a medical board consisting of the full-time civic medical officer of health and two nominees from the Winnipeg Medical Society. The names of doctors willing to participate in the plan would be posted in all relief offices in the city. After the first visit, doctors would notify the relief office of any need for follow-up visits; the medical society was to co-operate in preventing abuse through unnecessary follow-up care. This agreement was endorsed by the rest of the Civic Unemployment Relief Committee the following afternoon. Ratification from the city council was expected at the council's regular meeting on 13 February.[104]

To consolidate the profession's gains, Dr. Ross Mitchell, a former editor of the provincial medical *Bulletin*, wrote a press release for 1 February outlining the doctors' position. A zoned panel system was criticized on the grounds that it would attract only the junior members of the profession to take positions on the medical relief roster, since caring for all the relief patients in one-tenth of the city would preclude normal operation of a private practice. Given that there were more than fifty thousand relief recipients in Greater Winnipeg, this assertion was accurate. Mitchell also pointed out that the relief recipients were not an army of strangers:

> They are citizens, often citizens of many years standing, who for the most part paid their way before the wave of depression engulfed the Canadian west. . . . Does the city council seriously intend to propose to create new class distinctions, to say to those former taxpayers that they must accept a doctor of the city's choosing and desert the doctor who had been a tower of strength to them in some previous illness either of themselves or some member of their family?[105]

While the doctors waited for the city council to ratify the agreement, the Civic Unemployment Relief Committee had already sought and been refused aid from the provincial Public Works Department for the new plan.[106] The city council therefore faced the prospect of implementing an expensive program on a deficit budget. Nonetheless, there was very little choice. On 13 February the council resolved that its Unemployment Relief Committee be authorized to implement the plan immediately. Council was to reconsider the matter at the end of a three-month trial period.[107]

On 14 February civic officials advised the doctors' Special Relief Committee that an additional week would be needed for printing forms and attending to other administrative details for the new medical relief scheme. This delay was accepted and the escalation of the strike was averted in Winnipeg proper. The medical relief plan began operations on 21 February 1934, bringing with it an effective end to Canada's first medical work-action.[108] However, the suburban authorities had failed to respond to the doctors' threat, and the harder guidelines accordingly went into effect on 15 February affecting more than ten thousand recipients of relief in the outlying municipalities of Greater Winnipeg.

Discussions between the Special Relief Committee and the suburban municipal officials were quickly convened, and over the next two weeks East, West and North Kildonan, along with St. James and St. Vital, adopted the same plan as the City of Winnipeg.[109]

The resulting program, known as the Greater Winnipeg Medical Relief Plan, naturally encountered problems in its first year of operations. Predictably, the most serious difficulties were financial. By the end of the three-month trial period the City of Winnipeg alone was paying about seven thousand dollars a month for medical relief. Accordingly, on 22 May the city council resolved that its special Unemployment Relief Committee could renew the agreement with the medical profession for another three months, but was to negotiate in hopes of reducing fees for operations and hospital care.[110] Approaches were also made to both the federal and provincial governments, but no financial assistance was forthcoming. Thus, on 21 June the Civic Unemployment Relief Committee recommended to council that "the rates for Medical Relief be reduced by two-thirds after August 22nd, 1934 (the expiration of the present Agreement with the Medical Society) unless contributions are received from the Province or Dominion." The council approved this policy on 4 July.[111]

The doctors' Special Relief Committee, renamed the Committee on Sociology in the spring of 1934, was understandably determined to resist this downward pressure on the fee schedule.[112] In early August, Moorhead warned the city council that the profession would again refuse to provide routine care to relief patients if the reduction went into effect as planned. The council responded on 13 August by extending the standing agreement and fees for a month to allow further negotiations.[113] After some compromises on both sides, an agreement was reached in September to continue the plan with a 50 percent reduction in payments for major operations, and a 33 percent reduction in fees for hospital visits. The resulting savings, estimated at about $1 320 per month, were enough to permit maintenance of the plan.[114]

Given these budgetary problems, city officials were understandably worried about overuse of services. They alleged that patients were consulting doctors for trivial complaints,[115] and that doctors in turn were abusing the program by treating mild or chronic conditions that were "not disabling."[116] However, the profession's Committee on Sociology assisted in policing abuses, and despite these initial difficulties, within a year the Greater Winnipeg Medical Relief Plan was operating smoothly.[117]

After the Second World War Nova Scotia, Saskatchewan, British Columbia, and Alberta all followed Ontario's lead in establishing province-wide medical insurance schemes for recipients of social assistance.[118] In Manitoba, however, no such arrangement was made until the 1960s, and the Greater Winnipeg Medical Relief Plan accordingly endured in one form or another for almost thirty years.

Several features of this unusual incident in Canadian medical history deserve comment. First, no other Canadian medical group had ever before made such extensive use of political pressure tactics, and no other group was to withdraw services on such a scale until the Saskatchewan Medicare feud of 1962. Second, the solidarity of the profession was noteworthy, particularly since the work-action was maintained over several months in open contravention of the doctors' own ethical code. The unity of the Winnipeg doctors can obviously be attributed in part to their shared socioeconomic situation: only a small minority of practitioners who catered exclusively to the rich would not have suffered significant economic reverses as a result of the Depression, and some payment for medical relief services was better than none. Indeed, over its first seventeen months of operations, the Greater Winnipeg Medical Relief Plan paid out a total of more than $180 000 to participating practitioners — for an average of about forty dollars per doctor per month.[119]

Factors other than shared interests would also have contributed to the maintenance of a united front. The localization of the work-action to a single city meant that many of the practitioners knew each other well, and peer pressure must accordingly have been intense. Moreover, as the June 1933 editorial in the provincial medical *Bulletin* warned, economic repercussions had to be considered by any would-be strikebreakers, for they could pay a heavy price in lost referrals and refusals to renew clinic or hospital appointments.

The special circumstances of Winnipeg are underscored by the failure of the Committee on Sociology to organize a standardized medical relief plan for rural areas. In late 1934 only 65 of 113 rural municipalities in the province were making payments for medical relief, but despite several months' work, Moorhead and his colleagues were unable to recruit enough country doctors to mount a formal campaign.[120] Lower incomes and expectations,[121] the prevalence of payment in kind, less interaction with medical peers, and a closer bond to the community — all of these factors presumably reduced the rural doctors' interest in pressure-group tactics.

Also of note was the sophistication of the political elite that organized the Winnipeg work-action. The SRC recognized from the outset that it was important for the negotiating team to keep the city council from implementing a plan based around relief doctors on salary, for this would divide the profession and leave the majority without additional payments even as a small group gave up its independence for the security of a civic stipend. Moorhead and his committee worked hard to build solidarity through regular meetings that kept the rank and file informed of new developments. Internal communication was further enhanced by reports and editorials in the monthly *Bulletin of the Manitoba Medical Association*. At the same time, relations with the lay press were cultivated by release of newsworthy correspondence received or sent by the negotiating team, and formal statements for the newspapers were also submitted on occasion. In sum, the ethics of the doctors' work-action may be challenged, but their campaign was surprisingly well-organized and ultimately achieved its ends.

Not all the profession's political endeavours were equally productive. For example, in late 1934 the Committee on Sociology turned its attention to the broader issue of health insurance and, with the support of the MMA[122] and the health ministry, devised an insurance scheme to be tried on an experimental basis in the rural municipality of Woodworth. It is plain that Moorhead and other activists believed the profession must move ahead quickly to gain expertise in this new field. Dr. J.C. McMillan, the 1933–1934 MMA president, expressed these concerns succinctly in his valedictory address:

> In my judgement, the time has come, gentlemen, when we must decide if it is safe to continue our policy of watchful waiting and run the risk of having some new system forced upon us by outside agencies, or are we going to attempt to work out some new plan of our own for rendering medical services to the public.[123]

However, the council of the College of Physicians and Surgeons, which had used its revenue from licensing fees to help finance other MMA projects, refused to fund the trial insurance plan.[124] Indeed, criticism of the Committee on Sociology for its part in the project was such that Ernest Moorhead felt obliged to seek a vote of confidence from the MMA executive.[125]

Reasons for the rebuff from the College of Physicians and Surgeons are unclear. Certainly the success of the Greater Winnipeg Medical Relief Plan itself might have tempered any professional inclination to join with government in health services reorganization, since interest in payment for medical services to the unemployed was an integral part of the temporary enthusiasm for state intervention manifested by Canadian doctors during the Depression.[126] As well, editorials and articles in the *Manitoba Medical Association Review* during this period reflect a more negative view of government health insurance than in the early 1930s,[127] and the trial insurance scheme may therefore have been rejected simply because some regarded it as a step in the direction of "socialized medicine."

In fact, organized medicine's experimentation with health insurance served the opposite purpose, for, during the late 1930s, doctors in several parts of Canada started private medical services prepayment plans that eventually formed the cornerstone of the CMA's opposition to universal coverage under government auspices. Dr. Ernest Moorhead went on to play a key role in establishing both Blue Cross hospital insurance and a private medical-care plan in Manitoba. This pioneering organizer in medical politics had assured his colleagues in 1934 that their work-action was an important milestone: "Whatever happens in the future, the doctors of Greater Winnipeg have created for themselves a reputation for honesty of purpose, which will endure for a long time."[128] But by 1962, when Saskatachewan's doctors withdrew their services to protest the end of private medical insurance, Canada's first doctors' strike was largely forgotten, as were the lean times that prompted it: payment direct from government to practitioners had become an affront to professional pride, rather than an anodyne for economic woes.

Notes

1. The importance of government support and regulation in shaping the profession is documented in Ronald Hamowy, *Canadian Medicine: A Study in Restricted Entry* (Vancouver, 1984).

2. C. David Naylor, "Canadian Doctors and State Health Insurance, 1911–1918," *HSTC Bulletin* 6 (September 1982): 127-50.

3. C. David Naylor, "The Canadian Medical Profession and State Medical Care Insurance: Key Developments, 1911–1966" (D Phil. thesis, Oxford University, 1983), 82-108.

4. Ibid., 109-56.

5. Ibid., 157-202.

6. Ibid., 211-24.

7. Ibid., 314-24, 340-48.

8. There are many accounts of this dispute. One of the best is Robin F. Badgley and Samuel Wolfe, *Doctors' Strike: Medical Care and Conflict in Saskatchewan* (Toronto, 1967).

9. In general, a strike is regarded as the withdrawal of labour or services by an organized group seeking political or economic advantage. Terms such as job action or work action are sometimes used when the conflict has not yet escalated to the point that the group imposes outright work stoppages and instead resorts to various harassing tactics, including selective refusal to perform workplace tasks. The terms are applied interchangeably in this essay since the group in question withdrew all but emergency services for one segment of the population, yet otherwise worked normally.

10. *Report of the Royal Commission on Dominion–Provincial Relations: Canada 1867–1939* (Ottawa 1940), 1: 150.

11. *Report of the Committee on Economics of the Canadian Medical Association, as Presented at the Annual Meeting in Calgary, June 18–22, 1934* (n.p., 1934), 29. This pamphlet is widely available in university libraries, and can also be found as a supplement to the September 1934 issue of the *Canadian Medical Association Journal* (CMA Journal). It will be cited hereafter as CMA *Economics Committee Report, 1934*.

12. J.H. MacDermot, "The Medical Treatment of the Indigent in British Columbia," *Manitoba Medical Association Review* (*MMA Review*) 14 (January–February 1934): 13.

13. See CMA *Economics Committee Report, 1934*, 26-28.

14. For an account of the Pattullo administration's health insurance plan and its fate see Naylor, "The Canadian Medical Profession," 111-46.

15. "Provincial Association Notes," *CMA Journal* 35 (September 1936): 326-27.

16. For the profession's viewpoint we need only browse through the pages of the CMA Journal for 1932–1934. Specific provincial and civic situations are highlighted in the following articles, among many others: Lillian A. Chase, "The Economic Situation in Saskatchewan," *CMA Journal* 29 (December 1933): 661-62; G.E. Learmonth, "The Medical Relief Problem in Alberta," ibid., 30 (February 1934): 201-2; C.J. Veniot, "The Medical Economic Situation in New Brunswick," ibid., (May 1934): 551; CMA *Economics Committee Report, 1934*, 19-21.

17. "News Items: Saskatchewan," *CMA Journal* 29 (July 1933): 108.

18. "News Items: British Columbia," *CMA Journal* 29 (August 1933): 219.

19. J.H. MacDermot, "The Medical Treatment of the Indigent in British Columbia," *MMA Review* 14 (January–February 1934): 14.

20. "News Items: British Columbia," *CMA Journal* 29 (October 1933): 456.

21. "A Special Meeting of the Vancouver Medical Association," *CMA Journal* 30 (February 1934): 200-1. See also the "News Items" in the same issue, 227. The Vancouver reports make it plain that provincial health insurance was still seen at this stage as a preferable solution to short-term expedients such as municipal medical relief.

22. See, for example, *Bulletin of the Manitoba Medical Association (Bulletin of the MMA)* 101 (January 1930): 13; ibid., 105 (May 1930): 2-3; ibid., 109 (September 1930): 16-23; ibid., 111 (November 1930): 24; ibid., 113 (January 1931): 22-24; ibid., 114 (February 1931): 14-23; ibid., 118 (June 1931): 8-10, 29-31. (The name change from *Bulletin* to *Review* came in 1934.)

23. E.J. Boardman, "The Medical Services Committee," Bulletin of the MMA 111 (November 1930): 17-18. See also the minutes of the executive committee of the MMA, Bulletin of the MMA 113 (January 1931): 2-3.

24. An overview of Moorhead's career can be found in his obituary, Winnipeg *Free Press* and *Tribune*, 23 December 1957.

25. E.S. Moorhead, "A Report on the Feasibility of the Introduction of a Contributory Health Insurance Scheme to the Province of Manitoba," *Western Municipal News* 25 (October 1930): 333-36. See also *Free Press*, 8 October 1930.

26. *Journals of the Legislative Assembly of Manitoba* 65 (24 and 31 March 1931): 222-23, 248-49.

27. "Minutes of Executive Meeting,"*Bulletin of the MMA* 116 (April 1931): 2-4; "Medical Service Committee Report," ibid., 14-15.

28. Close contact was facilitated in part because Dr. F.W. Jackson, the provincial deputy minister of health, served as secretary to the House Committee and was also on stipend as the executive secretary of the Manitoba Medical Association. For some idea of other contacts see *Bulletin of the MMA* 124 (December 1931): 33-35; ibid., 12 (March 1932): 82.

29. "Medical Economics," *Bulletin of the MMA* 123 (November 1931): 12.

30. CMA *Economics Committee Report*, 1934, 30.

31. Ibid., 31. The provincial average amount of unpaid work was reduced from the Winnipeg figures because rural practitioners claimed only $1 631 in services provided without remuneration.

32. Ibid., 29

33. *Census of Canada*, 1931 (Ottawa, 1935), 5: 700.

34. Ibid.

35. An interesting series of comments on the impact of the Depression on doctors'

families can be found in Audrey Peterkin and Margaret Shaw, *Mrs. Doctor: Reminiscences of Manitoba's Doctors' Wives* (Winnipeg, 1976).

36. "Charity Begins at Home," *Bulletin of the MMA* 122 (October 1931): 29-30.
37. "Urgent Need for Action," *Bulletin of the MMA* 124 (December 1931): 13.
38. "Minutes of Special Executive Meeting of the Winnipeg Medical Society, Dec. 10th, 1931," from the minute book of the Winnipeg Medical Society for this period, a typescript volume now kept at the headquarters of the Manitoba Medical Association in Winnipeg. The minute book covers the period from November 1928 to December 1939. Cited hereafter as Minute Book.
39. *Journals of the Legislative Assembly of Manitoba* 66 (25 April 1932): 185-96.
40. H.I.P. O'Crates, "On Free Hospital Services," *Bulletin of the MMA* 12 (July 1932): 186-88.
41. Ross Mitchell, "Presidential Address—MMA," *Bulletin of the MMA* 12 (October 1932): 265-68. It should be noted that the Winnipeg Medical Society and Manitoba Medical Association had a close relationship, and many Winnipeg doctors were active in both organizations. However, membership dues for the two bodies were separate. MMA membership stood at about 310 in 1932, and fell to 260 in 1933; the membership figures of the Winnipeg Medical Society are not available. About 340 doctors lived in Greater Winnipeg alone—more than half the provincial medical community.
42. The number of persons on relief across the province rose steadily from 16 001 in November 1930 to a peak of 91 210 in March 1933, but began falling thereafter; see Alexander Brian McKillop, "Citizen and Socialist: The Ethos of Political Winnipeg, 1919–1935" (M.A. thesis, University of Manitoba, 1970), 101.
43. The editor of the *Bulletin* reprinted this speech under the title "The Worm Turns!" *Bulletin of the MMA* 12 (November 1932): 304-5.
44. Today, of course, this situation would be regarded as a significant conflict of interest.
45. Minute Book, 18 November 1932.
46. Minute Book, 16 December 1932. See also "Medical Services for People Who Are Receiving Government Relief Funds," *Bulletin of the MMA* 12 (December 1932): 327-28.
47. *Tribune*, 16 December 1932.
48. *Free Press*, 17 December 1932.
49. C.W. MacCharles, "On the Difficulties of the Medical Profession," *Bulletin of the MMA* 12 (December 1932): 328-29.
50. C.W. MacCharles, "Medical Services for People on Relief: Press Comments," *Bulletin of the MMA* 12 (December 1932): 335-36.
51. Minute Book, 20 January 1933. See also "Medical Care for Citizens Receiving Government Relief Funds," *Bulletin of the MMA* 13 (January 1933): 366-67.
52. Minute Book, 17 February 1933.
53. Ibid.
54. *Minutes of the City Council of the City of Winnipeg, Manitoba*, 13 February 1933, 110-19.
55. Minute Book, 17 February 1933.
56. *Minutes of the City Council*, 27 February 1933, 128.
57. "Medical Care for Citizens on Relief," *Bulletin of the MMA* 13 (March 1933): 399-400.
58. *Minutes of the City Council*, 13 March 1933, 160, 164-68.
59. E.S. Moorhead, "Medical Service to Indigents in Winnipeg," *CMA Journal* 29 (November 1933): 553.

60. As noted above, there were about 340 doctors living in Greater Winnipeg at this time.

61. Moorhead, "Medical Service to Indigents," 554. For further details see "Meeting of Medical Practitioners of Greater Winnipeg," *Bulletin of the MMA* 13 (April 1933): 441.

62. "The Place of an Out-Patient Department in the Medical Services for a Community," *Bulletin of the MMA* 13 (May 1933): 461-62.

63. Moorhead, "Medical Services to Indigents," 554.

64. Ibid.

65. *Tribune*, 14 June 1933; *Free Press*, 15 June 1933.

66. *Free Press*, 16 June 1933.

67. "Medical Services for Citizens on Relief," *Bulletin of the MMA* 13 (June 1933): 493-94.

68. The majority of those on relief were labourers, building tradesmen, and other tradesmen. Few clerical workers, and even fewer professionals registered on the relief rosters. See Michael R. Goeres, "Disorder, Dependency and Fiscal Responsibility: Unemployment Relief in Winnipeg, 1907–42" (M.A. thesis, University of Manitoba, 1981), 280, Appendix C.

69. E.S. Moorhead, "Relief Measures in Winnipeg," *CMA Journal* 29 (December 1933): 660.

70. *Tribune*, 4 July 1933.

71. "Recognition of Medical Services," *CMA Journal* 29 (August 1933): 192.

72. For a discussion of the national doctors' code see C. David Naylor, "The CMA's First Code of Ethics: Medical Morality or Borrowed Ideology?" *Journal of Canadian Studies* 17 (Winter 1982–1983): 20-32. This code was revised in 1936–1937 and the promise of free services to the poor was understandably one of the clauses altered; see Naylor, "The Canadian Medical Profession," 148.

73. *Free Press*, 6 July 1933.

74. Moorhead, "Relief Measures in Winnipeg," 660.

75. *Minutes of the City Council of the City of Winnipeg, Manitoba*, 17 July 1933, 431. The ideological split on city council is analysed by McKillop, "Citizen and Socialist." The Independent Labour party did not win control of the city council until 1935; prior to that, the majority of councillors were part of a loose coalition of Liberal and Conservative professionals and businessmen who called themselves the "Citizens Committee."

76. "Treatment of Venereal Disease among Indigents and Citizens on Relief," *Bulletin of the MMA* 13 (September 1933): 578-79.

77. Moorhead, "Relief Measures in Winnipeg," 661.

78. For details on the dispute see the *Tribune* 17, 18, and 23 October 1933.

79. Ibid., 23 October 1933.

80. Ibid.

81. "Medical Services for Citizens on Relief," *Bulletin of the MMA* 13 (November 1933): 607.

82. Ibid.

83. Minute Book, 30 October 1933. A second vote of thanks was passed by the executive on 17 November 1933.

84. Ironically enough, Bennett's assessment of the division of responsibilities in Confederation was proven accurate by the fate of his own government's 1935 package of social insurance measures.

85. "The Delegation to Ottawa re: Medical Care of the Unemployed," *CMA*

Journal 29 (November 1933): 554-56. See also a report under the same title in
Bulletin of the MMA 13 (November 1933): 610-13.
    86. *Tribune*, 18 and 22 November 1933.
    87. Ibid., 20 and 29 November 1933.
    88. Ibid., 28 November 1933, for a summary of the election results. The
Independent Labour party candidates fought the election on a platform of increased
welfare measures (see *Free Press*, 30 October 1933), while the Citizens Committee
argued that the civic debt was already too large to risk further deficit financing.
McKillop, "Citizen and Socialist," 126-41, provides a summary of the electoral
campaign and issues; his analysis, by omission, supports the concept that medical relief
and the doctors' strike were not central to the campaign debates. Indeed, this lack of
discussion may have led Professor McKillop to an erroneous conclusion, namely, that
"a temporary solution had been found through government–doctor negotiations and a
confrontation had been avoided" before the profession threatened to escalate the
work-action in early 1934 (149).
    89. Moorhead, "Relief Measures in Winnipeg," 661.
    90. *Tribune*, 13 December 1933.
    91. "Letter from Prime Minister to Premiers of Various Provinces," *Bulletin of the
MMA* 13 (December 1933): 629-30.
    92. *Tribune*, 6 January 1934; see also *Bulletin of the MMA* 13
(December 1933): 629-30.
    93. *Free Press*, 21 December 1933.
    94. *Tribune*, 25 December 1933.
    95. Ibid., 30 December 1933.
    96. *Free Press*, 6 January 1934.
    97. *Tribune*, 6 January 1934.
    98. The exchange of correspondence is summarized in the *Tribune*, 1 February
1934. See also Herbert Andrews' comments in the *Free Press*, 29 January 1934.
    99. *Free Press*, 29 January 1934.
    100. The letter is quoted in part by C.W. MacCharles in "Medical Services for
Relief Cases," *MMA Review* 14 (August 1934): 7-8.
    101. *Free Press*, 27 January 1934.
    102. Ibid., 29 January 1934.
    103. *Minutes of the City Council of the City of Winnipeg, Manitoba*, 29 January
1934, 71. See also the report in the *Tribune*, 30 January 1934.
    104. *Free Press*, 2 February 1934: *Tribune*, 1 February 1934.
    105. *Tribune*, 1 February 1934.
    106. *Minutes of the City Council*, 12 February 1934, 88.
    107. Ibid., 13 February 1934, 99. A complete text of the agreement with the
doctors can be found on 99-100.
    108. "Medical Services for Citizens in Receipt of Government Relief Funds: Plan
arranged with the City of Winnipeg," *MMA Review* 14 (March 1934): 14.
    109. "Medical Services for Relief Cases in Winnipeg," *MMA Review* 14 (April
1934): 13.
    110. *Minutes of the City Council*, 22 May 1934, 329.
    111. Ibid., 4 July 1934, 429.
    112. For the profession's viewpoint see "Medical Services for Relief Cases," *MMA
Review* 14 (August 1934): 7-8.
    113. *Minutes of the City Council*, 13 August 1934, 505-6.
    114. Ibid., 21 September 1934, 553-54.

115. See the letter from Alderman Herbert Andrews reproduced in *MMA Review* 15 (February 1935): 8.

116. "Medical Services for Relief Cases," *MMA Review* 14 (August 1934): 6.

117. "One Year of the Winnipeg Plan for Medical Services for Citizens on Relief," *MMA Review* 15 (June 1935): 9-14.

118. Malcolm G. Taylor, "Social Assistance Medical Care Programmes in Canada," *CMA Journal* 72 (1 January 1955): 45-50.

119. "Annual Meeting," *MMA Review* 14 (September 1934): 12. Note that the annual per capita costs after "taxing" accounts — that is, eliminating any inappropriate billings and pro-rating the payments against a $100 per month ceiling — was $2.76: *MMA Review* 15 (June 1935): 12. This was almost 60 percent higher than the original cost estimates made by the SRC, *MMA Review* 14 (January 1934): 9.

120. "Manitoba Medical Association: Minutes of Executive Meeting," *MMA Review* 14 (April 1934): 13-14; "Medical Services for Relief Cases in Rural Municipalities," ibid. (July 1934): 7; E.S. Moorhead, "Report from the Chairman of the Committee on Sociology of the Manitoba Medical Association," ibid. (December 1934): 15.

121. Rural doctors had pre-Depression average annual incomes that were $1 500 less than Winnipeg general practitioners. They also claimed about $900 less in unpaid office and hospital practice. See CMA *Economics Committee Report*, 1934, 30.

122. The plan was drawn up with the help of Dr. F.W. Jackson — the deputy health minister who was also on salary as secretary of the MMA. A delegation seeking the support of the College of Physicians and Surgeons included Moorhead and the two immediate past-presidents of the MMA, J.C. McMillan and Ross Mitchell. See "Executive Meeting," *MMA Review* 15 (January 1935): 12; "Executive Meeting," ibid. (March 1935): 10-11, 14.

123. Quoted in C. Howard Shillington, *The Road to Medicare in Canada* (Toronto, 1972), 58.

124. "Executive Committee," *MMA Review* 15 (March 1935): 15. Note that the college executive was sympathetic; in rejecting the health insurance experiment, the councillors were apparently at odds with leaders of both their own body and the MMA.

125. "Minutes of Executive Meeting," *MMA Review* 15 (April 1935): 14. Later in March, Moorhead consolidated his position by receiving formal approval from the Winnipeg Medical Society "to engage in propaganda among the lay population regarding health insurance"; Minute Book, 22 March 1935.

126. See Naylor, "The Canadian Medical Profession," 109-56, for details concerning the economic basis for the profession's interest in state health insurance.

127. See, on the editorial side, "Reformers and the Medical Profession," *MMA Review* 14 (March 1934): 16-17. See also two articles by Toronto actuary Hugh H. Wolfenden, "Insurance and Public Health," ibid. (September 1934): 13-18, and "The Problem of Health Insurance," ibid. (December 1934): 15-18. Wolfenden was known to be a strong opponent of social insurance in general. His critique is laid out in *The Real Meaning of Social Insurance* (Toronto, 1932). Wolfenden's views were quoted in a later editorial critical of state health insurance; "Sickness Insurance," *MMA Review* 15 (February 1935): 7.

128. Moorhead, "Report from the Chairman of the Committee on Sociology of the Manitoba Medical Association," 12.

THE HAMILTON BIRTH CONTROL CLINIC OF THE 1930s†

DIANNE DODD

The depression years in Canada, as in every other industrialized nation, saw great change and upheaval as people adjusted to financial insecurity, unemployment and deprivation. One consequence of the depression in Canada was the sudden emergence of a birth control movement. The dissemination of contraceptive information had, since 1892, been punishable under the criminal code. Prior to the 1930s, however, no individual or movement attempted to remove the legal prohibition on birth control.

A central figure in the Canadian birth control movement was A.R. Kaufman, a Kitchener industrialist. Kaufman established the Parents' Information Bureau[1] in Kitchener following his discovery of high fertility among the poor, unskilled workers whom he had been forced to lay off in 1929. The Bureau, which expanded rapidly in the 1930s, had as its goal in a number of Canadian cities, the distribution of low cost contraceptives to the poor and socially dependent through visiting nurses. Kaufman saw, as did a growing number of Canadians at this time, the dissemination of birth control to the poor, and sterilization of the unfit (loosely defined as the feebleminded, insane and diseased) as the solution to poverty, social unrest and general racial decline.[2] He lobbied governments to legislate in favour of birth control and sterilization, organized birth control groups and provoked a trial in 1936–37 which helped clarify the legal position of birth control work.[3] The Eugenics Society of Canada also emerged in the 1930s as the political voice of those who

† *Ontario History* 75, no. 1 (March 1983): 71–86. The author would like to thank Dr. Ruth Pierson of O.I.S.E. for her assistance and encouragement as well as Mrs. Thelma Will of Hamilton and the staff of The Hamilton Planned Parenthood Association.

hoped to cure all manner of social problems through restricting the reproduction of the feebleminded and genetically inferior.[4]

Attitudes towards birth control may have varied considerably from one community to the next. In Brantford, for instance, where the President of the Eugenics Society of Canada, Dr. William Hutton, was medical officer of health, birth control dissemination was carried out with official endorsement.[5] In Calgary, Toronto, Niagara Falls, York County and Essex County, however, efforts to place birth control dissemination in the hands of municipal authorities met with failure probably for a combination of political and financial reasons.[6] Most municipalities found it politically expedient to carry on the work quietly, thus minimizing opposition. Kaufman's nurses, in most communities, and birth control clinic workers in Hamilton, did the dirty work. These women received little thanks for their path-breaking efforts, being paid very little and at times being subjected to harassment and violence.[7]

The trial of one of Kaufman's nurses, who was charged in 1936 with disseminating contraceptive information in Eastview (now Vanier), Ontario, became the movement's platform for arguing the social, economic and political benefits of birth control.[8] At the Eastview Trial, birth control was presented as a technological solution to social, economic and political problems ranging from infant and maternal mortality to poverty, juvenile delinquency and racial tension, and thus legally pronounced to be for "the public good."[9]

The focus of this paper is on a women's organization involved in the birth control movement in Hamilton. This organization differed from the Parents' Information Bureau both in its motivation and in its approach to birth control. The literature of the Hamilton group indicates that the arguments used to justify birth control were similar to the economic arguments employed by the eugenicists and neo-Malthusians, although the methods of birth control promoted and the approach to distribution adopted were quite different. The eugenicists emphasized sterilization while the Hamilton women avoided it altogether. Kaufman's Parents' Information Bureau used "simple" methods of contraception (contraceptive jelly with a nozzle applicator and condoms[10]) which could easily and inexpensively be distributed through the mail without reliance on medical examinations. Kaufman preferred this method as he sought to reach large numbers of the poor. The women's organizations preferred to have a clinic with a doctor in attendance and generally prescribed the diaphragm method which is considerably more effective than the simpler methods. In contrast, Kaufman opposed the clinical method as he believed it reached too few women to warrant the expense and that the very poor (especially those on relief) would not attend the clinics. In short, the women's organization stressed quality as opposed to quantity and did not share the ambitious plans of eugenicists who hoped to reconstruct society through the manipulation of reproductive technology. Their clinic and organization served the needs of women in their community, and not the political ends of social reformers. Although they sometimes used economic and eugenic arguments in promoting birth control, these women very strongly believed that every married woman had a fundamental right to practise birth control. In this sense they can be termed proto-feminist, even though they did not describe themselves in this way.

The driving force behind the Hamilton clinic was Mary Elizabeth Hawkins, a prominent and wealthy Hamilton widow. Hawkins had worked with many charitable groups and from this experience had concluded that some community service, which could help women avoid unwanted children, was badly needed. An American-born Vassar graduate, Hawkins was also influenced by Margaret Sanger, a summer neighbour in Nantucket, Massachusetts, with whom she had discussed birth control.[11] She became convinced that the clinical method, employing fully certified medical practitioners to fit diaphragms and spot any gynaecological problems, was the best approach to birth control. Hawkins was, at least at the beginning, "dead against" Kaufman's visiting nurses.[12] She felt that the medical profession must be involved in the dissemination of information about birth control in order to "do the greatest good and least harm."[13] She also hoped to minimize opposition to birth control within the medical profession and the general public. She was careful to limit clinic patients to married women with at least two children and stated emphatically her opposition to abortion[14] in an effort to dissociate that practice from the work of the clinic.

Despite a few setbacks, a birth control clinic was opened in Hamilton in 1932. Dr. Elizabeth Bagshaw, one of the few female physicians in Hamilton, was persuaded to work as the clinic's medical director after the early resignation of Dr. Rowena Hume of Toronto, who had found the commuting distance too great.[15] Dr. Bagshaw was to remain with the clinic for more than thirty years, retiring at age eighty-four.[16] She attended the Sanger Clinic in New York for instruction in birth control techniques as medical doctors received no training in contraception.[17] Dr. Bagshaw received only a small honorarium for the two to four hours she donated to the clinic each week. Gertrude Burgar, a nurse and social worker who was also active in social service work in Hamilton, donated her Friday afternoons to the clinic, interviewing women and keeping records. She referred many patients from the TB sanitorium as well, patients who were well enough to go home on weekends, but who could not handle an unwanted pregnancy. This was certainly a more humane alternative than the eugenicists' suggestion that TB victims be sterilized.

Burgar and Hawkins investigated the legal position of birth control and found that dissemination of birth control information was a crime, punishable under the criminal code, but took comfort in a clause which provided that, where the "public good" was served, no conviction was possible. In 1932, they visited Crown Attorney George Ballard at the Wentworth County Court House in Hamilton, who told the women to continue their work as he was solidly behind the aims of the society.[18] Not yet satisfied, Mrs. Hawkins wrote her M.P., C.W. Bell, suggesting an amendment to the criminal code. He took this up with the Minister of Justice, Hugh Guthrie, receiving the polite but firm reply that legislation on this very important but controversial subject was not forthcoming. This lobbying activity got her nowhere and her lawyer informed her that such an amendment was unfeasible due to the expected opposition from the Province of Quebec.[19]

The clinic had to settle for working under the blind eye of the law, but, at least in Hamilton, that eye was sympathetic. It appears that many communities in the 1930s showed similar tolerance. Remembering that municipalities were responsible for doling out relief to the unemployed, one should not find it surprising that they showed an interest in birth control in the 1930s. Many local governments, some under pressure from eugenicists, considered resolutions in favour of birth control and sterilization — in fact it is at the local level that the birth control movement was most active.[20]

In many cases, although the attitude toward birth control was one of indifference, or even hostility, on the part of social agencies and relief authorities, the social workers themselves actually supported the cause. In the Hamilton case, public health nurses were forbidden to discuss birth control with clients.[21] Yet, by 1937 this same municipality passed on to the birth control clinic's nurse, Thelma Will, the names of people whom they felt needed birth control, so that she could bring them that information. It is not clear whether the authorities themselves supported birth control, yet were not prepared to admit as much in public or whether they genuinely opposed it, but were powerless to stop their workers from referring people to birth control workers.

Since birth control was considered opprobrious in Canada, the clinic had to work quietly and unobtrusively. Most of the clinic's advertising was [by] word-of-mouth.[22] In fact, it worked so quietly that Thelma Will, the registered nurse who worked for the clinic from 1937 to 1970, had not even heard of it until she was approached to work there. The clinic had been in operation for five years by that time.

Clinic workers received a small fee, "enough to keep us there," as Will, whose starting salary was fifty cents per day, described it.[23] Supplies of diaphragms, jelly, and condoms were provided by Kitchener capitalist A.R. Kaufman at cost, and workers claimed that no woman was ever turned away because she could not pay for supplies.

Most of the women's groups in the city supported the clinic in varying degrees. The clinic was financed by membership fees, an annual tea which was attended by many prominent Hamilton women, and the

donations of its founder Mrs. Hawkins.[24] The clinic had support from
a number of community services including the Samaritan Club, the Local
Council of Women, many of the Protestant churches, and some members
of the medical profession.[25] More vital, perhaps, in keeping the clinic
together was the dedication of women like Dr. Bagshaw, the clinic's
medical director, Mrs. Hawkins who "never missed a clinic" from its
founding to her death,[26] and Thelma Will, the nurse who began visiting
homes in 1937 and retired as the clinic's director in 1970. Although
Will singled out the continuity of Dr. Bagshaw's work as an important
factor in the clinic's longevity,[27] there were clearly others, herself
included, who made important contributions.

Several pamphlets, issued by the Hamilton clinic during the depression
years, highlight the social welfare approach of the clinic toward birth
control. To these committed women, birth control was a means of
reducing the evil of abortion and of ensuring healthier mothers and
children. One pamphlet states, for example, that "birth control is based
on love of children, more and more children who are well cared for, and
planned for, fewer and fewer the offspring of exhausted mothers, overburdened fathers and overcrowded homes."[28] Elsewhere, the view was
expressed that "the scourge of abortion is nothing more than the necessary consequence of a lack of birth control."[29] Hawkins stated that she
believed no child should be brought into the world who "hasn't a
reasonable hope of a healthy body, a sound mind, decent surroundings
and a fair chance."[30] Her stated aim was to "control the health and well-
being of women, children and families in her community."[31]

There was a tendency also to select the worst cases to be written up
in the pamphlets and reports. For example:

> Hamilton clinic case. Mrs. S., 9 living children, 2 dead children (2
> sets of twins in 12 months). Married 13 years. On city relief.

> Mrs. N., (Tubercular) 2 years in Sanitorium, 7 living children, 3
> dead children, 6 abortions, 16 pregnancies in 26 years married life.
> On city relief.[32]

These extreme and desperate cases probably appealed to middle-class
prejudices, as the false perception of excessively high fertility among the
poor was prevalent in the 1930s.

Mary Elizabeth Hawkins was not adverse to pointing out the economic costs involved in uncontrolled fertility, especially when appealing
for funds. Unwanted babies not only added to strain in homes, but
became a drain on the city's welfare and relief funds, she claimed, adding that many of the clinic's patients were on relief.[33] The clinic, she
argued, was not only alleviating the suffering of women and children,
and of families, but also reducing the load of the overburdened taxpayer.

Arguments of this sort were important in swaying public opinion in favour of birth control.

These "social good" arguments, however, were given a lower priority in the clinic's literature than arguments which placed a high value on the health and welfare of women and children. In contrast to the eugenicists' condescension and contempt for the poor, Hawkins repeatedly called for sympathy and understanding in dealing with the destitute, who were demoralized and dispirited as it was by relief and unemployment. She referred to poor women as heroines facing adverse conditions with courage and strength.[34] Thelma Will tells us that, despite her wealth, Hawkins identified with the women the clinic helped[35] and she took an active role in the clinic's day-to-day work. At the Eastview birth control trial, Hawkins protested against the Catholic Church's view that a woman's life must be sacrificed before that of her child. She also spoke to women's groups in Hamilton about birth control and was probably responsible for the Sanger visit to Hamilton to 1933.[36] Her distaste for abortion was clearly motivated by a sympathy with the risks it presented for women and a belief that birth control offered a saner, safer alternative.

Dr. Bagshaw was not a woman to worry much over moral dilemmas and does not appear to have developed any distinct political or social views on birth control. She was, however, very conscious of herself as a woman in a male-dominated profession and she showed considerable courage in supporting the clinic against the snubs of her male colleagues.[37] She found the lofty, theoretical condemnations of Hamilton's Roman Catholic Bishop J.T. McNally mildly amusing and liked to express the view that they served to advertise the clinic.[38]

Thelma Will was another woman of conviction and courage, who, during her thirty-three years at the clinic, also braved the sneers of public opinion. Although she, like Bagshaw, would not become entangled in moral debates about birth control, she believed it should be available to any married woman who wanted it and was not afraid publicly to endorse a practice which she and others of her class practised privately.[39] All of these women made, by their actions, definite statements opposing current social and sexual hypocrisy.

The clinic's methods of birth control dissemination and its indifference to eugenic sterilization, say much about its respect for women. At a time when many middle-class birth control activists were pushing the less effective methods (such as jelly or foam used alone) because they believed working class women were too ignorant to use a diaphragm properly,[40] the Hamilton clinic demonstrated that, with adequate instruction, most women could use the more effective means of birth control. It also refused to sacrifice the quality of service it offered to women for the sake of reaching greater numbers.

There was, of course, much opposition to the Hamilton clinic. Hawkins in one of her addresses condemned what she termed, "the socialist insistence that the poor should be able to have as many children as they wished, whatever the cost."[41] Hawkins clearly distorted the left's position on birth control, which was ambivalent at best. The left, quite understandably, suspected that birth control was being used as a means of avoiding economic reform and of blaming poverty on its victims.[42]

Probably the most significant opposition to the clinic came from the Roman Catholic church. Bishop McNally regularly and vehemently denounced the clinic from his pulpit.[43] When Margaret Sanger spoke on birth control in Hamilton in 1933, saying, among other things, that birth control would allow women more leisure for higher culture, the Bishop retorted that such "higher culture" would probably consist of sleeping until noon, playing golf in the afternoon, and bridge at night.[44] He also ridiculed women's emancipation, saying that, "although the woman stayed at home, and sewed, cooked or mended, she was monarch of all she surveyed, especially in a house filled with children."[45] He thought women already enjoyed greater freedom than men and denounced the clinic women as harlots, calling their philosophy degrading, blasphemous, depraved and atheistic.[46]

It would be unfair to present the Catholic opposition in a totally negative way. The Bishop's comments show that he believed birth control to be immoral and excessively materialist and it can hardly be denied that birth control gained widespread acceptance only with the rise in consumerism of the twentieth century. As the nation's advertisers pushed their new messages urging people to consume rather than to conserve, to indulge rather than restrain, sexual enjoyment without the sobering restraint of parenthood became more acceptable. The Bishop, however, felt that people who wanted fewer children should abstain from sexual relations, altogether failing to recognize the difficulty most women faced in marriage of imposing abstinence on husbands. Birth control allowed people to have sexual pleasure without facing its necessary consequence, procreation, and to the Bishop that was irresponsible, immoral, unnatural and contrary to God's will.[47]

The Bishop argued that Christian principles dictated society should care for its weaker members, rather than discard them in order to breed a race of supermen,[48] as the eugenicists would have it. He suggested that society should redistribute its wealth so that the poor could raise their children in peace and that feeblemindedness and other conditions which eugenicists continually pronounced upon were not inherited, but actually the product of "the exaggerated artificality and worry of modern life."[49]

The Catholic Women's League of Hamilton withdrew its membership from the Local Council of Women in 1933 in protest against a resolution the Council passed approving sterilization of the unfit.[50] The Hamilton Birth Control Society may have been the initiator of the resolution, although similar statements of support for birth control and sterilization were being made by women's groups all over the country in the 1930s.[51]

Catholic women were given an opportunity to abstain from the resolution while remaining in the Council—they refused. The Local Council of Women was not willing to expel the Hamilton Birth Control Society in order to accommodate the Catholic Women's League.[52]

The Catholic Women's League's opposition to birth control and its consequent withdrawal from the Local Council of Women was not forced upon them by the Bishop. They quite genuinely opposed birth control, seeing it as an assault on the dignity of motherhood and the vital institution of the family.[53] Catholic women felt that their special role as wives and mothers would be threatened by the sexual freedom which birth control offered.

In a letter to the editor of the *Toronto Daily Star*, one Catholic woman responded to Hawkins' plea that Catholic women be supplied with birth control as compensation for their church's doctrine of sacrificing women's lives to procreation. She replied that Catholic women knew what their church expected of them and gladly sacrificed their lives for the privilege of creating new life:

> I know . . . that the purpose of marriage is fulfilled in giving birth. I know that the God who gave me life, may see fit to see that life as the price of another life. I also know that God has a definite plan, has had from eternity, for each soul that is conceived and I know that just as surely as I interfere with the life of an unborn child I am as miserably guilty of murder, in the eyes of the God who ordained the life of that child, as I should be if I deliberately shot or poisoned a fellow man.[54]

This woman opposed efforts to bring motherhood onto the same plane as other forms of labour, preferring to see it as a divine mission.

It seems that Catholic women who were opposed to birth control and Protestant women who were birth control activists shared a desire to elevate the status of women through motherhood. Catholic women accepted the burdens of motherhood, opting for abstinence as a means of birth control in those few instances where it might be justified, while birth control activists embraced artificial means of fertility control. Catholic and Protestant women differed in their conceptions of sexuality: Protestants accepted the modern view of sexuality as a healthy form of expression for both men and women, while Catholics still viewed sexuality solely in terms of procreation. Both groups of women shared a belief in the family and a respect for women as mothers. They also shared a fear that birth control could destroy or weaken the family. As a consequence, birth control workers sought to limit the availability of birth control technology only to married women, whereas the Catholic Church opposed birth control altogether.

What Catholic women practised in private is not known, although birth controllers liked to emphasize that their clients included many Catholic women.[55] Of course Catholics were not alone in privately practising a measure which neither they, nor their organizations, could openly endorse. As was shown with the relief authorities, it is clear that Protestants were also capable of a two-faced approach to birth control.

There was at least one case of a Catholic woman in Hamilton who came to the clinic, but never returned due to the influence of her priest, at least as reported by the clinic worker.[56] Not all Catholic women approached by birth control workers rejected their Church's teachings. But as we will soon see, many women regardless of religious persuasion paid less attention to religious and moral pronouncements on birth control than to practical considerations.

Information about the women who availed themselves of the clinic is very difficult to obtain because the clinic's records were destroyed. Many birth control workers expected desperate women to come in droves to hear the birth control message, yet in Hamilton that was not the case, even though the clinic was usually busy. Thelma Will described the usual response to her door-to-door campaign as polite indifference.[57] Women would tell her whatever they thought she wanted to hear in order to get rid of her, but they never came to the clinic.[58] In short, they treated her like any salesperson who might show up at their door. In fact the fear of being associated with birth control was so strong that clinic patients generally preferred to go all the way downtown to pick up supplies, rather than go to the convenient "jelly stations" which were set up in board members' homes to be closer to patients.[59] But indifference may have been as big a factor as fear. No doubt there was also considerable suspicion regarding a middle-class woman, a nurse, who mysteriously appeared at the door and refused to reveal where she had gotten your name. In point of fact, a large part of her list came from the relief authorities, conditional upon that source not being disclosed.

Yet Thelma Will's work, even though she says they didn't get as many women as they should have, was successful. An increase in patients did result and the clinic, after seven years of work, could boast that patients had been helped, and that many patients had made return visits and referred friends and relatives.[60] Moreover, the clinic had to expand its hours of operation from one to two days a week.

Those women who did come were very appreciative of the service, Will says, although little was learned about each of them, except her medical history.[61] These records unfortunately no longer exist and no studies were done at the clinic so that we know neither the effectiveness rates nor the sociology of the patients. Will described her work as taking the medical histories of the women and advising them of the methods of birth control available. The women were then examined by Dr. Bagshaw and an appropriate method was prescribed. Usually the women were fitted for a diaphragm but other methods were also used.[62]

The letter of one woman which remains in the files is a touching testament. In it she submits one dollar, to help pay for contraceptive supplies which she had received free because her husband was unemployed. Now, after two years of unemployment, he was working again, and she had struggled to scrape together that dollar. She said she had thought of not sending the money, but decided that if too many people did that, well, there'd be no more clinic; so she sent the money. She did not know how she would have managed with a husband out of work and two children to look after, if it were not for the clinic.[63] Clearly the clinic was providing a valuable service for those women who wanted it badly enough to venture out.

When Thelma Will was asked what birth control methods the women whose homes she visited were using, she mentioned douching and withdrawal. Abortion was not mentioned by the women, as most women were reluctant to admit to it, even though there is evidence that it was a widespread practice. Hawkins complained of receiving requests for abortions.[64] Will says of the two popular methods, douching and withdrawal, "they're a good way to get pregnant,"[65] reiterating the birth controllers' denunciation of traditional methods which, though not as effective as the diaphragm, are actually more effective than they have been generally credited.[66] Middle-class women knew about condoms and vaginal suppositories, both available in the drug stores,[67] but these were too expensive for working-class women, especially during the depression. How many women were able to obtain a pessary (diaphragm) from their doctors is unknown. Very few of the doctors in Hamilton would openly endorse birth control—so much so that the clinic had trouble finding a replacement when Dr. Bagshaw went on holidays.[68] There may have been many more who were willing privately to fit diaphragms, although the lack of medical training in contraception must have been a handicap. The clinic itself corrected this omission by providing instruction to a number of doctors over the years. Probably the use of condoms, suppositories, sponges and douches were more common among the middle-class women than the diaphragm. Thelma Will herself obtained a diaphragm only after working at the clinic. Until that time she and her husband had used condoms, apparently a common practice.[69] The view expressed by many birth controllers, that middle-class women could easily get birth control from their doctors, while the poor were denied such access, may have been an exaggeration. It seems that middle-class couples got their birth control from the corner drug store.

Methods which the clinic relied upon were the diaphragm and jelly primarily, jelly and condoms, or, if either of these two methods were unsuitable for one reason or another, a tampon or sponge soaked in a contraceptive substance such as vinegar could be used. Women were given a choice, although it seems that most women preferred the diaphragm.[70] It is clear that the Hamilton group was not introducing the practice but rather new methods of birth control. They were also offering older methods (condoms and tampon) at a considerable saving.

The reaction of husbands to the clinic seems generally to have been indifference, although occasionally hostility emerged. Some men seem to have feared that birth control provided a means for a wife's infidelity, but generally it appears that men saw birth control as a woman's problem and let their wives deal with it in their own way.[71] When Thelma Will was asked if the husbands during the depression were concerned about restricting family size from an economic or financial viewpoint, she replied that men seemed relatively indifferent even to this consideration. "Well, that's mankind," she said.[72] In her opinion it was the women who worried about feeding and clothing all the children, not the men.

When attempting to get at the women's view of the moral controversy over birth control which raged in the press and the pulpits of Hamilton, one discovers that women generally did not think about it, nor did they seem to care.[73] They were attempting to survive as best they could, to care for themselves and their children, and the moralizing of social reformers and bishops meant nothing to them.

If there is any feminist motivation in the women birth controllers of Hamilton, it is a feminism which accepts women's place in the home as mothers. While none of these women demanded birth control in the name of women's emancipation from the family, all believed that simple justice dictated that women should control their fertility. Neither husbands nor the church had any right to interfere.

The idea of birth as a civil right, giving women the freedom to accept or reject motherhood, was quite foreign to this whole movement, including its women workers. Birth control would help women to be better, healthier mothers; it might alleviate poverty, decrease maternal and infant mortality, increase family stability, eliminate abortion, and as such women were entitled to it. In light of the distinction which is sometimes made between maternal feminism and equal rights feminism,[74] it is interesting to find that Mary Elizabeth Hawkins and most of her female associates did not find their belief in women's right to fertility control incompatible with their acceptance of women's maternal function in the home. Because these women reformers did not see women outside of the traditional family, they could defend the right of women to birth control and, at the same time, argue many of the social benefits of birth control which were attractive to public opinion. The alliance of feminism and neo-Malthusian reform is embodied in their literature.

While there was no radical critique of the patriarchal family, there was certainly a concerted push to elevate the status and conditions of motherhood. Birth control technology could give women rational control over the quantity and quality of their labour in the home, just as other technological advances had improved the workplaces where their husbands laboured.

From this look at the Hamilton Birth Control Clinic, it is obvious that the pattern for women birth controllers differed from the work of men such as Alvin R. Kaufman. The women were more active in the day-to-day work of birth control dissemination and stressed the effective methods in their concern for alleviating the suffering of individual women. Women also tried to instruct other women in birth control use rather than advocating sterilization. They worked quietly, on a small scale, and established community ties, staying clear of the political agitation of segments of the birth control movement.

In contrast, the men who were active in birth control work (as in the case of A.R. Kaufman) tended to stress sterilization of the unfit and to promote use of contraceptive techniques which, although lower in effectiveness, allowed for easy, inexpensive and widespread distribution. Male birth control advocates also tended to be much more politically active. The difference in approach probably stems from their different motivations. Women advocated birth control apparently out of an inchoate feminist desire to give women reproductive control, while men, it would appear, had larger, political ambitions for contraceptive technology.

Notes

1. A.R. Kaufman, "The Parents' Information Bureau," *The Journal of Contraception* (March 1938): 54-55.

2. Letter to H.L. Mencken for A.R. Kaufman, 10 August 1937, Gamble Papers, Francis A. Countway Library of Medicine, Boston, Massachusetts.

3. Gerald Stortz and Murray Eaton, "Pro Bono Publico: The 1936 Eastview Birth Control Trial" (unpublished paper, Wilfrid Laurier University, 1982). Also, Bill Stephenson, "The Great Birth Control Trial," *Macleans* (23 November 1957), and Dianne Dodd, "The Birth Control Movement on Trial, 1936–1937," *Histoire sociale/ Social History* (November 1983).

4. "The Aims and Objects of the Eugenic Society of Canada," File 43, Palmer Papers, University of Waterloo Library, Waterloo, Ontario.

5. Toronto *Mail and Empire*, 12 December 1932.

6. *Calgary Herald*, 1 December 1938; Toronto *Mail and Empire*, 12 December 1932; *Essex County Material Health League* (Pamphlet published by Essex County Maternal Health League, circa 1937).

7. Letter from Mary Bishop to the author, 10 December 1981.

8. Stortz and Eaton, "Pro Bono Publico," 2.

9. Dodd, "The Birth Control Movement on Trial."

10. Although Kaufman did distribute condoms, he based all of his effectiveness studies on the use of jelly alone, because he believed working class men were irresponsible and selfish in sexual matters: Letter to Clarence Gamble from A.R. Kaufman, 21 July 1937, Gamble Papers, Boston.

11. "Survives Despite Opposition," *Hamilton Spectator*, 1 March 1962, Uncatalogued Papers, Hamilton Planned Parenthood, Hamilton, Ontario. (This is an

uncatalogued collection of clippings, correspondence and miscellaneous material from the Hamilton Birth Control Clinic, approximately 1930–1960, hereafter referred to as the Hamilton Papers).

12. Letter to Mary Hawkins from Janet B. Whitenack, American Birth Control League, New York, 12 November 1936, File 33, Box 1, Palmer Papers, University of Waterloo Library, Waterloo, Ontario.

13. "President's Address," 15 January 1934, Hamilton Papers.

14. "Interim Report, Hamilton Birth Control Society, 1931," Hamilton Papers.

15. Letter to Mary Elizabeth Hawkins from Dr. Hume, 30 March 1932, Hamilton Papers.

16. Thomas Melville Bailey, *For the Public Good: A History of the Hamilton Birth Control Society* (Hamilton: Hamilton Planned Parenthood, 1974), 10-12. Dr. Bagshaw died in 1982 at the age of 100.

17. Ibid., 10.

18. Ibid., 14.

19. Ibid.

20. "Suggested Resolutions to be Passed or Rejected by Municipal Council," Hamilton Papers. In Orillia, such a resolution was passed concerning the sterilization of the "unfit" to be released from the Orillia school for the Mentally Retarded, Hamilton Papers.

21. Thelma Will, interview with the author, Hamilton, 22 January 1982.

22. Bailey, *For the Public Good*, 15, 16.

23. Thelma Will, interview with the author, Hamilton, 22 January 1982.

24. Bailey, *For the Public Good*, 19.

25. Ibid., 7.

26. Thelma Will, interview with the author, Hamilton, 22 January 1982.

27. Ibid.

28. "An Outline of the Work and Aims of the Birth Control Society of Hamilton, Indicating the Social, Economic, Political and Religious Aspects of the Subject" (Hamilton: Hamilton Birth Control Society, n.d.), Hamilton Papers.

29. Ibid., 11.

30. Bailey, *For the Public Good*, 21.

31. "Declares Aim is to Control Family Health," *Hamilton Spectator*, n.d., Newspaper Clippings, Hamilton Papers.

32. "An Outline of the Work and Aims of the Hamilton Birth Control Society," Hamilton Papers, 4-5.

33. Bailey, *For the Public Good*, 22.

34. Ibid., 4.

35. Thelma Will, interview with the author, Hamilton, 22 January 1982.

36. Bailey, *For the Public Good*, 22-23. Also, Toronto *Mail and Empire*, 5 August 1936; *Hamilton Spectator*, 6 April 1933; *Hamilton Herald*, 7 June 1933; and "Minute Book, Hamilton Birth Control Society, 1933," Hamilton Papers.

37. National Film Board, *Doctor Woman: The Life and Times of Dr. Elizabeth Bagshaw*, 1978.

38. Ibid.

39. Thelma Will, interview with the author, Hamilton, 22 January 1982.

40. James Reed, *From Private Vice to Public Virtue* (New York: Basic Books, 1977), 248-308.

41. *Hamilton Spectator*, circa 1934, Newspaper Clippings, Hamilton Papers.

42. For a treatment of views from the left on birth control in Canada, see Angus

McLaren, "What Has This to do With Working Class Women?: Birth Control and the Canadian Left, 1900–1939," *Histoire sociale/Social History* 14 (November 1981).

43. Bailey, *For The Public Good*, 18-19.

44. "Launches Attack on Birth Control," *Hamilton Spectator*, 11 October 1933, Newspaper Clippings, Hamilton Papers.

45. Ibid.

46. Bailey, *For the Public Good*, 35.

47. *Hamilton Spectator*, 11 October 1933, Newspaper Clippings, Hamilton Papers.

48. Ibid.

49. Ibid.

50. *Hamilton Spectator*, 5 March 1934, Newspaper Clippings, Hamilton Papers.

51. Bailey, *For the Public Good*, 7-8; Helen MacMurchy, *Birth Control? Sterilization? A Book For Family Welfare and Safety* (Toronto: Macmillan, 1934).

52. *Hamilton Herald*, 5 March 1934, Newspaper Clippings, Hamilton Papers.

53. The following statement came from the Catholic Women's League of Canada: "Whereas the Catholic Women's League of Canada, believing in the divine institution of marriage and its sacramental dignity, views with alarm the rise of false and perverse morality in the advocacy of birth control, and believes that the spiritual welfare of the state as well as the temporal happiness of its citizens, cannot remain safe and sound when the unit of society—the family—is threatened with destruction, by the actions of certain organizations who ask governments to establish clinics and facilities for birth control" (*Hamilton Herald*, 5 March 1934, Newspaper Clippings, Hamilton Papers).

54. "The Responsibility of Motherhood," *Toronto Daily Star*, 14 November 1936.

55. Bailey, *For the Public Good*, 18.

56. Thelma Will, interview with the author, Hamilton, 22 January 1982.

57. Ibid.

58. Ibid.

59. Ibid.

60. Bailey, *For the Public Good*, 25.

61. Thelma Will, interview with the author, Hamilton, 22 January 1982.

62. Ibid.

63. Letter to Hamilton clinic from Mrs. R.W. Dyet, R.R. 1, Selkirk, Hamilton Papers.

64. "Interim Report, Hamilton Birth Control Society, 1931," Hamilton Papers.

65. Thelma Will, interview with the author, Hamilton, 22 January 1982.

66. Reed, *From Private Vice to Public Virtue*, 11. For instance the actual-use effectiveness of withdrawal is 75-80 percent: *Our Bodies, Ourselves* (New York: Boston Women's Health Collective Inc., 1971), 185. (Quoted from *Contraceptive Technology, 1973–1974*).

67. Thelma Will, interview with the author, Hamilton, 22 January 1982.

68. Ibid.

69. Ibid.

70. Ibid.

71. Ibid.

72. Ibid.

73. Ibid.

74. Wayne Roberts, "Rocking the Cradle for the World: the New Woman and Maternal Feminism, Toronto, 1877–1914," in *A Not Unreasonable Claim*, ed. Linda Kealey (Toronto: The Women's Press, 1979), 15-45.

MONTREAL'S MUNICIPAL GOVERNMENT AND THE CRISIS OF THE 1930s†

TERRY COPP

The spring of 1940 is not likely to be remembered for the financial crisis that overcame the government in the city of Montreal. The invasion of France and the fall of the Chamberlain government occurred less than a week before the city was forced to default on the first of two bond issues which came due in May and June 1940. As the French army collapsed under the shock of the German offensive, Montreal passed under the control of the Quebec government's Municipal Commission. Camillien Houde and his City Council were relegated to an empty advisory role. The flamboyant mayor still had some months of freedom left before his internment for opposition to national registration, but his twelve-year struggle to dominate and shape the politics of his native city was over. Houde would return to the mayor's office with renewed popularity, but his role would henceforth be that of a figurehead, a rotund, comical "Mr. Montreal" symbolizing the élan of the city, but also symbolizing the end of the populist politics which Houde had stood for.

The humiliation of Camillien Houde and the takeover of his city were no doubt partly owing to political considerations. The volatile Houde had made enemies in all sectors of the highly partisan world of Quebec politics. But the new, deliberately undemocratic, form of government imposed on Montreal was a clear indication that Houde was correct when he charged that the Depression had ruined Montreal, and that now those who had tried to help the unemployed were to be replaced, "par les gens du Board of Trade, qui n'ont jamais aidé, qui n'ont offert que des critiques."[1]

† Alan J. Artibise and Gilbert Stelter, eds., *The Usable Urban Past*, Carleton Library Series, no. 119 (Macmillan for the Carleton Library, 1979), 112–29.

In a strong speech to the Quebec legislature, Houde reviewed his efforts to stave off bankruptcy. He defended the quality of municipal administration, pointed to the new tax measures he had introduced, recalled the representations he had made to senior levels of government, and told his silent audience: "If we had followed the advice of the bankers and economists, we would have had to leave the unemployed to die of starvation."[2]

Houde's speech won him renewed respect but no concessions. City Council would henceforth consist of ninety-nine members, one-third elected by property owners (only one in ten Montrealers owned their own home), one-third by all electors, with a final one-third appointed by various organizations. Council would appoint an executive committee, but the popularly elected mayor would not be eligible to sit on this all-powerful body.[3] The city was to be made safe for the bond holders.

The story behind the events of May 1940 is bound up in both the history of the city and in the particular circumstances of the Great Depression. The collapse of municipal credit, the dramatic career of Camillien Houde, and the "corporatist" city charter of 1940 are incident which serve as illustrations of structural problems in the evolution of Canada's metropolis, problems which reached crisis proportions during the 1930s. It would be foolish to suggest that all of these problems were unique to Montreal. Even a casual reading of the briefs presented to the Royal Commission on Dominion–Provincial Relations by various Canadian municipalities is enough to demonstrate that Montreal's agonizing struggle to maintain a minimal relief system during the 1930s was but a variation of the problems of other Canadian cities. A number of western cities had been forced to default well before Montreal was pushed to the wall. A detailed account of Montreal's story gives a valuable specificity and detail to an important problem in Canadian urban history and Quebec political history.

Montreal, similar to all Canadian cities, was a creature of its provincial government. The city's charter granted the popularly elected municipal council the power to raise revenue from a property tax, a business establishments tax, municipal licences, and from an occupant's levy known locally as a "water tax." The levels of such taxation were controlled by the provincial legislature and were subject to occasional readjustment when the "Montreal Bill" received its annual review by the Quebec Legislative Assembly and Council. Montreal also possessed the authority to borrow up to 15 percent of its assessed valuation, a privilege denied to many other Quebec municipalities.[4]

During the 1920s Montreal's ordinary revenues increased by 20 percent on a per capita basis, but this increase was grossly inadequate in view of the need for long overdue improvements in many municipal services. In 1926 Montreal's ordinary expenditure amounted to $39.60

per person in comparison to Toronto's outlay of $54.50. The vital field of public health received one-seventh of the allotment available in Toronto. Much attention was focused on the public health question after 1926, and expenditures in this area gradually rose to levels comparable to Toronto.[5]

Increasing revenues were quickly swallowed up by these and other improvements, but no additional money was made available to deal with the massive municipal debt which the city had accumulated during its hectic three decades of growth. By 1929 the city's net funded debt amounted to $185.2 million, or $238 per capita.[6] Montreal had become accustomed to solving its revenue shortages by extensive borrowing.

The provincial government, by contrast, pursued an extremely conservative fiscal policy, maintaining the lowest per capita expenditures of any province and the second lowest per capita debt. Representation in the provincial legislature was of course heavily weighted towards rural areas and Montreal's needs were usually accorded a very low priority.

The quality of Montreal's municipal administration had long been under attack from business organizations and self-styled reform groups. Local politicians were equally enthusiastic in levelling charges of maladministration at their opponents. There was no doubt a good deal of corruption in municipal politics; the normal lubrication of big city government, patronage, kickbacks, bribes, were generally believed to be commonplace and some of the charges may have been true. However, the fundamental difficulty confronting civic administration in Montreal was an inadequate tax base, not corruption at City Hall.

This problem was compounded by the existence of a number of autonomous municipalities within and around the city, each of which used the urban area without liability for costs incurred by Montreal. All of these suburban cities, including the predominantly working-class towns such as Verdun, Lachine, and Montreal East, were in relatively sound financial shape in the 1920s, and were far better able to cope with the financial pressures encountered during the 1930s.[7] The desirability of a genuine system of a metropolitan area government seems obvious, but there was in fact strong resistance from virtually all quarters to any expansion of the Montreal Metropolitan Commission's authority. Not only the suburban proponents of local autonomy but the Montreal politicians were opposed to metropolitan government which they associated with business and professional "good government" forces.

The relative prosperity of the late 1920s masked structural problems both in municipal finances and in the basic economy of the Montreal region. The city had tripled in size during the first thirty years of the century but its economy had experienced growth rather than modernization. The traditional mercantile functions of the city were as always dependent on servicing the growth centres of the Ontario and western Canadian economy. If such growth faltered, the harbour, the banks, the railways, and the other components of Montreal's metropolitanism would be highly vulnerable. The secondary manufacturing sector, which accounted for one job in four, was in many ways less diversified than it had been in the late nineteenth century. Almost all the new highly technical industries of the early twentieth century had bypassed the city. Instead of automobiles, agricultural implements, machine tools, steel, and electrical apparatus, the city continued to depend on food processing, textiles, the needle trades, and other low-wage, labour-intensive activities. Montreal had long been a magnet, selectively attracting a large pool of unskilled labour, the group most vulnerable in periods of economic contraction.[8] The impact of the Great Depression was felt immediately in Montreal. By June 1, 1931, 20 percent of the male labour force and 10 percent of the female labour force were without work. During the winter of 1931–1932 more than one hundred thousand Montrealers were on relief.[9]

Montreal's civic administration was in the hands of the remarkable Camillien Houde in 1930. Houde had been elected mayor in 1928, but during his first term City Council was firmly controlled by Alderman A.A. Desroches, representing Hochelaga, who was also chairman of the city's Executive Council. Houde organized a slate of candidates for the 1930 election and conducted a vigorous campaign against the "Desroches Clique" levelling the standard charges of maladministration and scandalous conduct. Houde's own program consisted of routine promises to improve public health, lower transit fares, and reduce utility rates. No particular attention was paid to the high unemployment levels of the winter season, which were not responding to the normal corrective, the arrival of spring. Houde and his slate swept all before them, capturing control of City Council. Houde received a majority of 40 847 votes, the largest in the city's history.[10]

The main thrust of federal, provincial, and municipal unemployment relief during 1930 and 1931 was towards public works projects, though provision was made for minor amounts of direct assistance. Montreal borrowed over twenty million dollars at the very high rate of 6 percent, to pay its share of expenditure on relief projects during the two years.[11] Houde and his associates spent public works money with a fine disregard for administrative niceties such as adequate accounting practices.[12] Work projects were oriented towards maximizing employment, and by 1932 Houde claimed that eighteen thousand additional workers, "the majority taken from the ranks of the unemployed,"[13] were at work on public works initiated by the city.

The federal Unemployment Relief Acts had made provisions for small amounts of direct relief in 1930 and 1931. In Montreal such assistance was channeled through the traditional private denominational organizations which distributed funds according to their own procedures. The St. Vincent de Paul Society maintained its responsibility for the French

Catholic community, 60 percent of the population, and by the end of 1932 it was providing support for an average of thirty-four thousand families a month, mainly the same families in each month. The Society was dispensing close to one million dollars each month, and more than three thousand volunteers were spending their evenings trying to maintain the policies outlined in the *Manuel du visiteurs du pauvre*.[14] The *visiteurs* were supposed to try and tailor their assistance to family needs and apparently did so. *Bons* or vouchers, redeemable at local stores, were issued. Other *bons* for rent, fuel, clothing and even school books were provided. The Society continued to visit the sick, provide counselling, help families find new accommodation, and run interference between the needy and their creditors.

Within the Protestant community, direct relief to the able-bodied unemployed was provided by the Emergency Unemployment Relief Committee, an organization established in the winter of 1924 to cope with seasonal unemployment. This committee worked in conjunction with the Protestant Employment Bureau and relief was available so long as the head of the family reported to the bureau every second day and had his card signed weekly by his local church minister. By 1933 between four and five thousand families were receiving rent assistance, a fuel allotment and a weekly ration as follows:

9 lbs. stewing beef	2 lbs. sugar
¾ lb. salt pork	½ lb. cheese
20 lbs. potatoes	2½ lbs. beans
4 lbs. carrots and onions	2 lbs. prunes
4 lbs. rolled oats	1 lb. peanut butter
2 lbs. rice	2 lbs. Lassie's syrup
3 bars Lennox soap	

This ration was supplemented by bread and milk to a maximum of two loaves and two quarts a day.[15]

English-speaking Catholics without work were the responsibility of agencies operated by the Federation of Catholic Charities, and more than two thousand families were registered with the Federation. A further one thousand families received assistance through the Baron de Hirsch Institute during a normal week in 1933, bringing the total number of families on relief to around forty-two thousand. This estimate does not include single men and women living outside family units, but it does include an unknown number of families for whom unemployment and dependency were old problems which predated the Depression. It would be reasonable to suggest that the number of Montrealers living on relief of one form or another reached the two hundred thousand mark during the winter of 1932–1933. When the civic authorities took over relief administration in August 1933, there were some sixty thousand names on the various relief rolls and an estimated 205 000 persons dependent on direct assistance.[16] These figures apply to the city of Montreal proper and not the metropolitan area, and, therefore, represent just less than one-quarter of the 874 000 residents of Montreal. The winter of 1933–1934 was the worst period of the Depression, with the total of municipal relief dependents reaching 250 000, 28 percent of the population.

A survey of the occupational background of relief recipients prepared in the winter of 1932–1933 indicates that the hourly wage earners bore a disproportionate burden of unemployment. Professionals accounted for just 2.6 percent of the total, and other white-collar workers 10.1 percent. The remaining 87.3 percent was made up of wage earners.[17] (Blue collar workers accounted for approximately two-thirds of the 224 000 males in the Montreal labour force.) In late 1933, then, one in every four males in the labour force was on relief, but the number of male *wage earners* on the dole was one in three. These figures also suggest that French-speaking Montrealers, heavily over-represented in the unskilled and semi-skilled occupations, bore a disproportionate share of unemployment and were much more dependent on relief than the English-speaking population.[18]

Between 1933 and 1939 the number of heads of families on relief never fell below thirty-three thousand. The "best" year, 1936, saw a monthly average of 114 988 heads of families, dependents, and single individuals on the dole. When the Department of Municipal Assistance discontinued the relief in 1940, there were still ten thousand families receiving aid.[19]

The distribution of government funds by private agencies came under vigorous attack in 1932. Local merchants frequently found that *bons* or other vouchers could not be quickly cashed and joined the chorus of criticism. The private agencies lacked the administrative facilities to "control" expenditure and were lumped together with the Houde administration as having engaged in "maladministration and ruinous extravagance."[20]

The municipal election of 1932 was fought essentially on this issue. Fernand Rinfret, a former minister in Mackenzie King's government, ran for mayor on a platform of financial reform. The goal, Rinfret said, was "the establishment of a new financial stability at City Hall." One of the first duties of a new administration would be "to restore the confidence of the bankers and financiers in the financial solidarity [sic] of the metropolis."[21] Taxes could not be raised, so strict economy must be enforced.

Rinfret's success in the 1932 election seems surprising in view of the efforts of Houde to combat unemployment. Perhaps the vote reflects the too-often ignored reality that the large majority of the population held on to their jobs during the 1930s and thus retained their notions of unemployment as a personal failing, an individual responsibility. Certainly Houde's vote dropped dramatically in most parts of the city. Even his home ward, Ste. Marie, was won by Rinfret.[22] Other explanations are equally possible, however, and only a very detailed study of the election would produce a more informed estimate.

Rinfret's election coincided with a general decline in government support for public works expenditures as the major form of depression relief. Direct assistance, the dole, became the favoured mechanism for dealing with unemployment. By 1933 more systematic methods of administering direct assistance were developing in most Canadian cities as officials attempted to bring expenditures under control.

Nowhere did the need for better administrative control of relief seem more serious than in Montreal. Dominion government officials were appalled by the casual accounting methods of the city's private agencies. One inspector dispatched by Ottawa for find out how the St. Vincent de Paul Society was operating reported that "although they handle a half a million dollars a month and maybe more, they have no office and no bookkeeping system."[23] The Society flatly refused to co-operate with the enquiry, to the point of rejecting a request to supply the government with the names of the presidents of the various parish councils. The inspector noted that the Society's director "could not describe the system in detail, but added some were receiving *bons*, others cash, and others goods."[24] The charitable practices of the Society were simply no business of the government.

The other Montreal agencies were more co-operative with Dominion government inspectors, but their information simply reinforced the picture of administrative chaos. No one seriously suggested that the private agencies were corrupt, but they did appear to be "extravagant" and, even worse, unsystematic. In February 1933, the St. Vincent de Paul Society forestalled further government interference by announcing that it would no longer handle unemployment relief. City Council moved to appoint a Civic Unemployment Commission (the Terrault Commission), which took over all direct assistance to able-bodied unemployed in the spring of 1933. Private charity was left with the responsibility for the sick, the aged, infirm, crippled, and widows.

The Commission quickly lost credibility when it resorted to a system of using the secretaries of city aldermen as agents for job hiring on city projects. A scandal developed in July 1934 when it was alleged that Commission employees had accepted bribes to redeem the *bons* of certain large companies while smaller merchants were being told that funds were not available.[25] Terrault was forced to resign and a new Unemployment Relief Commission under Brigadier-General E. B. de Panet was appointed. Panet, a "dollar-a-year" man borrowed from the CPR, moved to introduce "modern business practices" into relief administration.[26]

Camillien Houde had swept back into power in April 1934 in the aftermath of the worst winter in the city's history, and Panet's appointment was the first concrete fulfillment of his campaign promise to bring the best available men to the aid of the beleaguered city.

With a quarter of the population on relief, Montreal was barely maintaining basic services. Relief cheques were not sent out in April because the federal government refused to forward further funds until errors and irregularities in Montreal's accounts were corrected. Many landlords had not been paid in months and hundreds of evictions were reported.[27] The city's streets had deteriorated and no money was available for repairs or street cleaning. Houde ran a low-key campaign, making few promises but reminding his audiences that when he was in office he was accused of "having spent too much money. But you ate. . . . You had your boots, your clothes and your landlords got their rent."[28]

The new Unemployment Relief Commission moved quickly to set up a highly organized relief system. By mid-1935 there were more than eight hundred full-time employees working at the central office and in twenty district bureaus. A force of one hundred inspectors ran constant checks to ensure that no one was violating the rules, and much stress was placed on the penalities that would be incurred for giving a false oath or defrauding the city. In the first year of the Commission's existence, 866 cases were pursued by the investigators and 691 of these were cut off from relief or had their allocations reduced. Since more than forty thousand cheques were being issued each week, the number of cases of "fraud" uncovered by the vast investigating force seems quite small.[29] However, as the Depression continued it became harder and harder to get onto the relief rolls in the first place, and the investigators were strongly criticized for their inflexible interpretation of the rules.

Two categories of "employable unemployeds" were recognized by the Commission. Unattached men and women could obtain an allowance of $1.80 per week plus $1.38 as a rent allowance. The allotment for a family of five consisted of the following:[30]

	Food	Fuel (Summer)	Fuel (Winter)	Clothing	Rent	Electricity (Summer)	Electricity (Winter)
Weekly	$ 5.05	$0.75	$1.35	$0.75	—	—	—
Monthly	$21.88	$3.25	$5.85	$3.25	$10.50	$0.70	$ 0.90

Summer total	$38.58
Winter total	$41.38

Relief was paid by cheque with direct payments to landlords and the Montreal Light, Heat, and Power Company. A medical fund based on a city contribution of twenty-five cents per relief recipient was created and a panel of doctors recruited. The head of the household was allowed to earn up to three dollars per week without penalty and the wife and children could seek employment, providing 50 percent of their earnings was contributed to the family.[31]

Unattached men who were eligible for municipal relief found themselves under enormous pressure to enroll in the Dominion government's relief camps. When General Panet took over from the Terrault Commission, there were 8 614 bachelors, widowers, and separated husbands on the city lists. In less than a year that number had been cut in half. As Panet explained it, conditions of life in the camps might not be ideal but they were "at any rate a great deal better than life in the city at $1.80 a week."[32] Perhaps Panet was right, but when the King government cancelled the program in 1936, life-long residents of Montreal found that they had lost their residency status and could not get back on to the municipal rolls.

The Commission also enforced strict residency requirements, insisting that only persons resident in Montreal on May 1, 1933, were eligible for relief. During the winter of 1935–1936, *The Montreal Star* carried this account of the plight of "transient families":

> Denied the dole because they arrived here after May 1st, 1933, at the mercy of charity which has not the funds to maintain them, between six and seven thousand families embracing twenty thousand souls are in a desperate plight and the city administration is baffled because at least five hundred thousand ($500,000) would be required for winter food, fuel and shelter and the aldermen hesitate to tax real estate owners further for the benefit of people who drift during the crisis. Most of the families are from rural Quebec and in their home towns or villages there is no dole because their local communities cannot support it, so they filtered to the Metropolis in the hope of finding work or getting on the dole rolls.[33]

At first City Council accepted the Commission's ruling, but in January 1936 the residence requirement was moved forward to May 1, 1934, thus adding additional thousands to the city's relief rolls.[34]

The system of public relief developed by the Panet Commission was roughly comparable to the schemes in existence in other large Canadian cities. Toronto had established a municipal Department of Public Welfare in 1931 when it became apparent that the need for public assistance was likely to be prolonged. Relief assistance rates were generally higher in Toronto than in other Canadian cities, but then the amount of unemployment in the city was much lower and its financial resources were enormously greater than any other large Canadian urban centre. Hamilton operated its relief through a Public Welfare Board composed of private citizens and city council members. Winnipeg's Unemployment Relief Committee was appointed by city council, but operated as a separate organization. Vancouver, like Toronto, organized a civic relief department. Rates for these three cities were comparable to rates in Montreal.[35]

During his 1934 campaign Houde had made a specific commitment to conciliate the financial community by appointing an advisory committee composed of prominent businessmen. Dubbed the "Brains Trust," this committee found that its immediate task was to persuade the Banque Canadienne Nationale and the Bank of Montreal to refinance six million dollars due from the city on June 15. This crisis was overcome but it was clear than unless something drastic was done the city would go into bankruptcy. A wide variety of schemes to raise revenue were under discussion in the fall of 1934, but in the end Premier Taschereau rejected new provincial tax measures, though he did promise to accept a new tax proposal for Montrealers if City Council could agree on what was required.

The Montreal Bill considered by the Quebec legislature in February of 1935 was a very controversial document. There was some basic agreement that the city's projected current deficit of $8.2 million could only be dealt with by tax increases, but there was no agreement on the nature of the new taxes. Houde floated a number of trial balloons, including a tax on bank clearances, which brought outraged protests and threats to move bank offices to Toronto.[36] Eleven more or less distinct drafts of the tax proposals were required before the bill was actually presented. The final version was a much more regressive tax package than earlier versions.[37] The income tax component was reduced in importance, the 2 percent sales tax and the increases in "water taxes" (paid by occupants, not owners) were especially regressive. The business tax surcharge was quite moderate. Nevertheless, projected revenue figures indicated that Montreal would be able to balance its budget in 1935.

The strength of establishment opposition to the measures is somewhat surprising. Most of the press (French and English), the Board of Trade, the Retail Merchants' Association, the Chamber of Commerce, and, of course, Houde's political opponents, joined in a chorus of denunciation. In 1935 groups such as the Board of Trade argued that extravagance, high administrative costs, and outright corruption were responsible for the city's financial embarrassment, The Board of Trade, the Chamber of Commerce, and other business groups went so far as to declare, in a paid advertisement, that only 5 percent of the municipal debt was due to relief expenditures.[38] The large newspapers echoed this charge.[39] The statements of the official spokesmen of the business community are severe. No fair attempt at evaluating the origins of municipal debt could possibly lend support to their view, and their opposition to Houde's tax proposals requires further examination.

When the Board of Trade presented a brief to the Rowell-Sirois Commission, its analysis of the city's financial plight was little different than Houde's; it was generally a constructive and thoughtful study of the problems of municipal finance.[40] Why then did business groups behave in a narrowly partisan fashion in the arena of civic politics? The cause was most probably the exclusion of the business elite, particularly the anglophone elite, from power in civic politics. Ever since Médéric Martin had broken the gentleman's agreement to alternate English- and French-speaking mayors in 1914, City Hall had become potentially hostile, always foreign territory in the eyes of the anglophone-dominated business community. Houde, like Martin, described himself as a man of the people, a defender of the poor against the "interests," the east end against the western wards, the French against the English. Houde's populist rhetoric, his flamboyance, and his French-Canadian nationalism created further suspicion and fear. Houde's fascination with Italian fascism and his earlier links with anti-Semites such as Adrien Arcand raised additional barriers to a *rapprochement* between the Mayor and much of the anglophone community.

In 1934–1935 Houde seems to have been determined to try to end the bitterness and polarization along ethnic lines which had characterized the city since the First World War. He was equally ready to develop friendly relations with Taschereau and his ministers in Quebec City. No doubt political opportunism played a large role in these manoeuvres, but Houde was also motivated by the plight of the unemployed and the need to broaden support for the unemployment relief program. Unfortunately, no real *rapprochement* developed.

The election of Maurice Duplessis as Premier of Quebec created new difficulties for the city of Montreal. Houde had deeply offended the man who succeeded him as leader of the Quebec Conservative party, and Duplessis would not rest easy until Houde's power base was broken.[41] Duplessis had declared his intention to abolish Montreal's sales tax during his provincial election campaign, and shortly after "Le Chef" was installed in office Houde announced his resignation as Mayor of Montreal, declaring that the hostility of the new government made his task impossible.[42]

In the municipal elections of December 1936 Houde ran a poorly organized and badly financed campaign. He was narrowly defeated by Adhémar Raynault, a prominent *nationaliste* and Duplessis supporter. Raynault had vowed to abolish the sales tax but his commitment, like Duplessis's, was quickly forgotten. Duplessis and Raynault did take action designed to curb relief expenditures in Montreal, however. Relief eligibility regulations were sharply tightened and one entire category of recipients was struck off the relief rolls: female heads of families with young children. The rationale for this decision was that such women were not employable. In addition, it was suggested that the needy would be taken care of under the provisions of the new Mothers' Allowance Act passed by the legislature in March 1937. In fact, the first payments under the Act were not made until December 1938, and then only to mothers having two or more children.[43] The average monthly payment under the act was thirty dollars, a bitter joke indeed.[44]

Approximately three thousand women were declared ineligible for relief in the spring, including "females incapable of procuring work, those living in a state of concubinage, unmarried mothers, widows with young children, and women with husbands in jail."[45] A demonstration of seventy-five women at City Hall led to a temporary restoration of relief funds entirely at city expense, but after suggestions of Communist influence behind the demonstration and a commitment from Quebec to make such women eligible for assistance under the Quebec Public Charities Act, they were permanently removed from the rolls.[46]

Duplessis and Raynault were also determined to bring the Panet Commission under their control. A committee composed of four aldermen and three outsiders began an investigation of the Unemployment Relief Commission on the grounds that its administrative costs had risen to 5 percent of the budget. Before his committee reported, Duplessis ordered the provincial police to seize the records of the Commission. Panet, his fellow commissioners, and ten department heads were suspended because of "ruinous and intolerable abuses."[47] The Premier declared that Panet might be a friend of the autonomy of Montreal but that, as Attorney-General, he would not permit Panet to violate the autonomy of the province. The angry public response to this action caused Duplessis to retreat and the Commissioners were reinstated. However, three months later Mayor Raynault and his Executive Committee announced the abolition of the Commission and the transfer of its work to the Municipal Health Department. The Mayor claimed that this was done to cut administrative costs.[48] Direct relief costs did decline in 1937 and 1938, but as a result of the new regulations not lower administrative costs.

Houde was able to win back the mayor's office in the 1938 municipal elections, but he did not devote his major energies to combatting Duplessis's depression relief policies. Shortly after his defeat in 1936, Houde had contested a federal by-election in Montreal—St. Henri, a working-class area which had long been one of his strongholds. Houde's campaign was based on opposition to the increase in military expenditures announced in the 1937 federal budget.[49] The official Liberal candidate, bolstered by the anti-participation statements of Cardin and Lapointe, won handily but the by-election marked Houde's return to the *nationaliste* mainstream. During 1938 and 1939, Houde became one of the leading figures in the anti-war crusade which was taking hold in French Canada. At one point he declared that in the event of war between Britain and Italy, French Canada would favour Italy. He was forced to retract this statement, but the whole affair is indicative of Houde's new preoccupation.[50]

Montreal's financial situation had been temporarily improved by the

1935 tax measures, but the city's share of relief costs still had to be paid for by borrowing. Since the legal limit for municipal debt stipulated in the charter had long since been reached, the city had resorted to short-term loans authorized by the provincial legislature. This "Additional Debt" had gradually assumed quite impressive proportions and by early 1940 Montreal was in an even worse financial position than it had been in 1934. The projected deficit for 1940 was $11 million and there was no money available to redeem two bank loans, amounting to $6.6 million, due on May 15 and June 1.[51]

The new provincial administration of Adelard Godbout had given responsibility for municipal affairs to Télesphore-Damien Bouchard, a long-time mayor of Ste. Hyacinthe, and an activist in the Canadian Union of Municipalities. Bouchard though of himself as an expert on municipal administration. He was also an old enemy of Camillien Houde's. As rumours about Bouchard's plans for the city began to circulate, Houde launched a vigorous campaign to prevent a takeover by Quebec. He urged the government to wait for the publication of the Rowell-Sirois Report, which would include an analysis of municipal financial problems. During April and May 1940, Houde took his case into the enemy camp, speaking to a variety of business and professional groups. He proposed a number of alternative schemes, but the common thread was the gap between municipal responsibilities and municipal tax sources.

The recommendations of the Rowell-Sirois Report were finally made public on May 16. Houde must have felt thoroughly vindicated as local newspapers headlined the Commission's critique of Quebec provincial finances. The revelation that Quebec municipalities had paid 26 percent of direct relief cost as against a national average of only 15 percent was followed by a flat statement that Montreal's financial crisis was a direct result of relief expenditures. But it was too late. Montreal had passed under the control of the Quebec Municipal Commission the day before the Report was published. A civil servant, Honoré Parent, had been made sole administrator of Montreal's financial affairs until a new system of government was installed. Even more ironic was the announcement that Quebec would move to introduce a province-wide sales tax, an income tax, and substantial increases in corporate tax[52] — all measures which Houde had advocated for years.

During the 1930s the city of Montreal's share of direct relief costs amounted to some forty-four million dollars. Additional Depression-related expenditures on public works added at least another ten million dollars to the city's expenses. At the same time the level of spending on the reformed public health system rose by more than 100 percent (1929–1934). Overall, the city's ordinary expenditures rose by 25 percent over 1929 levels in a situation where traditional revenue sources were static or declining. Montreal had borrowed the entire cost of direct assistance, and had consequently increased its net funded debt from $185.2 million to $273.2 million (1938). In comparison, Toronto was able to survive the Depression without significant additional borrowing. At the end of April 1939, Montreal's net funded debt per capita (together with short-term bank loans) worked out to $338, in contrast to a figure of $145 in Toronto.[53]

The crisis in civic finances was, of course, only part of a broader problem. In 1926, manufacturing production per capita in Montreal had been equal to that of Toronto; by 1936 it had fallen to 71 percent of the Toronto level. Despite the severity of the economic decline experienced by Montreal, the population of the city had risen steadily during the 1930s.[54] There were 120 000 more residents of Montreal in 1939 than there had been ten years before.[55] Bad as conditions were in the city, they were better than in the rural areas of Quebec.

The 1930s were a disastrous decade for Montreal and its citizens. Considering the financial constraints under which the city operated, the response of the municipal authorities was comparatively constructive. The three Houde administrations (1930–1932, 1934–1936, 1938–1940), in particular, deserve at least sympathy for the defending of the city's relief system against constant attack.

Not even this much can be said for the provincial and federal governments. Unlike the cities of Canada, the senior levels of government possessed relatively great financial flexibility. The Taschereau government in Quebec met the crisis of the thirties by reducing expenditures, and in 1936 its per capita outlay was lower even that New Brunswick's. The provincial debt did rise slowly in the 1930s, but in 1937 the province had the second lowest per capita debt of the nine provinces.[56] Even after the relatively heavy expenditures of the Duplessis years, the province was, in comparison to Montreal, in sound financial shape, reporting budgetary surpluses. Moody's *Manual of Investments* continued to rate Quebec government bonds at Aa, the highest category.[57] Stewart Bates, in his *Financial History of Canadian Governments* prepared for the Rowell-Sirois Commission, noted that, "Considering the debt levels and tax systems of other Canadian provinces, Quebec appears still to have some latent reserves of credit and taxation with which to pursue new policies."[58] The same could not be said for Montreal, though Moody's, with its Ba rating for Montreal (a high rating compared to western Canadian towns), seems to have had more confidence in the city than the Canadian banks, which refused to extend further loans.

Professor John Taylor's stimulating article on "The Urban West: Public Welfare and a Theory of Urban Development," suggests that "in their unwillingness to face certain social responsibilities in the thirties and earlier, the cities established a pattern of provincial, federal, and private control that has made them today virtually impotent."[59] It can be argued that in Montreal at least there was more willingness to face social responsibilities among urban politicians and officials than among any other political elite. Montreal was powerless because it lacked any reasonable measure of financial autonomy, because it lacked political clout in the rural-dominated legislative assembly, and because the Depression in central Canada had remarkably little impact on the well-being of middle and upper classes who remained preoccupied with "sound" financial management.

Camillien Houde's role in defending the interests of the unemployed requires further comment. Houde was not a radical except in temperament; he sought no structural changes in society or government. He offered no solutions to the Depression but rather concerned himself with trying to prevent further suffering. Houde came out of Montreal's slum-ridden east end; he knew his constituency at first hand and tried to act on their behalf. But if Houde had achieved everything he wanted, the unemployed would have been only marginally better off. Slightly higher relief allowances, more public works, and less stringent relief regulations were all Houde really stood for. His emergence as a folk hero among working-class Montrealers stands more as a comment on Canadian political leadership in the thirties than as a tribute to Houde.

Notes

1. R. Rumilly, *Histoire de Montréal* (Montreal, 1974), 5: 20. An account of Houde's speech is in *Le Devoir*, 17 May 1940.

2. Rumilly, *Histoire de Montréal*, 17.

3. See Honoré Parent, "L'Administration Municipale," in *Montréal Economique* (Montreal, 1943), 325, for details.

4. City of Montreal, *Report of the Director of Finance 1932*, 3.

5. Figures from Huet Massue, "Financial and Economic Situation of Montreal Compared with that of Toronto" (McLennan Library, McGill University, 1940, Mimeographed), n.p.

6. Ibid., "Introduction."

7. Montreal Metropolitan Commission, *Financial Statements and Assessments, 1930–1940*.

8. See Terry Copp, *The Anatomy of Poverty: The Condition of the Working Class in Montreal, 1897–1929* (Toronto, 1974), 140-47.

9. Census of Canada, 1931.

10. Sabina Burt, "The Montreal Municipal Elections of 1930, 1932, and 1934" (Sir George Williams University, 1974, Mimeographed).

11. City of Montreal, *Report of the Director of Finance, 1932*, 4.

12. The files of the Dominion Government's "National Unemployment Assistance Commission," Public Archives of Canada (hereinafter PAC), Record Group 27, 70/303 are crammed with correspondence on Montreal's failure to provide adequate accounting of its disbursements.

13. *Montreal Star*, 25 March 1932, 3. All the major Montreal newspapers carry similar news reports of municipal affairs. Usually the *Star*, *La Presse* and the *Gazette*

carry the most complete accounts of City Council meetings and civic election campaigns.

14. Peter Kralik, "The Saint Vincent de Paul Society in Montreal During the Depression" (Sir George Williams University,1974, Mimeographed).

15. *Montreal Star*, 16 May 1931. Cited in Sally Jones, "Unemployment and Relief in Montreal 1930–33" (Sir George Williams University, 1974, Mimeographed).

16. E.B. de Panet, *The Work of the Unemployment Relief Commission 1934–35* (Montreal, 1935), 4.

17. Leonard Marsh, *Canadians In and Out of Work* (Montreal, 1936), 356.

18. This inference is borne out by the statistics on the percentage of families on relief by ward. Papineau, Ste. Marie, and Cremazie wards all had more than 40 percent on relief in 1934 while less than 1 percent were on the rolls in English-speaking Notre Dame de Grace and just over 7 percent in the predominantly English-language ward of St. Andrew. *Montreal Star*, 3 March 1934.

19. Montreal Department of Health, *Annual Report, 1933–1940*.

20. *Montreal Star*, 30 March 1932.

21. Ibid.

22. Burt, "Montreal Municipal Elections," 23.

23. Report of Inspector E. Trottier, 16 November 1932, PAC, RG 27, 70/303, Box 155, File "Correspondence-Quebec-Relief City of Montreal," n.p.

24. Ibid.

25. *Montreal Star*, 28 August 1932, cited in June Macpherson, "The Administration of Unemployment Relief in the City of Montreal 1931–1941" (graduate research essay, Concordia University, 1975).

26. Panet, *Work of the Unemployment Relief Commission*, 2.

27. *Montreal Star*, 24 February 1934.

28. Ibid., 6 April 1934.

29. Panet, *Work of the Unemployment Relief Commission*, 4.

30. "The Realities of Relief: A Report Submitted by the Unemployment Study Group of the Montreal Branch of the Canadian Association of Social Workers" (Montreal, 1938, Mimeographed), 12.

31. Ibid., 13.

32. Panet, *Work of the Unemployment Relief Commission*, 5.

33. *Montreal Star*, 2 December 1935.

34. Macpherson, "Administration of Unemployment Relief in Montreal," 25.

35. "The Realities of Relief," 6-9.

36. *Montreal Star*, 9 February 1935.

37. The most advanced tax proposal, which included a sharply progressive income tax to be levied on all citizens of the Montreal Metropolitan area, is described in the 24 January 1935 issue of the *Montreal Star*.

38. The advertisement appeared 20 February 1935.

39. The *Star*, *La Patrie*, *La Presse*, *Le Canada*, *Le Devoir*, and the *Gazette*.

40. *Brief of the Montreal Board of Trade to the Royal Commission on Dominion–Provincial Relations* (1938).

41. For an account of Houde's relations with Duplessis, see Conrad Black, *Duplessis* (Toronto, 1977).

42. Houde's letter of resignation was dated 27 August 1936, which was three and one-half months before the municipal election.

43. Macpherson, "Administration of Unemployment Relief in Montreal," 53.

44. *Quebec Statistical Yearbook, 1942*, 229.

45. City of Montreal, *Report of Investigating Committee re: Unemployment* (Montreal, 1937).

46. Macpherson, "Administration of Unemployment Relief in Montreal," 54-55.

47. Ibid., 21.

48. *Montreal Star*, 16 July 1937.

49. Rumilly, *Histoire de Montréal*, 225.

50. *Montreal Star*, 17 February 1939.

51. Ibid., 6 April 1940.

52. Ibid., 16 May 1940.

53. Ibid., 21 May, 1940.

54. Massue, "Financial and Economic Situation of Montreal Compared with that of Toronto."

55. Ibid.

56. Huet Massue, "Graphic Review of the Public Debt, Revenues and Expenses of the Dominion of Canada and the Provinces of Ontario and Quebec, 1914–1937" (McLennan Library, McGill University, 1938), n.p.

57. John Moody, *Moody's Manual of Investments — Government Securities* (New York, 1942).

58. Stewart Bates, *Financial History of Canadian Governments* (Ottawa, 1939), 173.

59. John Taylor, "The Urban West: Public Welfare and a Theory of Urban Development," in *Cities in the West: Papers of the Western Canada Urban History Conference*, ed. A.R. McCormack and Ian MacPherson (Ottawa, 1975), 286-313.

KEEPING CHILDREN IN SCHOOL: THE RESPONSE OF THE MONTREAL CATHOLIC SCHOOL COMMISSION TO THE DEPRESSION OF THE 1930s†

WENDY JOHNSTON

Restless children kept home from school for want of sturdy shoes and adequate clothing. Thin and sickly young students too hungry to concentrate on classroom lessons. Such images bear witness to the devastating impact of the Great Depression in Quebec. The children of the unemployed and working poor, no less than their more visible and vocal adult counterparts,[1] were prime casualties of the economic crisis. Yet the contours of the depression experience in the lives of children, and the response of Quebec's public and private authorities to the problems of juveniles, remain issues largely ignored by historians.[2]

Studies of social policy in Canada underline the importance of the depression period in the development of the modern welfare state.[3] In the context of an unemployment crisis of unprecedented proportions, traditional forms of local and philanthropic social assistance were tested and found wanting. Federal authorities were forced to introduce emergency relief measures financed under cost-sharing formulas with the provinces and municipalities. Yet the central government refused during the 1930s to assume responsibility for the elaboration of a permanent, comprehensive social security system.[4] In Quebec, as elsewhere in Canada, the unemployed, the working poor and their dependents paid a high price for the ad hoc, politically expedient approach of governments to the economic crisis.[5] By highlighting the inadequacies of existing welfare arrangements, the depression ultimately compelled a shift towards greater state intervention and rationalization of charity efforts. How did this

† Canadian Historical Association, *Historical Papers* (1985): 193–217. The author would like to thank René Durocher, Dominique Jean, Andrée Lévesque, Michael D. Behiels, and Bettina Bradbury for their valuable comments on earlier drafts of this text.

conjuncture affect the development of social welfare polices aimed at school-age children? Did the depression result in expansion and innovation in juvenile social services? To what extent did assistance measures meet the needs of Quebec youth during these "années dures?"

This paper aims to provide a partial response to these questions by examining the aid policies of an urban school system serving a mass juvenile clientele during the depression. This study focuses on the Montreal Catholic School Commission (MCSC), the largest of Quebec's local public school boards, during the period 1929 to 1940. The MCSC boasted in 1930 a predominantly French-speaking and working-class student body of nearly a hundred thousand, or approximately 20 percent of the province's total elementary school enrolment.[6] The commission's primary and secondary schools served the population of an industrial, commercial and financial centre hard hit by the international and Canadian trade slump. By 1932, some 30 percent of Montreal's 818 577 inhabitants[7] — a higher proportion than any other Canadian city — were on relief, and they were receiving less per capita than their counterparts elsewhere.[8] Economic "recovery" awaited war preparations at decade's end.[9]

Analysis of the origins, the nature and the impact of the commission's aid programmes will show that the Great Depression obligated the MCSC to adopt an enlarged, diversified and systematized role in juvenile welfare. Like many other depression relief efforts, similarly handicapped by lack of funds, the intervention of the MCSC proved woefully inadequate compared to existing needs. However, the initiatives of the thirties would set an important precedent in the expansion of the school's social role.

This article is divided into two major parts. The first section will discuss the principal socioeconomic problems facing commission students in the depression years. Part two will analyze the programmes developed by school authorities to address the material needs of their pupils — the fee remission policy and ventures in feeding and clothing students.

Students in Crisis

The repercussions of the Great Depression were felt severely in the mainly lower-class student population served by the Montreal Catholic School Commission. Few observers could fail to notice the signs of growing impoverishment among these school-children during the early thirties. Commission employees and agents in direct contact with the children — those on the front lines, so to speak — provided compelling evidence of a student body in crisis.

The distress of the commission's clientele was early reflected in the rise of absenteeism directly attributable to poverty. The commonly invoked excuses of illness and employment were, in large part, products of indigence. In addition, however, truant officers charged with the enforcement of regular attendance[10] often explicitly recorded poverty, indigence, or the lack of certain material effects as the specific source of truancy. During the 1930–31 school year, poverty was cited as the direct cause of 9 and 11 percent of the total volume of absences in the commission's western and central districts.[11] By 1933–34, material need alone motivated some 14 and 17 percent of absences in these same districts.[12] The statistical results of the truant officers' weekly investigations, combined with their occasional comments on individual cases, provide dramatic insights into the everyday misery of schoolchildren during the 1930s.

A frequently cited obstacle to regular school attendance was the lack of adequate clothing and footwear.[13] Many children were kept home from school for this pathetic but fundamental reason, especially during the long and difficult winter season. In a typical case in February 1932, a young boy without shoes of his own was obliged to don his father's galoshes to accompany the truant officer "chez la dame qui s'occupe d'habiller les pauvres."[14] In some cases, children needing clothing were reported to be "tout nu" or "presque nu" and some were therefore absent from school for periods exceeding a month.[15] The other constraints experienced by the young prisoners of overcrowded city apartments can only be imagined. Little wonder that a dictation for pupils published in the commission's pedagogical journal in 1933 argued that a good pair of shoes constituted "le premier désir des gens dénués de tout."[16]

In a context where parental revenues were often insufficient even to feed and clothe children properly school fees constituted another formidable barrier to regular attendance. At the MCSC, all children were required to purchase their textbooks, while certain categories of pupils were also subject to monthly tuition fees.[17] In poor families, especially those with several school-age children, it may often have been a choice between schooling and food. In other cases, children unable to afford corrective lenses stayed home rather than waste their time on lessons they could not comprehend.[18]

If the increasing rate of truancy due to indigence was cause for alarm, so too was the appearance and health of children in school. Clerical visitors and provincial school inspectors charged with the inspection of pedagogy, discipline and school facilities witnessed more than academic problems in depression-era classrooms. Widespread undernourishment among young pupils attracted the attention of many school commission agents, like the clerical visitor who in 1931 sadly reported on the large numbers of poor children who often came to school without breakfast.[19] From the comments made by these agents it is clear that inadequate nutrition interfered with the children's intellectual development. The direct link between hunger and learning difficulties was presented in stark terms by another clerical visitor in 1932: "La pauvreté . . . est un grand obstacle au développement des élèves. Il arrive que l'enfant n'a pas toujours de quoi se mettre sous la dent. Le ventre creux, comment peut-il fournir un bon travail intellectuel?"[20] The debilitating effects of extreme poverty and resulting underfeeding also struck the provincial inspectors. They noted in their 1933–34 joint report "la faiblesse physique et mentale"[21] among commission students.

The results of the medical inspection of schoolchildren carried out periodically by municipal health authorities reinforced these classroom observations. While the existence of malnutrition among students pre-dated the depression,[22] a growing proportion of children clearly were eating inadequately in the years of economic crisis. During the opening years of the decade, the proportion of schoolchildren suffering from malnutrition never fell below 13 percent of those examined.[23] The real incidence of malnutrition was probably much higher, as city health department figures during the thirties were based solely on a periodic weighing of children rather than on a combination of clinical and size factors or more sophisticated biochemical techniques.[24] Poor diet, com-bined with squalid living conditions and lack of adequate, affordable medical care had serious repercussions on student health. Medical inspec-tions diagnosed a wide variety of diseases and physical weaknesses, affect-ing at least 50 percent of all children examined throughout the thirties.[25] Vision defects and eye disease troubled numerous children, many of whom were unable to afford corrective eyeglasses.[26] The tonsils and glandular system proved another serious problem area and re-examin-ations indicated that relatively few children underwent surgery to correct their condition.[27] Many other pupils suffered from lung, heart and diges-tive disorders.[28] Dental problems appeared to be especially widespread. Some 50 percent of the children examined in the early 1930s displayed dental defects including cavities and gum disease, and many were unable to afford treatment.[29]

The fundamental problems experienced by Montreal Catholic school-children during the depression were certainly not novelties in the metrop-olis. During the supposedly prosperous twenties, life below the poverty line was the lot of many Montrealers.[30] Indeed it is largely because many were already living below or near the poverty line that the depression hit so quickly and so hard. Indigence-related difficulties took on critical proportions in the 1930s. The extreme misery strained the capacities of traditional private and public relief systems beyond the breaking point and overwhelmed the emergency assistance programmes introduced by the three levels of government. What was the reaction of the local school authorities to this dramatic state of affairs?

The Authorities Respond: Aid Programmes in the Schools

The MCSC response to the apparent state of emergency among its pupils was conditioned by the material and ideological situation of the organization. By 1930, the school commission had become a centralized and sophisticated administrative entity which an employee compared to a "colossale machine," tended by "ingénieurs," "mécaniciens" and "humbles manoeuvres."[31] Determining the policies of this modern bureaucracy were some nineteen appointed commissioners, without exception members of the city's clerical and lay elites.[32] Ultimate authority was vested in the president and director-general, a position held for much of the decade by Victor Doré, accountant, professor and active public figure. Doré's adherence to the prevailing ideology of economic liberalism, allied with a strong sense of social duty and a concern for educational reform, set the tone for commission operations during the critical depression years.[33] For the "machine" was experiencing difficulties. The depression seriously aggravated the commission's chronic financial problems, which stemmed from a dependence on local property taxes for the bulk of revenues.[34] In the face of spiralling costs, mounting deficits and declining revenues, the MCSC sought to minimize expenditures. The costs and benefits of additional financial or administrative undertakings would be carefully weighed within the parameters of a mandate for public instruction.

On the eve of the Great Depression, the MCSC already had a long-standing policy regarding student inability to pay tuition and book fees. Provincial regulations dating to the late nineteenth century required all Quebec school commissions to provide free education for indigent children.[35] The remission of school fees for the needy was to be financed directly from school commission funds. At the MCSC, eligibility for exemptions was traditionally determined by the parish priest or the president of the local chapter of the St. Vincent de Paul Society to whom school principals submitted requests for free schoolbooks.[36] Those receiving textbooks free of charge at the MCSC apparently were also supplied with such articles as notebooks, pens and pencils.[37] In the difficult financial context of the depression, school authorities modified and expanded these subsidization policies.

Faced with falling revenues and rising expenditures during the thirties, the MCSC implemented procedures designed to tighten control over the free schooling accorded to indigents. Official regulations were instituted to consecrate the existing procedures concerning free schoolbooks.[38] In 1935, moreover, a school commission directive urged greater vigilance. School principals and teaching personnel were instructed to use "beaucoup de prudence" and to obtain all the necessary information concerning demands for schoolbooks.[39] Cases of tuition fee remission were also subjected to closer scrutiny. In 1934, the research and statistics division added several special investigators to its staff. Their job was to make home visits in order to determine the validity of requests for tuition exemption and reduction in the advanced classes. Still serving the commission at the end of the decade, these agents had evidently proved their worth by increasing the sum collected.[40] The commission's truant officers also aided in this task during the period.[41] Finally, the decision to stop supplying notebooks, pens and pencils to indigent pupils as of January 1938 was another cost-cutting measure born of the depression.[42]

The restrictive regulations governing the free education policy were introduced in the context of expanding assistance. Two areas of policy were involved, the first of which was the remission of monthly tuition fees. As table 1 shows, the commission's financial commitment increased dramatically from $1 000 in 1932, to more than $40 000 in 1936. Tuition fee increases accounted in large part for this enormous rise in expenditure. Rates were increased as much as six-fold in certain cases in 1934. Nevertheless, local school authorities shouldered a greater responsibility for subsidization. The proportion of fees remitted in commission schools rose from just 3 percent of the total potentially imposable in 1931 to some 43 percent in 1936.

The existing sources do not allow one to evaluate the number of pupils admitted free of charge or at a reduced rate during the depression years because tuition fees varied according to the category of student.[43] Moreover, as previously noted, the rates increased during the period. However,

TABLE 1

Tuition Subsidization at the MCSC, 1931–1939

Year	Total imposable	Reduction and exemptions	%
1931–32[a]	$ 25 949.50	$ 723.00	2.79
1932–33[b]	23 618.00	1 773.00	7.51
1936–37[c]	97 216.00	41 526.75	42.72
1939–40[d]	112 321.50	43 898.00	39.08

SOURCES:
a. AMCSC, (5) Services, (14) Service de la Trésorerie, (10) Frais de scolarité — Rétribution mensuelle — Sommes perçues 1932 à 1960, CECM, "Rétribution mensuelle, Rapport au 30 juin 1932," 24 August 1932.
b. Ibid., CECM, Division des statistiques, "Relevé de l'imposition et de la perception de la rétribution mensuelle, exercice 1932–33," 28 November 1933.
c. AMCSC, CECM, "LDD," 3, 4 and 9 August 1937.
d. AMCSC, (5) Services, (8) Service de l'Informatique, (2) Statistiques — Frais scolaires, 1937–38 à 1949–50; CECM, "Rétribution mensuelle, Tableau sommaire de l'imposition et de la perception des frais scolaires couvrant la période du 1er septembre 1939 au 30 juin 1940," 26 July 1940.

it appears that a growing number of children benefitted from the increase in budget for the fee remission policy.

The commission also allocated a greater sum for free schoolbooks in the depression years. From less than $5 000 in 1928, the contribution rose to nearly $9 000 in 1930. As table 2 demonstrates, the budget for free schoolbooks attained its peak between 1931 and 1936, when it ranged from $11 000 to $16 000 annually.

Despite the expansion of commission expenditures and the subsequent increase in the number of fee remission cases, the subsidized schooling programme did not keep pace with existing need. The fragmentary existing evidence suggests that the number of demands for fee remission far exceeded those approved.[44] The commission president hastened to assure a union representative protesting the massive fee increases introduced in 1934 that the MCSC did not intend to close its doors to poor children.[45] Doré claimed moreover never to have refused admission to a child whom he knew could not pay. The veracity of these affirmations cannot be easily evaluated. But on the question of the application of free schooling policies for indigents, one might wonder, with the historian Gabriel Désert, "à partir de quel seuil commence la pauvreté, notion très relative?"[46] Even worse, how many children would have stopped attending school, or would simply have never enrolled, without ever having requested tuition fee exemption or free books?[47]

More innovative than the free schooling policy were commission efforts to feed and clothe its clientele. By the mid-1930s, the MCSC would introduce school canteens to distribute milk in the schools and would establish an agency destined to expand and administer the canteens as well as to provide clothing to needy children.

TABLE 2

Free Schoolbook Provision at the MCSC, 1928–1939

Year	Sum allocated
1928–29	$ 4 674.18
1929–30	6 057.59
1930–31	8 845.73
1931–32	13 731.38
1932–33	11 363.89
1933–34	15 122.24
1934–35	13 906.99
1935–36	13 647.68
1936–37	15 575.41
1937–38	8 537.59
1938–39	5 736.12
1939–40	7 493.19

SOURCE: MCSC, *Financial Reports*, 1928/29-1939/40

The state of chronic want in which many schoolchildren lived in the early thirties provoked numerous calls for the social intervention of the school commission. Commenting on "l'état miséreux dans lequel les enfants de certains quartiers se présentent à la classe,"[48] the commission's chief ecclesiastical visitor considered in 1930 that the authorities should organize a programme of school canteens. That same year, a truant officer suggested the creation of a charity association in the schools for the purpose of buying clothes and shoes for needy pupils.[49] Various women's organizations also called for commission aid programmes.[50] Commission failure to help the destitute was even partly responsible for a loss of clientele to the Protestant public schools whose charitable agencies apparently offered a better level of social services. The several apostasy cases reported by outraged truant officers in the early thirties were indicative of a larger trend viewed with anxiety by the city's leading clerical authorities.[51] Such pressures did not however lead to immediate action by the concerned school authorities. MCSC officials were aware of existing misery but considerable time passed before they executed a plan of attack.

The attention of the MCSC centred first on the problem of malnu-trition. On the agenda of the commissioners during the late autumn of 1929, the question was still at the study stage a year later. At that time, members considered the organization of school canteens for the distri-bution of milk to underfed young pupils whose health and "progrès scolaire" were judged to be in danger.[52] The project of milk distribution finally took shape at the close of the 1930–31 school year. The ground had been prepared by the work of a lobby composed of the super-intendent of the child hygiene division of Montreal's health department, several members of the commission's hygiene committee, and, import-antly, representatives of the Montreal dairy J.-J. Joubert et Compagnie.[53] Beginning in the fall of 1931, canteens were established on an experi-mental basis in selected schools. By springtime of that school year, some 60 percent of commission schools possessed a canteen. These operated under the supervision of the commission president, its direction of studies division, and of the nurse-hygienist Alice Lebel who represented the sole milk supplier.[54]

The programme was supposed to remedy the undernourishment of poor young pupils. Some children did benefit from a charity-subsidized distribution during the year. However, the canteens operated primarily as the vendors of milk at school recess breaks and the bulk of the milk supplied was sold not given to students.[55] On an average, nearly six thousand or only 6 percent of enrolled pupils per month purchased a daily half-pint of milk in 1931–32, at a cost of three cents per serving.[56] Lack of outside funding, as well as the commission's own severe financial problems, undoubtedly presented major obstacles to the introduction of a free milk programme. Commission efforts to obtain subsidies for such a project from societies such as the St. Vincent de Paul, proved vain at this time.[57] Moreover, school authorities appeared in principle reluctant to assume responsibility for the material welfare of their clientele. To suggestions that the commission either alone, or in conjunction with other authorities, undertake to feed or clothe schoolchildren, officials made it clear that the MCSC was in the business of instruction, not relief. School funds were to be used only for "des fins strictes d'éducation."[58] This attitude would however be modified with time.

The canteen experiment, judged successful by the commission, was continued in 1932–33. Ceding to the solicitations of city dairies, the commission accorded to several companies the contracts for the milk distribution that began in December in a greater number of schools. Despite the reduced price of 2.5 cents per half-pint, milk sales declined. As the ranks of the needy grew over this period, the nadir of the depression, fewer and fewer families could afford even this minimal expense. This deplorable situation, commented upon by school principals and milk company representatives alike, led the school authorities to suspend the canteens in June of 1933 in order to study the restructuring of the service.[59]

Throughout the summer and autumn of 1933, the commission studied the problem and called upon school principals to estimate the number of schoolchildren who should receive free milk. This preliminary inquiry produced a total figure considered extremely high by the authorities. As a result, the commission charged the canteen supervisor Alice Lebel with investigation of the criteria used to identify needy children.[60] Nurse and graduate of the public health programme of the Université de Montréal's École d'hygiène sociale appliquée,[61] Miss Lebel was considered the "expert" required to evaluate the situation correctly. Her discovery that the initial classification of pupils had been based on physical appearance and the list of those receiving free schoolbooks, evoked a response worthy of the professional administrator: more "scientific" procedures were necessary. Miss Lebel suggested the weighing of pupils to obtain "une sélection minutieuse"[62] of malnutrition cases. During the fall and winter of 1933, the municipal health authorities would help the commission identify the underweight, needy children.

The need had long been evident: the target clientele of milk distribution would now be "objectively" selected. And by the beginning of 1934, the commission had secured subsidies for the project. In January of 1934, President Doré announced the creation of the Catholic School Social Service (CSSS), which adopted the motto: "la joie de donner."[63] In addition to the distribution of free milk and the supervision of school canteens, the new service aimed to furnish clothes, shoes and other necessities to poor students and to promote hygiene, charity and civic duty.[64]

For the MCSC, the creation of an allied social service agency represented a significant initiative in the field of child welfare. Why did local school authorities assume a larger responsibility for the material well-being of their pupils, a domain they had previously considered outside their mandate? Were education officials acting out of genuine concern for student welfare? Or did public and milk company lobbying, or fears of the potential for social disorder and religious "defection" among destitute children and their families, constitute the prime spur to action? The question of motivations underlying policy decisions is a complex one, not amenable to monocausal explanations.[65] All these factors seem to have played a part in the decision to create the CSSS. However, even more important, one suspects, was the change of attitude forced upon the MCSC's conscientious administrators by the severity of the socio-economic crisis. It was clear that the task of public instruction could no longer by carried out when large numbers of children were malnourished, sickly and ill-clad.

The CSSS joined the ranks of the emerging French-Canadian social work profession whose origins lie in depression-era Montreal.[66] The founding in 1933 by prominent Catholic clergy and laymen of the Fédération des oeuvres de charité canadiennes-françaises reflected the growing movement to transform traditional charity practices in the interests of efficiency and the curative and preventive results of aid. This centralized organization grouped together a variety of philanthropic agencies and carried out annual collective funding drives.[67] The CSSS joined the Fédération in 1934. In 1935, the new umbrella organization established the Conseil des Oeuvres as a central planning and co-ordinating body. The Bureau d'Aide aux Familles, a social service agency dealing with all aspects of material and moral welfare, was added to the list of Fédération creations in 1938.[68] Trained social workers for these agencies would eventually be produced by the first francophone university school of social work, established at the Université de Montréal in 1940.[69]

The CSSS borrowed from the theory and practice of social service efforts elsewhere. Milk distribution programmes in the United States and Europe apparently inspired the MCSC venture.[70] Yet the service was also the product of a specific milieu. The CSSS declared its Catholic colours and operated within the confessional affiliated system based on the traditional institutions of parish, school and family.[71] Analysis of the structure and functioning of the CSSS reveals a welfare organization combining systematization and bureaucratic control of assistance with a reliance on parish action and private charity.[72]

The administration of the new service was under the immediate direction of Victor Doré and the direction of studies was entrusted to Alice Lebel. For this health care professional, forerunner of the school social worker,[73] the first major task was the implementation of operating and regulatory guidelines for the free milk distribution. The school canteens serving the daily half-pint of milk at recess time were open only during the five to six most physically trying months of the school year, generally from December to April. This was precisely the winter period when many children were unable to attend school regularly for lack of clothing or footwear.[74] Added to this unfortunate paradox was a set of cruelly parsimonious eligibility criteria combining "objective" standards and traditional means tests.

The practice of classification by weighing, elaborated previously by Miss Lebel, continued to serve as the basis for selection of recipients. Teachers were charged with the weighing of their pupils three times annually: at the beginning of the school year, towards the end of December and at mid-April. The results, recorded on forms supplied by the direction of studies, were compared with the table of normal weight and height furnished by the school medical inspection service. On the basis of these records, teachers prepared lists of the children corresponding to the standard fixed by the CSSS. Only those children whose weight was 10 percent or more below the normal for their height and age might receive free milk.[75] Moreover, mere physical deficiency did not suffice. Proof of indigence, as certified by the parish priest or local charitable agency representative, was also required to qualify for the programme.[76] While the distribution period was considerably lengthened towards the end of the decade, the strict and humiliating eligibility regulations remained in force throughout the thirties.

Fulfilment of the second aspect of the service's mandate, the provision of shoes and clothing, also entailed the development of a system of regulation and control, as well as collaboration with local charity authorities. During the 1934–35 school year, the CSSS established a central social filing index and adopted investigative casework methods to screen cases of absenteeism for lack of clothing.[77] Truant officers and the special investigators of the commission's research and statistics division carried out in-home visits of the poverty cases referred to the service by the school personnel or members of the public. In their determination of the validity of the claims and the extent of need, these agents were called upon to distinguish between the "deserving" and the "undeserving" poor. This categorization of the indigent was inherent in nineteenth-century poor law doctrine and prevalent in Quebec Catholic philanthropic circles.[78] The "deserving" cases were thereafter recommended to parish priests and local charitable organizations for aid.

The work of verification of material need, delivery of goods and the follow-up surveillance of those aided to ensure their appearance in school, seems to have preoccupied the service's limited and already busy investigatory staff.[79] Yet there is also evidence of a growing concern with the psychosocial and moral aspects of child welfare. As Lebel indicated in the service's 1934–35 annual report, CSSS inquiries concerning aid recipients permitted school authorities and educators to study "des misères qui seraient autrement inconnues."[80] The later 1930s saw a growing collaboration between the CSSS and other child welfare agencies.[81] The home visits to control assistance "abuses" may in fact be seen as a springboard to the broader and more intrusive investigation of the family environment by school and community social service agencies which would occur in the 1940s.[82]

Prejudicial conceptions of poverty clearly influenced the treatment of aid recipients at the MCSC. Yet the structural and regulatory limitations of the canteen and clothing provision programmes were in large part dictated by severe financial constraints. Locally administered, the service was also, in the main, locally financed. Maintenance of the milk programme depended upon subsidies from various organizations, primarily private charities (table 3). The Fédération des oeuvres de charité canadiennes-françaises and its anglophone equivalent, the Federation of Catholic Charities, provided the lion's share of the canteen funding. Milk suppliers were also called upon to contribute a remittance varying between one-half and three-quarters of a cent per half-pint furnished during the period. The MCSC itself contributed one-third of the cost of the service's staff salaries. From 1937, when the CSSS was reorganized under the name of the Catholic School Social Service Bureau,[83] the MCSC contributed a substantial fixed annual grant. Other groups and individuals, including the Provincial Dairy Commission and the city of Montreal, also participated in canteen financing during the 1930s. However, neither these subsidies nor the general increase in grants was equal to the need and the service recorded deficits during the first years of its existence.[84]

The service's clothing programme was even less well-endowed. Periodic and limited grants from commission coffers had been used since 1931 to clothe and provide shoes for a certain number of the most deprived children, on the president's authorization.[85] Private contributions allowed the CSSS to continue this form of assistance on a limited scale.[86] However, with the exception of the sum of five hundred dollars allocated by the MCSC in 1935 for the purchase of clothes, shoes and eyeglasses, the service did not dispose of revenues specifically for this purpose before the end of the decade. Beginning in 1939–40, commission grants financed shoe provision through the new programme, L'Aide à l'Écolier.[87]

The service's free milk distribution benefitted a significant and growing number of pupils during the depression years. From some six thousand schoolchildren during the programme's first year of operation, the number of participants rose to nearly eleven thousand—some 10 percent of commission clientele — in the peak year of 1940–41 (table 4). Those eligible for the programme evidently reaped profits: as for cattle reared under experimental feeding methods, the growth and weight gain of canteen beneficiaries were proudly noted in the service's annual reports.[88]

TABLE 3

Source of Funding, Free Milk Programme at the MCSC, 1933–1940

	Sources of Revenue ($)							
Year	FOCCF[a]	FCCI[b]	CILQ[c]	Dairies	MCSC	City of Montreal	Others	Total
1933–34	n.a.	n.a.	—	4 545.67	2 010.36	—	n.a.	—
1934–35	4 800.00	1 000.00	1 000.00	5 599.98	5 153.84	—	35.00	17 588.82
1935–36	8 100.00	1 000.00	1 000.00	6 051.36	4 112.33	—	25.00	20 288.69
1936–37	9 000.00	1 000.00	1 000.00	5 639.70	3 557.04	—	—	20 196.74
1937–38	9 500.00	1 000.00	1 500.00	6 569.74	3 750.00	—	1 039.17	23 358.91
1938–39	12 500.00	2 500.00	1 500.00	10 825.31	3 750.00	1 744.22	931.44	33 750.97
1939–40	12 500.00	2 500.00	1 500.00	13 122.99	4 750.00	1 500.00	984.52	36 857.51
1940–41	12 500.00	2 500.00	1 500.00	8 351.00	4 000.00	1 500.00	1 317.49	31 668.49

a. Fédération des Oeuvres de charité canadiennes-françaises.
b. Federation of Catholic Charities Inc.
c. Commission de l'Industrie Laitière de la Province de Québec.

SOURCES: AMCSC, Service des études, (4) Organisation scolaire, (6) Nutrition (bureau) — Bureau des oeuvres sociales scolaires catholiques et cantines scolaires — Rapports financiers 1935 à 1961, "Bilan financier des cantines scolaires," 1934/35 — 1940/41; ibid., BOSSC — Subventions, CECM, "Relevé des subventions versées au BOSSC d'après les états financiers annuels," 6 April 1962; MCSC, *Financial Reports*, 1933/34 — 1940/41.

TABLE 4

School Canteen Operations at the MCSC, 1933–1941

Year	Number of schools	Distribution days	Beneficiaries[a]	Underweight students[b]	Half-pints free of charge	Half-pints sold	Total consumed
1933–34	220	70	6 050	n.a.	369 500	552 346	921 846
1934–35	218	90	6 620	22 590	475 793	385 282	861 075
1935–36	216	92	7 599	19 965	536 881	396 425	933 306
1936–37	217	92	7 831	17 782	513 284	357 217	870 501
1937–38	217	87	7 884	n.a.	528 154	491 022	1 019 176
1938–39	213	105	9 327	n.a.	725 999	928 754	1 654 753
1939–40	216	120	9 019	11 340	798 140	1 200 864	1 999 004
1940–41	216	143	10 973	12 401	1 010 992	1 356 293	2 367 285
1941–42	217	160	9 176	n.a.	775 498	1 833 504	2 609 002

a. Students benefitting from free milk distribution during the school year.
b. Students showing a weight deficiency of 10 percent or more, according to the weighing reports.
SOURCES: AMCSC, "Rapport annuel du Service Social Scolaire Catholique/Bureau des Oeuvres Sociales Scolaires Catholiques," 1934/35–1941/42.

Yet the statistical record of CSSS activities also documents an alarming reality. The total number of schoolchildren underweight by 10 percent or more far exceeded the number of free milk recipients. Between 1934 and 1936, nearly one out of five enrolled pupils was classified in this underweight category (table 4). Yet less than 50 percent of this group were selected for the programme. During the second half of the decade the proportion underweight decreased, so that in 1940 there were nearly half as many as at the peak in 1934–35. Nevertheless, that year, 11 percent of the children enrolled still showed a serious weight deficiency. Were those children who were refused access to the programme actually able to pay for the daily half-pint? Examination of the quantity of milk sold during these years suggests that this was not the case. The expansion of the programme clientele was, according to the CSSS director, less a result of an increasing number of "deficient" and "deserving" school-children than of an increase in available revenues.[89]

Qualitative testimony to the programme's enduring inadequacies is provided by the results of an inquiry conducted by the direction of studies among teaching personnel in autumn 1937. The remarks added to questionnaires by some school principals provide a glimpse of the children behind the statistics. While few questioned the utility of the canteens for many children who would not otherwise be milk con-sumers,[90] the criteria used to select programme participants was fre-quently the target of attack. As one teaching nun stated: "J'ai vu défaillir par la faim des enfants qui n'étaient pas encore de dix pourcent inférieurs au poids normal, et qui pour ce motif ne pouvaient être secourus par les cantines scolaires."[91] Others evoked the inherent pathos of the situation created by poverty and rigid eligibility requirements. When a large number of poor students desiring milk were unable to purchase it, they were reduced at the time of milk distribution "à contempler d'un oeil d'envie leurs camarades mieux favorisés."[92] Anomalies such as the case of one sufficiently underweight child receiving milk while two or three of his siblings in similar need did not, also abounded.[93] Thus many of the school personnel asked that greater latitude be accorded to school principals or to the medical inspection staff in the choice of students.[94] Others went even further, suggesting that a noontime lunch or snack be added to the half-pint.[95] But in the context of the austerity reigning at the MCSC, a plan of school lunches — as existed in the United States under federal government auspices — proved impossible.[96]

The daily half-pint undoubtedly constituted too little for too few. At the end of the decade, school medical authorities reported that some 13 percent of the MCSC pupils were still suffering from malnutrition. This represented only a slight improvement over the mid-1930s high of 15 percent.[97] This constituted a stinging indictment of the CSSS canteen programme, certainly, but it was also a telling comment on national, regional and local policies which provided relief, and of a labour market offering salaries at levels below standards of subsistence.[98]

As for the clothing programme, it too reached but a fraction of the needy. The CSSS could only afford to serve as an intermediary between schoolchildren and local charitable organizations. During the 1934–35 school year, the service claimed to have secured assistance for 1 264 of the 1 595 cases referred to its office. But the following year, during the crucial month of November alone, over three thousand cases of children absent for lack of clothing were detected.[99] While two-thirds of these students were back in class "convenablement habillés" in January 1936 —largely as a result of Christmas season charity—a considerable number of new cases continued to be reported over subsequent months.[100] That year, Alice Lebel was obliged to admit defeat in the never-ending battle with poverty. She predicted that despite the combined efforts of the CSSS, the teaching personnel and charity agencies, "il y aura chaque année un nombre considérable d'enfants d'âge scolaire, surtout les enfants de chômeurs, qui seront privés des bienfaits de l'éducation parce que non suffisamment vêtus."[101] For Lebel, these children outside of school control represented a religious and social menace, inclined to juvenile delinquency and vulnerable to the lure of material aid offered by Protestant and "Communist" charitable associations.[102]

As late as 1938–39, the situation of children absent from school for want of clothing had improved little. That year some 1 871 cases were reported to the CSSS office. Of the 1 262 judged "deserving," less than half, some 520, received assistance.[103] Moreover, many other cases were not even reported because the direction of the studies knew that the service lacked the funds to remedy the situation.[104] The continued need prompted the creation in 1939–40 of a commission-subsidized programme, L'Aide à l'Écolier, which distributed some one thousand pairs of shoes and rubber boots during its first year of operation.[105] Yet in 1940, at least 14 percent of all the MCSC's truancy cases were still the direct result of indigence.[106] The investigations of the CSSS revealed in addition that if many "chefs de famille" now had jobs, there was little apparent improvement in family welfare.[107]

Conclusion

The Great Depression forced the Montreal Catholic School Commission to modify its role in child welfare. Extreme poverty among schoolchildren, as reflected in widespread malnutrition and illness, an alarming rate of absenteeism due largely to a lack of shoes and clothing and the inability of many children to afford school fees, interfered with the commission's mandate to dispense instruction to a mass clientele. Education, health and welfare could no longer be considered as separate categories. Existing relief provisions were clearly inadequate. As a result, local school authorities ultimately took the initiative to transform their aid policies and to develop new modes of social intervention. The school's new and broader responsibilities required innovation in the provision of social services. While continuing to rely heavily on the human and material resources of private charity, school officials employed emerging social work techniques in their aid programmes. The long-standing fee remission policy for indigents was simultaneously expanded and systematized and, in 1934, the commission created a social service agency to provide free milk and clothing to needy children. However, insufficient funding, provided largely by local and philanthropic sources, narrowly circumscribed the effectiveness of these aid programmes. MCSC assistance efforts proved hopelessly unequal to the magnitude of distress experienced by their predominantly lower-class clientele during the thirties. Comparative case studies of other school systems, both in Quebec and elsewhere, are needed. Yet given the commission's avant-garde position among Quebec's Catholic school commissions and the gravity of the problem it faced, it appears likely that the MCSC's response to the depression placed it among the leaders in school welfare ventures.

To appreciate the significance of the MCSC initiatives fully one must look beyond the depression decade. Poverty did not disappear with the outbreak of the Second World War, nor did the commission's social service agency. In 1944, the school canteens and the Catholic School Social Service Bureau gained permanent status and were incorporated as allied agencies of the MCSC. Still headed by Alice Lebel, the bureau was reorganized "sur un plan professionnel" in 1946. Social workers and health care professionals were hired to serve as liaison agents between the school, the family and community services.[108] At the Montreal Catholic School Commission, an improvised response to socioeconomic crisis thus paved the way for social work's entry into the school system.

Notes

1. Excluded from positions of power, rarely leaving behind first-hand accounts of their experience, children constitute one of the long-neglected groups in Canadian and Quebec historiography. The situation is changing, however; the history of childhood in Canada has been an expanding research field in recent years. For a sampling of historiography, consult the bibliography in Joy Parr, ed., *Childhood and Family in Canadian History* (Toronto, 1982).

2. Brief references to the situation of children and juvenile social services can be found in Claude Larivière, "Crise économique et contrôle social: le cas de Montréal (1929–1937)" (M.A. diss., Université de Montréal, 1976), and in Serge Mongeau, *Évolution de l'assistance au Québec* (Montreal, 1967), but in-depth analysis of these themes is long overdue. On the depression in Quebec, see for example: B.L. Vigod, "The Quebec Government and Social Legislation during the 1930s: A Study in

Political Self-Destruction," *Journal of Canadian Studies* 14 (Spring 1979): 59-69; Evelyn Dumas, *The Bitter Thirties in Quebec* (Montreal, 1975); Michel Pelletier and Yves Vaillancourt, Les politiques sociales et les travailleurs, Cahier II, *Les années 30* (Montreal, 1975); F.J. Frigon, "Catholicism and Crisis: L'Ecole sociale populaire and the Depression, 1930-1940," *Revue de l'Université d'Ottawa* 45 (1975): 54-70; Andrée Lévesque, *Virage à gauche interdit: les communistes, les socialistes et leurs ennemis au Québec, 1929-1939* (Montreal, 1984).

3. For an overview of social welfare developments in Canada from the pre-Confederation era to the 1980s, see Dennis Guest, *The Emergence of Social Security in Canada*, 2nd ed. rev. (Vancouver, 1985). On relief policy during the Great Depression, the following may be consulted with profit: James Struthers, *No Fault of their Own: Unemployment and the Canadian Welfare State, 1914-1941* (Toronto, 1983): H.B. Neatby, *The Politics of Chaos* (Toronto, 1972); L.M. Grayson and Michael Bliss, introduction to *The Wretched of Canada: Letters to R.B. Bennett 1930-1935* (Toronto, 1971); articles in the thematic issue, "Dependency and Social Welfare" of the *Journal of Canadian Studies* 14 (Spring 1979). See also the works cited in note 2 and the suggestions for further reading in Michiel Horn, *The Great Depression of the 1930s in Canada* (Ottawa, 1984).

4. See in particular the excellent recent study by Struthers, *No Fault of their Own*.

5. Quebec's welfare system offered only limited social assistance to supplement the inadequate emergency relief programmes sponsored by the three levels of government. Since 1921, the provincial Public Charities Act provided public funds for institutional care of the indigents under a cost-sharing formula with municipalities and institutions. Outdoor or noninstitutional relief was almost entirely in the hands of religious- and ethnic-affiliated charities. In 1932, the Act was interpreted to recognize English-speaking Protestant, Catholic and Jewish charitable agencies, almost exclusively centred on home care, as institutions "sans murs" eligible for small grants. The French-speaking social service agencies only availed themselves of this possibility some ten years later. The decade of the 1930s was not rich in government-sponsored social welfare developments. Though the provincial regime appointed a Social Insurance Commission (1930-33), most of its recommendations, including family allowances and subsidized health insurance, remained dead letters. It was only during the period 1936-39 that modest pension schemes for the aged, the blind, and needy mothers were implemented. For a discussion of the Act and social assistance developments during the 1920s and 1930s, consult Mongeau, *Évolution de l'assistance*, 44-70 and B.L. Vigod, "The Quebec Government and Social Legislation."

6. In 1929-30, there was 564 374 students enrolled in the primary level schools of the Protestant and Catholic sectors in Quebec. The MCSC alone accounted for 97 556 of these, of whom approximately 10 percent were enrolled in its English-language schools. Quebec, Bureau des statistiques, *Statistiques de l'enseignement pour 1930-31*; Archives of the Montreal Catholic School Commission (hereafter AMCSC), (5) Services, (8) Service de l'Informatique, (2) Statistiques—Inscription par degré 1923 à 1973; Commission des écoles catholiques de Montréal (hereafter CECM), "Relevé de l'inscription par degré du cours (1928-1967)," undated. The numbers in parentheses used in document references throughout this article correspond to the classification system for papers at the AMCSC.

7. According to the *Census of Canada*, 1931, 2: 277.

8. Struthers, *No Fault of their Own*, 49.

9. Larivière, "Crise économique," 12-14.

10. Although school attendance to age fourteen became compulsory in Quebec only in 1943, the MCSC established its own truancy control service as early as 1928.

For more on the structure and evolution of this service, see AMCSC, (4) Élèves, (7) Contrôle des absences—Généralités 1924 à 1969, CECM, Service des archives, "Mémoire relatif au contrôle des absences des élèves," 24 February 1944.

11. Percentages calculated on the basis of data contained in the "Rapport hebdomadaire des contrôleurs d'absences," 1930–34, in AMCSC, (4) Élèves, (7) Contrôle des absences—Rapports hebdomadaires des contrôleurs d'absences, 1929–1942 (hereafter RHCA). Absences for which the truant officer recorded the cause as poverty/indigence, lack of shoes, clothing, eyeglasses or books were considered as motivated directly by poverty in this compilation. Note that these rates underestimate the full weight of the poverty factor as they fail to take account of indigence-related excuses like sickness or work, and of the reticence of families before the truant officer. For more concerning the methodology employed and the series of statistics for the 1930s, see Wendy Johnston, "La Commission des écoles catholiques de Montréal face à la Crise des annees 1930" (M.A. diss., Université de Montréal, 1984), 163-76.

12. See note 11.

13. Judging by the letters by Prime Minister R.B. Bennett, many children throughout Canada suffered the same fate in the depression years. See L.M. Grayson and Michael Bliss, introduction to *The Wretched of Canada*, xiv.

14. AMCSC, RHCA, J.-M. Brosseau, "RHCA pour le District Ouest," week of 29 February 1932.

15. Ibid., weeks of 30 January and 6 November 1933. According to Brosseau's 30 January report, an almost naked boy had been absent from school since Christmas.

16. Marcelle Tinayre, "Chaussures d'enfants," *L'école canadienne* (February 1933):274.

17. Examples of truancy caused by the inability to pay school fees can be found in AMCSC, RHCA, E.-B. Brunelle, "RHCA pour le District Centre," week of 5 September 1932; AMCSC, Contrôle des absences, Rapports-Généralités 1929 à 1938, W. Gravel to E. Leblanc, 26 September 1931. While Montreal city residents in the preparatory to seventh grades attend school free of charge, non-residents, non-Catholics, as well as students in the advanced classes were subject to monthly tuition fees ranging from fifty cents to two dollars on the eve of the depression. Under the pressure of financial difficulties, the commissioners even introduced substantial increases in these rates during the thirties. Moreover, as stated, all categories of pupils were obliged to purchase their schoolbooks. For the evolution of tuition rates, see Johnston, "La Commission des écoles catholiques de Montréal face à la Crise," 55-59. Free tuition to age fourteen and a free textbook policy were introduced by provincial legislation only in 1943 and 1944.

18. For examples, see AMCSC, RHCA, P.-N. Carle, "RHCA pour le District Est," week of 6 to 13 March 1932; ibid., week of 18 to 25 September 1932.

19. AMCSC, (7) Inspections—Visites des écoles—Visiteurs ecclésiastiques d'école—Visiteurs ecclésiastiques, Rapports—J. Eugène Gareau, 1929 à 1931, "Notes tirées des rapports de M. L'abbé Garneau pour le District Nord," weeks of 8 to 28 February 1931, 3 March 1931.

20. AMCSC, (7) Inspections—Visites des écoles—Visiteurs ecclésiastiques d'école—Visiteurs ecclésiastiques, Rapports—H.-A. Forget, 1929 à 1932, "Rapport de H.-A. Forget à J.-O. Maurice," 19 January 1932.

21. AMCSC, (7) Inspections—Visites des écoles—Inspection des écoles—Rapports des inspecteurs d'écoles—J.-R. Côté 1931 à 1953, "Rapport conjoint des inspecteurs d'écoles de la CECM pour le 2e semestre scolaire 1933–34," 4.

22. During the 1927–28 school year, 8 998 city students "ayant des affections de la nutrition" were identified by the medical inspection; the following year, the number

rose to 9 943 or 15 percent of children examined. *Rapport annuel du Service de Santé de la Cité de Montréal* (hereafter *RASSCM*) (1928), tableau 4, 88; and ibid., (1929), tableau 4, 96.

23. The statistics on malnutrition and student health are drawn from the reports of the doctors, nurses and dentists of the city medical inspection service. See AMCSC, (10) Service du personnel, (2) Bureau médical — Rapports des médecins-inspecteurs et des infirmières-visiteuses 1929–1940, "Rapports des médecins-inspecteurs," "Rapports des infirmières-visiteuses," "Rapports des inspecteurs-dentaires," 1929/30-1939/40. These figures are compiled in tables 29, 30 and 31, pp. 197-203 in Johnston, "La Commission des écoles catholiques de Montréal face à la Crise."

24. Before 1930–31, it appears that malnutrition was diagnosed by the medical authorities on the basis of a "subjective" evaluation of skin appearance and other indicators. The superintendent of the city's child hygiene division maintained that the adoption of a "more rigorous" method (based on periodic weighings) in 1930 was responsible for the decreasing rate of malnutrition recorded between 1929 and 1933: *RASSCM* (1934), 125. The inadequacy of weight as the sole criterion of nutritional state was signalled by McGill University social scientist Leonard Marsh in his depression-era study, *Health and Unemployment* (Montreal, 1938), 53, 155.

25. AMCSC, (10) Service du personnel, (2) Bureau médical — Rapports des médecins-inspecteurs et des infirmières-visiteuses 1929–1940, "Rapports des médecins-inspecteurs."

26. Ibid.

27. Ibid.

28. Ibid.

29. Ibid.; see also AMCSC, Rapports médicaux, "Rapports des inspecteurs-dentaires."

30. In 1919, the clerical visitor for the commission's western district identified poverty among the principal causes of absenteeism. AMCSC, Visiteurs ecclésiastiques-Généralités 1917 à 1964, Joseph-H. Dupuis, "Notes pédagogiques pour l'annee 1918–19," 10 September 1919. For a description of working-class life in Montreal before the depression, see Terry Copp's excellent study, *The Anatomy of Poverty: The Condition of the Working Class in Montreal, 1897–1929* (Toronto, 1974).

31. AMSCS, Visiteurs ecclésiastiques — Rapports annuels 1925/26 — 1957/58, "Rapport annuel du visiteur ecclésiastique en chef 1931–32," 3.

32. The commissioners were named for a five-year mandate by four public authorities: the Quebec government, the municipal council, the Archbishop of the diocese of Montreal and the Université de Montréal (*Statuts de Québec*, 1928, chap. 50, art. 4). In 1937, the number of commissioners was reduced to nine and a consultative twenty-member Pedagogical Council was added (*Statuts de Québec*, 1937, chap. 65, art. 3).

33. Doré was obliged to trade his post of commission president for that of secretary-treasurer in 1937, following the victory of Duplessis's Unionistes over the Taschereau Liberals. In 1939, he left the commission to serve as the province's superintendent of public instruction. Doré's later career included stints as Canadian ambassador to Belgium and Switzerland and as first president of UNESCO. During the thirties, Doré headed a team of commissioners which included such prominent "progressive" Liberals as Édouard Montpetit, who presided over the Social Insurance Commission (1930–33). On the links between the Montreal education officials and the Taschereau regime, see B.L. Vigod, "Qu'on ne craigne pas l'encombrement des compétences: Le gouvernement Taschereau et l'éducation 1920–1929, "*Revue d'histoire de l'Amérique française* 28 (September 1974): 224-25, 235-37.

34. An analysis of the depression's impact on the financial situation of the MCSC can be found in Johnston, "La Commission des écoles catholiques de Montréal face à la Crise," 40-99.

35. *Code scolaire de la province de Québec* (Quebec, 1899), art. 215, 249; ibid. (Quebec, 1931), art. 221, 261. The legislation concerning the MCSC confirmed this duty (*Statuts de Québec* 1928, chap. 50, art. 24).

36. AMCSC, (7) Service des études, (3) Recherches et programmes, (5) Manuels scolaires — Manuels fournis gratuitement aux élèves par la C.E.C.M., Généralités 1912 à 1946, J. Casgrain to V. Doré, 16 September 1931.

37. AMCSC, CECM, "Livre des délibérations" (hereafter LDD), 28 December 1937, Res. XIX; AMCSC, Circulaires, "Lettre circulaire de la Direction des études à la direction des écoles," 7 January 1938.

38. AMCSC, Manuels fournis gratuitement, R. Desjardins to V. Doré, 27 August 1936; CECM, "Règlement no. 35," 27 August 1936. A subsequent revision of the regulations in 1940 allowed the presentation of the father's Commission de Chômage card for francophone students and the father's relief card for anglophones, to be accepted in the place of local charity organization approval ("Règlement no. 35," 3e révision, September 1940).

39. AMCSC, Circulaires, "Lettre circulaire de la Direction des études à la direction des écoles," 3 September 1935.

40. See note 44, below. The number of investigators went from three in 1934 to four in 1937-38. AMCSC, Contrôle des absences, Généralités 1924 à 1969, J.-F. Vincent to V. Doré, 17 October 1936; AMCSC, Service de l'Informatique, Frais scolaires, J.-F. Vincent to R. Delcourt, 8 April 1940; CECM, "LDD," 19 October 1937.

41. AMCSC, Contrôle des absences, Généralités, CECM, Direction des études, "Rapport no. XI," 27 October 1938. From five in 1930, the number of truant officers passed to nine at decade's end.

42. AMCSC, Circulaires, "Lettre circulaire de la Direction des études à la Direction des écoles," 7 January 1938.

43. See note 17.

44. Between 1934 and 1938, commission truant officers and special investigators carried out on average two thousand case investigations each year concerning requests for total or partial exemption of fees in the advanced classes. The commission saved considerably from their efforts: in 1936, for example, total remission was granted to only 32 percent of the demands made in the commission's eastern district. AMCSC, RHCA, P.-N. Carle, "RHCA pour le District Est," weeks of 6 to 27 September 1936; CECM, Direction des études, "Rapport no. XI," 27 October 1938.

45. AMCSC, (14) Service de la Trésorerie, (10) Frais de scolarité — Rétribution mensuelle — Généralités 1896 à 1966, V. Doré to L. Girard, 7 August 1934.

46. G. Désert, "Alphabétisation et scolarisation dans le Grand-Ouest au 19e siècle," in *The Making of Frenchmen. Current Directions in the History of Education in France 1679-1979*, ed. Donald N. Baker and Patrick J. Harrigan (Waterloo, 1980), 160.

47. Note that a drop and subsequent stagnation of enrolments in the primary superior classes at the MCSC is evident beginning in 1934 when substantial tuition increases were introduced. AMCSC, Service de l'Informatique, CECM, "Relevé de l'inscription par degré du cours (1928-1967)."

48. AMCSC, Visiteurs ecclésiastiques, Rapports annuels, "Rapport annuel du visiteur ecclésiastique en chef pour 1928-29," 13 March 1930, 15.

49. The associations administered by the pupils of each school would collect

contributions from children and their parents for the needy. AMCSC, Contrôle des absences, Généralités, W. Gravel to J.-M. Manning, 27 October 1930.

50. See note 58.

51. In 1932 the truant officer for the central district reported concerning a girl registered in a Protestant school that he had "réussi à la faire changer d'idée après l'avoir habillée et lui avoir procure les livres nécessaires" (AMCSC, RHCA, E.-B. Brunelle, "RHCA pour le District Centre," week of 5 September 1932). See also ibid., P.-N. Carle, "RHCA pour le District Est," week of 29 November to 6 December 1931. Archdiocese and school commission sources reveal that from 1930 to 1938 some 2 865 Catholic Montrealers officially renounced their faith. These apostasies were in part apparently motivated by a lack of interest on the part of French and Irish welfare agencies towards non-francophones, as well as by the inadequate quality and limited accessibility of English-language teaching in the Catholic schools. See AMCSC, (5) Services, (7C) Services aux étudiants, (3) Bureau de l'accueil et de l'admission-Néo-Canadiens — Élèves non-catholiques et non-protestants — 1941, "Rapport du J.-Rod Thibodeau à l'Hon. Hector Perrier re: Prosélytisme Protestant et instruction aux enfants non-catholiques romains, non-protestants," 17 November 1941, 2.

52. AMCSC, CECM, "Rapport du Comité d'enseignement d'hygiène," 22 November 1929, Res. IV; ibid., 26 November 1930, Res. VI, VIII, in "LDD de la Commission Pédagogique."

53. Dr. J.-A. Beaudoin, professor at Université de Montréal's École d'hygiène sociale appliquée, was also present. AMCSC, CECM, "Rapport du Comité d'enseignement d'hygiène," 2 June 1931, Res. XI, 15 June 1931, Res. I; V. Doré to members of the Commission Pédagogique (hereafter CP), 11 January 1934, in *L'école canadienne* (February 1934): 248-49; AMCSC, (7) Service des études, microfilm reel no. 58, Cantines scolaires, Fournisseurs 1931 à 1939, J. Casgrain to C.B. Price, 3 November 1931.

54. V. Doré to members of the CP, 11 January 1934.

55. Ibid.; AMCSC, Service des études, microfilm reel no. 58, Cantines scolaires, Fournisseurs, J. Casgrain to W. Mitchell, 6 December 1932. The St. Vincent de Paul Society and the Canadian Progress Club apparently furnished milk tickets to poor children, a practice they continued in 1932–33. The number of children aided by this is unknown.

56. CECM, in "Rapport du Comité d'hygiène" 13 June 1932, Res. V, "LDD de la CP."

57. V. Doré to members of the CP, 11 January 1934.

58. Response of CP to letter from l'Alliance canadienne pour le vote des femmes in "LDD de la CP," 6 October 1931, Res. XXVIII. On another occasion, the president noted that the school commission was obligated by law to provide instruction to school-age children and to furnish indigents with free school articles but "non à les nourrir et les vêtir." Since 1931, however, the commission had voluntarily provided shoes and clothing to a few of the most needy children. See AMCSC, Service des études, Manuels scolaires fournis gratuitement, V. Doré to Marie Claire Laroche, 5 October 1933.

59. AMCSC, Service des études, microfilm reel no. 58, Cantines scolaires, Fournisseurs, Soeur Sainte Céline to J. Casgrain, 16 December 1932; ibid., M. Valiquette to J. Casgrain, 17 June 1933; CECM, "LDD de la CP," 20 June 1933, Res. VI.

60. AMCSC, Service des études, (4) Organisation scolaire, (6) Nutrition (bureau) — Bureau des oeuvres sociales scolaires catholiques et cantines scolaires, Rapports

mensuels 1934 à 1936, A. Lebel to V. Doré, 8 January 1934. The total figure reported by the school principals is not mentioned.

61. Founded in 1925, the École d'hygiène sociale appliqué dispensed a one-year public health programme to qualified nurses. Lebel also completed a practicum at Columbia University before 1940.

62. See note 60.

63. In school commission documets, the service is generally referred to by its French title, Service Social Scolaire Catholique.

64. V. Doré to members of the CP, 11 January 1934.

65. The limitations of a rigid "social control" approach to social welfare and educational developments — the tendency to neglect the reactions and experience of the "controlled," and to underestimate the role of conflicts within the ruling class and unintended outcomes — have been signalled by a number of historians in recent years. For an influential statement of the social control thesis and a sampling of its critics, consult the following: Frances Fox Piven and Richard A. Cloward, *Regulating the Poor: The Functions of Public Welfare* (Toronto, 1971); Joan Higgins, "Regulating the Poor Revisited," *Journal of Social Policy* 7 (April 1978): 189-98; J. Donald Wilson, "Some Observations on Recent Trends in Canadian Educational History," in *An Imperfect Past: Education and Society in Canadian History* (Vancouver, 1984), 12.

66. On the beginnings of social work in French Canada, consult the following: Hayda Denault, "L'insertion du service social dans le milieu canadien-français," *Service Social* 10 and 11 (October 1961–April 1962): 3-29; Serge Mongeau, *Évolution de l'assistance au Québec* (Montreal, 1967), 49-70; L. Groulx, "Le service social confessionnel au Canada français — ses énoncés et son rôle," *Canadian Social Work Review/Revue canadienne du Service social* (1983), 141-60.

67. The Fédération was preceded by less successful attempts at co-ordination: in 1927, the Fédération des Oeuvres sociales de santé, superseded in 1929 by the Fédération des Oeuvres d'hygiène infantile. Mongeau, *Évolution de l'assistance au Québec*, 49-50; Groulx, "Le service social confessionnel," 141-42.

68. Groulx, "Le service social confessionnel," 141-42.

69. Since 1932, however, courses in social work were offered by the Soeurs de Notre-Dame de Bon Conseil — a religious institute involved in parish social services — for their members and interested laics. Denault, "L'insertion du service social," 10-11. The first professional school, organized by priests trained in social work at the Catholic University of Washington, was officially annexed to the Université de Montréal in 1942. Nicole Vanier, "Aperçu historique de l'école de Service Social de l'Université de Montréal," *Service social* 10 and 11 (October 1961–April 1962): 95-101; Denault, "L'insertion du service social," 10-11. One might note the parallels between these developments in the Quebec francophone community and the movement towards "scientific" charity in Britain during the nineteenth century and in English Canada and the United States during the opening decades of the twentieth. The current reflecting "the growing concern about inefficient and palliative relief, the duplication of charitable services and the perceived perpetuation of pauperism" gave birth in Montreal to centralized charity organizations and a school of social work serving the English and Jewish milieu in the wake of the First World War. Yet despite certain common developmental imperatives, the young social service sectors in Montreal remained divided along sociocultural and confessional lines, each group maintaining its network of social service agencies and institutions. See Patricia T. Rooke and R.L. Schnell, "Child Welfare in English Canada, 1920–1948," *Social Service Review* 55 (September 1981): 484-88; Mongeau, *Évolution de l'assistance au Québec*, 49-50, 63.

70. Édouard Montpetit, "L'école primaire est-elle américanisée?" *Revue trimestrielle canadienne* 26 (1940): 63-64.

71. A recent study argues that the social work field born in depression-era Montreal was not a professional and "progressive" import, but a product of the milieu, wedded to the values of social catholicism and aiming to introduce new measures of moral control over the lower classes. To Groulx's otherwise convincing arguments this author would like to point out the similarities between elements of social work ideology and practice in Montreal, English Canada and the United States. See Groulx's arguments in "Le service social confessionnel."

72. A prominent commissioner, the author and educator Édouard Montpetit, underlined the CSSS's preference for parish action and private charity to social organizations "à tendance rigide et enregimentée" of the United States. See Montpetit, "L'école primaire est-elle américanisée?" 63-64.

73. With only four to five hundred trained social workers in all of Canada throughout the depression, many public health nurses, policemen and other civil servants were pressed into service for relief administration. See Struthers, *No Fault of their Own*, 49.

74. The canteens re-opened in February 1934. Thereafter, and until 1936, they operated from December to April; in 1937–38, from mid-December to mid-May; in 1938–39, from mid-November to the end of April; and in 1939–40, until mid-May. AMCSC, Service des études, (4) Organisation scolaire, (6) Nutrition (Bureau) — Bureau des oeuvres sociales scolaires catholiques et cantines scolaires — Rapports annuels 1932 à 1962, "Rapport annuel du SSSC/BOSSC 1934/35-1940/41."

75. AMCSC, Circulaires, "Lettre circulaire de V. Doré à la direction des écoles," 16 January 1934. Beginning in 1934–35, it appears that certain weak, sickly children recommended by the school medical inspectors could also participate, to the measure that service funds permitted. Teachers were urged to make a "judicieuse" selection of beneficiaries and they were forbidden to substitute children to those on the list who were absent. AMCSC, Circulaires, "Lettre circulaire du Bureau du SSSC à la direction des écoles," 26 November 1934.

76. The CSSS relied on the recommendations of these agents concerning the recipients of free schoolbooks. CECM, "Rapport du Comité d'Hygiène," 29 September 1933 in "LDD de la CP."

77. "Rapport annuel du SSSC," 1934/35, 3-4.

78. Truant officers at times demonstrated astonishing harshness in their judgements and treatment of parents and children, not hesitating to threaten parents perceived as negligent. See for example, AMCSC, RHCA, J.-M. Brosseau, "RHCA pour le District Ouest," week of 6 November 1933; E.-B. Brunelle, "RHCA pour le District Centre," week of 28 September 1936. Studies of the depression era in Canada indicate that such traditional attitudes towards the poor persisted in official circles, despite the emergence of a professional social work ethic which claimed to abandon the judgemental and punishing approach to dependency. See, for example, James Struthers, "Two Depressions: Bennett, Trudeau and the Unemployed," *Journal of Canadian Studies* 14 (Spring 1979), 70-80; Roger E. Riendeau, "A Clash of Interests: Dependency and the Municipal Problem in the Great Depression," ibid., 50-58; Elwood Jones, "Dependency and Social Welfare," ibid., 2.

79. See the truant officers' reports for the period.

80. "Rapport annuel du SSSC," 1934/35, 5.

81. Co-operation with the Colonie de Vacances Jeanne d'Arc (summer camp for girls), the Bureau d'assistance aux familles, the juvenile court and other organizations.

82. For a critical view of the nature and techniques of social services in Quebec during the 1940s, consult Groulx, "Le service social confessionnel."

83. The new French name was Bureau des oeuvres sociales scolaires Catholiques (hereafter BOSSC). The service thereby gained a greater budgetary and adminstrative autonomy, although its administrative committee was responsible to the MCSC and its expenditures had to be approved by the commission president and treasurer. CECM, "LDD," 15 November 1937.

84. Before 1937, the MCSC absorbed those deficits. See the canteen's "Bilan financier" for the period and table 3.

85. AMCSC, Service des études, Manuels scolaires fournis gratuitement, V. Doré to Marie Claire Laroche, 5 October 1933.

86. See "Rapport annuel de SSSC," 1936/37.

87. AMCSC, Service des études, microfilm reel no. 58, Vêtements aux indigents, Correspondance générale 1934 à 1936, A. Lebel to V. Doré, 10 November 1936; "Rapport annuel du BOSSC," 1939/40, 3.

88. "Rapport annuel du SSSC/BOSSC," 1934/35-1940/41.

89. See the service's "Rapport annuel," 1938/39-1940/41.

90. AMCSC, Service des études, microfilm reel no. 58, response of James Lyng to "Questionnaire au Personnel enseignant," 1937.

91. Ibid., response of Soeur St-Joseph-de-Sion.

92. Ibid., response of Frère Maximilien.

93. Ibid., response of Soeur Marie-Gatienne.

94. See, for example the response of Soeur St-Joseph-de-Sion, and that of Sister Margaret Mary.

95. For example, the response of James E. Barry.

96. Since the early 1930s, however, hungry children in several English-language schools of the commission snacked on bread rolls supplied by the Canadian Progress Club. AMCSC, Service des études, microfilm reel no. 58, Cantines scolaires, Fournisseurs, Charlotte K. Penner to J.-M. Manning, 24 April 1933. Introduced during the 1930s under FERA and WPA auspices, the United States national school lunch programme had a budget of $12 million in 1940. R. Freeman Butts and Lawrence A. Cremin, *A History of Education in American Culture* (New York, 1953), 58. In London, England, charity-subsidized lunches date back to the nineteenth century. Tax-supported feeding of schoolchildren was authorized by a British act of parliament in 1906 and began in London under county council auspices in 1909. See David Rubinstein, *School Attendance in London: A Social History* (Hull, 1969), 81-83.

97. AMCSC, "Rapports des médecins-inspecteurs," 1935/36-1939/40. See also note 24.

98. As Alice Lebel noted in 1936, "Les allocations de chômage suffisent à peine aux besoins de familles et . . . les enfants sont les premières victimes de ce déplorable état de choses" ("Rapport annuel du SSC," 1935/36, 2).

99. Ibid., 1934/35, 4; and 1935/36, 5. This situation prompted the commission grant of five hundred dollars in 1935, which purchased clothing and other necessities for some 189 pupils.

100. Ibid., 1935/36, 6.

101. Ibid.

102. Ibid.

103. AMCSC, BOSSC et CS, Rapports annuels, A. Lebel to Armand Dupuis, 31 July 1939; "Rapport annuel du BOSSC," 1938/39, 3.

104. "Rapport annuel du BOSSC," 1938/39, 3.

105. "Rapport annuel du BOSSC," 1939/40, 3.

106. Compilation based on data contained in CECM, "Rapport annuel des contrôleurs d'absences," 1940/41. See also note 11.

107. "Rapport annuel du BOSSC," 1940/41, 2.

108. AMCSC, BOSSC et CS, Rapports annuels, *Bonheur et santé de l'écolier: l'apport de 30 ans! 1931–1961* (BOSSC brochure, n.d.).

MOULDING THE MIDDLE CLASS: STUDENT LIFE AT DALHOUSIE UNIVERSITY IN THE 1930s†

PAUL AXELROD

Historians have studied Canadian universities primarily from the perspective of presidents, principals and administrations. Too many "biographies" of universities extol great men and great buildings but fail to place the study of higher education adequately within the context of Canadian social and intellectual history. In particular, historians of post-secondary education in Canada have tended to devote too little attention to the participation of students in university life. This is unfortunate, since one of the central purposes of the university has been to prepare Canadian youth to fill appropriate social roles in the adult world.[1]

The following case study examines the experiences of students at one Canadian university during the decade of the 1930s. Opened on a permanent basis in 1863, Dalhousie University of Halifax was, by 1930, a non-denominational university offering both a liberal arts degree and professional education in medicine, dentistry and law; in addition, King's College, the affiliated Anglican institution, offered degrees in Divinity.[2] In 1930 the student body was made up of 970 students, 70 percent of whom were in Arts and 30 percent in professional programmes. Two-thirds of the students came from Nova Scotia, and women, who were admitted to Dalhousie in 1881, made up 27.5 percent of the student

† *Acadiensis* 15, no. 1 (Autumn 1985): 84–122. It gives the author great pleasure to acknowledge the following contributions to this study: Hedy Armour for superlative research assistance; Charles Armour for his co-operation at the Dalhousie University Archives; Debbie Stewart, Joann Trypuc, Anne Oram and Paul Craven for technical assistance and/or advice; Craig Heron and John Webster Grant for helpful suggestions; and the Social Sciences and Humanities Research Council for generous funding support. An earlier version of this paper was delivered to the 1985 meeting of the Canadian Historical Association in Montreal.

body in 1930.[3] In the following pages the analysis begins with an assessment of the economic impact of the Depression of the 1930s on the resources of the university and its students. The class origins and occupational destinies of Dalhousie's graduates are examined. The intellectual and learning environments of the university are described, and the social life and political attitudes and activities of Dalhousie students are also explored. What emerges from this case study is a picture of an educational institution which weathered the uncertainties of the 1930s with some measure of success in meeting the needs and aspirations of its middle-class constituency.

The Great Depression disrupted and sometimes debilitated Canadian universities, but it did not destroy them. Austerity cost some professors their jobs while many more survived by enduring salary reductions. Enrolments, which had climbed considerably during the 1920s, levelled off. Straitened financial circumstances prevented many aspiring students from attending and compelled others to drop out. But the absence of employment opportunities convinced students, if they could find sufficient funds, to stay in university for as long as possible. Canadian universities initiated few new programmes in the 1930s. With some exceptions, plans for expansion, particularly in professional education, were delayed or cancelled. At best, the universities "marked time," carrying on in a sober atmosphere of diminished expectations.[4]

Dalhousie's experience fit the Canadian pattern. In the absence of government support, a $400 000 grant from the Carnegie Foundation in 1930 kept the university afloat for much of the Depression, but its accumulated deficit exceeded $230 000 by June of 1939.[5] A new gymnasium, replacing the old one destroyed by fire, was built in 1932, and on the strength of a grant from the Rockefeller Foundation, the university opened an Institute of Public Affairs in 1936. Apart from the addition of a medical library in 1939, no other capital construction occurred during the decade. Indicative of the financial strain was the elimination for one year of the Depression of funding for the Law School Library. When the Dean informed Stanley that the school could not function

TABLE 1

Number and Gender of Dalhousie Students, 1930, 1935, 1939

| | 1930 | | 1935 | | 1939 | | Total | |
	%	Number	%	Number	%	Number	%	Number
Male	72.5	737	78.3	692	76.5	686	75.6	2115
Female	27.5	279	21.7	192	23.5	211	24.4	682
Total	100	1016	100	884	100	897	100	2797

SOURCE: Registration Books, 1930/31, 1935/36, 1939/40, Dalhousie University Archives. Based on registrations in September; official registrations are lower after drop-outs.

without at least three hundred dollars to purchase current journals, Stanley replied, "You say you *have to have more*. I do not dispute that. I only say, and you must treat this as final, that there is no possibility of my finding the money for it."[6]

Several staff members, demonstrators and instructors were laid off in the early 1930s, including a librarian with fourteen years' service. These austerity measures were especially hard on female employees of Dalhousie.[7] Unlike other Canadian universities, Dalhousie never reduced the salaries of its full-time faculty. Carleton Stanley, the university president, was certain that salary reductions would cost the university heavily in academic terms by encouraging good professors to leave, or by convincing them not to come.[8] However, Stanley was rebuked by the Board of Governors when he offered to subsidize the salary of a new professor out of his own pocket. Appalled by this lack of professionalism, board chairman Hector McInnes declared: "This Board cannot approve any professor's salary being supplemented by the President. I speak for the board when I state this as a principle."[9]

The proportion of educational costs borne by Maritime students increased significantly throughout the 1930s, rising from 29 to 40 percent between 1926 and 1939, compared to a national average increase from 21 to 33 percent over the same period.[10] How expensive was higher education? Dalhousie Arts students, who paid lower fees than those in professional programmes, needed $390 for tuition and lodging in 1938–39. Tuition in Arts, set at $125, had been increased from $112 in 1932.[11] Books, equipment, library fees, student activity fees, and personal expenses added at least another 50 percent to a student's costs, making it difficult for students away from home to live on less than $600. (More than 70 percent of Dalhousie students were from outside Halifax).

Increasing costs were not offset by adequate scholarship funds at Dalhousie or elsewhere in Canada. In 1933 Dalhousie reduced the number of awards available, the result of "a substantial shrinkage in income from the investment set aside to produce the moneys for prizes."[12] The president even suggested that students who won scholarships but who did not require the award, be asked to "turn back to the university this money."[13] In 1938–39, approximately 11.6 percent of Maritime students held entrance or undergraduate scholarships which were worth an average of $113 per year. (This compared to 13.7 percent in Ontario and 6.7 percent in western Canada, with average annual values of $121 and $89 respectively).[14] Emergency loan funds, frequently over-subscribed and later uncollectable, were provided by number of universities, including Dalhousie. Only students who had attended the university for at least one year were eligible for the maximum annual loan of a hundred dollars.[15] Male students commonly helped finance their education through part-time and summer work, but job opportunities for women were scarce throughout the 1930s.[16]

At one level the financial obstacles facing aspiring students reinforce the traditional image of the university as a haven for the affluent, particularly in the Depression, when many parents were so badly squeezed. Indeed, Canadian educators were convinced that universities were becoming more elitist than ever. G.J. Trueman, president of Mount Allison University in Sackville, New Brunswick, admitted that his institution was fighting a losing battle in its efforts to draw students from the small villages and rural areas of the region.[17] President Stanley of Dalhousie confirmed this trend in a speech to the National Conference of Canadian Universities in 1934:

> Canadian university students have always included a number of exceedingly poor boys, some of them even desperately poor. In the last two or three years all of the desperately poor have been obliged to desist altogether. Since, on the whole, the numbers of Canadian students have not diminished, it is obvious that their ranks have been filled . . . by those who are not so poor.[18]

To submit, however, that higher education excluded the children of the "desperately poor" by no means proves that universities were mere bastions of the rich. While there were very few working class youth at Dalhousie, the typical Dalhousie student came from modest means. Lawrence Read, the son of a minister "who had no money," entered Dalhousie only after his father borrowed five hundred dollars from a friend.[19] Gene (Morison) Hicks' father was a civil servant who had taken two salary cuts in the early 1930s. He, too, borrowed money to send his daughter to university.[20] Her future husband, and future premier of the province, Henry Hicks, grew up in Bridgetown, Nova Scotia, where

TABLE 2

Place of Residence, Dalhousie Students, 1930, 1935, 1939

Place of Residence	%
Halifax	28.4
Other Nova Scotia	38.7
New Brunswick	9.9
Prince Edward Island	5.1
Newfoundland	4.8
Other Canada	2.9
United States	8.9
British Isles	.2
West Indies	.8
Other	.3
Total	100
Known Cases	2792

SOURCE: Registration Books, 1930/31, 1935/36, 1939/40, Dalhousie University Archives.

his father drew a salary of $3 500 from J.H. Hicks and Sons Ltd. While his was one of the wealthier families of the county, the senior Hicks "lost almost everything" in the crash of 1929–1932, and was forced to mortgage his home. A scholarship and part-time work as chapel janitor helped put Henry Hicks through his undergraduate years at Mount Allison and Dalhousie.[21]

According to William J. Archibald, who came to Dalhousie in 1929, "in those days the farmer would mortgage his farm to send his kids to college." He recalls both the presence of some children from wealthy families "who lived on Young Avenue," and the absence from the university of "blue collar people," who went to school until grade eight and then learned a trade. "Most of us came from middle class families," with limited resources and a strong devotion to self-improvement. Gene Hicks concurred: "My father and mother were both of Presbyterian-Scottish background, and these people put a great emphasis on education. The idea of furthering your education was not strange at all in our family."[22]

University registration records from 1930, 1935 and 1939, which include information on the occupations of students' fathers, provide further insight into the class origin of Dalhousie students. The results of this analysis are presented in table 3.[23]

What do these findings reveal about the class backgrounds of Dalhousie students with respect to the population as a whole? Certainly the children of professionals, who constituted between 2 and 3 percent of the Nova Scotian male working force, were over-represented in the university. Farmers, who made up 32.5 percent of working Nova Scotians in 1931 and 25.7 percent in 1941, accounted for only 6.7 percent of students' fathers. And while miners comprised about 9 percent of the

TABLE 3

Fathers' Occupations, Dalhousie Students, 1930, 1935, 1939

Occupational Category	%
Professional	28.4
Business	31
Supervisory	10.8
White Collar	8.7
Artisan-Skilled	7.8
Semi-skilled and Unskilled	5.6
Farming, Fishing	7.6

Total number of known cases	2271
Total number of missing cases	526

SOURCE: Registration Books, 1930/31, 1935/36, 1939/40, Dalhousie University Archives.

labour force between 1931 and 1941, their children included only .4 percent of Dalhousie students in the 1930s.[24]

The largest single category of Dalhousie students consisted of children of "Merchants," who made up almost 11 percent of the student body. Additional information was obtained on 36 percent of this group from Nova Scotia. According to Dun and Bradstreet business records, 21.3 percent of them had "pecuniary strength" under five thousand dollars, and two-thirds had assets under twenty thousand dollars. On the other hand, 12.4 percent had assets of over fifty thousand dollars. The typical Nova Scotian merchant owned a clothing, grocery, dry goods, furniture, or general store. At the one end of the scale was E.J. Murphy of Halifax (father of Charlotte), whose dry goods business produced an "estimated pecuniary strength" of $300 000 to $500 000 in 1934. At the other end of the scale was Philip Kristol of New Waterford (father of Louis), whose assets were estimated to be under five hundred dollars.[25] When one considers the 64 percent of merchants of Nova Scotia for whom information and/or ratings were unavailable, and who in all likelihood were proprietors of very small businesses, one is left with the impression that to be a Nova Scotian merchant in the 1930s was to be of modest, though (particularly in light of the times) by no means destitute, circumstances.

Thus a handful of Dalhousie students came from extremely affluent families. The sons and daughters of labourers seldom attended. The majority came from a broad range of middle class backgrounds, for whom a university education was an expensive proposition. Frequently, students' fathers worked in high status but not especially lucrative occupations, such as teaching or the clergy. These patterns were typical of students' social origins in other parts of Canada.[26]

When this information is combined with an analysis of the post-university experiences of Dalhousie students, we can draw meaningful conclusions about the role of the pre-Second World War university in the process of social mobility. Without question, some former students secured positions within what sociologist John Porter called "the Canadian corporate elite."[27] Donald McInnes (LLB 1926), who later became chairman of the Dalhousie Board of Governors, rose to the presidency of the Eastern Trust Company. Charles Mackenzie (LLB 1928) became President of Canada Permanent Mortgage Corporation and of Canada Permanent Trust, and A. Gordon Archibald (B. Comm. 1933) worked his way to the top of Maritime Telephone and Telegraph. Robert Stanfield (BA 1936 and LLB 1940), apart from his family connection with the successful Stanfields Ltd., later became Premier of Nova Scotia and national leader of the Progressive Conservative Party.[28] By virtue of their importance in the political and economic affairs of the region, and occasionally the country, these graduates stand out, but they are by no means typical. The Canadian corporate elite, as defined by Porter, was far too small (985 individuals), and the number of university graduates in the 1930s far too large (more than 56 000), to guarantee the majority of former students such privileged futures.[29] What became of the vast majority of them?

Judging from the Dalhousie experience, the evidence is clear. Most of the "middle class" students who graduated in the Depression ultimately, though not necessarily immediately, improved their positions *within* the middle class—though important distinctions must be made between the experiences of male and female graduates. Of the 326 cases of male graduates from Dalhousie in 1931, 1936, and 1940 whose careers were known (representing 75 percent of all male graduates), virtually all became professionals.[30] The Depression, however, may well have delayed their entry into these fields. Frequently, students spent a year or more after graduation at odd jobs or were unemployed before obtaining work in the fields for which they were prepared. Those graduating towards the end of the 1930s often enlisted in the armed forces and either resumed or took up careers when the war ended.[31] The Depression was less kind to many others. Approximately 25 percent of the male graduates from the same three years were unable to be traced. Some of these remained unemployed, died in the war, worked at less prestigious jobs, or simply did not report on their subsequent careers. Similar research methods showed that only 8 percent of the male graduates from 1921 and 1926 fell into the "unknown" category. Fully 92 percent of the graduates from those two years profited from better times and became professionals.[32]

In all likelihood, the women who graduated from Dalhousie in the 1930s also improved their positions within the middle class — but through marriage not through careers. While 72 percent of the thirty-six women who graduated from Dalhousie in 1921 were found to have worked for at least part of their adult life in professional occupations (mostly at teachers, librarians, nun, and nurses), only 29 percent of the fifty-nine women who graduated in 1936, and 27 percent of the forty-one women who graduated in 1940, were known to have found such work.[33] These figures must be interpreted cautiously. It is probable that the percentage of women who worked, at least for a short time before marrying, was far higher than the figures for 1936 and 1940 suggest. The alumni magazine, from which this information was derived, was clearly more successful at tracing graduates from the 1920s than those from the late 1930s and early 1940s. Even allowing for these statistical imperfections, the difference in the career experiences of Dalhousie women in the 1920s and 1930s is pronounced. Notably, the enrolment of female students at Dalhousie dropped significantly during the Depression. If they worked, women remained in professions that were less well paying and less prestigious than those occupied by men, a conclusion supported by further evidence with respect to the country as a whole. The Depression appeared to impose high costs on women aspiring to professional careers.[34] Since women seldom broke into the prestigious male professions, collectively they probably achieved the same degree of social mobility as men only if they married other professionals. Since it was assumed (without ever being statistically validated) that women students came from more affluent families than men, their relative degree of social mobility may have been less significant.[35]

Thus while Dalhousie was home to a minority of extremely privileged youth, the "average" Dalhousie student was the son of a merchant, who after facing lean times, became a lawyer or a doctor with a modest, but secure practice. Certainly the university turned out upwardly mobile men, and it rewarded them with privilege that the general population would never know. They were an elite, but of a less exalted status than generally believed. Dalhousie, in the main, was a middle class institution.

Between the world wars Canada's non-denominational universities became fully integrated into the secular and material worlds. Unmistakably (in view of the fate of graduates), their main function was to train men (and to a limited degree, women) who would occupy society's leading professions. Universities faced increasing pressure, particularly in lean economic times, to demonstrate their relevance and social utility. The high priority given agricultural studies in western Canada,[36] the emergence of Bachelors of Commerce courses in a number of universities,[37] the commissioning by government of numerous economists and political scientists to help chart the country's future (accelerated by the creation in 1937 of the Royal Commission on Dominion–Provincial Relations),[38] and the near replacement on some campuses of classical and ancient philosophy by American-oriented behavioural psychology,[39] all speak to these trends. Dalhousie felt the impact of such demands, and with the creation of its Institute of Public Affairs in 1936, and an Honours course in Public Administration a year later, it even claimed a pioneering role in the preparation of future government employees. "Hitherto," noted the *President's Report* in 1936, "no Canadian university has consciously set itself to give a special training for those of its students who look ahead to the civil service or to direct participation in government of municipalities or provinces."[40]

Yet these developments did not proceed with unanimous consent on campuses across the country. "Conservative" academics in English-Canadian universities were appalled by, and sometimes tried to thwart, the continental, material and utilitarian influences around them. Like the colonial philosophers of an earlier era, they favoured more training and classical education over "faddism" and "jargon," a "disciplined intelligence" over "intellectual anarchy."[41] Dalhousie was a prime example of a university embodying this tension, partly because its president, outraged by the twentieth century, had heart and soul firmly planted in the nineteenth.

Carleton Stanley, educated at the University of Toronto and Oxford, taught Greek and served as assistant to the principal of McGill before coming to Dalhousie in 1931. He replaced Stanley Mackenzie who had been president since 1911.[42] Canadian university presidents in the early twentieth century were cast from a similar mould. Mackenzie, Stanley, Robert Wallace, Arthur Currie, Walter Murray, and G.J. Trueman (among others), were austere, Christian gentlemen; kindly, wise and paternalistic, these were the type of community leaders in whom Canadian parents could faithfully and confidently entrust the custody of their children.[43] The public image of university presidents expressed the righteousness, sobriety, and "myth of concern" deeply embedded in the high culture of English Canada.[44] Intellectually, however, the presidents differed. Some, such as Robert Wallace and Walter Murray, were pragmatic, utilitarian men, conciliators with little patience for romantic, philosophical dirges on the poor quality of students or the erosion of traditional education. They presided over universities which enthusiastically embraced "public service," an approach found wanting by their colleagues, such as James S. Thomson, Hamilton Fyfe, and Carleton Stanley.[45]

Like University of Chicago president Robert Hutchins, who "was at war with the insidious combination of progress, evolution and empiricism in jettisoning the past, in promoting adjustment as an ideal, and in substituting vocationalism for thought as the focus of the university,"[46] Stanley railed against universities in which

> students are struggling during the first two years or so, to compensate for inadequate schooling, and even at a later period they are more concerned with attending lectures, preparing for examinations and the getting of marks, than with the fields of literature or scientific thought. Meantime, faddists, masquerading as educational authorities, fill the air with jargon about technocracy, and researching for a Ph.D degree.[47]

The dismal state of public education he blamed on the plethora of poorly trained women teachers. Schooling would improve only if "the colleges take it as one of their chief practical duties, if not the chiefest of all, to send back some of the *very best male brains* into the school. . . . After a certain age boys can be educated only by men."[48] He considered university students "illiterate" if they had not read the classic works of Thucydides, Aristotle, F.P.G. Guizot, W.F. Maitland, and Sir Paul Vinogradoff.[49]

When Stanley came to Dalhousie, he found an academic programme described to him by one authority "as an example of something worse than anything found in the United States." Matriculation requirements had been loosely enforced, and as Stanley noted, students were allowed to take their twenty credits for the B.A. degree "in any order," with the result that the demanding compulsory subjects (Latin or Greek, Mathematics, French or German) were put off until the fourth year, where they proved to be a "nightmare."[50] Quality education demanded both more rigour and the restoration of Classics and Mathematics, "the foundations of scholarship," to high priority in the undergraduate programme. Riding the crest of early popularity, Stanley succeeded in reforming the curriculum in 1932. Despite funding restraints, he convinced the Board of Governors to offer two scholarships "for boys only" in each of Honours Mathematics and Classics.[51] In addition, the university introduced an Honours programme of "advanced study" in Mathematics, Classics, and Modern Languages and History, designed for "exceptional" students from Grade XII. Finally, students were no longer permitted to postpone all difficult subjects to their final year. But Stanley's attempt to create a course in Greek and Biology, in which the classics of science would be read in "the original tongue," was, to the relief of many, "successfully resisted."[52]

Stanley took pride in these early feats of curriculum reform, but his remaining years at Dalhousie were spent in frustration. In an angry statement to the Board of Governors in 1940, he expressed resentment at the energy he had expended in raising money for the university, a task he felt belonged to the Board alone. He deplored the annual drain on university resources by the Public Health Clinic, and he decried the high costs of maintaining professional education at the expense of arts and science:

> I tried to make you Governors of the University aware . . . that you had been attempting to do something that had never been attempted elsewhere, that is, maintain Medical and Dental Faculties without endowments and without public assistance. I tried to make you see that such an attempt was not heroic, but foolish, and that it ultimately could not succeed. Finally, I told you that it went against my own conscience, as one of the trustees of the University, to cramp the work of the Arts Faculty in such an attempt, and to bolster up by funds, which in strict rights should be used by the Arts Faculty.[53]

The priority given to preserving the costly professions was heightened in 1938–39, when Dalhousie, at risk of losing its standing as an accredited medical school with the Association of American Medical Colleges, was forced both to improve clinical training facilities and construct a new medical library.[54]

Although Stanley retained the presidency until 1945, he was far from popular among Dalhousie students. At first intrigued by his provocative, blunt speeches, students grew to resent his rigid, traditional ways. When the university announced a ban on mixed badminton in the gymasium except on Saturday afternoons, the editors of the student newsaper mocked Stanley in a cartoon and denounced his "reform school methods."[55] Viewed in retrospect as an "ivory tower man," an "egomaniac," and a devotee of the anachronistic ideal that students "should talk and think Greek,"[56] Stanley distanced himself in a manner that concealed his true compassion and concern. His former secretary recalls a sensitive, principled man who met personally with all new students (including the women), offered them considered guidance, and found ways to provide financial assistance to the very poor. She admitted, however, that his formality sometimes intimidated the shy.[57]

Stanley's concern about incompetent students and the materialistic, frivolous culture which engaged them, was probably more applicable to the 1920s than the 1930s. The post-war atmosphere of Canadian campuses was frequently raucous, explained in part by the inability or unwillingness of university officials to impose traditional discipline upon those student veterans who had fought life and death battles overseas.[58] Though frivolity hardly disappeared, during the Depression Canadian students appeared more serious academically. Stanley himself observed that at Dalhousie it was "a matter of common remark that the library is used five times as much as formerly." He noted on another occasion the "common sense which marks our student body as a whole and the high seriousness of our best students."[59] As *Pharos*, the student yearbook, commented in 1933, "This sudden desire for knowledge is one of the several beneficial results of The Great Economic Depression."[60] Occasionally, student columnists expressed concern with the very cultural issues that preoccupied Stanley. A *Gazette* editorial in 1930 defended the classical subjects, which, "though regarded as useless and dead, are really courses which inspire thought and give a broad culture otherwise unobtainable."[61] In an article entitled "Something to Think About," one student tackled the central dilemma of higher education, "its attempt to make a compromise between two irreconcilable principles":

> The system makes a half-hearted attempt to achieve the glorified trade school ideal as typified by the university that gives a degree in hotel management and at the same time to achieve the classical ideal as typified by Oxford and Cambridge with their prerequisites of Latin, Greek and philosophy. The universities do not make a sincere attempt either to teach students how to make a living or how to live. They give the student a smattering of both and as a result he leaves the university knowing nothing of either.[62]

Students also debated the quality and methods of teaching, particularly the lecture system, which was defined by one writer, "as a process by which the notes of the lecturer are transferred to the notebook of the student without ever passing through the minds of either."[63] Remembered with special displeasure were those professors, such as Herbert L. Stewart, who read their notes word for word, year in and year out. A stimulating writer and nationally known broadcaster on political affairs, Stewart taught Philosophy I in a notoriously tedious fashion. Lecture notes purchased from previous students, and in at least one case provided by a parent who had studied under Stewart a generation earlier, helped some students through the year. The bold suggestion by one student that Stewart distribute his notes to class and then "talk to us like you do on the radio" was greeted coldly by the lecturer.[64] More stimulating was the teaching of historian George E. Wilson, whose lectures "painted a vivid picture of the past and of the forces at work."[65] Political scientist R.A. Mackay was described as an "ideal" professor, whose warm-hearted manner accompanied his determination to have students "think about political matters on their own."[66] Economist W.R. Maxwell, renowned for his barely audible speaking voice, examined economic issues without dogmatism, "from all points of view, conservative and radical." Wilson, Mackay and Maxwell provided Lawrence Read, who later became a university professor, with the type of quality teaching he never encountered elsewhere.[67]

Dalhousie offered students a strong, traditional, liberal arts education, breaking little new ground in the arts or sciences. With heavy teaching loads, enabling its youthful law faculty barely "to keep one jump ahead of the students,"[68] Dalhousie professors, like others in Canada, had little time and few resources to engage in extensive research and publication. Departments seldom had more than two professors who shared responsibility for up to a dozen courses. The English Department, under C.L. Bennett, focused almost exclusively on the literature of England. The calendar of 1939 offered some fifteen courses in British subjects, but none in Canadian or American literature. Until his death in 1933, the dominant figure in arts was the prolific Archibald MacMechan, professor of English, who taught at Dalhousie for more than forty years. A romantic, Victorian idealist, MacMechan wrote stories of eighteenth-century privateers, merchants and sailors, imbuing them with a deep sense of "Christian morality," and hearkening back to a more "heroic age," out of which the Nova Scotian community emerged as a noble and spirited British colony.[69] The imperial connection—always strong in Nova Scotia — was reinforced by the History Department, which in 1939 offered eight courses in European or British history, two in American, and two in Canadian, one of which put special emphasis on the history of the province. As with political science, where the textbooks included W.P.M. Kennedy's *The Constitution of Canada*, and A.V. Dicey's *Law of the Constitution*, history courses emphasized political and legal developments with[in] the British Empire. Possibly the most enduring publication by a Dalhousie arts professor was R.A. Mackay's classic, *The Unreformed Senate of Canada.*[70]

In science, students received a strong basic training from professors who had been taught by Lord Rutherford, the discoverer of the nucleus. According to William Archibald, a student who later taught physics at Dalhousie, the university in the 1930s was "twenty years behind the times," a common problem at small institutions cut off from the centres conducting new research. Archibald learned nothing of quantum mechanics at Dalhousie, and little about Einstein's theory of relativity— subjects he studied in depth only after he went to graduate school in the United States. The physicists and chemists who did publish (such as H.L. Bronson and G.H. Henderson) "did an awful lot of good work—within conventional areas."[71]

Though the teaching styles of professors varied, classes were generally conducted in an air of formality, with students addressed as Mr. or Miss. The men dressed in jackets and ties, the women in skirts and sweaters —never pants. As students "prayed"[72] for professional employment and worried about their futures, they worked their way through a curriculum which steeped them in the cultural heritage and intellectual traditions of British North American civilization. At Dalhousie Carleton Stanley's academic conservatism was combined with an increasingly utilitarian curriculum in an institution devoted to turning out respectable professionals—young adults who were civil, refined, and respectful of tradition. If students sometimes questioned the university's methods and rules, they did not seriously challenge the socialization process.

Universities and colleges of the 1920s and 1930s inherited children affected by the shifting social and economic forces of the late nineteenth and early twentieth centuries. As child labour was mechanized and disappeared, as professional training increasingly found its way into institutions of higher learning, as business diversified and government expanded, demanding better educated managers and supervisors, students spent longer in school, and the period of adolescence, only recently "invented," was prolonged.[73] This hiatus between childhood and adulthood drew more public attention both to new theories of child rearing, and to the spirited culture of middle class youth.[74] According to Paula Fass, "the young became more independent and newly dependent; independent of strict adult supervision but dependent for longer and longer periods upon the adult world that made peer groups necessary and upon the peers who made a transitional independence possible."[75]

Academic training constituted only part of the university's role. Students spent at least as much time participating in a wide array of "extracurricular" activities which on the one hand served as a necessary outlet for self-expression, and on the other hand demanded a culture of conformity consistent with the "respectable" middle-class lives for which they were being prepared. In the prosperous 1920s university officials sometimes feared they were losing control of carefree, undisciplined, and cynical students. The Depression, however, dampened the taste for anti-social behaviour, and as even Carleton Stanley noted, the balance between self-expression and conformity was restored: "Student life is always healthiest and sanest when it is spontaneous, and not too much observed and commented upon by elders and authorities. At some risk of infringing this rule, I should like to say that for the most part the life of our students is wholesome."[76] If the atmosphere of North American universities was generally subdued in the 1930s, at Dalhousie it was positively tranquil.

For Canadian students, the university was less an ivory tower than a sanctuary, offering welcome if temporary respite from an uncertain world. Dalhousie students may not have loved Carleton Stanley, but they loved their university. They poured enormous energy into the associational network available to them. Clubs, drama groups, fraternities, student government, dances, journalism, and athletics — as participants and cheering spectators — occupied their time outside the classroom. Peer culture placed a premium on "belonging," and most students, craving acceptance and fearing exclusion, joined something.

Loyalty to the university, encouraged by the administration, was expressed in a variety of ways, notably through celebrations carried on during "Munro Day," an annual event commemorating the university's past and optimistically revelling in its prospects.[77] The student newspaper greeted with jubilation the announcement of the $400 000 grant from the Carnegie Foundation in 1930, as it did the news in February 1938, that the Rt. Hon. R.B. Bennett, "Dalhousie's Most Distinguished Graduate," who had recently endowed a chair in the Law School, would be visiting the university. According to the *Gazette*, "Dalhousians will rejoice to hear that such a distinguished son and sturdy supporter of the University is to be in our midst, and we will no doubt give him a hearty welcome."[78]

The dates of upcoming sporting events, and particularly the football, hockey, or basketball victories they produced, bellowed from the front pages of the Gazette throughout the 1930s. When school spirit showed signs of flagging, the newspaper, along with the student council, lectured Dalhousians on the need to restore it. University-wide pep rallies sent the teams off to battle and greeted them upon return.[79] However popular their teams, Canadians universities devoted far less attention to inter-campus sports than did their counterparts in the United States, where the 1920s witnessed the appearance of a rash of "million-dollar stadiums" and lucrative athletic scholarships, and where sports became some colleges' biggest businesses.[80] Lacking both the financial resources and the inclination to corrupt academic life with "professionalism in athletics," Canadian universities could celebrate their teams' victories but take equal pride in keeping sport in its proper place.[81] Instead, Dalhousie students successfully agitated for compulsory physical education, which was instituted for freshmen in 1934. Carleton Stanley opposed the new regulation, viewing it as yet another example of the university yielding to a popular demand outside its legitimate prerogative: "Why any of you should wish compulsion in the matter of taking exercise and the enjoyment of young health I cannot understand." Students told him that compulsory physical education logically followed from compulsory mental preparation, and that it might increase participation in university sports.[82] Eventually, the Senate concurred.

Public health in general, particularly in Halifax with the memories of the 1917 explosion, the flu epidemic of 1918, and the physical costs of the First World War, received growing attention in universities. Educators increasingly viewed this aspect of adolescent development as part of the school's responsibility. In 1931 Dalhousie instituted compulsory medical examinations for all students, when, if necessary, they were immunized against smallpox, diphtheria and scarlet fever. In addition, doctors and nurses inspected "the living quarters of every student."[83] After it was reported in 1933 that 11 percent of students were not in good physical condition, the university sponsored, beginning the following January, a series of lectures on Hygiene and Health, compulsory for all new registrants. Students stayed away in droves.[84]

The university's involvement in the preparation of responsible leaders extended to student government. An elaborate organizational system, complete with bureaucracy, constitution and electoral process, provided interested students with managerial and political skills. In a characteristic editorial, the *Gazette*, playing the role of the Council of Students' watchdog, outlined the qualities that student leaders should possess:

> Upon the makeup of the student council will depend its efficacy. Its members should be conversant with the university and with university life and problems, for without these attributes it cannot act with authority and efficiency. The members should be "level-headed," that is, they should be capable of dealing circumspectly with problems. Haphazard and snap judgements leave many pitfalls in their train. On the other hand, the council should have initiative or stagnation will be the results of its rule.[85]

Once elected, the Council of Students' main function was to collect student activity fees and distribute them responsibly to approved campus organizations, ensuring that spending was in the "best interests of the student body as a whole, and [not] detrimental to the name of Dalhousie. . . . The Council shall be the only recognized medium between the student body and the University authorities and also between the student body and the general public."[86]

The Depression imposed special challenges on student councillors acting out their role as managers-in-training. In the spirit of "profession-alism," the council appointed veteran student leader and alumnus, Mur-ray Rankin, to the position of "permanent secretary-treasurer" at the honorarium of $350, and in 1934, like the university, the council grap-pled with the problem of diminishing revenues. Foreseeing a two-thou-sand-dollar drop in income, the result of declining enrolment, it ordered the *Dalhousie Gazette* to distribute the paper off-campus only to those with prepaid subscriptions. To save money, a less expensive printer was hired.[87] In addition the council could not afford to publish *Pharos*, the student yearbook, in 1934.

Despite its professional pretensions, the student council functioned within well-defined boundaries. Consistent with its role as overseer and guardian of student affairs, the University Senate exercised its power to approve the student council's constitution and any revisions. Student activity fees could be increased only with Senate sanction — which was withheld in 1936.[88] When student organizations occasionally failed to behave in a business-like manner, particularly in their relations with the public, the university was forced to bail them out. One such incident occurred in 1937, when the Dalhousie Glee and Dramatic Society per-formed three plays without paying the required copyright fees to a Toronto company. President Stanley's intervention eventually resolved the problem, but it left him exasperated with the students' irresponsibil-ity, and he offered this advice to companies dealing with them: "I cannot understand why business organizations give credit to any student organiz-ation, whatsoever. . . . A student organization, from the nature of things, has a personnel that changes annually and consequently is incapable of corporate responsibilty. . . . Any dealings with an organization so con-stituted should be on a strictly cash basis."[89]

Well beyond childhood, students were still at a stage of life demanding from their elders sometimes an iron hand and sometimes a velvet glove. Every fall a handful of Dalhousie "men" began the year by making a nuisance of themselves in the Halifax community. According to the Chief of Police, they "interfered with traffic, pushed cars from parking places, and accosted people on the streets."[90] In the latest incident they tossed an apple through the window of a doctor's home on Coburg Road. Understanding that boys would be boys, the Chief told Stanley that "we have always endeavoured to deal with them as leniently as possible." The president was grateful: "You have been very human and tolerant about the pranks of young blood, and we have tried to see to it that you will have few pranks to overlook."[91]

Mindful of its public image, and resolved to police itself, the university groped for a formula allowing students an outlet for animated but socially acceptable behaviour. The preferred approach on Canadian campuses involved a process through with student councils would voluntarily enforce university rules, acting as their own policemen. According to the Dalhousie calendar, "students conducting themselves in an unbecoming manner on or beyond the premises of the University during the session, may be fined, suspended, or expelled from the University. Since the formation of the Council of Students in 1912, that body holds an investigation and reports its findings to the Senate for action and may recommend penalties to be inflicted."[92]

Although student antics seldom got out of hand at Dalhousie in the 1930s, there was some confusion over the responsibility for establishing and administering regulations. In the mid 1920s, the university had created a "Committee of Nine," consisting of three faculty, three students, and three alumni, whose purpose was to act as a "final authority" in the "interpretation, construction and application" of rules governing student activities. By 1935, however, the Committee, though officially alive, was in practice "defunct."[93] In its place rule-breakers were punished usually by the Senate and occasionally by President Stanley or the Council of Students. Smoking in the halls or gymnasium earned a two-dollar fine for first offenders. A student who tore pages from several books in the medical library was fined one hundred dollars. At the insistence of the Council of Students, the Senate took measures to eliminate "cribbing" or cheating on examinations by "giving more attention to seating of candidates in the examination room." While students were required to attend lectures, and subject to fines if they did not, it was an open secret that this regulation was enforced only loosely, if at all, during the 1930s.[94] Drinking was prohibited on campus, though some students in Shirreff Hall, the women's residence, were known to imbibe in the privacy of their rooms. When prohibition ended in Nova Scotia in 1930, men who were old enough did their drinking openly and legally in Halifax hotels. While university officials frowned on the practice, they could not prevent it. Public drunkenness, however, was condemned by students, professors, and administrators alike.

Indicative of growing sober-mindedness in the 1930s was the elimination of the practice of hazing. This initiation ritual, in which freshmen were put through a series of humiliating and "sadistic" indignities by those in upper years, officially ended at Dalhousie in the fall of 1933.[95] Universities had tolerated this practice as part of freshmen orientation because it quickly integrated new students into campus culture. But violence, injuries, and a successful fifty-thousand-dollar law suit by one victim at the University of Alberta, convinced administrators and students at a number of Canadian universities that the socialization of students could be effectively conducted through less extreme methods.[96]

Dancing, the most popular extra-curricular activity, aroused the most discussion in the early 1930s. A *Gazette* editorial in 1930 claimed that Dalhousie was "on the verge of going dance crazy." Though Carleton Stanley tried to reassure the public that the problem had been exaggerated, he reported in 1933 that in February alone "at least sixteen dances had been held by Dalhousie students," the vast majority of which took place off-campus.[97] Dances were sponsored by various clubs and fraternities, and any attempt to deny them met with stern resistance. Facing enormous pressure from students in the professional schools, the Council of Students was forced in the fall of 1932 to rescind a ban on all off-campus dances.[98] While the socially less confident students avoided such events, confining their entertainment to such things as movies, for others they were the main forums through which the sexes mingled, where women were courted, and social graces learned. Aside from the more casual sock-hops in the gymnasium, dances were usually formal events, with men dressing in tuxedos and women in gowns. Orchestras were hired, dance cards were filled before the programme, and men enhanced their prestige by dancing with the most popular women. Officially, dances ended at 1:00 a.m., though special events, such as the Delta Games Ball, might go until 2:00 a.m. Customarily, faculty who were willing served as chaperons.[99]

Sexual activity among Dalhousie students remains something of a mystery. An American study on the sexual habits of college students concluded that in comparison with the more free-wheeling 1920s, students in the 1930s were more conservative and certainly more discreet. According to one American magazine, "sex is no longer news. And the fact that it is no longer news is news."[100] American college women evidently believed that intercourse with one's future husband was acceptable, though with anyone else it constituted promiscuous behaviour. One survey found that while half the men had had intercourse, only one-quarter of the women had, indicating the American students were more liberal in attitude than practice.[101] At Dalhousie the rules may have been broken occasionally, but men were not allowed to visit women in their residence rooms at Shirreff Hall. According to one former student, some men found sexual partners off-campus. Another claimed that there was little peer pressure to "go all the way."[102]

Almost as controversial as the amount of dancing was the appropriateness of university fraternities and sororities. Fraternities were first formed in the United States in 1820s, as self-governing social groups that "released students from the once stringent supervision that obtained in American academies."[103] They grew rapidly at the end of the nineteenth and in the early twentieth centuries, reaching a total of 3 900 chapters by 1930. While never as widespread in Canada, throughout the 1920s and 1930s Canadian students established "branch plant" chapters, receiving permission to affiliate with American fraternities. The first began at Dalhousie in 1930 and by 1937 there were seven fraternities and two sororities. Approximately 20 percent of Dalhousie students were fraternity members.[104] Dalhousie never actually recognized fraternities. Instead, the administration chose not to ban them. Carleton Stanley despised the institutions, believing them "discredited almost everywhere" in the United States and that they acted as a wasteful drain on the energies of students. That their members behaved irresponsibly by sometimes failing to pay their bills or by creating "grave disorders" on and off campus, also aroused Stanley's ire.[105] The *Gazette* also debated their value, opponents finding them guilty of making "invidious" distinctions among students, and of attempting to control campus politics.[106]

Despite these objections, fraternities thrived for two reasons. First, they provided a practical solution to the problem of residential housing for male students. Because Dalhousie had no male dormitory (though some men boarded at the Pine Hill Divinity Hall residence), students depended in part on the lodging provided by fraternity houses to help fill that need. There was no possibility of finding funds for the construction of a male residence during the Depression, though everyone recognized the need.[107] Secondly, the fraternities served as additional agencies by which the energies of students could be channelled and controlled, particularly at poorly facilitated campuses. In the absence of dining rooms and common rooms, they were an outlet for "the healthy, gregarious instinct of the college students."[108] Despite their periodic excesses, fraternity men and women projected an image of confidence, leadership, and wholesome competition that university officials and parents generally admired. "Conformity to what was believed to be a collegiate style epitomized by fraternity men and women was already self-imposed before a youth ever became a member."[109] Because fraternity leaders were anxious to gain credibility, they sponsored good-natured events on and off campus, and usually agreed to abide by university regulations with respect to smoking, drinking and initiation. If they confined their reckless activities to unsupervised fraternity houses, no one was the wiser. While Stanley believed that fraternities "added little to the progress of the University," he conceded they were under control at Dalhousie, "interfering much less with study" than elsewhere. As on other issues, he resigned himself to a youthful mode which he could temper but could not change.[110]

Fraternities at Dalhousie and elsewhere in Canada shared one set of values with the white, Anglo-Saxon culture around them. They were steeped in racial and religious prejudice. When critics denounced fraternity "cliquishness," they were referring not simply to the criteria for admission, which included a "good" family background, fashionable clothing, high grades, and a "friendly manner," but to unwritten codes barring non-whites and Jews. The Pi Beta Phi Sorority at Dalhousie officially rationalized its anti-Jewish policy on the grounds that the group's ritual was based on the New Testament, which Jews could not accept. Thus, even those who satisfied other admission standards, including a Jewish girl from Shirreff Hall "who everyone liked," could not make the grade because of their religion. The Law School fraternity, too, was "opened to everybody except Jews."[111] While the university made no attempt to challenge these prohibitions—indeed Jewish students themselves responded not by petitioning for entry, but by forming their own fraternity—Dalhousie's own admission policies were considerably more liberal than those of the fraternities.

Most Canadian universities began as religious colleges, and in the early twentieth century, even non-denominational institutions in English Canada, including Dalhousie, would have been pleased to think of themselves as "Christian" institutions. Indeed, Dalhousie officially required all students "not residing with parents of guardians . . . to report to the Office on or before October 15th the churches which they intend to make their places of worship during the session."[112] Issued probably more in prayer than conviction, this regulation seemed mostly designed to reassure parents, since failure to attend chapel was one student sin that the university tended to overlook.[113]

Still, amid an aura of Christian tradition and morality, how did Canadian universities deal with those outside the Christian faith? Some universities, notably McGill and Manitoba, actively, if not openly, discriminated against Jews by requiring them to achieve higher grades out of high school, or by imposing rigid quotas limiting their numbers in professional programmes.[114] Dalhousie's record compares favourably. There is no evidence that it followed such practices in the 1930s. Certainly, continuing concern about declining enrolments had some bearing on this policy of openness. Yet the figures speak for themselves. In a province where Jews made up .37 percent of the population in 1941, Jewish students comprised about 11 percent of Dalhousie's student

TABLE 4

Religious Affiliations of Dalhousie Students, 1930, 1935, 1939

Religious Denomination	Dalhousie Students 1930, 1935, 1939 %	Nova Scotia Population 1941 %	Canadian Population 1941 %
United	34.4	21.5	19.2
Anglican	22.6	17.9	15.2
Roman Catholic	15.1	32.7	43.4
Jewish	11.3	.4	1.4
Presbyterian	7.6	8.2	7.2
Baptist	6.3	15.4	4.2
Lutheran	.5	1.6	3.5
Other	2.2	2.3	5.9
Total	100 (2794 known cases)	100	100

SOURCE: Registration Books, 1930/31, 1935/36, 1939/40, Dalhousie University Archives; *Census of Canada, 1941*, Vol. 4, 56-60.

body.[115] Since a very high proportion of Dalhousie's Jewish students came from the eastern United States, where quotas in universities were notorious,[116] Dalhousie obviously did not follow the University of Alberta's policy, which refused admission to the medical school to Jews who lived outside the province.[117] In 1939, fourteen of the thirty-six graduates from Dalhousie medical school were Jews, all but one of whom were American. While these students were not welcomed socially, the university did not thwart their academic progress.

With respect to "coloured" students, very few went to Dalhousie during the 1930s. A small number (most of whom were Indian not black) were admitted each year from the West Indies, a practice followed in other Commonwealth universities.[118] Black youth from Halifax, however, virtually never attended the university. In 1920, President Mackenzie admitted that "if there were coloured men here in large numbers we might have [difficulties] develop." In Mackenzie's period the university denied black students who were not "British subjects" entry to the medical school.[119] In the 1930s all but one of Nova Scotia's hospitals (the Tuberculosis Hospital) refused to allow blacks to practise. Because of this the university chose in 1932 to refund tuition fees to a black student who was unable to do his internship.[120] Like other white Canadians, Nova Scotians recoiled at the prospect of physical contact with black doctors.

At one-quarter of the student population, women were Dalhousie's largest minority group. By the 1930s, the phenomena of women at work and in university were no longer novelties, though feminism as a political movement diminished in Canada following the achievement of universal suffrage at the end of the war in all provinces except Quebec. Magazines of the 1920s and 1930s devoted attention to the young business woman, to the profession of social work in which women were newly engaged, and to the remarkable lives of accomplished pioneers such as Agnes Macphail and Cora Hind.[121] At the same time advertising, features, and advice columns addressed women where most actually were—at home performing the roles of wives and mothers.[122]

The issue of "co-education" was discussed from time to time, usually with jocularity, in the *Dalhousie Gazette*—and more seriously by academics in the *Dalhousie Review*. Because their presence made the social life of the campus far more interesting, men appreciated having women at the university. Still, males tended to accept the prevailing view that women were primarily interested in being "social butterflies," which made them both light-hearted and light-headed. "The Women — Ah, God Bless all of 'em," declared Thomas A. Goudge, "but keep 'em away when we are trying to study."[123] Men had only to cite the more respectable views of *Dalhousie Review* contributors such as J.A. Lindsay and William D. Tait to confirm their prejudices: "The maternal instinct . . . makes [the woman's] view of life more personal, more bound up with the activities and sanctities of the home, likelier to be that of the family than of the tribe or the nation, more partial in judgement, less willing to be guided by the canons of abstract justice than the male." According to Tait, men had a greater facility for abstract thought owing to the larger size of their "frontal lobes."[124]

Periodically, outspoken women felt compelled to defend both the principle of co-education and their intellectual integrity, but feminism, as a philosophical issue, did not preoccupy them. Most were not interested in professional careers. At best, they intended to work for a short time after graduation until they married.[125] And without question, they cared intensely about campus social life (as did men); among them was a minority of upper class "peacocks" who fit the stereotype for whom the university was merely a "finishing school."[126] But to dismiss university women as "social butterflies" was a demeaning exaggeration. What most Dalhousie women sought from the university was not full equality but the type of independence and social skills that would improve their lives as women — whether at work or at home. To the degree that the university provided this, they cherished the experience and tolerated discrimination, both on and off campus, as a fact of life.

Women encountered special paternalism with respect to living arrangements. Unlike men, women away from home were required to live in residence (at Shirreff Hall) "except in very unusual circumstances."[127] Because Shirreff Hall was never fully occupied, the university had an economic incentive to increase the enrolment of women, which declined in the mid-1930s.[128] Within the residence they lived under a variety of regulations, mostly self-policed, and not considered especially oppressive, though they did carry on under the watchful eye of a "Warden." They were allowed to be out four nights a week until 11:00 p.m. (10:30 on Sundays), and later on weekends and dance nights. Those who broke curfew were punished with extra telephone duty, though chronic violators faced more serious discipline.[129]

As at other campuses, all Dalhousie women belonged to a single organization — the Delta Gamma Society (as distinct from the exclusive Delta Gamma Sorority). No such body existed for men. Delta Gamma was responsible for the initiation of "freshettes," and sponsored a variety of teas and dances throughout the year. Though men sometimes ridiculed its preoccupation with these social activities, women jealously guarded and defended Delta Gamma. It was the one institution in which they had exclusive autonomy and which addressed their interests uniquely.[130]

Those few women who studied "male" subjects such as law or commerce were perhaps viewed as "oddities," but they were not ostracized. If they openly expressed interest in a professional career, this too their female peers could accept, even if the men who controlled the professions were less open-minded. But these women were assumed to be choosing a vocation over marriage, a choice still considered by the majority to be second best.[131] On the other hand, working for a year or two after graduation as a teacher or secretary was deemed a useful and admirable way of making the transition from youth to full adulthood. The university facilitated this passage. Because women were not expected to become professionals in high status occupations, they lacked the reinforcement and reward network that motivated — and probably increased the pressure on — men. Still, society viewed highly educated women as more refined, better conversationalists, and even better homemakers, all qualities which made the university degree a valued commodity in middle class families.[132]

Neither feminism nor political radicalism in general fired the souls of most students in the Depression. Despite the propaganda of media barons, such as Randolph Hearst, who claimed communism was rampant in North American universities, more serious journalists and social psychologists in the United States found little evidence of "dangerous" ideas percolating among the vast majority of college youth.[133] Undeniably, American organizations such as the League for Industrial Democracy; the National Student League, and university-based "social problems" clubs actively campaigned for fundamental and sometimes revolutionary change; and periodically, pacifist groups organized impressive demonstrations, drawing thousands of students.[134] But militant political activity in the United States was sustained only among the ranks of the committed minority. At best students were found to be more "intellectually curious" and "slightly" more liberal than their parents; at worst they were "sheep-like," apathetic," and "fatalistic." The "Fitzgeraldian cockiness" of the 1920s, the passion for self-expression without ideology, had not congealed into a broad collective movement for political change in the 1930s.[135] The Depression made American students more serious, not more radical. Similar attitudes prevailed north of the border, where political activism was even more tempered, less threatening, and more easily contained by university officials when it did erupt. Dalhousie students were generally peaceable.

While Canadian campuses were sometimes illiberal, they were by no means consistently oppressive.[136] Universities normally faced little provocation from their students, and with notable exceptions, allowed debate on a wide variety of topical issues. In a period offering numerous possibilities for political discussion, debating was in fact a popular pastime on Canadian campuses. Judging from the issues argued at Dalhousie between 1933 and 1937 — sometimes before very large audiences — the anxious observer might have concluded that heresy permeated student life: Resolved that "this House deplores the policies of the Bennett government," that "this House would rather live in Moscow than Berlin"; that "Democracy in the past ten years has been proven to be a failure," that "the sit-down strike is a just weapon in the hands of organized labour"; that "this House approves an order based on socialist principles"; that "Hollywood should be razed."[137] Even if their supporters lost the arguments, Bennett, big business, and Hollywood need not have feared. Debating, like football, initiation, and student council elections was a spectacle—judged more on style than substance. Students enjoyed the intellectual tussle; they were impressed by the articulate, intelligent, and witty debaters — all social skills prized by cultured and educated middle class youth. When Dalhousie's debaters defeated those from Mount Allison, McGill, or better yet Oxford, students thrived in the glow of institutional superiority. But they did not make plans to move to Moscow.[138]

The main forum for the expression of student opinion was the *Dalhousie Gazette*, a weekly publication that reflected well the mood of the campus. Student newspaper editors in Canada sometimes ran into trouble with student councillors and university presidents if their printed opinions violated discretion and good taste. Publicly supporting petting cost a *Varsity* editor his position at the University of Toronto, probably the least tolerant university in the country. When the editor of the *Ubyssey* at the University of British Columbia criticized the provincial government's spending policies in 1931, he was suspended by the Board of Governors. When such incidents occurred, a code of solidarity was expressed in student papers across Canada. Like the *Dalhousie Gazette*, they normally took the side of the punished editors, and nobly defended the principle of free speech.[139] However, this was about as overtly political as the *Gazette*, under a variety of editors, ever became. Apparently, no such major confrontations occurred between the *Gazette* and its readers in the 1930s, though the paper closely and critically evaluated the performances of student politicians. Over the years, the tone of the *Gazette* was less feisty than that of other student papers.[140]

The *Gazette* took a back seat to no one in its role as a campus booster. Criticized on one occasion for its content, the paper explained its publishing philosophy. It claimed to be caught between those who wanted it to be a "tabloid, Winchellian" type of journal, and those who sought a mere literary publication. The editor claimed that the *Gazette* was neither. It was instead a "glorified bulletin board for student activities," and an organ of "student opinion." The paper's platform in 1936 called for such developments as a "vigorous arts and science society," a college band, a skating rink, friendlier relations with other colleges, and more efficient management of student affairs.[141] News, per se, played a minor role in this brand of journalism.

Muckraking did not interest the *Gazette*. Asked why the newspaper refused to identify students caught smoking in the gym in January 1935, the *Gazette* explained, somewhat melodramatically:

> The policy of the *Gazette* is to keep scandal out of its columns. We might print the actual names, if say, the parties concerned were

dismissed from the University. The students have a right to such news. But the harrowing details that mark the wreck of someone's reputation or life are not news; they are always abnormal and often debasing. We feel that the wreck of the reputation is bad enough, but to pry among the wreckage is ghoulish.[142]

The *Gazette* preferred good news, and let nothing, not even the outbreak of the Depression, stand in its way. The New Year's editorial called for 1930 to be "another wonderful year of progress," and the Depression itself was not deemed worthy of comment in the *Gazette* until 28 January 1931.

Student activism was muted at Dalhousie, but it was not absent. As institutions that dwell in the world of ideas and that temporarily free young people from the drudgery of earning a living, universities have always inspired a degree of unorthodox thinking. Circulated in the 1930s, the provocative writings of F. Scott Fitzgerald, John Dos Passos, Sinclair Lewis, Thomas Wolfe, and Bertrand Russell captured a mood which combined cynicism, alienation, black humour and the spirit of reform.[143] Once touched by radical thinking, some students became deeply committed to political action, particularly if their iconoclasm received positive reinforcement from a tight network of family and peers.[144] For these students—the socialists, communists, humanitarians, and pacifists—the substance of political debate mattered far more than the style.

The most enduring of such groups at Dalhousie was the Student Christian Movement. Founded in Canada in 1920 amid a post-war quest for permanent peace and moral order, the SCM was a creature of the social gospel, a Christian reform movement "seeking to realize the Kingdom of God in the very fabric of society."[145] SCM study groups convened on campuses across Canada, and gathered at conferences throughout the 1920s and 1930s. While other reform groups came and went during the Depression, the SCM's moderation and righteousness earned it a secure place at "Christian" institutions such as Dalhousie. A number of faculty members, including Carleton Stanley, regularly donated money to the organization. Some of the SCM's members participated in seminars led by H.L. Bronson, who conducted sessions on the "synoptic gospel," or the search for the true meaning and applicability to contemporary social problems of the life of Jesus.[146] Though nominally evangelical, the SCM did little aggressive recruiting among Dalhousie students. With an annual membership of twenty-five or thirty, it sponsored talks on the "world in crisis," and "practicality and Christianity," and provided an important outlet for the minority devoted to combining Christian living with social change.[147]

Less interested in social change than student services, the National Federation of Canadian University Students (NFCUS) received the regular support of student councillors and editors. Established in 1926 in the spirit of internationalist idealism, NFCUS interpreted its mandate conservatively, and committed itself not to disturbing political convention, but to serving the special material needs of college youth. Best known for its sponsorship of the popular exchange programme, in which students from one part of Canada would spend a year of university in another region, NFCUS also arranged discount travel rates and sponsored debates and other competitions.[148] Each year a small number of Dalhousie students participated actively in the organization.

For some Canadian students, however, the NFCUS approach to students' concerns was too narrow and its actions too timid. As the result of an impressive organizational effort by the SCM, a national conference of students was arranged in December 1937 at the University of Manitoba in Winnipeg. More than three hundred student representatives from twenty campuses attended, and they tackled issues ranging from the quality of education to Canadian foreign policy. They listened to speeches by reformers such as Reinhold Niebuhr from New York, and King Gordon, vice-chairman of the Cooperative Commonwealth Federation (CCF). For many students, the conference represented the first time they had travelled out of their own province, and they were absorbed in debates such as that between Catholic activist students in Quebec (who defended the repressive Padlock Law) and defenders of Communists' right to free speech. Gene Hicks, a member of the Dalhousie delegation, recalls the conference, with its left-of-centre orientation, as a moving and stimulating experience.[149] Out of the conference emerged a left-wing rival to NFCUS, the Canadian Student Assembly, whose major activity, supported by Dalhousie, was a successful campaign for a programme of national scholarships, instituted in 1939.[150] In the period following the Spanish Civil War, communists carried their campaign against fascism onto campuses across the nation. They were especially active in Montreal. While some Dalhousians recall a small number of communists on the campus, and forums sponsored by the communist-led League Against War and Fascism, communists had virtually no impact on Dalhousie student life.[151]

Some Dalhousie students sympathized with the democratic socialist CCF but its influence on the campus was also limited. John Webster Grant, a CCF partisan, attended meetings of the organization in Halifax while enrolled at Dalhousie from 1935 to 1938, but he and others recall that the campus proved to be far from fertile recruiting ground for the CCF.[152] Dalhousians such as Angus L. Macdonald, a law student in the early 1920s and a professor of law later in the decade, channelled their reformist energy into the Nova Scotia Liberal Party, which came to power under Macdonald's leadership in 1933.[153] On the whole, however, Dalhousie students during the Depression distanced themselves from political movements promoting far-reaching social change.

That the collapsed economy of the 1930s provoked more debate than political activism among Dalhousie students—and others in Canada—is not surprising, and perhaps in a small way reflected the mood in the country as a whole. The Depression was an ordeal requiring from its victims creative strategies for survival. People, especially young people, were cynical of politicians, and as Gene Hicks noted, not conditioned to believe that government could "do much in the field of economics and welfare." The need to survive overwhelmed any inclination among most students to join movements for social reform—on or off-campus. Socialists, and even communists, were listened to with interest, but then dismissed as well-meaning dreamers. For struggling middle class students, the university was an important part of their formula for survival. It armed them with a degree which, in the long run, they hoped to turn into secure professional employment. In the short term the university was a temporary oasis, which, for most students, helped make the Depression bearable.[154]

One issue did spark more than passing interest among Dalhousie students in the 1930s. The legacy and prospect of war hovered over and even haunted the lives of young people growing up in the Depression. Students in North America, and particularly in Europe, were sometimes jarred from political stupor and youthful gaiety to express genuine alarm over the possibility of a renewed bloodletting into which they might be drawn.[155] While a Depression economy was something they quietly endured, the prospect of world war roused active concern precisely because it brought survival itself into question. Though students were hardly obsessed with the issue on a daily basis, it occupied a permanent place in the recesses of their minds, and even before 1939, was periodically pushed to the forefront.

A national petition campaign was organized in late 1931, encouraging Prime Minister Bennett, in rather vague terms, to push for peace at the upcoming Geneva Peace Conference on Disarmament. In urging students to sign, the *Gazette* denounced the "hypocritical platitudes" of politicians who talked peace while preparing for war. That peace was not simply a student concern was indicated by a front page letter in the *Gazette* from President Stanley, urging everyone to take an active interest in the campaign.[156] Another peace plebiscite, following the Italian invasion of Ethiopia in 1935, asked Canadian students whether the League of Nations should confront invading powers with economic and/or military sanctions, and whether students would be "prepared to bear arms." While more than 50 percent of Dalhousie students answered the questionnaire, the results were far from clear-cut. The *Gazette* concluded that "Dalhousie students . . . want to punish Italy but they don't want to have any part in the punishing."[157] In March of 1936, in solidarity with peace actions elsewhere in the country, Dalhousie students elicited the agreement of the university to cancel classes for a meeting to discuss "Dalhousie's contribution to the peace movement."[158]

Like others in Canada, Dalhousie students were somewhat slow to recognize the threat of fascism, particularly in Germany. In early 1934, the *Gazette* carried an article defending the German sterilization act, under the headline "Hitler: Scientist of Progress."[159] Two months earlier, an article by a member of Dalhousie's Officer Training Corps defended Hitler's success at bringing the "German people out of their slough of despondency by a system of organization and national thought."[160] Somewhat uncharacteristically, however, a commentary in October 1936 challenged the British policy of appeasement: "It is difficult to reconcile the tremendous warlike preparation 'in Germany,' their persecution of innocent Jews, and the suppression of truth as compatible with peace."[161]

When war finally did erupt, most traces of isolationist sentiment disappeared. The pro-imperial bias, deeply rooted in the Halifax community, found renewed expression at the university.[162] Just as "Dalhousians" had "Mourned the Death of their Beloved Sovereign" in 1936,[163] so too they enthusiastically joined the national crusade on behalf of the empire in 1939. The Dalhousie branch of the Canadian Officers' Training Corps, in existence since 1915, saw its membership triple (voluntarily) in the fall of 1939 to more than four hundred students and graduates.[164] Once compulsory military training was imposed on male students in Canada in 1940, the problem of "conscientious objectors" did not emerge at Dalhousie, though as Carleton Stanley noted, "there has been a lot of trouble at other institutions."[165] When Dalhousie students voted to withdraw from the Canadian Student Assembly early in 1940, along with a number of other Canadian campuses, they disassociated themselves from any political actions that could be interpreted as unpatriotic. The CSA held a conference in January 1940, in which considerable sentiment (especially among Quebec students) was expressed against the possible imposition of conscription for wartime service. Opinions polarized, and the Mount Allison delegation led a walkout claiming that the conference was being manipulated by those who were "anti-British, anti-war, and anti all those principles which form our ties with the British Empire."[166] Though opinions were divided at Dalhousie, the anti-CSA and presumably "pro-British" forces carried the day.

Canadian universities had not been spared the injurious impact of the Depression. But in spite of severe financial difficulties, they carried on their role of reproducing and perpetuating the culture of middle class Canada. By training professionals, universities enabled students from modest backgrounds to achieve lives, not of luxury, but of relative comfort and assured status. In one way, a collapsed economy made this process more difficult by delaying the delivery of secure employment. But in another way it made the process easier, for the Depression took the fight, if not the fear, out of most students. They studied harder, and outside the classroom they lived vigorously within a peer culture

approved and overseen by adult educators. When students occasionally
got out of hand, a well-defined system of social control restored order.
Universities attempted, in ways that would be impossible in future generations, to govern the behaviour of students both on and off campus.
Transgressors were sometimes punished and sometimes protected by the
tolerance shown youthful indiscretion. University officials may have
worried about the emergence of a broadly based oppositional culture,
but the one political campaign out of which this threatened to develop
— the peace movement — was, before the war, more respectable than
menacing. If Canada's Prime Minister could flirt with the politics of
isolationism, so too could Canadian students. When the war broke out
English-Canadian students, like their parents, willingly joined the parade.

Like other universities, Dalhousie weathered the Depression and successfully managed the lives of the middle class youth placed in its custody.
The university was neither a narrow-minded nor an irreverent educational institution. Its students inherited the civility, the respect for education, the cultural prejudices, and the liberal-conservative temperament
of the community which enveloped them. Undoubtedly they would pass
these values on. In December 1929 a *Gazette* correspondent wrote,
prophetically:

> College students today will be the citizens of the world tomorrow,
> and the spirit which today seems to flame in revolutionary colors
> will tomorrow infuse new life and vigor into society. The college
> man who is the ring leader in the so called "college pranks" may
> become the strong and just leader of the law court. The co-ed who
> is forever "on duty" for staying out too late will want her daughter
> to keep within her leave. The students who kick hardest against
> the rules and regulations will be the staunchest, the sternest uphold-
> ers of university traditions against the surging tide of youth.[167]

Notes

1. Some recent histories of Canadian universities which have broken out of this
traditional genre are John G. Reid, *Mount Allison University: A History to 1963*, 2
vols. (Toronto, 1984); Charles M. Johnston, *McMaster University*, 2 vols. (Toronto,
1976, 1981); Frederick Gibson. *Queen's University: To Serve and Yet Be Free*, vol. 2,
1917–1961 (Montreal, 1983); and George Rawlyk and Kevin Quinn, *The Redeemed of
the Lord Say So: A History of Queen's Theological College*, 1912–1972 (Kingston, 1980).
2. There is no full scale history of Dalhousie. Historical information can be found
in D.C. Harvey, *An Introduction to the History of Dalhousie* (Halifax, 1938); John
Willis, *A History of Dalhousie Law School* (Toronto, 1979); Centenary Committee,
Dalhousie University, *One Hundred Years of Dalhousie* (Halifax, 1919); Peter Waite.
"Playing at Universities: Dalhousie and the Sectarian Struggles in Nova Scotia," in
Higher Education in Canada: Historical Perspectives, ed. A. Gregor and K. Wilson
(Winnipeg, 1979), 67-81; Judith Fingard, "They Had a Tough Row to Hoe,"
Dalhousie Alumni Magazine (Winter 1985): 27-30; Robin Harris, *A History of Higher*

Education in Canada: 1663–1960 (Toronto, 1976); Patrick Keane, "Dalhousie University and the Nontraditional Student: The First Century," *Dalhousie Review* 63 (Summer 1983): 277-97. On the development of professional education, see A. Flexner, *Medical Education: A Comparative Study* (New York, 1925); Colin D. Howell, "Reform and the Monopolistic Impulse: The Professionalization of Medicine in the Maritimes," *Acadiensis* 11, no. 1 (Autumn 1981): 3-22; C.B. Stewart "One Hundred Years of Medical Education at Dalhousie," *Nova Scotia Medical Bulletin* 47, no. 5 (1968): 149-52; W.S. Learned and K.C.M. Sills, *Education in the Maritime Provinces of Canada* (New York, 1922); Harris, *History of Higher Education in Canada*, 259-306 and "Legal Education in Canada," *Canadian Bar Review* 1 (1923): 671-84, and 2 (1924): 376-89.

3. The figure of 970 students is lower than the actual number of registrants (before drop-outs), 1 016, which forms the basis of statistical analyses later in this paper. Official figures can be found in Dalhousie University, *President's Report, 1931–32*, Dalhousie University Archives (hereinafter DUA). On the distribution of students in various programmes see Fred Pearson to Carleton Stanley, 17 December 1931, Correspondence—Fees File, President's Office Papers, DUA. The calculation of the sexual distribution of students is based on registrations in September, found in "Registration Book, 1930–31," DUA. See table 1.

4. D.L. Thomson, "McGill Between the Wars," cited in Harris, *History of Higher Education*, 353. There were 35 926 full-time students in 1930–31, 35 108 in 1935–36, and 36 386 in 1940–41: *Historical Compendium of Education Statistics: From Confederation to 1975*, Statistics Canada, 81-568 (Ottawa, 1978), 208. For other accounts of the financial problems of Canadian universities in the 1930s, see Gibson, *Queen's University*, 2: 83-155; Johnston, *McMaster University*, 2: 39-83; Michael Hayden, *Seeking a Balance: The University of Saskatchewan 1907–1982* (Vancouver, 1983), 153-99; John G. Reid, *Mount Allison University*, 2: 60-143. In addition, interviews conducted by the author with students in Western Canada and from Dalhousie provided considerable information about the impact of the Depression on their lives.

5. Dalhousie University Board of Governors' Minutes, 24 November 1939, DUA.

6. Willis, *History of Dalhousie Law School*, 125.

7. Board of Governors' Minutes, 19 December 1932, 26 January and 26 April 1933, DUA; Fingard, "They Had a Tough Row to Hoe," 29.

8. Carleton Stanley, "Dalhousie Today," *Dalhousie Review* 18 (1938–39): 216-28.

9. Board of Governors' Executive Minutes, 2 September 1932, DUA.

10. "Financial Statistics of Universities and Colleges in Canada, 1921–1939," in Dominion Bureau of Statistics, *Higher Education in Canada, 1938–40* (Ottawa, 1941), 54-56. In a 1931 speech to the National Conference of Canadian Universities, W.E. McNeill from Queen's University claimed that some students were paying up to 50 percent of costs: cited in Gwendoline Pilkington, "A History of the National Conference of Canadian Universities, 1911–1961" (D.Ed. thesis, University of Toronto, 1974), 271-72.

11. Over President Stanley's objections, the Board raised tuition fees in 1932: Carleton Stanley to Board Executive, "Matter of Raising Fees," 9 June 1932, Correspondence—Fees File, President's Office Papers, DUA. And over the objection of students, the university imposed incidental library and diploma fees of five and twenty dollars respectively in 1934: Howard Oxley to Stanley, 16 February 1934; and Stanley to Oxley, 7 March 1934, Correspondence—Council of the Students' File, President's Office Papers, DUA. In addition, students from outside the British

Commonwealth paid higher fees ($300) than other Dalhousie students. Law students paid fees of $250 in 1932. See also Dominion Bureau of Statistics, *Higher Education in Canada, 1936–38* (Ottawa, 1939), 13; and Stanley, "Dalhousie Today."

12. Dalhousie University Senate Minutes, 13 May 1933, DUA.

13. Ibid.

14. Dominion Bureau of Statistics, *Higher Education in Canada, 1936–38*, 16-18; Jack Chernick, "National Scholarship," *The Manitoba Arts Review* 1, no. 2 (Fall 1938): 30-32.

15. *Calendar, Dalhousie University, 1939–40*, 18; C.H. Mitchell to Board of Governors, Board of Governors' Minutes, 7 April 1932, DUA.

16. Interviews: Eric Mercer, 11 August 1983; Jean Begg, 13 August 1983; Henry Hicks, 8 August 1983; William Archibald, 12 August 1983.

17. The percentage of Mount Allison students from communities of under a thousand people had fallen from 36.2 to 29.3 between 1930 and 1939, while those from cities and towns over 10 000 increased from 19.6 to 27.7: Reid, *Mount Allison University*, 2: 143.

18. Carleton Stanley, "School and College," speech to National Conference of Canadian Universities, 6 June 1934, Correspondence—Conference of Canadian Universities, President's Office Papers, DUA, also cited in Pilkington, "National Conference of Canadian Universities, 1911–1961," 253.

19. Lawrence Read, interview with author, 8 September 1983.

20. Gene Hicks, interview with author, 12 August 1983.

21. Henry Hicks, interview with author, 8 August 1983.

22. William Archibald, interview with author, 12 August 1983; Gene Hicks, interview with author, 12 August 1983. Other interviews that confirmed these impressions were conducted with Dr. Ian S. Robb, 11 June 1985; Dr. Harry D. Smith, 12 June 1985; John Webster Grant, 20 June 1985. Grant, whose father was a minister, recalled, "we were economically poor but respectable."

23. The construction of an occupational scale was made possible by registration forms filled out by students which, among other things, asked them to identify their father's occupation. Before creating an occupational class scale, the following sources were consulted: Bernard Blishen, "The Construction and Use of an Occupational Class Scale," *Canadian Journal of Economics and Political Science* 24 (November 1958): 519-31; Bernard Blishen, "A Socio-economic Index for Occupations in Canada," *Canadian Review of Sociology and Anthropology* 4, no. 1 (February 1967): 41-53; P.C. Pineo and John Porter, "Occupational Prestige in Canada," ibid., 24-40; Michael B. Katz, "Occupational Classification in History," *Journal of Interdisciplinary History* 3, no. 1 (Summer, 1972): 63-88; Donald J. Treiman, *Occupational Prestige in Comparative Perspective* (New York, 1977); Allan Sharlin, "On the Universality of Occupational Prestige" (review of Treiman), *Journal of Interdisciplinary History* 11, no. 1 (Summer 1980): 115-25; Andrea Tyree and Billy G. Smith, "Occupational Hierarchy in the United States: 1789–1969," *Social Forces* 56, no. 3 (March 1978): 881-99. The scale created is similar, though not identical, to a number of those used in the sources cited above. As always, the categorization of some occupations demanded choices which some might dispute. For example, should a self-employed "photographer" be categorized as skilled worker-artisan or as a businessman? (I chose the former.) Is a "foreman" a supervisor or a skilled worker? (I chose the latter.) I was guided, in part, by Donald Treiman's book, which argues, on the basis of occupational scales used in more than sixty societies, that with few exceptions, the "prestige" of occupations has been remarkably consistent over time. Treiman's scale was consulted for advice on controversial rankings. However the handful of difficult placements are ranked, the

overall percentages would be only marginally affected. Finally, it should be noted that the "Business" category makes no attempt, since the registration forms do not allow for it, to distinguish between "big" business and "small" business. I have tackled this problem by following up those Nova Scotian businessmen identified as "merchants." I would like to thank Gordon Darroch for his advice on this issue.

24. *Census of Canada,* 1941 (Ottawa, 1946), 7: 6-7. Working-class youth may have comprised a larger proportion of students attending Nova Scotian universities such as Acadia and St. Francis Xavier.

25. Information on the assets of students' fathers comes from R.G. Dun and Co., *The Mercantile Agency Reference Book for the Dominion of Canada,* various issues, 1920–1932; and R.G. Dun and Bradstreet, *The Mercantile Agency Reference Book for the Dominion of Canada,* various issues, 1933, 1934. The limitations of the Dun and Bradstreet records should be noted. Family income or wealth derived from sources outside the individual business are not recorded.

26. Analysis of the background of students at the University of British Columbia and at the University of Alberta shows similar trends, with the exception that at Alberta a far higher percentage of students came from farming families. Though comparable data are not available, students at the University of Saskatchewan appeared to have been the poorest in Canada. According to an ex-president of this university "in 1934–35, [promissory] notes were accepted from 600 students, approximately one-third of the total in attendance," who could not pay tuition: W.P. Thompson, *The University of Saskatchewan: A Personal History* (Toronto, 1970), 124-25. While no analysis has yet been done of the backgrounds of students from the University of Toronto and McGill University, this author would not be surprised to find that students at those institutions were more affluent than those in the Maritimes or Western Canada. See also Gibson, *Queen's University,* 11: 110.

27. John Porter, *The Vertical Mosaic* (Toronto, 1965), 274, 282-83.

28. *The Alumni News* (Halifax) various issues, 1930–1980.

29. *The Canada Year Book,* 1941 (Ottawa, 1941), 892-94.

30. Information on students' careers comes from *The Dalhousie Alumni News* (Halifax), various issues, 1920–1927, and *The Alumni News,* various issues, 1938–1980.

31. Leonard Kitz, interview with author, 9 August 1983; Eric Mercer, interview with author, 11 August 1983.

32. *The Dalhousie Alumni News,* and *The Alumni News,* various issues.

33. Ibid.

34. In 1930, thirty-one women graduated as doctors in Canada compared to twenty-seven in 1939, while over the same period, the number of male graduate doctors increased from 518 to 565. Eight women lawyers graduated from Canadian universities in 1930 compared to ten in 1939; by contrast, the number of male lawyers rose from 211 to 254. While the number of male engineering graduates rose from 324 to 629 between 1930 and 1939, Canadian universities produced one female engineer in the former year and none in the latter: *The Canada Year Book,* 1941, 892. According to the 1931 census, 14 percent of all female teachers, 16 percent of all nurses, and 90 percent of all nuns were unpaid. In total, 20 percent of women in "professional" occupations were unpaid compared to less than 6 percent of men. Valuable information on the Canadian experience can be found in Marjorie Cohen, "Crisis and the Female Labour Reserve: The Canadian Depression Experience," unpublished paper, presented to the Blue Collar Workers Conference, Windsor, Ontario, 1979. I am grateful to Marjorie Cohen for providing me with access to this paper. For discussions of the American experience, see Jane Humphries, "Women:

220   PAUL AXELROD

Scapegoats and Safety Valves in the Great Depression," *The Review of Radical Political Economics* 8, no. 1 (Spring 1976): 98-121; Ruth Milkman, "Women's Work and Economic Crisis: Some Lessons of the Great Depression," ibid., 73-97; Frank Stricker, "Cookbooks and Law Books: The Hidden History of Career Women in Twentieth-Century America," *Journal of Social History* 10, no. 1 (Fall 1976): 1-19; Susan Ware, *Holding Their Own: American Women in the 1930s* (Boston, 1982), 69-72. See also Susan Carter, "Academic Women Revisited: An Empirical Study of Changing Patterns in Women's Employment as College and University Faculty, 1890–1963," *Journal of Social History* 14, no. 4 (Summer 1981): 675-99.

35. The occupational-class background study of Dalhousie students showed no significant differences between men and women. But since this study contains very little information on the incomes of students' families, it is possible that such differences did exist. The fact that women found it more difficult to find summer employment suggests that their families needed access to greater resources to keep daughters at university. Most ex-Dalhousians interviewed were under the impression that women came from more affluent families. For example, interview with Grace Wambolt, 13 June 1985.

36. On courses in agriculture, see *Report of the Board of Governors and President of the University of Alberta, 1935–36,* 15-16. University of Alberta Archives, Edmonton. The Faculty of Agriculture included Departments of Poultry, Horticulture, Dairying, and Field Crops. See also Robert Newton, "The University: A Laboratory for Alberta," *The Trail* 49 (December 1941), the alumni magazine. On the University of Manitoba, see F.W. Ransom, "How Has the M.A.C. (Manitoba Agricultural College) Helped the Community," copy included in University of Manitoba: Correspondence, 3210/5-4, President's Papers, University of Alberta Archives. On Saskatchewan, see "Report to Advisory Council on Agriculture," *President's Report, University of Saskatchewan, 1931–32,* and *Calendar, The University of Saskatchewan, 1935–36,* 92-103, Archives, University of Saskatchewan, Saskatoon.

37. Queen's University introduced the first commerce course in Canada in 1919: Gibson, *Queen's University,* 2: 35-37. Dalhousie introduced a Bachelor of Commerce degree in 1928, and the University of British Columbia did so in 1931: *Graduate Chronicle,* University of British Columbia (April, 1931), 12.

38. See Gibson, *Queen's University,* 2: 169-71; see also Barry Ferguson and Douglas Owram, "Social Scientists and Public Policy from the 1920s through World War II," *Journal of Canadian Studies* 15, no. 4 (Winter 1980–81): 3-17.

39. For example, what had been the Department of Philosophy in 1931 at the University of British Columbia had become, by 1939, the Department of Philosophy and Psychology: *Calendar, University of British Columbia, 1930–31,* 159-62; and *Calendar, 1939–40,* 160-65. Dalhousie's Philosophy and Psychology Departments were also combined. For a discussion of trends in the teaching of psychology, see Peter Hampton, "Schools of Psychology," *Queen's Quarterly* 46, no. 3 (1939): 287-93.

40. Dalhousie University, *President's Report, 1935–36,* 1-2, DUA.

41. On the colonial philosophers, see A.B. McKillop, *A Disciplined Intelligence: Critical Inquiry and Canadian Thought in the Victorian Era* (Montreal, 1979), 5, 232. S.E.D. Shortt refers to the conflict as one between "idealism" and "empiricism": *The Search for an Ideal: Six Canadian Intellectuals and their Convictions in an Age of Transition, 1890–1930* (Toronto, 1976).

42. F. Ronald Hayes, "Two Presidents, Two Cultures, and Two Wars: A Portrait of Dalhousie as a Microcosm of Twentieth-Century Canada," *Dalhousie Review* 54, no. 3 (Autumn 1974): 405-17. According to material in the McGill University Archives, Stanley's ideas and approach to his work were not popular in all

administrative circles at McGill. McGill Principal Arthur Currie initially opposed
Stanley's appointment as Assistant to the Principal. After Stanley's departure from
McGill, there was considerable resentment at McGill of the media's portrayal of
Stanley as an "indispensable" aide to Currie. See Dalhousie University File, Principal's
Papers, RG2 G43, McGill University Archives, Montreal.

43. Wallace was President of The University of Alberta (1928–36) and Principal of
Queen's (1936–51). Arthur Currie was Principal of McGill (1920–1933). Walter
Murray was President of the University of Saskatchewan (1907–1937). G.J. Trueman
was President of Mount Allison University (1923–45).

44. McKillop, *A Disciplined Intelligence*, cites Northrop Frye on "concern," by
which he means "something which includes the sense of the importance of preserving
the integrity of the total human community," ix.

45. On J.S. Thomson, President of the University of Saskatchewan (1937–1949),
see Hayden, *Seeking a Balance*, 193-205; and on Hamilton Fyfe, Principal of Queen's
(1930–1936), see Gibson, *Queen's University*, 2: 88-132. A revealing exchange of
views can be found in Thomson to Stanley, 16 December 1938 and Stanley to
Thomson, 21 December 1938, series II, B-138, Presidential Papers, Archives,
University of Saskatchewan. According to Thomson, with the typical university
curriculum, students "pay your money and take your choice."

46. Frederick Rudolph, *The American College and University: A History* (New York,
1965), 479-80. Hutchins' famous work was *The Higher Learning in America* (New
Haven, 1936).

47. Stanley, "School and College."

48. "Inauguration Address," 9 October 1931, Board of Governors' Minutes, 29
October 1931, DUA. The speech was reprinted in *The Halifax Chronicle* and
accompanied by favourable editorial comment under the headline, "The Best Male
Brains," 10 October 1931. Stanley's views were shared by Robert Falconer, president
of The University of Toronto, who complained about the domination of school
teaching by women: Pilkington, "National Conference of Canadian Universities,
1911–1961," 222.

49. As cited in Hayes, "Two Presidents," 409-10.

50. Stanley claimed to be citing the views of W.S. Learned, co-author of the 1922
report on higher education in the Maritimes for the Carnegie Foundation for the
Advancement of Teaching: Stanley to J.S. Thomson, 21 December 1938. According
to Stanley, "After announcing that there were seven matriculation subjects, the
calendar went on to say that those who had passed English and any other three
subjects would be admitted to Dalhousie," with the effect that "the boys looked over
the list, of course, and decided that Latin, Mathematics, French, or German were the
best three subjects to miss. In my first year here 28 percent of those in the Arts faculty
— and this included many in the fourth year — had not matriculated."

51. Board of Governors' Minutes, 29 October 1931, DUA.

52. Senate Minutes, 21 April 1932 reflect some tightening of the rules, though the
university did not go as far as Stanley would have liked: Hayes, "Two
Presidents," 409.

53. Board of Governors' Minutes, 26 April 1940, DUA.

54. Board of Governors' Minutes, 7 April 1937, 3 March and 31 August 1938,
DUA. The new library cost $106 758, of which $50 000 was provided by the
Carnegie Foundation.

55. "Student Government History, #59," *Dalhousie Gazette* (Halifax), 8 January
1976. See note 77.

56. Interviews with: Lawrence Read, 8 September 1983; Leonard Kitz, 9 August

1983; Zilpha Linkletter, 11 August 1983; Eric Mercer, 11 August 1983; William Archibald, 12 August 1983; Dr. Harry Smith, 12 June 1985; Grace Wambolt, 13 June 1985. However, Dane Parker (15 June 1985) liked Stanley because he believed that the president was a defender of those who expressed dissident views.

57. Lola Henry, interview with author, 16 August 1983. Files in the President's Office reveal a good deal of personal interest taken by Stanley in the problems of students. There are several cases of his arranging for bursaries or loans for students who could not otherwise afford to come to Dalhousie. He wrote elaborate letters to students or their parents. His tone was always sympathetic though he was more than usually frank about the academic potential and performance of students. He had a number to dinner. See the following correspondence: George Sellars to Stanley, 7 October 1935; Stanley to Sellars, 15 October 1935; Margaret Kendall to Stanley, 3 February 1935; Stanley to Mrs. Kendall, 6 February 1935, Student Correspondence Files, President's Office Papers, DUA.

58. See Gibson, *Queen's University*, 2: 66-68; Hayden, *Seeking a Balance*, 139-50; W.H. Johns, *A History of the University of Alberta, 1908-1969* (Edmonton, 1981), 92-94.

59. Stanley, "Dalhousie Today," *Dalhousie Review* 18 (1938): 219; *President's Report, 1931-32*, 3, DUA.

60. *Pharos* (1933), 53.

61. *Dalhousie Gazette*, 29 October 1930.

62. *Dalhousie Gazette*, 2 October 1936. Many columns, including this one, were unsigned.

63. W.M., *Dalhousie Gazette*, 3 December 1937. See also Robert F. Legget, "The Lecture System," *Queen's Quarterly* 46, no. 2 (1939): 207-14.

64. Zilpha Linkletter, interview with author, 11 August 1983.

65. Lawrence Read, interview with author, 8 September 1983.

66. Ibid.

67. Ibid.; Gene Hicks, interview with author, 12 August 1983; John Webster Grant, interview with author, 20 June 1985.

68. Willis, *History of Dalhousie Law School*, 137.

69. Shortt, *The Search for an Ideal*, 41-57.

70. Dicey's *Introduction to the Study of the Law of the Constitution* was published originally in 1889. Mackay's book was published by Oxford University Press in 1926.

71. William Archibald, interview with author, 12 August 1983.

72. Henry Hicks, interview with author, 8 August 1983: "We used to translate Dalhousie's motto, Ora et labora—pray and work—into pray for work."

73. Joseph Kett, *Rites of Passage: Adolescence in America, 1790 to the Present* (New York, 1977), 215-72; John Gillis, *Youth and History*, expanded ed. (New York, 1981), 169; Dominion Bureau of Statistics, *Dependency of Youth* (Ottawa, 1937), 9. In Canada the school-leaving age rose from fourteen to sixteen between 1911 and 1931. See also Selwyn K. Troen, "The Discovery of the Adolescent by American Educational Reformers, 1900-1920: An Economic Perspective," in *Schooling and Society: Studies in the History of Education*, ed. Lawrence Stone (Baltimore, 1976).

74. Norah L. Lewis, "Creating the Little Machine: Child Rearing in British Columbia, 1919-1939," *B.C. Studies* 56 (Winter 1982-83): 44-60; Norah L. Lewis, "Physical Protection for Spiritual Welfare," in *Studies in Childhood History: A Canadian Perspective*, ed. P.T. Rooke and R.L. Schnell (Calgary, 1982): 135-66; Veronica Strong-Boag, "Intruders in the Nursery: Childcare Professionals Reshape the Years One to Five, 1920-1940," in *Childhood and Family in Canadian History*, ed. Joy Parr (Toronto, 1982), 160-78; Robert Stamp, "Canadian High Schools in the 1920s

and 30s: The Social Challenge to the Academic Tradition," *Historical Papers/ Communications historiques* (1978): 76-93.

75. Paula Fass, *The Damned and the Beautiful: American Youth in the 1920s* (New York, 1977), 57.

76. Dalhousie University, *President's Report*, 1931–32, 2, DUA.

77. "Student Government History, #48, #50," *Dalhousie Gazette*, 27 March, 2 October 1975. Some of the information on student activities comes from a remarkable series of sixty-nine articles by Dan O'Connor, published in the *Dalhousie Gazette* from 1974 to 1976. I am grateful to Michael Lynk for bringing this series to my attention.

78. "Student Government History, #46," *Dalhousie Gazette*, 13 March 1975, and *Dalhousie Gazette*, 24 February 1938.

79. *Dalhousie Gazette*, 8 November 1935, 10 January 1936, 30 October 1936; "Student Government History, #47," *Dalhousie Gazette*, 20 March 1975.

80. Robert Cooley Angel, *The Campus: A Study of Contemporary Life in the American University* (New York, 1928); Michael Pearlman, "To Make the University Safe for Morality: Higher Education, Football and Military Training from the 1890s through the 1920s," *The Canadian Review of American Studies* 12, no. 1 (Spring 1981): 37-56; Calvin B.T. Lee, *The Campus Scene, 1900–1970: Changing Styles in Undergraduate Life* (New York, 1970), 7; Paula Fass, *The Damned and the Beautiful*, 182.

81. Dalhousie University, *President's Report, 1931–32*, 2, DUA.

82. Senate Minutes, 11 October 1934, DUA; *Dalhousie Gazette*, 18 October 1934, 1 December 1932, 23 November 1932.

83. Stanley to Frank G. Pedley, 26 November 1943, Correspondence—Student Health Service, President's Office Papers, DUA. This letter reviews health service activities over the previous ten years at Dalhousie.

84. *Dalhousie Gazette*, 1, 8 February 1933; H.G. Grant, Chairman, Committee on Student Health, memo. to Stanley, 5 January 1934, Correspondence—Student Health Service, President's Office Papers, DUA. See also *Canadian Public Health Journal* 31, no. 3 (1940): 146, which reports on "Students' Health Service at Dalhousie University."

85. *Dalhousie Gazette*, 17 February 1928.

86. "Revised Constitution of the Student Body of Dalhousie University, Approved by Senate, 14 May, 1938," Council of Students' File, President's Office Papers, DUA.

87. "Student Government History, #50, #60," *Dalhousie Gazette*, 2 October and 11 December 1975.

88. Senate Minutes, 26 March 1936, DUA.

89. Stanley to Samuel French Canada Ltd., 11 June 1937, Correspondence— Council of Students' File, President's Office Papers, DUA.

90. Judson Conrad to Stanley, 2 October 1939, Correspondence—Student Misdemeanours, President's Office Papers, DUA.

91. Stanley to Conrad, 3 October 1939, Correspondence—Student Misdemeanours, President's Office Papers, DUA.

92. *Dalhousie University, Calendar, 1930–31*, 18.

93. Committee of Nine File, 17 March 1927, Stanley to W.M. Rogers, 23 March 1935, Correspondence—Committee of Nine File, President's Office Papers, DUA. The Committee was officially disbanded in April 1935: Senate Minutes, 18 April 1935, DUA.

94. Senate Minutes, 14 February 1939, 13 December 1934, 11 April 1935, 2 February 1939, DUA.

95. *Dalhousie Gazette*, 28 September 1933.

96. Johns, *University of Alberta*, 139-42.

97. *Dalhousie Gazette*, 3 December 1930; Dalhousie University, *President's Report, 1932-33*, 2, DUA. Stanley said that he was convinced that one-third of the male students did not attend dances at all: Senate Minutes, 23 March 1933, DUA.

98. "Student Government History, #54," *Dalhousie Gazette*, 6 November 1975.

99. Interviews with: Jean Begg, 15 August 1983; Henry Hicks, 8 August 1983; Leonard Kitz, 9 August 1983.

100. "Youth in College," *Fortune Magazine* (June 1936), 101.

101. Ware, *Holding Their Own: American Women in the 1930s*, 61-63; "Youth in College," 155; Fass, *The Damned and the Beautiful*, 76; Maxine Davis, *The Lost Generation: A Portrait of American Youth Today* (New York, 1936), 83. The major survey to which these accounts referred was Dorothy Dunbar Bromley and Florence Haxton Britten, *Youth and Sex: A Study of 1300 College Students* (New York, 1938).

102. In the interests of discretion, these interviewees will remain anonymous.

103. Fass, *The Damned and the Beautiful*, 142. Gillis, *Youth and History*, 77-90, discusses the European origins of fraternities.

104. Correspondence — Fraternities' File: President's Office Papers, DUA; *Pharos, the Dalhousie Yearbook* (1938).

105. Dalhousie University, *President's Report*, 1933-34, 13; Stanley to J. William Fisher, Treasurer, Delta Tau Fraternity, 7 March 1934; Stanley to P. Oyler et al., Phi Kappa Pi, 2 May 1933—where he scolds them for not paying bills: Correspondence — Fraternities' File, President's Office Papers, DUA.

106. *Dalhousie Gazette*, 12 October 1934.

107. Dalhousie University, *President's Report*, 1933-34, 13; Stanley to Sherwood Fox, 21 February 1935, Correspondence — Fraternities' File, President's Office Papers, DUA.

108. *Dalhousie Gazette*, 12 October 1934.

109. Fass, *The Damned and the Beautiful*, 152.

110. Stanley to W.E. Thompson, 26 February 1935; Stanley to Sherwood Fox, 21 February 1935, Correspondence — Fraternities' File, President's Office Papers, DUA.

111. Interviews with Gene Hicks and Leonard Kitz.

112. *Dalhousie University, Calendar, 1930-31*, 18.

113. Interview with Eric Mercer.

114. Percy Barksy, "How Numerus Clausus Was Ended in the Manitoba Medical School," *Canadian Jewish Historical Society Journal* 1, no. 2 (October 1977): 75-81. For a detailed discussion of the exposure of anti-semitism in the admission policies of the University of Manitoba, see *The Winnipeg Free Press*, 16 March and 14 September 1944, 20 March 1945. See also Frost, *McGill University*, 2: 128. Amazingly, one learns far more about the McGill policy from Gibson, *Queen's University*, 2: 199-202, than from Frost's superficial and apologetic treatment of McGill's anti-semitic admission policies.

115. *Census of Canada, 1941*, 4: 58-60; "Registration Book, 1930" and the same document for 1935 and 1939, Dalhousie University, DUA. The average annual figure was probably less than 11 percent, since 1935 was an exceptionally high year; 19.6 percent of the students were Jewish.

116. Marcia G. Synott, "The Admission and Assimilation of Minority Students at Harvard, Yale and Princeton, 1900-1970," *History of Education Quarterly* 19, no. 3

(Fall 1979): 285-304; John Kenneth Galbraith, *A Life in Our Times: Memoirs* (Boston, 1981), 19-20, 51.

117. R.C. Wallace to Sidney Smith, 13 February 1936, University of Manitoba: Correspondence, 32/10/5-4, President's Papers, 1928-36, University of Alberta Archives.

118. Reid, *Mount Allison University*, 2: 102.

119. Stanley Mackenzie to Andrew T. Drummond, 24 November 1920, Correspondence—Admission of Coloured Students, President's Office Papers, DUA.

120. The case is discussed in Board of Governors' Minutes, 9 June 1932, DUA.

121. Mary Vipond, "The Image of Women in Mass Circulation Magazines in the 1920s," in *The Neglected Majority*, ed. Alison Prentice and Susan Mann Trofimenkoff (Toronto, 1977), 116-24; Katherine M. Caldwell, "College and Then What?" *Canadian Home Journal* (September 1929); James Struthers, "Lord Give Us Men: Women and Social Work in English Canada, 1918-1953," *Historical Papers/Communications historiques* (1983): 96-112; Mollie McGee, "Four Women in Parliament," *Chatelaine* (May 1938). On working class women in the 1920s, see Veronica Strong-Boag, "The Girl of the New Day: Canadian Working Women in the 1920s," *Labour/Le Travailleur* 4 (1979): 131-64; and on women doctors, see Strong-Boag, "Feminism Constrained: The Graduates of Canada's Medical Schools for Women," in *A Not Unreasonable Claim: Women and Reform in Canada 1880s-1920s*, ed. Linda Kealey (Toronto, 1979), 109-29.

122. The March 1937 issue of *Chatelaine* contains the following items: "Kitchen Idea Contest," "Home Improvements," "Housekeeping," "Recipes," and "Fashion." There are ads for soap, cleanser, and drapes.

123. "A Feminist World?" *Dalhousie Gazette*, 11 January 1929; ibid., 8 November 1929, 2 March 1932, 16 November 1933, 8 November 1934.

124. J.A. Lindsay, "Sex in Education"; William D. Tait, "Some Feminisms," *Dalhousie Review* 10 (1930-31): 148-49, 52-53.

125. Interviews with: Gene Hicks, Jean Begg, Zilpha Linkletter. Jean Begg, who became the first woman bank manager in Nova Scotia in 1962, recalls that the idea of getting a job in the 1930s "never entered my head."

126. For an attack on female "peacocks" in universities, see Frank Underhill, speech to the National Conference on Canadian Universities, 1930, cited in Pilkington, "National Conference of Canadian Universities," 220. See also Carleton Stanley, "Inauguration Address," Board of Governors' Minutes, 29 October 1931 and *President's Report, 1932-33*, 2. Stanley laments the fact that some parents encouraged daughters at Shirreff Hall to attend dances in order to learn "social graces."

127. *Dalhousie University, Calendar*, 1930-31, 18.

128. "It was hoped that the course in Household Science [at the Halifax Ladies' College] might also be a means of increasing registration in Shirreff Hall": Florence Blackwood to Stanley, 21 January 1939, Correspondence—Halifax Ladies' College, President's Office Papers, DUA. The percentage of women dropped from 27.5 to 21.7 between 1930 and 1935 and rose to 23.5 in 1939.

129. Interviews with Jean Begg and Zilpha Linkletter; and "General Report" by Margaret E. Lowe, Warden of Shirreff Hall, Shirreff Hall—General, President's Office Papers, DUA.

130. *Halifax Daily Star*, 22 January 1938.

131. Interviews with Gene Hicks, Jean Begg. Willis, *History of Dalhousie Law School*, 139, points out that there were one or two women in the law programme every year. Grace Wambolt, the first woman to open a law office in Halifax, recalled some of the difficulties that women lawyers faced breaking into the legal profession. Davis, *The*

Lost Generation, 89-90, claimed that women in the 1930s were less anxious to secure careers than those in the 1920s, no longer viewing a career as "the be all and end all."

132. Allison Richards, "Are You Spoiling His Chances?" *Chatelaine* (March 1937). Also, "As well as making her life more enjoyable and providing a more profitable way of spending unemployed hours, a higher education enables a woman to be a more interested and interesting companion of her husband. A college career does not change the woman to a pedant; her education is a social asset." This typical defence of co-education appeared in *The Sheaf* [student newspaper, University of Saskatchewan], 21 January 1929.

133. "Youth in College," *Fortune Magazine* (June 1936): 99, also cited in *The Manitoban*, 3 February 1937. See also Davis, *The Lost Generation*, 39-46; C.L. Morgan and H.H. Remmers, "Liberalism and Conservatism of College Students as Affected by the Depression," *School and Society* 41, no. 1067 (8 June 1935): 780-84; Vernon Jones, "Attitudes of College Students and the Changes in Such Attitudes during Four Years in College," *The Journal of Educational Psychology* 29, nos. 1 and 2 (January and February 1938): 14-25, 114-34.

134. Ralph Brax, *The First Student Movement: Student Activism in the United States during the 1930s* (London, 1981); R.L. Schnell, *National Activist Student Organizations in American Higher Education, 1905–1944* (Ann Arbor, 1976); Philip Altbach, *Student Politics in America: A Historical Analysis* (New York, 1974); John P. Diggins, *The American Left in the Twentieth Century* (New York, 1973). Probably the largest demonstration occurred on 13 April 1934, when something between 500 000 and 1 000 000 American students staged peace demonstrations across the country. See also Eileen Eagan, *Class, Culture, and the Classroom: The Student Peace Movement of the 1930s* (Philadelphia, 1982); Louis Filler, *Vanguards and Followers: Youth in the American Tradition* (Chicago, 1978); Frederick Lewis Allen, *Since Yesterday: 1929–1939* (New York, 1965 [1940]); Seymour Martin Lipset, *Rebellion in the University: A History of Student Activism in America* (London, 1972).

135. Davis, *The Lost Generation*, 27, 39, and "Youth in College," 156; Filler, *Vanguards and Followers*, 77-78. As *Fortune Magazine* (June 1936) put it, students "are passive more than apathetic. They know more but act less," 100.

136. For discussion of academic freedom in Canadian universities in the Depression, see Frank Abbott, "Academic Freedom and Social Criticism in the 1930s," *Interchange* 14, no. 4 and 15, no. 1 (1983–84): 107-23; Douglas Francis, "The Threatened Dismissal of Frank Underhill from the University of Toronto, 1939–41," *CAUT Bulletin* (December 1975); Michiel Horn, "Academic Freedom and the Canadian Professor," *CAUT Bulletin* (December 1982).

137. In March 1929, the debate between Dalhousie and the Methodist College Literary Institute in St. John's, Newfoundland, drew 650 to 700 people: J.M. Barbour to Stanley Mackenzie, 15 March 1929. A 1934 debate at Dalhousie drew 500: Sodales File, President's Office Papers, DUA. Carleton Stanley was a debate enthusiast. See *Dalhousie Gazette*, 1, 15 March, 9 November 1933, 23 October, 27 November, 12 November 1937.

138. The political attitudes of Canadian students were reflected in a poll conducted at the University of Saskatchewan in 1935. Asked whom they supported federally, the students gave the Liberals 45 percent, the CCF 25 percent, Conservatives 21 percent and Communists 8 percent. According to the editor of *The Sheaf*, 21 March 1935, the straw vote "will certainly put an end to a very popular misconception of the university as a hotbed of radicalism."

139. *The Globe* (Toronto), 4, 8 February 1929 described the University of Toronto incident. On the UBC conflict, see *The Ubyssey* (Vancouver), 10 to 28 February 1931,

and *Dalhousie Gazette*, 4 March 1931. The *Gazette* also sided with student journalists at the University of Saskatchewan who were forced to resign following the publication of anti-war statements in 1938: *Dalhousie Gazette*, 25 November 1938.

140. Other newspapers examined include *The Ubyssey, The Sheaf, The Gateway* (University of Alberta), *The Manitoban* (University of Manitoba), and selections from *The Varsity* (University of Toronto).

141. *Dalhousie Gazette*, 19, 2 October 1936.

142. *Dalhousie Gazette*, 31 January 1935.

143. Filler, *Vanguards and Followers*, 77-78; Hugh MacLennan, "What it Was Like to be in Your Twenties in the Thirties," in *The Great Depression: Essays and Memoirs from Canada and the United States*, ed. Victor Hoar (Toronto, 1969), 152.

144. For recollections of those who were politically active, see David Lewis, *The Good Fight: Political Memoirs, 1909–1958* (Toronto, 1981); H.S. Ferns, *Reading from Left to Right: One Man's Political History* (Toronto, 1983); Merrily Weisbord, *The Strangest Dream: Canadian Communists, The Spy Trials, and the Cold War* (Toronto, 1981).

145. Richard Allen, *The Social Passion: Religion and Social Reform in Canada, 1914–1928* (Toronto, 1971), 219-23.

146. Ibid., 221; Interviews with: Lawrence Read, Eric Mercer, John Webster Grant, Grace Wombalt, Dr. Harry Smith, Dane Parker, Dr. Ian Robb.

147. *Dalhousie Gazette*, 19 October 1933; "Annual Report of the Student Christian Movement, Dalhousie University, 1933–34," Student Christian Movement File, 8 March 1934, President's Office Papers, DUA; Hugh MacMillan "21st Anniversary, Student Christian Movement," *Saturday Night*, 27 December 1941. See also Gibson, *Queen's University*, 2: 147.

148. *Dalhousie Gazette*, 25 January 1929, 7 February 1935. Also see *Report of the Conference of Representatives from the Students of the Canadian Universities, Held in Montreal at McGill University, 28-31 December 1926*, National Federation of Canadian University Students Collection, McMaster University Archives, Hamilton. The McMaster Archives contains reports of subsequent NFCUS conferences throughout the 1930s.

149. Interview with Gene Hicks; Armour Mackay, "Canadian Students Draw Together at Winnipeg," *Saturday Night*, 15 January 1938; *The Manitoban*, 7 January 1938; *The Ubyssey*, 7 January 1938.

150. The scholarships were incorporated into the Dominion-Provincial Youth Training Act. See *The Ubyssey*, 22 September 1939; *The Sheaf*, 22 September 1939.

151. Interviews with: Lawrence Read, Leonard Kitz, and Gene Hicks. One member of the Communist Party, who knew the Halifax situation at the end of the decade, agreed with this assessment. While the Young Communist League, the youth branch of the Communist Party of Canada, had active branches in Montreal, Toronto, and Winnipeg, it had no branch in Nova Scotia: Ivan Avakumovic, *The Communist Party in Canada: A History* (Toronto, 1975), 122-23.

152. Interviews with John Webster Grant and Dane Parker.

153. John Hawkins, *The Life and Times of Angus L.* (Windsor, N.S., 1969), 54-70.

154. Interviews with: Gene Hicks, Leonard Kitz, Dr. Ian Robb.

155. Students at Cambridge and Oxford were more active politically than those in Canada, owing in part to the proximity of European hostilities. When a Cambridge student leader was killed in the Spanish Civil War, many students were politicized in the struggle against fascism. For a particularly vivid portrayal of student life at Cambridge, see Victor Kiernan, "Herbert Norman's Cambridge," in *E.H. Norman:*

His Life and Scholarship, ed. R. Bowen (Toronto, 1984), 27-45. See also Ferns, *Reading from Left to Right*, 81-82, 116-28.

156. *Dalhousie Gazette*, 24, 31 October 1931.

157. *Dalhousie Gazette*, 10, 17 October 1935. A similar poll in the United States produced equally mixed results: Davis, *The Lost Generation*, 99.

158. "Student Government History #65," *Dalhousie Gazette*, 4 March 1976. See also Johnston, *McMaster University*, 2: 75. This particular campaign was organized by the Student Peace Movement, an organization that founded chapters on a number of Canadian campuses.

159. Interview with Henry Hicks; "Fascism in Italy Not a Dictatorship" [reports on speeches by Italian government representatives who toured Canada in 1934], *Vancouver Sun*, 16 February 1934; *Dalhousie Gazette*, 11 January 1934.

160. *Dalhousie Gazette*, 2 November 1933.

161. *Dalhousie Gazette*, 2 October 1936.

162. Arthur Lower claims in his memoirs that Professor R.A. Mackay was hesitant to support an isolationist organization because he feared that "if he became too conspicuous in such a movement, there would be so much pressure in Halifax that Dalhousie would probably be forced to dismiss him!" (Arthur R.M. Lower, *My First Seventy-five Years* (Toronto, 1967), 205).

163. *Dalhousie Gazette*, 24 January 1936.

164. Board of Governors' Minutes, 10 October 1939, DUA.

165. Stanley to Colonel C.B. Smith, 16 October 1940, Correspondence—COTC File, President's Office Papers, DUA. On Dalhousie's other war activities, see *The Alumni News*, April 1943, 16-18.

166. Cited in *The Ubyssey*, 16 January 1940 and *The Gateway*, 26 January 1940. Dalhousie's response is in the *Dalhousie Gazette*, 26 January, 2 February 1940. See also, Gibson, *Queen's University*, 2: 182; Reid, *Mount Allison University*, 2: 153-54.

167. *Dalhousie Gazette*, 3 December 1929.

A PROFESSION IN CRISIS: CHARLOTTE WHITTON AND CANADIAN SOCIAL WORK IN THE 1930s†

JAMES STRUTHERS

The 1930s produced an explosion of public welfare in Canada as governments at the federal, provincial, and municipal level spent more than a billion dollars on the care of the unemployed and their families.[1] The suddenness and sheer magnitude of this expenditure forced major changes in Canada's social welfare structure. Before the Depression private charities played a dominant role in caring for the victims of joblessness. By 1940, however, the federal government had created a national system of unemployment insurance and employment offices and most of the provinces along with the larger municipalities had developed permanent welfare bureaucracies with at least the rudiments of professional administration. Out of the "dirty thirties," then, came a belated acknowledgement that social welfare was a major responsibility of the state.

Perhaps no group benefited as much from this transition as the social work profession, one of the few occupations to experience "practically one hundred percent employment" during the Depression.[2] Yet we know little about the role social workers played during the decade in shaping government policy. It is usually assumed that the lack of an experienced welfare bureaucracy was largely responsible for the abysmal conditions endured by those on the dole. In this view, public welfare became "professionalized," during the thirties, in order to improve living standards for the unemployed and their families.[3]

However, an examination of the role of Charlotte Whitton, executive director of the Canadian Council on Child and Family Welfare (CCC & FW), in shaping the relief policies of the Bennett and King governments

† *Canadian Historical Review* 62, no. 2 (1981): 169–85. The author would like to thank Veronica Strong-Boag for her helpful comments on this paper.

casts serious doubts on this assumption. In the mind of Canada's "best known social worker,"[4] at least, the interests of the unemployed and of the professionals entrusted with their care were by no means identical.

Like the rest of Canadian society, social workers were unprepared for the Depression. Although the 1920s had been formative years for the profession,[5] for the most part what little expertise the country possessed in welfare matters still existed within its private charities and this did not amount to much. There were only two schools of social work in the entire country and even Ontario, Canada's wealthiest and most industrialized province, had "practically no such thing" as a "corps of trained social workers," according to a 1930 Royal Commission report. The profession itself had only organized its first national associations during the 1920s and possessed but a fledgling status on the eve of the 1930s.[6]

The public welfare field had expanded significantly during the preceding decade, but for the most part this occurred within patronage-ridden provincial bureaucracies with the result that complaints about partisanship, inefficiency, and corruption in the administration of mothers' allowances and old age pensions were widespread throughout the country.[7] Consequently, many Canadian social workers shared their American colleagues' "long tradition of disdain" for state relief. Its bureaucratic emphasis upon "classification, determination of eligibility, and routine surveillance" seemed scarcely related to their own more "scientific" skills of investigative casework and professional counselling.[8] Canada thus entered into the greatest crisis of dependency in its history armed with only a few well-organized charities in its larger cities, a municipal relief structure built upon the nineteenth-century poor law, and an underdeveloped social work profession that viewed the whole field of public welfare with some skepticism.

As long as government officials viewed the Depression as a temporary "emergency," this lack of expertise and organization in the welfare field was not considered alarming. R.B. Bennett, after all, had been elected in 1930 on a promise that he would "abolish the dole" through stiff hikes in the tariff.[9] As a result, he had little interest in perfecting public welfare administration. Out of the twenty million dollars provided in his first relief act, sixteen million went for public works and only four million was slated for direct relief. Not a cent of this was spent on developing competent local welfare bureaucracies. The same pattern prevailed the following year despite the fact that Ottawa's expenditure on direct relief almost doubled.[10] Adamant that the care of the jobless was primarily a municipal obligation, Bennett washed his hands of any responsibilty for ensuring that federal money was expended in an equitable and decent fashion.[11]

The consequences of this policy were horrendous. By the winter of 1932 Canada's few well-organized charities were overwhelmed as unemployment rose above 20 percent of the workforce. Their plight was effectively described by one harassed official in Toronto's Neighbour-hood Workers Association:

> [I]n 1930 we thought . . . that we were pressed to the uttermost and that we could not possibly drive the staff any harder. Never in our experience have we faced anything to equal this winter. The staff is working literally day and night to deal with the situation. . . . The District Offices are interviewing anywhere from 50-90 clients daily. The toll on the physical and nervous energy of one's workers, who day in and day out, are interviewing 20-30 clients each is appalling. . . . Just how we can go on facing it I do not know. We are trying to secure additional workers, but even that does not solve the problem. One reaches the saturation point when further supervision and guidance are difficult, if not impossible.[12]

The problems of the private charities, however, paled in comparison to those of the municipal relief offices. The charities, at least, were experienced in the welfare field. The cities were not. Only four had bothered to establish permanent welfare departments to distribute public relief before 1930.[13] More importantly, the sheer cost of financing their one-third share of direct relief upon a rapidly declining property-tax base did not incline most communities towards developing elaborate or overly-generous structures for relieving human need.

This fact was made abundantly clear by a devastating indictment of Ontario's relief system, published by Harry Cassidy, [later] director of the University of Toronto's School of Social Work, in the spring of 1932. After surveying the relief practices of the province's twelve largest municipalities, Cassidy discovered that, depending on where they lived, an Ontario family of five could receive anywhere from $3.50 to $8.50 a week in direct relief food orders. In two-thirds of the cities he studied, relief officers themselves admitted that their food allowances were inadequate to maintain health. Most municipalities, moreover, did not even attempt to determine what a minimum food budget should be and in no city did Cassidy discover a budget which came even close to existing nutritional guidelines. Since neither the province nor the dominion provided any assistance towards the cost of relief administration, trained social workers were in charge of dispensing aid in only four of the cities he studied. Residence and eligibility requirements for relief varied from town to town; few cities provided any facilities for relieving unemployed single men and none aided single women.[14]

Cassidy held the provincial and federal governments directly to blame for this situation. By assuming that the unemployment crisis was an emergency "likely to be of brief duration," they had taken no steps to replace the present haphazard organization of relief with "adequate governmental machinery of a permanent nature." Most importantly, their policy of holding the municipalities primarily responsible for the care of the jobless guaranteed "neither uniformity of treatment nor even distribution of justice for the unemployed."

As a solution, Cassidy recommended permanent provincial and federal "leadership" in the welfare field to ensure well-planned public works; food allowances that provided the "minima requisite for the maintenance of health"; adequate rent and clothing allowances; uniform eligibility requirements that guaranteed a right to relief regardless of where one lived; and the placing of trained social workers in charge of social aid. These recommendations might require a "large increase in relief expenditure," Cassidy realized, but to skimp on the care of the unemployed now would only lead to the "deterioration in the quality of our working-class population" and "huge social service expenditures later on."[15]

When it became clear, in the spring of 1932, that the Bennett government was about to abandon relief works entirely and rely solely upon direct relief in order to conserve funds, other members of the profession began to echo Cassidy's concerns. At a social work conference in April some welfare administrators, disgusted at the spectacle of "families who had become sick on the miserable relief minima that had been paid," urged their colleagues to "take [a] stand for adequate relief" and "express their conviction that people could not be kept idle, dragged on the most miserable rations, from day to day."[16]

Their most influential colleague, however, disagreed. Although better known today for her tempestuous career as mayor of Ottawa, Charlotte Whitton, by 1932, was already acknowledged as "one of the outstanding women of her generation"[17] through her prodigious work in the area of child welfare. Born in Renfrew, Ontario, in 1896, Whitton attended Queen's University and graduated with a brilliant academic record and an MA in history in 1918. That same year she entered the burgeoning field of social work by becoming assistant secretary to Dr. John Shearer of the Social Service Council of Canada.

A diminutive woman with a sharp wit, a fiery temper, and enormous energy, Whitton lost no time in moving to the top of her profession. In 1920 she was appointed honorary secretary of the newly-formed Canadian Council on Child Welfare, a national federation of social agencies established to promote the development of child welfare programmes across Canada. Starting with "no office and no money," Whitton six years later (with the help of federal government funding) was the full-time director of Canada's most influential social work organization. For the remainder of the decade she worked tirelessly, arranging conferences, conducting research surveys, and publishing reports in order to bring professional standards and prestige to the rapidly expanding sphere of family welfare.[18]

Even before the Depression struck, Whitton had been convinced that the growth of social aid programmes was far outstripping the supply of people who could capably run them.[19] As a result, she was hardly surprised when Bennett's first unemployment relief effort collapsed in disarray in the spring of 1932. The problem, she wrote the prime minister that April, was not lack of money, but rather the way it was being spent. At present, she noted, the provinces and municipalities were packing relief rolls with thousands of indigents who, under normal circumstances, would be not considered unemployed, simply to get a federal subsidy. In Quebec, relief funds were being distributed according to the "racial or religious proportions of the population," not actual need. Finally, Whitton pointed to the wide variation in relief expenditure among Canada's six largest cities (from $0.84 per person in Montreal to $6.80 in Winnipeg) as evidence of the need for imposing a "more rigid schedule of conditions" upon the way federal money was spent. And here her profession could help. Social workers had a "wealth of knowledge in the annual administration of hundreds of thousands of dollars" for social aid, she argued, that was "open and ready" for Ottawa's benefit if it seriously wanted to bring relief costs under control.[20]

More than generosity lay behind Whitton's offer. Her outrage over the waste and the inefficiency surrounding relief reflected a strong sense of professional alarm at the rapid changes overtaking Canada's welfare structure. Thousands of untrained and frequently patronage-appointed personnel now staffed municipal and provincial relief offices across the country. Unless her profession could somehow gain control of this swelling bureaucracy, Whitton was convinced that social workers would soon be by-passed within their own field by a new class of government employees, particularly now that investigative casework, the skill upon which they rested their professional identity, was being undermined by the sheer volume of applicants for aid.[21]

The abandonment of public works as Bennett's chief form of unemployment aid in the spring of 1932 seemed to offer just such an opportunity for "professionalizing" the dole. The "whole aspect" of relief, Whitton argued, had now changed "from one of . . . registration and employment to one primarily of social welfare." Such a "changed situation" demanded "different procedure . . . knowledge and experience" and presumably different administrators as well. "Social work has its own technique as have engineering and construction," she pointed out to Bennett a few months later, "and the processes and personnel of the one cannot be automatically interchanged with the other without serious mismanagement and loss."[22]

Coming at a time when Bennett was gravely worried that the ballooning cost of relief might bankrupt the country, Whitton's arguments could not have been more apropos. While Cassidy's study, with its recommendation for a "large increase in relief expenditure," evoked a negative response from the Prime Minister's Office, Whitton was called to a meeting with Bennett in early April in order to "talk over" the contents of her memo. A month later she was hired by the federal government to "work as quietly as possible" on a study of unemployment relief in western Canada, the area of the country hardest hit by the Depression.[23]

After four months of extensive travelling throughout the prairies, Whitton submitted a two hundred page report that autumn. Since it was the only detailed unemployment relief study that Bennett ever commissioned during his five years in office it had enormous influence in conditioning his subsequent response to the Depression, although in ways Whitton hardly suspected at the time.

Her most startling conclusion was that almost 40 percent of those presently receiving relief in the West did not really need it. In fact, over the past two years Bennett's relief work programme had succeeded in actually "raising . . . the standard of employment and living of the great volume of the underemployed."[24] Farmers and their sons, for example, had been employed on relief projects in large numbers "when there was no actual question of the need of food, fuel, clothing or shelter for themselves and . . . when ordinarily the winter was a period of idleness." In southern Alberta the widespread availability of direct relief had "arrested . . . any natural disintegration" of dying mining communities and "served to 'suspend' them on direct relief." The same was true of "dead communities" in the northern fringes of all provinces that had been "swept back or left behind as settlement moved elsewhere." The plight of their people was pitiful but it was "not one deriving from the present emergency" and therefore should not be supported by federal relief.

Jobless women fell into the same category. Their problems arose primarily from desertion, death, and illegitimacy, not from unemployment; therefore, they did "not form a justifiable charge on . . . (relief) legislation." Direct relief was also raising the living standards of unemployed single men and immigrant families. Too many of the former, who could have stayed on farms during the winter, were "going to the cities where 'they could get two good meals and a bed a day on relief' and 'have a real rest for the winter.'" Immigrant families were receiving "supplies on a scale neither attained nor desired by these people from their own resources or efforts."[25] In short, lax standards of administration were allowing thousands of casual workers who were *normally* unemployed six to eight months of the year to "swarm . . . into relief . . . on a 'year round basis'" and thus raise their standard of living "beyond anything that they have ever known."[26]

The problem, Whitton concluded, was that western municipalities had neither the incentive nor the expertise to restrict relief to only the genuinely unemployed. Fear of bankruptcy had acted as a deterrent to generosity in the past, but now many cities were so hopelessly in debt there was a real danger they might "cut loose" from all fiscal restraint in order to avoid social unrest,[27] particularly now that Ottawa was paying such a large share of their costs. More importantly, municipal administration of relief had subjected it to "the most contemptible type of local . . . politics." Relief offices were being staffed "on the . . . basis of party preferment," and as a result, most of the people Whitton found in charge of the dole "would never be considered by even a small business for any responsible position."[28]

Not surprisingly, her principal recommendation was that trained professionals be placed in charge of relief administration throughout the entire country. This had to be made the "*sine qua non* of any continuance of federal aid." By attaching rigorous conditions to its relief grants, demanding "minimum standards of education, experience and similar qualifications for all appointments in provincial or municipal relief offices," Ottawa could, in effect, "professionalize" the dole, improve its efficiency, and thus reduce its costs. Unlike Cassidy, however, Whitton counselled against any national minimum standard of relief itself. This would make the dole too attractive in too many communities. Her object, in contrast, was to tighten up relief administration before the casually unemployed became "permanently dependent at a scale of living which they never had and never will be able to provide for themselves."[29]

Whitton's October report with its confused distinctions between "casual" and "genuine" unemployment confirmed Bennett's worst fears that widespread abuse of the dole lay behind its rapidly increasing costs. This was certainly no coincidence. Exaggerating the extravagance of the present system was her most effective means of stressing the importance of her profession's administrative skills to the government. However, although Whitton's analysis made an impact upon Bennett, it was not in the way she had hoped. Although his suspicions of waste were now confirmed by "the most capable woman engaged in social welfare in the Dominion,"[30] Bennett did not believe that forcing the provinces to hire trained social workers was the answer. Instead, he opted for a quicker remedy. If the provinces and municipalities were wasting federal money, the solution was simply to give them less money to waste. Rather than spurring Bennett on to exert bold new leadership in the relief field, Whitton's report merely increased his desire to get out of the whole business as soon as possible. By emphasizing the extravagance rather than the suffering surrounding the dole, Whitton thus destroyed whatever chance there was that it might be reformed.

Over the next two years those without jobs paid the price. Although unemployment rose to 30 percent of the workforce during 1933 and the number dependent upon the dole climbed to over a million and a half,[31] Bennett and his labour minister W.A. Gordon turned a deaf ear to the growing demand from across the country that Ottawa assume a larger responsibility for relief. People were flocking to the dole, Gordon told the premiers in 1933, because "sufficient emphasis was not being placed upon the responsibility of the individual to maintain himself." If

Ottawa assumed a larger portion of the relief burden, "administration will be without restraint."[32]

As a result, the federal share of direct relief costs was held at one-third and an arbitrary million-dollar ceiling was placed on the budgetary deficits of the western provinces as a condition for further federal loans.[33] Apart from establishing relief camps for single men, Bennett's government refused to take any responsibility for the way relief was administered. Faced with absorbing the largest share of the dole's soaring costs, the provinces and municipalities thus had little incentive to ensure equitable and decent treatment for the unemployed.

By the beginning of 1934, this continued federal indifference towards the chaotic state of relief had produced a growing "sense of futility and frustration" among Canadian social workers who, as Whitton pointed out, were the ones "closest to actual evidence of . . . [its] . . . course and effects."[34] But while calls for "more centralized leadership" were wide-spread throughout the profession, there was less agreement over where exactly Ottawa should lead.[35] On the left, critics such as Leonard Marsh and Harry Cassidy demanded a "much greater degree of dominion participation and control" in the care of the unemployed simply to ensure that the dole was made "as adequate and as fair as possible."[36]

Whitton, however, continued to undercut their arguments by insisting that the real victim of Ottawa's laissez-faire policy was not the unemployed but the taxpayer. In a memo sent to Bennett's office early in 1934 she argued that by leaving responsibility for relief in the hands of the "unit of government most susceptible to direct political control and manoeuvre" Bennett had created a "wide open" system of relief administration that encouraged "loose organization and lavish expenditure."[37] As one relief administrator complained to Whitton, cities such as Calgary, where labour exerted a strong political influence on city hall, were "giving us all a lead which the unemployed cannot be blamed for urging we should follow and which fifty percent of the members of our City of Winnipeg council are trying hard to catch up and pass."[38] Small wonder, Whitton concluded, that there was a "growing tendency to seek relief and to stay on it over an increasing period of time. The system has bonussed such developments."[39]

The director of the Council on Child and Family Welfare undoubtedly hoped these sweeping accusations would finally convince Bennett to rationalize relief administration through enacting stiff conditional grants that would place trained social workers in charge of the dole. Instead, the prime minister once again moved in the opposite direction. Frustrated by the failure of the numbers on relief to decline in reponse to his economic policies, Bennett seized upon Whitton's arguments during the summer of 1934 to justify a severe reduction in Ottawa's support for the unemployed. At first threatening to terminate all contributions to relief, he ultimately settled for a 22 percent cut in federal spending, achieved through replacing Ottawa's one-third percentage contribution to the dole with a system of fixed monthly grants-in-aid.[40]

Relief had become a "racket," he told the premiers in justifying his move. Twenty percent of its cost was going not to the genuinely unemployed, but to "partially employed" workers whose wages were as high as before the Depression. "Relief conscious" municipalities had thus accustomed many of the jobless to a "hitherto unknown" standard of living. Moreover, nearly every province was attempting to "scrap the constitution" by packing the dole with indigent unemployables who normally were an exclusively local responsibility.[41]

Although his arguments were borrowed almost entirely from Whitton's 1932 report on relief in western Canada, Bennett drew a different conclusion. For Whitton, the logical remedy to these abuses was closer federal supervision of relief through more stringent conditional grants. The prime minister rejected this approach on the grounds that "divided authority was not efficient."[42] Instead, the "proper method," he argued, was simply "to make the grant-in-aid and to place the whole responsibility upon the Provinces and Municipalities." Up to now, local governments had "not taken any steps to prevent abuses."[43] Limited to a fixed federal grant, they might.

In effect, Whitton was hoist upon her own petard. Using her arguments, Bennett opted for a change in relief policy which, as she ruefully admitted, was "almost directly contrary" to her suggestions.[44] Instead of increasing federal supervision of the dole, he simply cut back Ottawa's support. The ledger, not the social work profession, the prime minister obviously concluded, would provide the most efficient check upon "waste" and "lavish expenditure" in relief.

Bennett adhered to this policy for the remainder of his administration. Even the introduction of unemployment insurance as part of his famous "New Deal" in 1935 contained no provisions for the reform of relief.[45] In frustration, Whitton turned to the business community for support in her attempt to change government policy.[46] This time she found a receptive audience. By the beginning of 1935 businessmen across the country were becoming increasingly alarmed at both the growing leftward trend in municipal politics and the threat to government solvency posed by soaring relief costs, developments which many felt were not unrelated.[47] Thus, when Whitton's annual "Relief Outlook," at the end of 1934, pointed to the "increasing core of permanent dependency developing from the tendency to exploit the vote of the dependent unemployed and to offer more and easier relief," business organizations quickly began to echo her call for the "removal of relief standards, practices, and administration from the realm of political influence and manoeuvre."[48]

Early in 1935 the Canadian Chamber of Commerce noted, in a letter forwarded to all members of Parliament, that although the dole was now the "heaviest burden on . . . government treasuries," it was "loosely integrated" and "subject in many cases . . . to political influence." As a result, the chamber demanded that Ottawa "should immediately take such action as will result in lifting control of relief administration and financing directly out of the field of the local political influence" in order to "conserve public funds."[49]

With the victory of Mackenzie King's Liberal party at the end of the year, the time for such a step seemed to have come. Although King had never insisted that Ottawa should administer relief itself, he had called, while in opposition, for a national commission that would investigate the real conditions surrounding relief administration and keep a close eye upon the way federal money was spent. True to his word, in April 1936 King established the National Employment Commission to "find ways and means of providing remunerative employment," to register and classify those on relief, and to supervise and audit provincial and municipal relief expenditures.[50] By bringing to light the "obvious abuses, rackets, overlapping and [the] like" surrounding the dole, he was convinced the NEC would soon "save the Treasury & . . . the taxpayers many millions of dollars."[51]

For help in discovering how to do this the NEC hired Canada's foremost authority on the subject, Charlotte Whitton. Now she had the chance to put into effect all the recommendations which she had so fruitlessly urged upon Bennett over the past five years. Whitton wasted no time in returning to her familiar theme. "[T]he most important phase of the whole problem," she warned the commission upon taking the job, was the "continuous interference and exploitation of the situation" by the municipalities. Consequently, the first step in reforming relief was to guarantee the social work profession "administrative freedom [and] adequacy of personnel" by attaching strict conditions to the new relief agreements with the provinces.[52]

Within a year the NEC's interim report made public her ideas of what should be done. They had changed little since her first report to Bennett in 1932. The dole, Whitton told NEC commissioner Tom Moore when the interim report was released, was providing many people with a "regularity of income" they had "not known in their usual occupation."[53] Not surprisingly, then, the thrust of her recommendations was to tighten up control over those on relief.

Whitton suggested three principal ways this could be accomplished. First, those now receiving unemployment aid should be divided into two categories: those who could work and those who could not. Ottawa would be financially responsible only for the first group. In this way, the federal government could both limit its expenditure and concentrate all its efforts upon devising efficient policies for getting the employable unemployed off relief.[54]

Second, the actual administration of unemployment aid should remain with the provinces and municipalities. Although this recommendation would fly in the face of the NEC's final report which argued that the federal government should assume total responsibility for the jobless, it nonetheless reflected Whitton's belief (shared, as it turned out, by King as well) that a nationally-administered relief system could not effectively keep payments to the unemployed below regional and local wage rates.[55] In other words, a national dole would erode the work ethic.

While these two proposals would have limited Ottawa's responsibilities, Whitton's third recommendation involved an important extension of federal authority. The present unconditional block grants for relief, introduced by Bennett in 1934, should be replaced by new agreements which attached strict and comprehensive conditions to all federal aid. The goal, Whitton argued, was to "make it certain that those unemployed . . . will move into employment as rapidly as employment opportunities offer."

To ensure this would take place, she recommended surrounding local administration of relief with close federal supervision to guarantee that work was kept more attractive than the dole. The new relief agreements, Whitton argued, should contain provincial "standards of eligibility"; a "limitation of shelter allowances to a definite relationship with assessments"; and procedures for maintaining a "running record of earnings" of those on relief in order to "facilitate the acceptance of casual employment" through quick "cancellation of aid." In addition, there should be reports on "schedules of allowances, costs of living and average earnings of unskilled workers" as well as those "in receipt of Aid continuously for 12 months"; and above all, constant "investigation" into the "circumstances of individual relief recipients."

But while all these recommendations called for increased standardization of unemployment aid across the country, in one crucial area flexibility would remain. The new relief agreements, Whitton stressed, should enforce "the principle of maintenance of incentive to accept employment by relating the *maximum* Aid to actual earnings of unskilled labour in each centre or regional division"[56] [emphasis added]. There was to be no "national minimum." The goal of reforming relief was not to abolish the poor law doctrine of "less eligibility," but to make it work more effectively by removing control over relief rates from the unit of government "most susceptible to every wind of popular demand."[57]

Six months after she submitted her report Whitton's recommendations began to take effect. In January 1938, as part of a series of cost-cutting measures designed to reduce Ottawa's expenditure on the dole, Norman Rogers, King's minister of labour, inserted into relief agreements with the provinces the new stipulation that "material aid given to any family head or individual . . . must be less than the normal earnings of an unskilled labourer in the district as averaged over the preceding year."[58] When CCF spokesmen denounced this change as an attempt to reduce the living standards of the unemployed, Rogers denied that the government had "in any way brought pressure to bear upon provincial governments with respect to any change in relief scales."[59] This was simply untrue. While not interested in ensuring a *minimum* standard of support, the federal government was now actively enforcing a *maximum* on the level of relief provided by any community. Whitton's advice had finally triumphed at the expense of those on the dole.

Her contribution in pushing Ottawa towards a reform of relief thus sheds significant light upon some of the motivations behind the professionalization of public welfare in the 1930s. Although other social workers (such as Leonard Marsh and Harry Cassidy) were equally vigorous in their condemnation of Canada's obsolete municipal relief structure,[60] none was as successful as Whitton in seeing their suggestions translated into federal policy during the Depression.

Whitton's influence stemmed not simply from her reputation, her expertise, or her position as head of Canada's most important social work federation, but also from the fact that she told businessmen and federal leaders what they wanted to hear. By claiming that municipal politicians were "exploit[ing] the vote of the dependent unemployed and . . . offer[ing] more and easier relief," she implied that Ottawa should be spending less, not more, on the dole. By arguing that 40 percent of those on relief in the West did not really need it, she hinted that efficient social administration could succeed, where economic policies had failed, in reducing the volume of the unemployed. Finally, by stressing that relief scales had to be kept below the "actual earnings of unskilled labour," Whitton, unlike some of her colleagues, never lost sight of the fact that the primary goal of public welfare in any market society is not simply to relieve human need, but to maintain the work ethic.[61]

Her reward, by the end of the Depression, was to see legislation in place ensuring that trained social workers, not local politicians, would be in charge of administering social aid in the years to come. For her colleagues, however, it was a dubious legacy. Ultimately, the skills Whitton made most attractive to the government were those of a profession that could limit the costs of social welfare and keep a close surveillance over the unemployed. In return for such services, social workers could expect increasing employment within a burgeoning state sector. In effect, they, not the jobless, would become the chief beneficiaries of Canada's "reformed" relief system.

Notes

1. Canada, *Report of the Royal Commission on Dominion–Provincial Relations*, Book 2 (Ottawa, 1940), 18.
2. Dorothy King, "Unemployment Aid (Direct Relief)," in *Canada's Unemployment Problem*, ed. L. Richter (Toronto, 1939), 94-95.
3. Ibid. For recent versions of this argument see Linda Grayson and Michael Bliss, eds., *The Wretched of Canada: Letters to R.B. Bennett 1930–35* (Toronto, 1971), x, xii, xvi, xxi; or H. Blair Neatby, *The Politics of Chaos: Canada in the Thirties* (Toronto, 1972), 25-27.
4. The phrase is from an article on Whitton in *Canadian Welfare* 8, no. 7 (January 1942).
5. Particularly through the developments of mothers' allowance and minimum wage commissions and systematic child welfare surveys in the 1920s. On these developments see Veronica Strong-Boag, "Wages for Housework: Mothers' Allowances and the Beginnings of Social Security in Canada," *Journal of Canadian Studies* 14, no. 1 (Spring 1979), and by the same author, "The Girl of the New Day: Canadian Working Women in the 1920's," *Labour/Le Travailleur* 4, no. 4 (1979).
6. Ontario, *Report of the Ontario Royal Commission on Public Welfare* (Toronto, 1930), 6. In 1929 there were one hundred openings for every thirty graduates from Canada's two schools of social work. James Pitsula, "The Emergence of Social Work in Toronto," *Journal of Canadian Studies* 14, no. 1 (Spring 1979): 41.
7. Public Archives of Canada (hereinafter PAC), Canadian Council on Social Development [CCSD] Papers, 25, "Retrospects and Prospects: Canadian Council on Child and Family Welfare, 1922–1935," 5-7. See also Kenneth Bryden, *Old Age Pensions and Policy-Making in Canada* (Montreal, 1974), 84; Veronica Strong-Boag, "Wages for Housework," 27-28; and Peter Oliver, *G. Howard Ferguson: Ontario Tory* (Toronto, 1977), chaps. 11 and 15.
8. Roy Lubove, *The Professional Altruist: The Emergence of Social Work as a Career, 1880–1930* (Cambridge, 1965), 53-54.
9. Canada, House of Commons, *Debates*, 9 September 1930, 21-27.
10. Harry Cassidy, *Unemployment and Relief in Ontario, 1929–1932* (Toronto, 1932), 91-92. Canada, *Report of the Dominion Commissioner of Unemployment Relief*, 30 March 1935, 33. It should be noted that the federal government itself spent only $43 000 of its first relief grant on administrative expenses. Ibid., 47.
11. Canada, House of Commons, *Debates*, 11 September 1930, 91; 12 September 1930, 174
12. PAC, CCSD Papers, vol. 14, file 68, J.S. Driscoll to Charlotte Whitton, 8 January 1932.
13. King, "Unemployment Aid (Direct Relief)," 89.
14. Cassidy, *Unemployment and Relief in Ontario*, 202-11, 256.
15. Ibid., 276-89.
16. PAC, Bennett Papers, vol. 706, "Summary of the Proceedings of the Second Bilingual Conference on Family and Child Welfare," Montreal, April 1932.
17. *Canadian Welfare* 8, no. 7 (January 1942): 1. Whitton's pre-eminence was revealed when she became one of seven Canadian women to receive a CBE upon the resumption of the Crown's Honour List in Canada in 1934. See *Child and Family Welfare* 9, no. 5 (January 1934).
18. Phyllis Harrison, "In the Beginning Was Charlotte . . . " *Canadian Welfare* 51, no. 2 (1975): 14-15; *Canadian Welfare* 18, no. 7 (January 1942): 1-3.
19. See her comments in PAC, CCSD Papers, vol. 25, "Retrospects and Prospects:

Canadian Council on Child and Family Welfare, 1922–1935," 5-7, and Pitsula, "The Emergence of Social Work in Toronto," 41.

20. PAC, Bennett Papers, vol. 798, memo from Whitton to Bennett on the "Distribution of Unemployment Relief," 9 April 1932. See also vol. 706, Whitton to Bennett, 18 April 1932.

21. See for example, the complaint of Whitton's colleague Dorothy King that "Few of those employed have had training in social welfare administration. . . . In the administration of unemployment aid, in, for example, Northern Alberta, the Royal Canadian Mounted Police are the agents; in other provinces, Provincial and City Police, Public Health Nurses and officers of the Children's Aid Society, have been pressed into investigation services. 'White collared' and other unemployed, have been used freely, the general supervision being usually assigned to officers of the municipal or provincial government, whose previous experience has been in other fields" (King, "Unemployment Aid (Direct Relief)," 94-95). On Whitton's fears for her profession see PAC, CCSD Papers, vol. 25, "Retrospects and Prospects: Canadian Council on Child and Family Welfare, 1922–1935" (n.d.); vol. 21, file 85, Whitton to CCC & FW Board of Governors, 6 May 1931; and memorandum by Whitton to Canadian Chamber of Commerce, 31 August 1932, on "Public Welfare in Canada."

22. PAC, Bennett Papers, vol. 779-80, "Report *re* Unemployment and Relief in Western Canada, Summer 1932," 478107-9.

23. Ibid., vol. 789, Bennett to W.F. Nickle, 26 April 1932; Nickle to Bennett, 3 May 1932; ibid., vol. 706, Bennett to Charlotte Whitton, 26 April 1932; Whitton to Bennett, 31 May 1932.

24. Ibid., vols, 779-80, "Report *re* Unemployment and Relief in Western Canada," 478800-1, 478928-30.

25. Ibid., 478093-99, 478105, 478823, 478858-59.

26. Ibid., 478946-47, 478812.

27. Ibid., vol. 706, Whitton to Bennett, 16 June 1932.

28. Ibid., vols. 779-80, "Report *re* Unemployment and Relief in Western Canada," 478125-28, 478848.

29. Ibid., 478848-55, 478812.

30. Ibid., vol. 706, Bennett to J.T.M. Anderson, 4 June 1932.

31. "Monograph on Unemployment," in *Census of Canada, 1931*, 13: 374; Canada, Department of Labour, *Report of the Dominion Commissioner of Unemployment Relief*, 30 March 1935, 52.

32. PAC, Bennett Papers, vol. 561, "Minutes of the Dominion–Provincial Conference, 17-19 January 1933," 346894-955.

33. Ibid., vol 566, Bennett to the four western premiers, 9 March 1933.

34. PAC, CCSD Papers, vol. 15, file 68, Whitton to A.A. Mackenzie, 4 January 1934; Bennett Papers, vol. 798, Charlotte Whitton, "The Essentials of a Relief Programme for Canada, 1934–35," 19 January 1934.

35. See, for example, "Problems in the Social Administration of General and Unemployment Relief," the discussion and findings of a conference on this subject, called at Ottawa from 1-4 May 1933, under the auspices of the Canadian Council on Child and Family Welfare, reprinted in *Child and Family Welfare* 9, no. 1 (May 1933). Disagreement was particularly sharp over the issue of unemployment insurance. Harry Cassidy and Leonard Marsh insisted it could relieve "the major part of distress occasioned by unemployment," while Whitton maintained that any "actuarially sound" scheme would only absorb the "smaller part" of any future relief load. See Whitton, "The Essentials of a Relief Programme for Canada, 1934–35," and the

criticisms of it by Cassidy and Marsh in PAC, CCSD Papers, vol. 16, Leonard Marsh to Whitton, 13 February 1934.

36. Harry Cassidy, "Is Unemployment Relief Enough?" *Canadian Forum* (January 1934); PAC, CCSD Papers, vol. 16, Leonard Marsh to Whitton, 13 February 1934.

37. PAC, Bennett Papers, vol. 804, Charlotte Whitton, "The Challenge for Relief Control," March 1934.

38. PAC, CCSD Papers, vol, 16, file 68, A. MacNamara to Whitton, 5 February 1934.

39. Whitton, "The Challenge for Relief Control."

40. The first suggestion that Ottawa would withdraw from relief was a warning by W.A. Gordon to the premiers at the January 1934 dominion–provincial conference. Subsequently, Gordon was forced to back away from his proposed June 15 cut-off date because of severe pressure from the premiers and from within his own party. For further details on this episode see Struthers, "No Fault of Their Own: Unemployment and the Canadian Welfare State, 1914–1941" (Ph.D. thesis, University of Toronto, 1979), chap. 6. The percentage cut in Ottawa's relief spending is calculated from the *Report of the Dominion Commissioner of Unemployment Relief*, 30 March 1935, 5-6, 34; and ibid., 31 March 1936, 36.

41. PAC, Bennett Papers, vol. 182, "Minutes of the Dominion–Provincial Conference," 31 July 1934.

42. Ibid.

43. Ibid., vol. 182, Bennett to Jimmy Stitt, 30 July 1934.

44. PAC, CCSD Papers, vol. 15, file 68, Whitton to W.H. Lovering, 1 August 1934.

45. Much to the chagrin of one of the consulting actuaries who worked on the bill. See PAC, Department of Insurance Records, vol. 1, "Actuarial Report" by H.H. Wolfenden, 1 February 1935.

46. In this endeavour, Whitton had a well-placed ally. Wendall Clarke, secretary of the Canadian Chamber of Commerce, was also a member of the CCC & FW governing board. As early as 1932 Clarke had suggested to Whitton the "need for a more intimate tie-up with the business interests in this very important work of yours" since "the importance of Social Service [was] growing increasingly in Canada" (PAC, CCSD Papers, vol. 21, file 85, W. Clarke to Whitton, 14 March 1932).

47. See, for example, John Taylor, "Urban Social Organization and Urban Discontent: the 1930's," in *Western Perspectives* 1, ed. David Bercuson (Toronto, 1974), 1: 33.

48. PAC, CCSD Papers, vol. 15, Charlotte Whitton, "The Relief Outlook in Canada," December 1934.

49. PAC, Bennett Papers, vol. 812, letter and memo from Wendall Clarke, secretary of the Canadian Chamber of Commerce, to all members of Parliament, 13 April 1935. See also vol. 790, resolution forwarded to Bennett by the Ontario Associated Boards of Trade and Chambers of Commerce, 14 January 1935, urging the same policy in almost identical language.

50. PAC, Department of Labour Records, acc. 70/382, vol. 60, copy of the National Employment Commission Act, 1 Edw. 8, c. 7, 47-50, 8 April 1936.

51. PAC, King Diary, 8 April 1936.

52. PAC, Department of Labour Records, National Employment Commission (hereinafter NEC) files, vol. 66, Charlotte Whitton to Harry Baldwin, 22 July 1936.

53. Ibid., Charlotte Whitton to Tom Moore, 24 July 1937. See also her article, "The Relief of Unemployment," in *Child and Family Welfare* (May 1936).

54. NEC, *Interim Report* (Ottawa, 1937), 15-16.

55. Ibid. A position Whitton made quite explicit in her criticisms of the Rowell-Sirois Report's recommendation that Ottawa should administer unemployment aid itself. "I am . . . appalled," she wrote to Harry Cassidy, "to find that plans apparently contemplate the actual setting up of staff and budgets and the actual administration of aid in cash or in kind—I presume the former—right across Canada in city, rural, mining and widely differing areas. Mr. MacNamara and I have both been telling them that a Dominion power will not be able to pay $27.00 in Saint John, $13.00 in a nearby town, $40.00 in Calgary and $45.00 in Winnipeg; that these differentials must be left to local authority" (CCSD Papers, vol. 99, file 179, Whitton to Cassidy, 16 December 1940).

56. NEC, *Interim Report*, 16-17 (my emphasis).

57. PAC, Department of Labour Records, NEC files, vol. 75, memo by Whitton on "The Organization of Aid to Persons in Distress," March 1937. See also her article on "The Relief of Unemployment."

58. Queen's University Archives, Norman Rogers Papers, copy of statement released by Rogers, 12 March 1938.

59. Canada, House of Commons, *Debates*, 28 April 1838, 2379.

60. See, for example, Harry Cassidy, *Unemployment and Relief in Ontario, 1929–1932* (Toronto, 1932); Leonard Marsh, *Health and Unemployment* (Montreal, 1938); or the collection of essays in L. Richter, ed., *Canada's Unemployment Problem* (Toronto, 1939).

61. A theme elaborated eloquently in Frances Fox Piven and Richard A. Cloward, *Regulating the Poor: the Functions of Public Welfare* (New York, 1971).

"RELIEF FROM RELIEF": THE CITIES' ANSWER TO DEPRESSION DEPENDENCY†

JOHN TAYLOR

Relief of the unemployed was the cities' major problem of dependency in the depression of the thirties. "Relief from Relief" emerged as their central solution.[1] The slogan, concocted by the great Dominion Conference of Mayors of 1935, was shorthand for total federal assumption of relief of the unemployed. Once made the demand was reiterated by local, and particularly city organizations to the end of the decade, heedless of federal obduracy or of consequences to local government.

As an answer to the major problem of dependency in the thirties, it was a policy of social nihilism, a crude cutting of a Gordian knot. It disregarded both the complexities of "state-willed parasitism" in an industrial society, as well as the niceties of responsibility in a federal system.

Yet it was not simply a policy of catastrophe or a gesture of urban desperation. It was thought out. It was justified in endless speeches, addresses and resolutions. It was sanctioned by city organizations in every region of Canada. It begat an organization of mayors to promote it. And it persisted. It did *not* represent social breakdown, though that was predicted; nor did it represent financial collapse, though that was apprehended, especially in the West.

The roots of such a policy lay, rather, in the crisis politics of urban-industrial society. "Relief from Relief" was not so much a social policy as a political catch-phrase masquerading as one. It was brought to life by a curious, strident, charismatic group of mayors who sprang into power in mid-depression in nearly every major city in the Dominion. "Relief from Relief" was their magic potion. It would help dissolve away an

† *Journal of Canadian Studies* 14, no. 1 (Spring 1979): 16–23.

emerging politics of confrontation that was embedded in the social structure and social ecology of their cities, and sharpened to the point of conflict by the depression crisis.

"Relief from Relief" represented a change in city attitudes. It was by no means their first, or up to 1935 their only answer to dependency in modern industrial society. During the teens, twenties and into the early thirties, city governments and city chief magistrates in particular had been among the leaders in the Dominion in urging a reworking of systems of support, especially for the unemployed, a reworking, moreover, that would heavily engage the public sector.[2] They were uncertain in these decades about what to do, and in their own practices tended to be both parsimonious and crude. But they were asking, persistently and repeatedly, for three-level discussions on the care and cost of the unemployed. Whatever their motives — and financial expediency was probably high on the list — they had broken away, as few others had done, from the concentric circles syndrome for relief of the unemployed.[3]

The concentric circles syndrome governed both the ethos and the machinery of relief (and much other welfare) before and through much of the depression. Under it, welfare began as a responsibility of the individual and the family, a notion held in most parts of the country and a provision of the Quebec Civil Code. It is "a humane provision," argued the Montreal *Gazette*, and one "based upon the natural law . . . it is one which, in its acceptance and operation, strengthens family ties and has been a steadying and altogether good influence in the lives of the people."[4] Should individual or family resources become exhausted, private sector support could be drawn on, usually in the form of denominational charity. This ancient system was most favoured in Quebec and Ontario, was somewhat weaker in the West where it had partially collapsed in the period around the First Great War, and was abetted by a primitive if somewhat more "modern" Elizabethan Poor Law System in Nova Scotia and New Brunswick that specified areas of local, public responsibility. Lacunae or breaches in the individual and private support systems were traditionally filled by local governments, though usually only to drag a man back from the edge of the grave. Some partial links between the private and various public sectors, and among the public sectors themselves had been forged by the twenties in most regions, for example in the form of the Public Charities Act of Quebec or the emergency relief grants of the senior governments to the municipalities. But they were not predicated on any new perception of the relationship of the indigent individual and the state. The old catechism persisted. Mackenzie King, prime minister and social scientist, sketched it as well as anyone:

> the obligation of looking after men who are unemployed . . . should be understood to be primarily a matter for individuals in the first instance, between municipalities and the people living within their

bounds, in the second instance, next, between the provinces and
the citizens of the respective provinces, and only finally a matter
of concern in the federal arena.[5]

Should we do otherwise, echoed his Conservative rival, Arthur Meighen,
" . . . we land ourselves in a Serbonian bog from which we will not
emerge. . . . "[6]

The endemic nature of industrial unemployment in twentieth-century
Canada, its increasing scale and the inadequacy of private sector or local
government machinery to deal with it had led local governments, especially in the twenties, to demand of the senior governments a negotiation of responsibilities and financing to meet the problem. Local
governments were especially strident about revision in the sharp depression of the early twenties, but maintained at a less heated level their
position of three-level negotiation of responsibility and financing through
the latter part of the twenties and into the thirties. By 1931 they had
convinced R.B. Bennett's Minister of Labour, Gideon Robertson, that
" . . . there should be a Federal–Provincial Conference, attended by the
Mayors of the largest cities . . . ," to discuss some of the issues.[7] Though
some local politicians in these years were advocating single-level (usually
federal) assumption of relief—mainly because they perceived unemployment as a direct consequence of national immigration policies — they
were mainly in the west and in a minority. They did not represent the
primary thrust of the local demands, that is, to move relief of industrial
unemployment into the public sector on a co-ordinated basis. Under
such a proposition, the concentric circles philosophy would be turned
inside out.

For a variety of mainly political reasons — however much they were
dressed up in Kingsian piety or the threat of yawning Serbonian bogs—
the senior government persistently rejected such ideas,[8] and were ably
seconded by the various provincial authorities for a number of reasons,
most of them still unresearched in any detailed fashion.[9] Through the
twenties and into the thirties they insisted on local responsibility as the
last line of defence, though there seem to have been few impediments
to provincial intervention or even federal.

Where the oft-repeated notion of local responsibility came from is by
no means clear. Many types of social welfare were traditionally the
domain of the provinces in Canada (including Quebec); others were
traditionally handled by the private sector. Explicit statutory responsibility of local governments for social welfare was rare, confined to Vancouver and the Alberta cities in the twenties, and the Ontario
municipalities in the thirties. Some local responsibilities were imposed
through ancillary legislation, like the poor laws of the Maritimes or the
Public Charities Act of Quebec, but though relief of the indigent was
within the general powers of most charters and municipal acts, it was

mainly optional. Formal lines of responsibility before and during the depression were tangled and unclear, especially where the "involuntary unemployed" were concerned. As a result, both the type and degree of local, public sector intervention was a bewildering, almost anarchical hodgepodge. It was an uneven, unrationalized "system" that was neither completely in nor completely out of the local, public sector. Nonetheless, senior governments continued to insist on the notion of local responsibility.

By 1934—and in most cases much earlier—the notion that the individual, the family or private sector charity could either sustain or be held responsible for the unemployed had been stripped away by the depression or made untenable in a practical sense. Traditional arguments that the individual could or even ought to be held responsible for his own work and welfare faded with a general acceptance that he was a victim rather than a cause of his unemployment.

> The old argument of the school of rugged individualism that all government schemes for assisting the unemployed are evil devices which encourage the work-shy to live at the expense of the community, is no longer acceptable.
>
> A new and vital social consciousness has been born and it will not tolerate involuntary destitution as an inevitable part of human life.[10]

The author of those lines, Vancouver Mayor Gerry McGeer, was prone to hyperbole, but he probably reflected fairly accurately the feelings of most of the big city mayors. The individual, as a cause of unemployment, was dethroned. He had been reduced, in Toronto Mayor Jimmie Simpson's phrase, to "but a cumber of the ground."[11]

Likewise, the private sector as a basic support system, or even as an effective administrative medium for public support, had virtually collapsed by 1931, though the fiction of denominational charity was maintained in Quebec through the depression and for two decades after. For the mayors themselves, there was little but contempt, by 1935, for "Mr. Bennett's idea . . . that the care of the unfortunate in our communities is still a charge on the great majority of our fortunate men. . . ."[12]

That the urban leaders should be concerned . . . is not to be wondered at. Local governments, willy nilly, within a few years of the crash were quite alone in their responsibility for the bulk of the unemployed, though they were aided financially by a system of federal and provincial emergency matching relief grants, and by the assumption of the responsibility for certain categories of relief, most particularly the single man. Private sector relief was by 1932 directed largely to providing "amenities" beyond basic subsistence, or supporting certain kinds of relief, like the Oriental in Vancouver, or the single female parent in Montreal, who was denied relief on the grounds of immorality. The concern of the big city governments was likewise heightened by the fact that they had the lion's share of the problem: " . . . the larger cities with about 30 percent of the country's population contain about 50 percent of the unemployed and incur nearly 70 percent of the total cost of relief."[13]

The scale of the problem, in addition to its persistence, had led most cities by 1934 into serious financial difficulties, though none of the central cities had defaulted, and only Windsor had been put under supervision.[14] It is even debatable how serious their plight was, and it is certain that the difficulties varied widely.[15] The problem, however, was the same, whether imminent bankruptcy was real or apprehended: uncontrollable expenses, mainly for relief and interest, were growing, while the tax base was shrinking. Assessments were declining, collections were down, revenue sources were eliminated by some provincial governments, outright destruction of property was practised, and thousands of properties were falling to the cities for non-payment of taxes. "At the rate we are going now it won't be long before the entire city is owned by the city,"[16] an Edmonton mayoral candidate observed.

In such circumstances, almost every device to reduce controllable expenses — less than half of most city budgets — was tried. Some efforts were predictable: cut back work, wages and establishment. Others were unorthodox: charging non-residents for education, turning off street lights, or resorting to scrip for payment. Attempts were made to expand the tax base as Camillien Houde did in Montreal, and to avoid responsibilities, as McGeer in Vancouver did by threatening to cut bond interest rates unilaterally, or as Mayor Andy Davison in Calgary did by paying his American bonds in discounted Canadian dollars.

But the demands of relief overwhelmed every expedient and only added to statutory obligations, especially obligations to pay interest on loans. By 1934 nearly every major city in Canada was funding its relief, either directly through borrowing, or indirectly by suspending sinking fund payments. And such borrowing produced no civic assets (as traditionally supposed to) except, as Toronto's Conservative Mayor W.J. Stewart argued to his equally Conservative council, "an asset in man's humanity to man."[17]

Municipalities in general and the big cities in particular were not only isolated and on a financial rack, they were in a policy vacuum. The individual could not be held responsible. Traditional modes of support, like the private sector, had fallen away and non-traditional ones, like the senior governments, were adamant in their repeated refusal to assume any responsibility. The local governments were alone with their dependents and their bankruptcy, and repeatedly frustrated in their efforts to move back to old ways or to introduce new ones.

Even had the municipalities somewhere to go, they had no clear idea by 1935 what direction to take or how to get there. There was an almost complete vacuum in terms of social policy, or possibly such a bewildering variety of often hare-brained schemes that a single strategy was difficult to find. Few local politicians had a comprehensive program or alternatives, though unemployment insurance tended to be a perennial though not pre-eminent element in their deliberations and resolutions. Even it was abandoned in 1935. There was virtually no direction from the senior governments. Nor was there any significant body of research on which to base a program. The mayors of the big cities in late 1934 and 1935 " . . . failed utterly to obtain from any government, with the exception . . . of Nova Scotia, information which would guide us in any way towards a solution of the problem."[18] The mayors, as a result, generated their own comparative statistics, one of their number remarking that it was a "sad commentary" on Canadian governments that [they] lacked information that was "vitally important and necessary" to direct the relief system.[19] Not until December of 1935, for the purposes of the Dominion–Provincial conference, was comparative information generated by the federal authorities, and, as a result of that conference, was machinery established to develop comprehensive, comparable, and regular information on relief and its costs. The whole nation was without a social compass, even had it known where it wanted to go.

The absence of social policy can be explained in part by the sheer lack of information and perhaps the absence of specialists who had some idea of how to generate information and what to do with it. But lack of information and technicians was an excuse more than a reason. That modern public social work was at a discount in the depression reflects an unwillingness to confront a problem and to develop machinery and strategies to resolve it.

There is also a considerable element of truth in the argument that the city fathers were congenitally incapable of meeting problems of economic contraction and social responsibility,[20] and thus turned to "Relief from Relief' as a logical consequence of that incapacity. Their ethic, from an earlier period, was based on economic expansion of the individual city, or every city for itself, coupled with social irresponsibility, or every man for himself. They simply lacked the imagination or motivation to break out of an ethic better adapted for a quite different environment. This was no doubt why retrenchment and autarky, as the reverse of expenditure and expansiveness, were the chief economic strategies of most city governments, not to mention those of the senior levels. Still, it was very traditional councils and traditional mayors who brought much welfare into the public sector, admittedly with reluctance and mainly because they wanted some control over the public funds they were pumping into private sector organizations. It was *not* traditional mayors who argued in mid-depression for the abandonment of relief responsibilities. This idea was pressed, rather, by the mid-depression radicals, the quixotic charismatics who reached the zenith of their activity in the Dominion Conference of Mayors of 1935.

Doctors and lawyers may well have been on relief rolls in the thirties, but they were the dramatic and dramatized exception to the rule that the bulk of the unemployed was drawn from the lower levels of the industrial structure. Canada's census takers in mid-depression were quite explicit: " . . . there [was] a class differentiation between the employed and the unemployed . . . created in part by the industrial structure, in part by extraneous forces."[21] To be more specific, the unemployed were the workers who had the weakest attachment to the most vulnerable parts of the industrial structure. Recent immigrants and young people, for different reasons newcomers to the labour force, were unemployment prone, as were the construction workers and general labour.

The articulation of depression joblessness and anxiety in a class or vertical sense through the industrial structure also had its visible manifestation on the city-scape. Socio-economic segregation was characteristic of the Canadian urban landscape, and in its twentieth-century form was tied to the emerging industrial structure.[22] People with similar places in the industrial structure also tended to live in similar parts of the city. In the depression, the unemployed, tending to come from certain groups or classes, also therefore tended to come from certain, quite specific areas of the cities. They resided, for the most part, in the Skid Road and working-class sections. Conversely, the employed appear to have lived in other, distinctive areas. The unemployed were *not* diffused through the industrial structure; equally they were *not* spread evenly across the urban landscape.

In a period of fairly widespread local democracy — though property qualifications for office, a property franchise for money bills, and plural voting were general — the segregation of the employed and the jobless presented a political reality that could not be ignored and a dilemma that did not admit of easy resolution. Urban ecology, industrial class and city politics were thus linked.

The emergence of large numbers of unemployed identified with specific areas of the city tended to accentuate political divisions that traditionally had existed, but which in most cities had been expressed politically in only a limited way. Among the major centres, only in Montreal and Edmonton had the poorer or working-class areas been able to translate their dominant numbers into political control prior to the depression. In Montreal's case, it was done through the vehicle of Populists like Médéric Martin and at the end of the twenties and in the early thirties by Camillien Houde; in Edmonton, through a labour party that obtained majority control of city council in the late twenties and sustained it (adding the mayor's chair) until 1934. In most other cities, working-class representation on council was weak, though in the west some form of labour/socialist politics was perceived as a real alternative to "business" politics, most notably in Winnipeg.

For the most part, cities in the pre-depression and early depression periods were controlled by conventional coalitions, that is to say Liberals and Conservatives, who represented themselves as the non-partisan directors of the city corporation, and above invidious distinctions of class or neighbourhood, as they were above invidious distinctions of political party.

The depression, however, intensified any existing threats of non-partisan politics. Prosperity had offered the prospect of mobility to all, and individual initiative had offered the means. With the fall of prosperity and the discounting of the role of the individual, prospective mobility, so corrosive of working-class consciousness, became less appealing to groups seemingly frozen into a life of intermittent work and the dole. That is, at least one major inhibition to an occupational group sense, perception or consciousness was removed by the depression. It also provided a major incentive to group identification. Relief was basically a transfer of money from one group in one part of the city to another group in another part of the city. And both groups mightily resented the transfer, or the need for it. The depression opened the chasm between the victims of industrial society and the merely victimized. Class or group action, encouraged by a common experience and propinquity, emerged as a more plausible strategic alternative to individual effort and non-partisan politics. Since working-class areas, if organized, had numbers, political groups, especially of the socialist species, appeared a real threat to traditional civic government.

The threat became increasingly real with the mobilization of the socialist/labour groups in the thirties, though at the local level, as elsewhere, they tended to be a confused and often warring collection of communists, CCFers (after 1932), and labour fronts. They clearly recognized the social and the spatial divisions in the cities and were attempting to translate them into political control via the party. Conventional politics for the nonce was at a discount. Its business strategies of autarky and retrenchment and vapid expressions of goodwill to the unemployed were disenchanting. Mere stress, created by economic collapse, was made a crisis for many by a collapse of conventional imagination, and the threat of socialist alternative. In such a situation, "Fear . . . is replaced by anxiety . . . ," and society rapidly "becomes more preoccupied with alleviating its state of anxiety than its fear, and practically ceases to do anything about the danger which elicited the fear in the first place. Figuratively speaking, a society in crisis clamours for 'cultural bromides' rather than for tools and weapons."[23]

By 1934, in most of the major cities, the call for bromides was being answered by a curious group of radical mayors that might, after Weber, be called charismatics, but after Cervantes, be called quixotic. They had mass appeal, but were unable to institutionalize it. They represented a temporary alternative to both the socialist and conventional impulses. In most cases they were strident, enthusiastic individuals who made great point of their independence from establishments of all kinds. Fightin' Joe Clarke of mid-depression Edmonton was typical of the genre when he claimed that the conventional local politicians had put the city "on the bum" and labour had kept it there. Others were Camillien Houde of Montreal, Gerry McGeer of Vancouver, and Cornelius Rink of Regina. Their kind were reasonably common to local politics in the twentieth century, and they seemed to emerge from time to time as a check or warning to establishment forces or, more common to the depression, to transcend the warring divisions in the cities. The exception was Montreal where they remained in the twentieth century as an almost permanent check. For the most part they were able to cut into areas of support traditionally claimed by both the left and the right in local politics (except for their core areas), the most spectacular success coming in Vancouver where in 1934 Gerry McGeer won every poll in the city. Invariably their appeals involved a scapegoat that lurked in the class, cultural or regional mists of their various cities. Very often it was the "socialists" (who wished to turn the cities into warring camps), but their targets also included corporations, financial conspiracies, eastern power brokers — in short, establishments of one sort or another that had generated resentments in a particular region or culture. Finally their programs generally involved crusades of one sort or another, whether against "redwings," bond-dealers, immorality or atheism. They were active. Such politics of crisis produced a policy of crisis, "Relief from Relief," and the crusade of the mayors in the spring of 1935 to Montreal and their subsequent confrontation with the government in Ottawa.

The policy and the crusade had much to recommend it. "Relief from Relief" would shift responsibility for the unemployed out of the local political arena where the business of taking from Peter and giving to Paul was proving to be politically dangerous. It would at the same time resolve the serious strain on city budgets and prevent further expansion of indebtedness, thereby appeasing the taxpaying class, and providing more certain funding to the tax-using class. A taxpayers' revolt and a proletarian revolution would both be defused.

The program was accepted by both conservative and socialist in the cities: for the former, perhaps, because it had nothing better to offer, and for the latter because such a strategy conformed closely enough to their broader policy of centralized planning and administration of social services. In both cases political expediency demanded participation in a people's crusade.

The mayors' proposals were rejected by the senior governments. They chose another strategy, one of separating power and responsibility, a practice that the Prime Minister, Mackenzie King, was denouncing even as he was helping to put it into effect. The cities ultimately were given the task of delivering services, the provinces of regulating them, and the provinces and the federal . . . [government the task] of funding them.

Neither the mayors' program nor that of the senior governments was, however, primarily a solution to a type of urban dependency. Neither program recognized unemployment as a class problem supposedly susceptible to a class solution, or any other solution that focussed on the dependants themselves. Both were, rather, policies their proponents saw as productive of political harmony and political success: for the mayors in the face of intolerable social cleavage; for the senior governments, especially the federal, in the face of constitutional cleavage. The greater relief was relief for the politician.

In all of this, the greater victims, arguably, were the cities themselves, which came out of the depression lumbered with a burden of fiscal and statutory controls that effectively tied their future development to the realities of senior government planning and politics, not civic ones. Perhaps the process was inevitable, as K.G. Crawford argues, in order to obtain a modicum of equity in a federal and plural state.[24] Or perhaps the effective dethronement of the city flowed from broader, more powerful secular forces, as Hugh Whalen argues:

> Local self-government as it exists in most industrial democracies today can no longer be considered a major instrument of control. In an era of expanding communities, growing mass publics, and intricate and expanding technologies, mechanisms of democratic control must be located at the vital centres of power of each national community.[25]

But whatever the cause, at least one effect was to fudge the class nature of dependency and, in many cities, though not all, the class nature of politics. Though the solution was not that demanded by the mid-depression mayors, the effect probably was. What they hadn't anticipated, however, was that the abrogation of responsibility for social policy—in effect what "Relief from Relief" was — opened in the way for other strategies that reduced the cities, in the main, to delivery systems. In one sense, urban dependency by the Second Great War was as applicable to the cities themselves as to the social casualties in them.

Notes

1. Three policy resolutions were approved at the conference. Federal assumption of relief was the first and central one. The second was a proposal for federal refunding of local and provincial debt, in effect a call for relief of past relief. The third was a proposal for constitutional revision that was necessarily implied by the first two.

While the first was greeted with universal enthusiasm, the other two, especially that for refunding, which was pressed by the western cities, met some resistance.

2. See resolutions of the Union of Canadian Municipalities, as reported in *The Municipal Review of Canada*. Typical of many years in the twenties was that in vol. 25, no. 9 (September 1929): 369.

3. The phrase "concentric circles" if not invented by, was used by Esdras Minville, in *La Législation ouvrière et le régime social dans la Province de Québec*, a study prepared for the Royal Commission on Dominion–Provincial Relations, Ottawa, 1939. The idea was pervasive at the senior levels of government, as debates in the various legislatures make abundantly clear. For some recent, detailed scholarship on relief and welfare in which the notion is expressed, see James Struthers, "Prelude to Depression: The Federal Government and Unemployment, 1918–29," *Canadian Historical Review* 58, no. 3 (September 1977): 277-93; and B.L. Vigod, "Ideology and Institutions in Quebec. The Public Charities Controversy, 1921-1926," *Histoire sociale/Social History* 11, no. 21 (May 1978): 167-82.

4. Editorial, *The Gazette* (Montreal), 14 January 1929.

5. Canada, House of Commons, *Debates*, 24 April 1922, vol. 2, 1073.

6. Ibid., 1078.

7. Roberston to R.B. Bennett, Ottawa, 6 May 1931, Public Archives of Canada, Bennett Papers, Micro M-1448, 487162.

8. See Struthers, "Prelude to Depression."

9. See Vigod, "Ideology and Institutions."

10. G.G. McGeer, "An Address," typescript of a radio address on CBO, Ottawa, 11 May 1938, McGeer papers, Provincial Archives of B.C.

11. Dominion Conference of Mayors, Montreal and Ottawa, 25-28 March 1935, *Report of Deliberations*, 2nd session, 25 March, unpag.

12. *Report of Deliberations*, James Simpson, 1st session, 25 March 1935.

13. H. Carl Goldenberg, *Municipal Finance in Canada*, a study for the Royal Commission on Dominion–Provincial Relations (Ottawa, 1938), 69.

14. Ibid.

15. For the variety, see: Department of Social Research, McGill University, *Comparative Statement of the Relief Situation in Canadian Municipalities*, in Mayors, *Report of Deliberations*, and Thomas Bradshaw, "The Maintenance of Public Credit," Ontario Municipal Association, *Proceedings* (1934), 75. For a sceptical comment on the degree of the problem, see the latter.

16. Mayoral candidate James H. Oglivie, quoted in *The Journal* (Edmonton), 7 November 1934.

17. "Inaugural Address," January 1934, Toronto City Council, *Minutes*, Appendix C, Reports and Returns.

18. Halifax Mayor E.J. Cragg, "To MPs and Senators," Mayors' Conference, *Report of Deliberations*, 7th session, 27 March 1935.

19. Ibid.

20. The argument is set out in Alan F.J. Artibise, "Patterns of Prairie Urban Development," paper presented to The Great Chautauqua, Western Canada Studies Conference, University of Calgary, February 1978, and the Atlantic Studies Conference, University of New Brunswick, April 1978.

21. "Unemployment," in *Census of Canada*, 1931, 13: 358.

22. The whole subject of human ecology, especially social segregation, is full of pitfalls, and much punctuated with debate. The best Canadian material so far is Peter Goheen, *Victorian Toronto, 1850-1900: Pattern and Process of Growth* (Chicago, 1970).

Nonetheless, the fact of segregation and some relationship to group and class structure is clear.

23. George Devereaux, "Charismatic Leadership and Crisis," *Psychoanalysis and the Social Sciences* (New York, 1955), 4: 147.

24. K.G. Crawford, *Canadian Municipal Government* (Toronto, 1964), 337.

25. Hugh G. Whalen, "Ideology, Democracy, and the Foundations of Local Self Government," *Canadian Journal of Economics and Political Science* 26, no. 3 (August 1960): 394.

THE LIBERAL WAY: FISCAL AND MONETARY POLICY IN THE 1930s†

H. BLAIR NEATBY

It would be foolhardy to suggest that the Liberal way was a clearly defined thoroughfare in the 1930s. More often it resembled a network of aimless paths, more concerned with avoiding obstacles than arriving at a destination. Yet it is possible to distinguish movement and direction. The "dirty thirties" is a more distinct era or historical period than most decades. It has a beginning and an end — from the Wall Street crash to the outbreak of war — and it has the depression as the focus of talk and action. The Liberal party, of necessity, was forced to respond, to debate fiscal and monetary policy, to contemplate radical economic initiatives, and tentatively to experiment with unprecedented measures. There was no revolution, but the Liberal Party of 1939 had travelled a long way from the Liberal party of 1930.

In this decade, Mackenzie King seemed almost an anachronism. His career went back to the pre-war era of Laurier, and his policies and his style seemed inappropriate at a time when the eternal verities were being challenged and when a new generation was hankering for revolution. In the words of Frank Scott, who has never suffered conservatism gladly:

> He blunted us,
> We had no shape
> Because he never took sides,
> and no sides
> Because he never allowed them to take shape.
>
> . . .

† Victor Hoar, ed., *The Great Depression: Essays and Memoirs from Canada and the United States* (Toronto: Copp Clark Ltd., 1969), 84–114.

Truly he will be remembered
Wherever men honour ingenuity,
Ambiguity, inactivity, and political longevity.[1]

I don't propose to challenge this version of Mackenzie King. He did avoid confrontations with ingenuity and ambiguity. Instead of innovation and change he counselled caution and patience. Yet even King could not ignore what was happening in Canada. His was the politics of survival but to survive he had to adapt. He did react to the pressures on the federal government for dynamic leadership, for initiative and experiment, for government intervention, although he reacted in his own inimitable way. His response to these pressures is a case-study of a political leader and also of the country which he led for so long.

Even without the depression, the 1930s would have marked a new beginning in Canada. Physical problems had dominated Canadian life since the days of John A. Macdonald. The National Policy had been the focus of politics for two generations because without immigration, railways and the tariff there would have been no integrated national economy and no Canada. By the 1920s however, the aims of the National Policy had been achieved. The railways were built, the west had its settlers and the east had its industries. There was still some tidying up to do. The 1920s were the decade when bankrupt railways were melded into the Canadian National Railways, when the flow of immigrants was slowly turned off, and when the King government tinkered with minor tariff reductions.

Thus Canadians of the 1930s would have had to grope for a new national policy even without a depression. Canada was established as a geographical and an economic entity but within this framework there were social realities which could no longer be ignored. There were economic disparities between rich and poor, regional rivalries dividing east and west, cultural divergences between French and English — and already there were signs that Canadians would challenge the inequities and iniquities so long overshadowed by the more urgent problem of establishing a national economy.

The depression added a new element to the debate on the new national policy. In one sense, the depression was a catalyst because it accentuated social, regional and cultural divisions and so added emotional depth to the confrontations. It was more than a catalyst, however, because it focussed attention primarily on the regional disparities. Social and cultural differences did not disappear. Industrial workers became more conscious of the class struggle — in British Columbia, the CCF was primarily a labour party and polarized provincial politics by that fact; in Ontario the industrial unionism of the CIO threatened to have the same effect. French Canadians too, became more conscious of their cultural identity. But these developments seemed almost peripheral because the

depression struck the western provinces so disastrously and so dispro-
portionately. The temptation to see the problem in regional terms was
too strong to be resisted.

The context of the depression affected more than the intensity of
east–west rivalry. It also determined the issues that were debated. There
was now a consensus on immigration — few people wanted newcomers
at a time of industrial unemployment and agricultural surpluses. Railways
were an issue only because of the CNR deficits. Even tariffs, the touch-
stone of the prairie politics for a generation, had lost their relevance for
farmers who had almost no income. In this period of desperate crisis the
nostrums of the cranks and heretics of a few years before were now
seriously debated, and socialism and Social Credit flourished where the
Progressives had once seemed radical. The conviction that traditional
social institutions had failed forced men to consider revolutionary
alternatives.

Money was one such institution. There is no need to stress the
importance of money in a capitalist economy. To be sound as a dollar is
to be very sound indeed, and if the dollar is weakened, the fabric of this
society is surely rent asunder. In western Canada the traditional reverence
for a sound dollar was swept away by the hot dry winds of the 1930s.
In some areas of southern Saskatchewan there were nine successive years
of crop failure because of drought and grasshoppers or, when the rains
came, because of rust and frost. This was enough to make men irrational.
Crop failures alone, however, might have been accepted with resignation
because no mortal could be blamed for them. But even for those farmers
who did harvest a crop in some of those years, the price they received
for their wheat was so low that three or four bushels were needed to
buy what one bushel had bought before. For farmers with mortgages,
interest rates had not declined, although the land had so depreciated in
value that arrears of interest alone often exceeded the present value of
the mortgaged property. Something was radically wrong when the men
who tilled the soil could be exploited in this way by the price system
and by banks and moneylenders. "There were two ways one could
become popular in the west," J.G. Gardiner told King in 1932; "one
was to hammer the banks and one was to hammer the Tories."[2] In the
next few years hammering the bankers, who reputedly controlled credit,
was to become an even more popular sport that hammering Tories, who
controlled the tariff. Bankers were blamed for not making loans, for
keeping interest rates high — in short for all the ills of a debtor society
in a depression. From bankers it was a short step to monetary policy.
Why shouldn't the government put more money into circulation? More
money would mean higher prices, lower interest rates and the repayment
of mortgages in inflated dollars. The government had printed money to
pay the cost of the war. Why not now? One responsible and balanced
Liberal reported to King in January of 1933 that "inflation has swept

like a fire over the prairies."³ The fire was to sear many political fingers before it burned out.

Political leaders may also be institutions in their day. In many provinces politicians were the first institutions to be overthrown. It was all too easy to make them the scapegoats for the depression and to cast them aside. It is true that established politicians were unreceptive to new and radical proposals. They could not easily believe that the society which had recognized and rewarded their talents was fundamentally unsound, and, as men in power, they tended to equate radicalism with sedition. But there is no need here to analyse the defeat and often the disgrace of once-respected leaders. For our purpose their defeat is significant for what it reveals about the 1930s. In Quebec, the dignified and aristocratic Taschereau is deserted by the young Liberals, is identified with corruption and is replaced by Maurice Duplessis, who is neither dignified nor aristocratic. In Ontario George Henry, sound and stolid, is replaced by "Mitch" Hepburn, who flouted conventions.

In Alberta, J.E. Brownlee, such a respected lawyer that he had become leader of a farmer's party, was accused of personal immorality and his party was defeated by Social Credit under "Bible Bill" Aberhart, who knew more about biblical prophecies than world wheat markets. And in British Columbia, the cautious Dr. Tolmie was swept out of office by the reckless "Duff" Pattullo, who offered "work and wages" and "socialized credit." In short, the traditional political leaders, with middle class origins, good social connections, and once admired for their unimaginative integrity, were replaced in the 1930s by men without social prestige, uninhibited men who spoke in the vernacular of the under-privileged, who may have been more demagogic than radical but who symbolized the rejection of middle class leadership.

At the federal level, five years in office was enough to destroy the reputation of R.B. Bennett and his Conservative party. In 1930 Bennett believed that higher tariffs would end unemployment in Canada. When unemployment grew worse he reacted like a traditional Tory and looked to the Empire and imperial preferences for the cure. His mission as he saw it was to preserve the society which had been so satisfactory in the past; a cynic might say that he naturally admired a system which had enabled him to become a millionaire. In 1932 he announced bluntly that his government would "stand for sound money. Let there be no mistake about that."⁴ In each successive session the objective of his government was to balance the budget, and unemployment and farm relief was begrudgingly conceded as a regrettable obligation of the federal government. Indeed Bennett seriously considered sacrificing certain political institutions in order to preserve financial stability. In 1933 he toyed with the idea of appointing a federal receiver to take over the financial administration of the western provinces which could not meet their own relief costs. Even legislative assemblies were less important than a sound dollar. In his draft letter to the western premiers he explained: "It is with regret that I find myself obliged to write to you in these terms but the fact is that the credit of the Dominion is just now the most vital factor affecting the welfare of the people of Canada, and I dare not omit any step necessary to protect that credit."⁵ Western Conservatives such as M.A. Macpherson in Regina could see the logic of this argument but felt that "one's eyes must not be closed to the political effect of decisions of this kind."⁶ This idea was dropped but the paramount importance of preserving a sound dollar was never questioned.

In 1934 Bennett did establish a central bank. Even this, however, was not intended to be a radical innovation. The new Bank of Canada was a privately owned institution with directors elected by the shareholders. This cumbrous system, Bennett explained, was designed to remove the bank as far as possible from partisan politics. Monetary policy was too important to be entrusted to governments.

The traditional policies proved to be sterile in these years but Bennett had little else to offer. The frustration of impotence provoked vehement denunciations of his opponents. To Bennett, critics of his monetary and fiscal policies were dangerous because they were attacking the foundations of society. He labelled the advocates of inflation indiscriminately as socialists or communists. In 1932 he exhorted all loyal Canadians "to put the iron heel of ruthlessness" on such revolutionaries, as he himself invoked Section 98 of the Criminal Code to put Tim Buck and other communists in jail. How could society strengthen itself against its enemies? One minor measure was to restore the conferring of titles on meritorious Canadians and thus to reward the faithful and enhance the prestige of the ruling class. It goes without saying that his critics were neither awed nor silenced. Farm titles seemed more important than knighthoods to many Canadians.

R.B. Bennett never took the road to Damascus. His New Deal was not a sudden conversion to radical measures. His New Deal broadcasts had some of the rhetoric of a revolutionary: "The old order is gone. It will not return." "If we cannot abolish the dole we should abolish the system." But Bennett's solution was not to transform but to reform the system. Laissez-faire was dead and government regulation and control was necessary: "In what way and to what extent must the Government intervene? That is a difficult question. All I can tell you is that we will go just as far as is necessary to reform the system and make it effectively work again."⁷

The New Deal legislation of the session of 1935 was radical in constitutional terms, since it would have extended federal authority significantly, but it was not radical in social terms. Unemployment insurance would not abolish the dole; anti-combines legislation would not abolish the capitalist system. The New Deal was an essay in political psychology. It was intended to convince Canadians that their government was taking action. It failed because Bennett was no longer credible as a reformer. His vaunted charisma went unperceived by the depression audiences in the election of 1935. Bennett felt betrayed by a colleague—H.H. Stevens —in 1935, betrayed by the party which chose Manion as his successor in 1938, and went home to England with the taste of Canadian ingratitude bitter in his mouth.

William Lyon Mackenzie King had a very different fate. He might have had a reputation as a reformer or even as a radical Minister of Labour under Wilfrid Laurier, but King had been Prime Minister through the 1920s and had a well-earned reputation for judicious caution and for carefully calculated compromise. Neither he nor his party were linked to any radical nostrums or to any New Deal in the years in Opposition. Yet in 1935 King was returned to office with the largest majority of any government up to that time. His majority was less impressive in terms of the popular vote—48.6 percent, only slightly up from the Liberal vote in 1930—but still striking for an electorate which by 1935 was choosing between CCF, Social Credit and the Reconstruction Party as well as Conservative and Liberal. King was one of the exceptional politicians who survived the transition from the 1920s to the 1930s and, indeed, went on to survive the 1940s as well. How did King and his party adapt to the "politics of discontent" during the depression? What was the "Liberal way" which led to the seats of the mighty in 1935 and which left the party securely ensconced for the rest of the decade?

Mackenzie King never thought of the depression as an economic problem. To him it was a political problem. His objective in its simplest terms was to get into office and to stay in office. And for the first years of the decade the depression had remarkably little impact on his thinking. He had, after all, come into office in 1921 during a depression. In the years that followed, his government had gradually reduced tariffs and taxes; the economy had recoverd and gone on to unparalleled prosperity. It was natural for King to see a cause and effect relationship and to take it for granted that the same policies would again be effective.

His defeat in 1930 did not force him to question the validity of his past experience. He had expected to win on his government's record and it was easy to rationalize Bennett's victory as the temporary triumph of a demagogue who had promised the impossible and would reap the whirlwind. It was also easy for King to avoid nagging doubts or changing his perspective because Bennett gave priority to the traditional Tory panacea of higher tariffs. King would have been quite happy to hammer on the tariff for the next four years, confident that high tariffs were a bad thing and that Canadian voters would soon agree. As King wrote to T.A. Crerar after the special session in 1930:

How much we have to thank Bennett for I do not imagine we will ever know. There had been something more or less unreal about most of our tariff discussion. The country as a whole has never had to face the effect of extremes in policy. . . . That there is a difference is now wholly apparent and we are going to see what the effects of the difference really amount to.[8]

Not all Liberals were as patient as their leader. By the spring of 1932 many western Liberals were convinced that the depression was an unprecedented crisis which called for unprecedented measures. The official Liberal response to the Conservative budget of that year, however, was still a reflection of King's views. The Liberal amendment insisted that lower tariffs were "essential to a revival of trade, and improvement of business, and the return of prosperity."[9] The surviving Progressives in the House, impelled by economic disaster, took a radical leap by demanding government control of the financial system and a policy of monetary inflation. J.S. Woodsworth supported the Progressives. In the Liberal caucus, according to King, "One member after another from the West and B.C. declared they would vote for the progressive amendment." King pleaded for party unity. He pointed out that this amendment implicitly rejected lower tariffs as a reform measure. Why not vote against the Progressive amendment on those grounds, while still expressing their personal views on monetary reform?[10] In the end all Liberals did vote against the radical amendment. King was able to continue his dogmatic slumber.

His sleep was disturbed, not by R.B. Bennett but by "thunder on the left." The CCF party was provisionally organized at a conference in Calgary in 1932. The conference at Regina a year later established the constitution of the new party and approved a program which had already been outlined at Calgary. Labour and Progressive MPs at Ottawa had succeeded in bringing together the western labour movements, splintered since the days of the OBU [One Big Union] and the Winnipeg Strike but still active and still radical, and the radical western farmers' movements which had survived King's blandishments in the 1920s. The details of the formation of the CCF are not central to the story of King's adjustment to the economic crisis. The emergence of a new political party, a socialist party, a party which menaced the Liberal position in western Canada — this was the crucial fact for King.

Thus after the summer of 1932 it was obvious that the political situation had changed. No longer could King take it for granted that the almost certain Conservative defeat at the next election meant almost certain Liberal victory — the CCF would give voters a third choice. No longer could King talk only of the iniquities of the Bennett tariff and the beneficent effects of increased trade — he now had to counter the policies advocated by the CCF as well.

It was not the socialism of the CCF that he considered to be the threat. Tories, he believed, wanted to exploit political power for the benefit of capitalists; socialists wanted to exploit it for the benefit of the lower class. Liberals, in King's lexicon, offered the middle way, using political power to protect the interests of all. This rather simplified version of the three political ideologies made it easy for King to believe that real socialists, like real Tories, would always be a minority. Liberally minded men would always be the largest group. Some liberally minded men, however, might be so misled or so misguided as to mistakenly support the CCF party (as some had supported the Conservative party in the past) regardless of its ideology. It was King's task to keep them from going astray.

The danger was not socialism but inflation. The CCF was a socialist party, but it was a socialist party that gave a high priority to monetary policy as a means of establishing a socialized economic order. In the Regina Manifesto, the first item is planning; the second is socialization of finance. The nationalization of other institutions, the policies for agriculture and labour, welfare policies, constitutional policies; all these came later because in the words of the Manifesto, "control of finance is the first step in the control of the whole economy." Mackenzie King saw the danger — liberally minded men might vote for a socialist party because it was an inflationist party. As he wrote to a friend in England in January of 1933:

> If we had an election tomorrow, we would, without question, sweep the country. I doubt if Mr. Bennett's fate would not be equal to Mr. Meighen's when we came into office in 1921 and [he] did not have a single seat in six provinces out of nine. Unfortunately, we would meet to some extent with the same kind of misfortune as we did in 1921, through the inroads of a third party — a combination of farmer and labour — the Cooperative Commonwealth Federation they call themselves. Inflation of the currency and freeing society of the capitalist system is, at the moment, their main objective. Western Canada, in particular, where the farmers have suffered terribly through low prices, appears to be ready to support anything which promises to increase the nominal values which they are called upon to meet.[11]

Thus it was inflation, not socialism, which worried King.

Western Liberals saw an easy answer — the Liberal party should also opt for a policy of inflation. Many eastern Liberals, however, were more respectful of the value of money, and King himself was inclined to see inflation as a form of robbery. But King was first and foremost a party leader, and it was as party leader that he responded. "I fear we are going to have a difficult time in reconciling the views of some of the members of the party on currency and credit problems," he wrote to Crerar, again in January of 1933. It might be difficult but it was essential if the party was to appeal to all liberally minded men.

In the early months of 1933 King managed to create the optical illusion that he had squared the circle. He did not opt for either inflation or sound money. Instead, he opted for a publicly controlled central bank. A central bank was not a policy. It was an institution. But it was an institution which provided the machinery for manipulating currency and credit for social purposes. Even though a central bank might implement rigidly conservative policies, it was identified in the minds of many Canadians with a policy of inflation. By advocating a central bank, the Liberal party would not necessarily be committed to inflation but to radicals at least, it would appear to be.[12]

It was not easy for King to persuade the party to advocate a central bank. The compromise was too radical for some and too conservative for others. The issue was debated bitterly for six weeks in caucus. King used his remarkable skills as a diplomat to engineer an agreement. Eventually the Liberals went a little farther than King had originally hoped. In addition to a central bank, the official statement of party policy went on to say that supply of currency and credit should be determined by the needs of the community.

This was more than a platitudinous declaration. Nobody knew how a Liberal government would assess the needs of the community. Nevertheless, it stated that monetary policy should be a government responsibility, and this was a revolutionary idea when viewed in the context of government policies in the past. The Liberal party was adjusting slowly, but it was adjusting.

Bennett's Bank of Canada legislation in 1934 provided useful publicity for the Liberal new look. By attacking the idea of a privately owned bank and by championing the principle of government control, the Liberal party at least identified itself more closely with a potentially radical policy.

This potential as a party of reform was an asset in the election of 1935. Mackenzie King made few promises and offered the healing hand of the physician rather than the mailed first of a revolutionary. With R.B. Bennett discredited, King was the choice of the cautious. Some Liberals, however, were less restrained. As J.W. Dafoe admitted, it was easy for monetary enthusiasts to interpret the "somewhat adaptable Liberal formula" as a policy of inflation.[13] In an election in which three new parties had appeared — CCF, Social Credit and Reconstruction — the Liberals had the advantage of appearing both reliable and a reform party at the same time.

Once in office, King burnt no bridges behind him nor did he leap enthusiastically into the unknown. His first major decision in domestic affairs was to name Charles Dunning Minister of Finance. Dunning had been a westerner and the leader of a party in Saskatchewan which had been a farmers' party in all but name. But Dunning, like Tom Crerar, was more Whig than radical and his experience as a successful business executive during the depression had, if anything, confirmed his orthodoxy. In 1932 he could calmly argue that the optimism of the 1920s had caused the disaster and that "Humanity is now doing penance in an economic sense for its infraction of the laws of sound economics." When the debt had been paid the immutable law of supply and demand would once more hold sway in the land.[14] With such a man as Minister of Finance, King could be sure that the orthodox views of sound money and balanced budgets would have an influential spokesman in the Council chamber.

True to his traditional assumptions about the nature of economic crisis and its solution, King gave priority to trade matters. Negotiations for a trade agreement had already begun under R.B. Bennett but the long discussions had been broken off during the election campaign. King had promised the electors at the time that he could succeed where Bennett had failed. Negotiations were re-opened after the election and within two weeks of taking office, King himself was in Washington to see Roosevelt. This summit meeting made it possible to rule promptly on some difficult points and an agreement was quickly reached. The treaty was a significant reversal of the economic nationalism of Smoot-Hawley and the Bennett tariffs — and may be seen as the starting point for the symbiotic trade relations between Canada and the United States which is the central feature of Canadian trade today. Needless to say, however, the agreement did not end the depression.

In the months after the election of 1935, the impression of dynamic leadership was sustained. Shortly after the trade agreement came the Dominion–Provincial Conference of 1935. King's election campaign had stressed the benefits of co-operation between the federal and provincial governments and anything seemed possible with the Liberal party in office at Ottawa and in every province except Alberta. The federal government offered at the Conference to increase the federal grants-in-aid for relief to the provinces by a dramatic 75 percent. This heightened the image of a government at Ottawa sensitive to the personal tragedy of individual Canadians suffering from economic forces over which they had no control, and a government which could act decisively.

The honeymoon did not last. Disillusionment was inevitable for the harsh reality was that no Canadian government could exorcize a depression which was blanketing the entire world. But disillusionment was more pronounced because the impression of dynamic leadership was soon dispelled.

Mackenzie King had not been converted to radical ideas and even his sympathy for the plight of the suffering was qualified by his more immediate concern for the solvency of his government. Sir Charles Gordon, President of the Bank of Montreal, must have been reassured by a letter from King shortly after the election, in which King explained that "My own view is that the most effective means of ending the drain of relief expenditures on our financial resources and of making bearable the burdens of existing debt is to be found in the revival of trade." There is no suggestion here of deficit financing or of an inflationary monetary policy—only the policy of tight belts until prosperity returned. The only thing to fear in the meantime was the drain of relief expenditures on the federal budget.

This policy of retrenchment was not inconsistent with the decision at the Dominion–Provincial Conference to increase grants-in-aid for relief. The increase was only for the winter months and was seen as an emergency measure. The provincial premiers had agreed, at the same time, to a National Employment Commission which would supervise all relief expenditures. For the provincial premiers it was enough that they would have more money for the next few months; the Commission, it was doubtless assumed, would recognize the continuing need for federal grants when the time came. Behind this federal proposal, however, was the unstated belief that a good deal of extravagance and waste would be eliminated by the federal Commission, and that in the future, the drain of relief expenditures on the federal treasury could be controlled.

Mackenzie King, it must be remembered, was not the leader of a national government but of a federal government. His primary concern was inevitably with the federal treasury. From the vantage point of Ottawa, the provinces were spending money on relief but the federal government had to issue the cheques. Small wonder that King wanted to ensure that provincial governments spent the money wisely—which meant ensuring that they spent as little as possible.

Some provincial governments, unfortunately, could not manage their own affairs. The four western provinces, at least, were already virtually bankrupt and could not continue without federal funds. The interest on provincial debts alone absorbed almost half of their provincial revenues. If one adds to this the dependence of most municipalities on provincial subsidies and the impossibility of collecting taxes from people who needed relief, it was clear that these provincial governments had to find money somewhere and had nowhere to turn but to Ottawa. Nobody else would lend money to provinces in such desperate straits.

Charles Dunning produced a plausible solution at the Dominion–Provincial Conference of 1935. He offered to guarantee the interest on future provincial bond issues, thus making it possible for the western provinces to borrow money. There was, of course, a *quid pro quo*. This guarantee was to be dependent upon each province agreeing in advance to the establishment of a Provincial Loan Council, consisting of the federal and provincial Ministers of Finance and the Governor of the Bank of Canada. The Council would first have to approve the loan, which meant, in effect, approving the fiscal policies and financial administration of the province. Clearly Dunning believed that the federal government would be able to re-establish control over its own budget by establishing some control over provincial budgets.

Initially the provincial governments showed little opposition to the Loan Council proposal. The federal and provincial finance ministers had two meetings early in 1936 and Dunning believed that an agreement had been reached. It seems likely that the provinces which could still issue bonds without a federal guarantee did not care and that the other provinces were desperate. Duff Pattullo, however, soon realised that his platform of large-scale capital expenditures financed by "publicly created credit, non-interest bearing"[15] would not have the enthusiastic support of a Loan Council. The federal government decided to delay the formal amendment to the BNA Act until the unanimous consent of the provinces had been obtained. "Meanwhile," King noted in his diary, "if they apply for loans, they should be refused further loans even if it means their defaulting."[16]

Alberta became the test case. An Alberta debenture issue for some three million dollars fell due on April 1, 1936. Dunning refused a federal loan to meet this maturity unless Alberta accepted the Loan Council idea. Cockcroft, the Provincial Treasurer, had seemed to favour the idea on his visits to Ottawa but Mr. Aberhart was made of sterner stuff. He refused, and the province of Alberta defaulted — the first default of a Canadian government. The Loan Council idea was quietly buried.

The federal government continued to toy with the idea that it could keep solvent by leaving the provinces to sink or swim. Saskatchewan and Manitoba were, if anything, worse off than Alberta, and in December of 1936 King recorded his opinion and the opinion of most of the Cabinet that these two provinces should also be allowed to default.

By then, however, Dunning had changed his position. The federal Minister of Finance had large-scale operations on the money market in 1937. Dominion war loans were maturing and new series of bonds would have to be issued. Dunning was naturally eager to refund this maturing obligation at lower interest rates—interest on the existing debt was a major item, annually absorbing one third of federal revenues and any reduction would be a significant item in his budget. But the credit rating of the federal government would not be based on federal policies alone. The money market would be affected by provincial defaults. For federal reasons, therefore, Dunning now favoured loans to Saskatchewan and Alberta. Over the few weeks King shifted from opposition to reluctant acceptance of Dunning's point of view.

His decision to save the provinces from default was combined with a decision to name a Royal Commission on federal–provincial financial relations. Not that this implied any change of heart by King. He still gave a high priority to protecting the federal treasury against provincial raids. His concern is reflected in the terms of reference of the Commission, in which the division of powers between governments was directly related to the aim of keeping the burden of public expenditures to a minimum. The appointment of such stable and reliable men as N.W. Rowell and J.W. Dafoe was to be a guarantee of "responsible" recommendations. It is also relevant to note that in midsummer, when the Commission was still being discussed, King thought of it as no more than a fact-finding commission which would report before the next session. To the extent that King had any policy at this time, it seems still to have been a policy of retrenchment.

It should have been clear by then that retrenchment was a failure. The Loan Council idea had been abandoned. The National Employment Commission was also a disappointment. It had been expected to reduce relief expenditures by eliminating extravagance and duplication. It had prepared the way by establishing a register of all direct relief recipients. It got no farther, however, because any effective administrative role was blocked by the provincial governments which refused meekly to surrender their authority to a federal Commission. Relief costs remained an uncontrollable item in the federal budget.

The depression had also survived efforts to use monetary policy as an instrument of government. The Bank of Canada Act had been amended in 1936 in order to allow the government to name the majority of the Bank's directors. Neither King nor Dunning, however, had any intention of imposing an inflationary policy. Graham Towers, the Governor, seems to have been responsible for a policy of easy money by gradually and steadily expanding chartered bank funds. The results were modest. The availability of money at reduced interest rates did not trigger private investment. The Bank of Canada Act was amended again in 1938 when the shares in private hands were redeemed by the government. This amendment, however, had nothing to do with monetary policy. It was a political gesture to placate the radical Liberals who would be satisfied with nothing less than a government-owned bank. Easy money was as far as the government or the Bank of Canada would go.

The next phase of the government's response to the depression can only be understood by referring once more to the National Employment Commission. In addition to its administrative responsibilities the Commission was also an advisory Commission. Its final report was submitted to the government in 1938.

King's first reaction to the report was that it was an unmitigated blunder. Late in 1937 he had learned from a member of the Commission that the report would recommend full federal responsibility for unemployment relief. He was aghast that men like Purvis, the chairman, and W.A. Mackintosh, a Queen's University economist, could be so irresponsible and so disloyal. He was then flabbergasted to discover that Norman Rogers, Minister of Labour, also from Queen's University, agreed with these men. When O.D. Skelton, again from Queen's, expressed some sympathy with the proposal, and when Clifford Clark, Deputy Minister of Finance, another Queen's man, did not object, it all became clearly an academic plot. "The more one sees of the academic mind," wrote King,

> the more one feels how necessary it is that it should be supple-
> mented or balanced by wide political outlook or experience, to
> save [avoid] courses of action which mean defeat in the end of the
> causes it is intended to support. Logic is a means to an end. The
> academic mind is apt to make, of logic, an end in itself.[17]

The cause which King intended to support was still the solvency of the federal government. It was too late to block the report of the Commission, which was already drafted. It was not too late, however, to modify it. King's attitude and that of most of his colleagues, was conveyed to the Commissioners, some of whom now saw the enormity of their offence. To avoid a complete split within the Commission a compromise was reached. The final version of the report still argued that the federal government should be responsible for administering direct relief but now it went on to say that recommendations for allocating the financial responsibility should be left to the recently appointed Rowell Commission. King still regretted that the issue had ever been raised but at least this compromise would be less compromising for the federal government.

The National Employment Commission thus passed into oblivion, unhonoured and soon forgotten. It deserves more than an epitaph, however, because it marks a significant advance in the analysis in Canada of the role of government fiscal policy. The co-ordination of relief and employment measures by the federal government, which had so infuri-ated King, was justified in the report by a sophisticated advocacy of contra-cyclical financing, and the need for increased expenditures, reduced taxation and the easing of credit during periods of unemploy-ment. King did not get the message at this time but Norman Rogers did, and even the intransigent orthodoxy of King and Dunning may have been subtly undermined. How important this was it is not easy to say, but the Commission may have prepared the way for the shift in federal fiscal policy in 1938. In this year, the disastrous recession of 1937 increased the pressures on the government for action, and at least the ideas of the Commission were there for a government that desperately needed ideas.

Certainly the session of 1938 was a turning point. Initially Dunning and King both assumed that the objective was still a balanced budget — an objective which seemed more urgent than ever because this might be the last budget before the next election. Rogers, however, wanted to increase government expenditures and to budget for a deficit. There were heated Cabinet meetings at which first Rogers and then Dunning threat-ened to resign. Rogers had the support of many Ministers who wanted to increase their departmental estimates even though they may not have fully shared his broader view of fiscal policy. Dunning was probably under pressure from Clifford Clark, his Deputy Minister, as well. King himself was not convinced by the newfangled economic theories. He still believed that government investment would only reduce private investment, and so accomplish nothing. What was worse, a reliance on government initiative might make the people increasingly dependent on the state[18]—a menace which a subsequent generation would label "creep-ing socialism." Again, however, it was clear that his personal view would have to be sacrificed to the cause of party unity. He accepted the idea of pump-priming, contenting himself with fighting a rearguard action and limiting the increases in the estimates.

From our vantage point, thirty years later, the government measures do not look radical. Some forty million dollars were included in the estimates for various relief projects, which meant a probable deficit of twenty-three million dollars. It must be remembered that this was out of a total budget of five hundred million dollars. And in addition to the budget, there was a Municipal Improvements Assistance Act, providing up to thirty million dollars in loans to municipalities at 2 percent, and a National Housing Act which would provide up to sixty million dollars in loans. The budget itself also eliminated the sales tax on construction items as well as income tax exemptions for investments in new mines. There were no tax increases. The idea of a static and balanced budget was gone; in its place was a fiscal policy of stimulating economic recovery by modest government deficits and by direct economic incentives.

The new policy did not work any miracles. Significantly, however, Dunning's budget of 1939 confirmed the new approach to fiscal policy. Taxes were slightly reduced once more and expenditures were again to be increased. Dunning forecast a deficit of sixty million dollars this time. And instead of an apology, his budget speech was now a forthright defence of this deficit. Prosperity was now directly linked with expansion and "in times of depression," he declared, " . . . increased expenditures on the part of governments are a sheer necessity."[19] The policy of retrenchment was now in limbo and the government had become the advocate of contra-cyclical budgeting.

Mackenzie King did not speak on the budget during the session. Even in his diary he made few references to it. In April of 1939 he was naturally preoccupied with the European crisis. He also devoted a great deal of his time to plans for the Royal visit in May. His relative silence can be interpreted as consent. King was not inclined to brood over past decisions and for him the decision on fiscal policy had been made in 1938. He would live with the new policy without qualms unless there were signs that it had become a political liability.

One comment by King at this time deserves to be quoted. In referring to Dunning's budget speech, he recorded "It was evident he [Dunning] was reading a Professor's statement and not speaking his own mind from conviction."[20] The professor, of course, was Clifford Clark. A year before King had noted that the Queen's academics had been trying to impose their ideas on the government. However, academic logic had prevailed. The experienced politician had been flexible enough to adopt the ideas of academics when his own traditional policies had proved ineffective.

It would be an exaggeration to say that Mackenzie King had been completely converted by the end of the decade. He had begun with the assumption that the Liberal policies of the 1920s were the final answer — that prosperity would return if the government could economise, could reduce tariffs and taxes, and so let free enterprise flourish. Ten years later he still hoped the day would come when the budget could be balanced, when governments could reduce expenditures and leave details of economic planning to private citizens. For King, the politician, however, this attitude had not been an insurmountable handicap. The economic orthodoxy of his youth was less important than the political orthodoxy of party government. He could accept the idea of a central bank which might manipulate currency and credit, and if Loan Councils and Employment Commissions didn't work, he was prepared to accept deficit financing and pump-priming. He instinctively preferred the check-rein to the whip but he never forgot that leader and party, like rider and horse, must always go at the same speed in the same direction. There was no reckless galloping but the Liberal party did cross over new terrain during these years, and at the end, Mackenzie King was still firmly in the saddle. Uninspiring he was, but as a political leader he presided over a government which did respond to the pressures of a revolutionary decade. His "Liberal way" at least had some relevance to the Canada of the 1930s.

Notes

1. F.R. Scott, "W.L.M.K.," *Selected Poems* (Toronto: Oxford University Press, 1966), 60.

2. J.G. Gardiner to William Lyon Mackenzie King (hereafter W.L.M.K.), 5 October 1932, King Papers, Public Archives of Canada (hereafter PAC).

3. W.L.M.K., Diary, 30 January 1933, PAC.

4. Canada, House of Commons, *Debates*, 10 October 1932, 53.

5. Meighen Papers, vol. 151, 091676, PAC.

6. M.A. Macpherson to R.R. Finlayson, 21 November 1933, Bennett Papers, PAC.

7. The five radio broadcasts of January 1935 were published by the Conservative Party in a booklet entitled "The Premier Speaks to the People."

8. W.L.M.K. to T.C. Crerar, 28 November 1930, King Papers, PAC.

9. House of Commons, *Debates*, 11 April 1932, 1903.

10. W.L.M.K., Diary, 13 April 1932, PAC.

11. W.L.M.K. to Violet Markham, 28 January 1933, King Papers, PAC.

12. This policy might be paraphrased, "inflation if necessary, but not necessarily inflation."

13. J.W. Dafoe to J.M. Macdonnell, 27 August 1935, J.W. Dafoe Papers, PAC.

14. C.A. Dunning to J.A. Cross, 27 December 1932, Dunning Papers, Queen's University Archives.

15. T.D. Pattullo to W.L.M.K., 14 February 1935, King Papers, PAC.

16. W.L.M.K., Diary, 18 March 1936, PAC.

17. Ibid., 25 June 1938.

18. Ibid., 25 May 1938.

19. House of Commons, *Debates*, 25 April 1939, 3150.

20. W.L.M.K., Diary, 27 April 1939, PAC.

THE GREAT DEPRESSION: PAST AND PRESENT†

MICHIEL HORN

Is something like the Depression of the 1930s about to be repeated? The question is heard with growing frequency. Predictions of economic gloom are becoming common, and the gloomiest economic event that most of us can think of is the Great Depression.

That the question should be asked at all testifies not only to the pervasiveness of the current anxiety but also to the hold which an historical event can have on the minds of people, including some who know it by hearsay only. For hundreds of thousands of Canadians now in their forties and older the 1930s are still the most shattering time they have ever known. "Hard times," "the winter years," "the dirty Thir-ties": these are book titles, clichés perhaps. They nonetheless have the power still to disturb people as they recall the things that were. Unem-ployment at its worst reached 30 percent, transient men roamed the country in box-cars looking for jobs that did not exist, drought and grasshoppers plagued the West, and most commodity prices dropped disastrously low. Many buildings and people looked ever shabbier, cor-porations and municipalities feared debt default, farmers and home-owners dreaded mortgage foreclosure or tax sale, and pauperization became the fate or fear of millions of Canadians, not only many who had always lived in poverty but also some who had never before felt reason to be insecure.

All the same, some Canadians look back with affection on those years. They remember the Depression as a time when people learned the value of a job and of simple pleasures. Life could be good if you had a little

† *Journal of Canadian Studies* 11, no. 1 (February 1976): 41–50.

money, for you had learned to make a little go a long way, even to do without on occasion. As I tried to show in my documentary history of the Depression in Canada, *The Dirty Thirties* (1972), the experiences of Canadians varied widely. The Depression was far from all bad or all bleak.

Certainly life was cheap. A newspaper cost two cents and a pound of sirloin steak less than a quarter. A Ford or Chevy was six hundred dollars and a good house six thousand dollars. Even in Toronto rents were less than fifteen dollars a month for a small bungalow or apartment; a Rosedale mansion could be rented for a hundred dollars. Shoes sold at Eaton's for two dollars; a blue serge suit cost fifteen dollars at Simpsons. A housemaid would work all day, six days a week, for room, board and eight dollars per month, and line up for the privilege. Materially, at least, life was good to that minority who had the incomes that allowed them to take advantage of deflated prices and the glut of sellers in the labour market. Income taxes were low, moreover, although they went up modestly during the decade while exemptions were lowered to bring in more taxpayers. On the whole, however, governments continued to rely mainly on time-tried indirect taxes which weighed more heavily on the poor than on the well-to-do or the comfortable middle class.

There were far more of the poor than of the latter two groups. If we follow L.C. Marsh in identifying the well-to-do as families in receipt of ten thousand dollars or more per annum (1931 figures), we find that between one in a hundred and one in two hundred families could be so classified. A further 20 percent constituted the middle classes. Their family heads were small- and medium-scale business operators, professionals, technical, managerial, commercial, and other white collar workers, and "responsible and independent industrial workers."[1] In these groups family income ranged from approximately fifteen hundred to ten thousand dollars per annum, with most families near the bottom end.

At least half of Canadian families could be described as working class in the 1930s, while Marsh called the remaining 30 percent the farming class. One thing can confidently be said of many farmers and the great majority of the working class: at best they lived only just above the poverty line, with little left over for comforts or savings for a rainy day.[2] Many of them slipped into destitution during the early Thirties; many more survived on its ragged edge. Some drifted into a chronic dependence on the state from which they did not escape even during the war-stimulated boom after 1939.

The deprivations of the farming and working classes have done much to shape the image which Canadians have of the Depression. Perhaps more important in the longer run, however, was the experience of the middle classes. They suffered much less from unemployment than the working class, but they had also been much less used to it before the Depression. The insecurity which many of them felt was a psychological deprivation that has left its marks. Their dread of unemployment and its results, added to the much better founded fears of the working class, has been perhaps the most potent legacy of the Depression years.

Fear and psychological loss can hardly be measured. The material losses and deprivations of the Depression can be measured with some accuracy. We have figures on the declines in foreign trade, Gross National Income, Gross National Product, and Gross National Expenditure, during the downswing of 1929–1933. From a variety of sources we can draw unemployment figures and, even more central to this essay, statistics on the granting of relief. These are a clear indication of the extent of pauperization in the country, most of it due to unemployment. Relief was almost everywhere made available only as a last resort, and grudgingly at that, to people who had exhausted all other resources. By the spring of 1933 at least 1 500 000 Canadians, or approximately 15 percent of the population, depended on unemployment and drought relief for subsistence. Estimates of the numbers of public dependents in 1934 and 1935 were 2 000 000 and 1 900 000 respectively, although some of these did not owe their condition to the Depression. In 1938 no less than 845 000 Canadians still depended on urban unemployment assistance, while 170 800 received farm relief and a further 100 000 were getting provincial and municipal poor relief.[3]

The incidence of relief was very unevenly distributed among communities. This reflected not only differing regional and industrial incidences of unemployment, but also differing relief policies, which continued to be the responsibility of municipalities and provinces even when the federal government was supplying a large part of the money. H.M. Cassidy found that the percentage of people on relief in the larger Ontario municipalities in April 1932 ranged from 7.3 percent in Kitchener to 38.6 percent in East Windsor. In every town for which comparable figures were available for April 1930 the increases were startling, being as high as 1 000 percent and more in Hamilton, Stratford and East York Township.[4]

The situation in the four Western provinces was explored by Charlotte Whitton of the Canadian Council on Child and Family Welfare (later in the decade to become the Canadian Welfare Council) in the summer of 1932. It ranged from alarming to disastrous. The relief population in British Columbia was estimated at 7.5 percent in Victoria, 12 percent in Vancouver, and 22 percent in Burnaby. Single industry towns were faring worse: the Vancouver Island mill town of Port Alberni had 37 percent on relief, and the interior coal-mining town of Fernie 47 percent. Calgary and Edmonton had approximately 13 percent each. Regina and Saskatoon had 20 percent, as did Greater Winnipeg. In the latter case as in several others, notably Vancouver and Toronto, the city proper had a considerably lower rate than the suburbs. Brandon had only 10 percent on relief; Swift Current, on the other hand, had reached 35 percent when the town was forced to cease relief payments on August 15th, 1932.[5] The growing burden of relief expenses forced scores of municipalities, especially in the West, to default on their indebtedness and to look to provincial governments for the money to keep the relief recipients alive. These governments, in turn, were forced to look to Ottawa.

By March of 1933 almost one third of the population of Montreal was on relief, including 38 percent of French-speaking Roman Catholics.[6] Here and elsewhere in Quebec the system of private poor relief, in which the Church was central, was breaking down. In the Maritimes the contrast with the 1920s was less dramatic because large areas of the Atlantic region were already depressed. A report on unemployment and relief in the mining towns of Nova Scotia in 1931 indicated, however, that things were getting worse. In Glace Bay, with a population estimated at 21 000, "during July 1 250 people received relief. Practically all are heads of families. Anticipated that the number will increase from time to time."[7] The situation in Sydney Mines was at least as bad, and in most of the other towns it was little better.

These figures understated the extent of destitution somewhat. Single people usually found it difficult to get relief in their own right. They were apt to become transients and then had to depend on private charity and casual labour, or else enter the relief camps which were established by several provinces in 1931 and 1932, and in the latter year by the Dominion government as well. In rural areas relief was often very hard to obtain. (An exception, though not a happy one, was drought-stricken southern Saskatchewan, where in 1931 the Saskatchewan Relief Commission became the guardian of two hundred thousand farming people.) The tax base was narrow in most rural districts, especially in the West. Examiners of relief applications in the Manitoba countryside were instructed that "persons signing this recommendation, should do so, only after careful inquiry and consideration and with the realization that granting relief means extra taxation."[8] The deprivation became stark indeed. Harry Avison, a United Church minister in Deloraine, Manitoba, found in 1934 that many farm families lacked underwear, bedding and even shoes. Yet these families were not on relief and were often loath to ask for help. Charity was not welcome, just the chance to make a go of things. To go on relief was the ultimate indignity to people who saw themselves as being independent.

Going "on the pogey" was not lightly undertaken by many city dwellers either. But these did not have the opportunity, at least enjoyed by poor farmers, of growing some food for home consumption and cutting firewood. Canada had no unemployment insurance, and few people had the private resources to keep going for long after they lost their jobs. A common though inadequate defence was for a woman to work if the male breadwinner was laid off. Two incomes had for many families always been a necessity if a subsistence level was to be maintained or slightly exceeded. Wage discrimination against women tended to work in their favour when workers were being dismissed. For most families it was only a question of time before unemployment brought about pauperization, however. "We must assume, and the assumption is supported by investigations," a Winnipeg report stated in 1931:

> that practically all families that come on relief are experiencing a measure of destitution at the time they come on relief.
>
> The relief schedule of the City of Winnipeg provides only for food and fuel necessities, and water, light and rent where absolutely necessary for maintenance of services and shelter. In the case of water and light, payments are made by our Committee only after the services have been discontinued.

Yet hundreds of families had to be helped in this way, and the report predicted that their number would increase sharply. Then there was the need for clothing: "The need for clothing allowances for all members of the family is very urgent and cannot be disregarded much longer. Many of our families have been on relief for nine months and are absolutely destitute of clothing. It is safe to assume that all families now on relief will require to be clothed next winter."[9] Bedding, cooking utensils, furniture: all these things wore out. What, if anything, was to be done? James Gray has in *The Winter Years* described with grim humour what it was like to be on relief in Winnipeg. Much of the humour, one suspects, was scarcely evident at the time.

Unemployment rose with only seasonal interruptions from the fall of 1929 to the spring of 1933. According to a report to R.B. Bennett it reached 32.1 percent on May 1st.[10] That may have been the peak: the uneven recovery which began in 1933 led to a gradual reduction of unemployment during the next four years to less than 10 percent. Relief proved to be even more persistent, however, because seasonal unemployment quickly put back on relief families whose reserves had been completely exhausted in their earlier bout of joblessness. And hundreds of thousands never got off the pogey at all. It proved possible to restore production by and large to the level of the late 1920s without drawing on the entire labour pool. This was partly because some industries lagged, notably agriculture, transportation, and construction, partly because some workers had become unemployable because they lacked appropriate skills and education, and partly because the labour force had been growing by natural means. Furthermore, unemployment increased again in the recession which began in 1937 and lasted into the war. That conflict virtually ended unemployment as a problem for the time being, but the relief population never did return to the low levels of the middle and later 1920s.

The sharply increased economic activity which came with World War II masked for a while the effects of chronic unemployment and under-employment in the 1930s. Ever vigilant against a weakening of the national moral fibre, however, Charlotte Whitton had identified some of the dangers as early as 1934. The relief system was "actually penalizing the low paid wage earner, especially if his work be subject to short-term and seasonal shifts." The man on relief was "really far better off," especially because the growing practice of paying relief in cash rather than by means of vouchers had "wipe[d] out the last distinction between the family on relief and the struggling low paid wage earner's family. . . . It is not surprising that there is a growing tendency to seek relief and to stay on it over an increasing period of time."[11] This painted the situation a bit too bleakly. Still, to some Canadians who had become virtually unemployable even though able-bodied, life on the dole was probably coming to be seen as certainly no worse and possibly better than the fitful, menial and badly paid employment that had been theirs.

Another informed observer, Leonard Marsh, also warned of dangers ahead. A tenth or more of Canadians were drifting into chronic indigence, he wrote. Unemployment was the chief cause of this, and working class Canadians were the main victims.

> It is not possible to characterize unemployment as solely a working-class problem, because there are large margins of farm labourers and lesser white-collar workers who have been left stranded by depression; but by far the larger part undoubtedly is. Relief, or the destitution directly attributable to unemployment, is even more concentrated than unemployment; though here again conditions of chronically unstable work and below-minimum incomes are not confined to the bottom of the occupational structure. . . . [U]nemployment drags men down. Prolonged unemployment is a leveller, which creates unskilled and unemployables as frequently as the reverse situation of lack of skill increases the risk of inferior employment and frequent lay-off. And below the white-collar line it is often easier to fall than to rise.[12]

The great majority of those who slipped into chronic dependence during the 1930s were from that one half or more of the Canadian population who had lived in poverty or near poverty during the relatively prosperous 1920s. For many people the Twenties had not roared.

We can discern in this an important contribution to the building of the welfare trap of the post-World War II years. A study done four years ago found that more than a quarter of men on welfare were second generation relief-recipients.[13] But our current awareness of the Depression probably owes more to the deprivations of farmers in the West and middle class Canadians everywhere than to the sufferings of the working class. For many people today the 1930s are connected especially with images of the western dustbowl, possibly also with dim recollections of low prices for farm products. The latter hurt farmers everywhere, but especially grain growers and stockmen in the three Prairie provinces. The decrease in average net money income from agriculture in Manitoba, Saskatchewan and Alberta was 94 percent between 1928–29 and 1932–33, as compared with a decrease in total national income of 41 percent. Canada's per capita net income declined by 48 percent from 1928–29 to 1933; Manitoba's per capita income dropped by 49 percent, Alberta's by 61 percent, and Saskatchewan's by 72 percent. They were the only three provinces which underperformed the Canadian economy as a whole.[14]

These percentages give only a notion of the material and psychological deprivation experienced by the people of these provinces, the farmers above all but also railway workers, tradesmen and shopkeepers, artisans, professionals and the employees of many enterprises, all of whom were affected by the collapse of the western economy. Physicians and dentists had to be subsidized by the Saskatchewan Relief Commission so that they could afford to stay in the drought-stricken rural areas, and the teachers were put on relief, "to be repaid when their salary arrears were met."[15] A novel by Robert Kroetsch, *The Words of My Roaring*, demonstrates more convincingly than any official report how the penury of the farmers also impoverished local tradesmen. In Alberta and Saskatchewan the political scene changed markedly during and in the aftermath of the Depression, mainly because most farmers became disaffected from the parties in power.

Drought and low prices lasted the entire decade. The year 1937, reasonably good in Central Canada, was the worst year yet on the Plains. Farmers in the rest of the country did not have life easy. Like most producers of primary goods, fishermen, lumbermen and workers in non-ferrous mining, many had it very difficult. It is the Western farmer, however, his land dried out and threatened by mortgage foreclosure, who stands out as a symbol of Depression suffering.

About the middle classes one generalization holds: they fared a good deal better than the industrial working class and the primary producers. As the national income declined, wage and salary earners were getting a larger share of it, with the latter doing better than the former. People who kept their jobs may, indeed, have been better off in 1933 than they were four years before. Wage and salary rates tended to be sticky, falling more slowly than the general deflation. A 25 percent decline in the consumers' goods index from 1929 to 1933, followed by only a slow, slight rise during the next six years, benefited those Canadians on fixed or nearly fixed incomes. One might not get a raise for years, but if one did not have to take a reduction life was not too bad.

Wage and salary cuts were common, however, and many workers paid directly or indirectly out of government funds also experienced them. The Royal Commission on Price Spreads (1934–35) unearthed plenty of evidence that employees could be squeezed hard in this way if they worked in vulnerable industries or for unconscionable employers. Businessmen could be squeezed hard, too. The garment industry in Montreal and Toronto, for example, broke the hearts of many proprietors even while the workers in their shops were being sweated ruthlessly. The Depression reinforced a trend which had been evident for some decades already: smaller enterprises were driven out of existence by larger competitors. The files of R.B. Bennett's Minister of Trade and Commerce, Harry H. Stevens, are filled with complaints from small shopkeepers about the "unfair" competition with which the supermarkets were facing them. The existence and continued consolidation of oligopolies in many branches of Canadian industry became obvious as the struggle for survival grew more vicious. For employees this added to the climate of fear. What if, for whatever reason, one were to lose one's job? There were, after all, plenty of people who were eager to get going, and who would take a lower wage or salary in the bargain. This was especially true of younger people, who often had nowhere to go when they got out of school. That is no doubt an important reason why, in spite of the personal expense, university enrolments held more or less steady throughout the decade. "The essence of being in your twenties in the Thirties," Hugh MacLennan has said, "was that no matter how well tuned up you were, you stayed on the ground."[16] And while they were there they undercut the incomes and security of older people.

Many professional men and women discovered that the traditional independence of their professions was no consolation when those who could afford to pay for their services were too few. Those professionals who had traditionally entered public employment, notably teachers, found that school boards which were hiring were ill-inclined to set much of a price on the services of a group so obviously in over-supply. In a contracting economy there were simply too many young people, with too much training. After 1933 matters improved somewhat, but only World War II ended the unemployment and underemployment of highly trained white (and blue) collar workers.

It is not known how many Canadians were personally stung in the stock market crash of 1929 or in the subsequent decline to the lows of 1932. We may surmise, on the basis of American evidence, that they were a small minority, 2 to 3 percent at most. That dividends dropped sharply after 1931–1932 can also have affected only a small number of Canadians. Undistributed corporation profits were negative in 1932 and 1933, and business failures increased, though it is worth noting that neither in number nor in dollar value did they reach the levels set in the post-inflationary depression of 1920–1922. Not surprisingly, income tax statistics indicate that high income earners became fewer. Canadians declaring incomes over ten thousand dollars dropped from 13 477 in

1929 to 6 440 in 1934, before recovering to 8 085 in 1938.[17] Further-more, the average amount of income tax paid by them doubled during this period. It is most unlikely, however, that the inconveniences under-gone by some families in this unrepresentative group are what we think of when we recall the Depression. Some wealthy families may have seen their incomes or wealth seriously eroded and may have slipped into the ranks of the middle class. We may safely assume, nevertheless, that most families that were well-to-do at the beginning of the decade were still in that happy condition at its end, and were well-equipped to improve their fortunes in the war-time boom and after.

It is a mistake to think that the 1930s themselves were devoid of opportunities for money-making or the safe investment of one's savings. Even people of small means got ahead in the worst years. In 1930 W.A.C. Bennett opened a hardware store in Kelowna, B.C.; the following year Roy Thomson started a radio station in North Bay, Ont. Neither found the early going easy, but both laid the basis for business success.

Wealthier people had a number of rewarding possibilities. Not only did common and preferred stocks reach bargain basement lows in 1932, but the real estate market was severely depressed. Bonds and de-bentures on which interest was in arrears traded at a discount; many of these eventually satisfied creditors in full. There were few quick gains to be realized in the investment climate of the 1930s — gold shares were a notable exception — but those who had been reasonably prudent in the 1920s, and were able to take the long view, could enjoy a steady income and later reaped handsome and untaxed capital gains. Propertied people never had to undergo the trauma of seeing their banks close and go into receivership, moreover. To be sure, the liquidity and soundness of the Canadian banking system was achieved in part at the expense of borrowers who lost their lines of credit, some of whom went bank-rupt as a result. But *sauve qui peut* is a motto well understood in the financial world.

To return to the middle class experience: it presents a complicated picture. There were winners and losers, as well as many who simply held their own. Unemployment was far less common among managerial, professional, commercial, "responsible," and clerical workers — in that order — than it was among all groups of industrial workers. Service workers not elsewhere specified were roughly halfway between the two larger groups.[18] But many middle class people had some reason to feel threatened. As early as 1931 some 6.8 percent of managerial, 11.5 percent of professional, 14.7 percent of commercial and 19.5 percent of clerical workers had already "lost some time."[19] These percentages were low in comparison with those for skilled, semi-skilled and unskilled workers, which ranged between 50 and 60 percent. The length of job-lessness was also greater among the latter categories. To middle class workers who felt themselves endangered, however, and who perhaps had never felt this way before, the greater suffering of others is likely to have been scant consolation. The implications of unemployment were too disturbing. To lose one's savings, to lose one's possessions, to lose one's house: all these possibilities led to a very painful insecurity. Not for nothing did F.D. Roosevelt tell Americans in his Inauguration Address: "The only thing we have to fear is fear itself." He was wrong, of course, but he was nearly right enough for his remark to hit home.

Fear of unemployment and its consequences stains the image that Canadians have of the Depression. That fear still manifests itself in odd ways. For example, a small headline in the Ottawa *Citizen* of November 13th, 1974, stated: "Most fear depression." The story referred to a Gallup Poll in October in which Canadians were asked whether they thought that "this country is heading into a depression within the next year or so," and, if they belonged to the 51 percent who answered in the affirmative, whether they thought it would be "a serious depression, such as that in the Thirties, or more likely a less serious recession."[20] There was no reference to fear in the questions. However, in the newsroom of the *Citizen* a depression is apparently something one can only fear, even at a time when inflation has become a grave menace to pensioners and many other low income earners. It is unlikely, moreover, that readers of that story, including most pensioners, noticed anything out of the ordinary.

Working class people have reason to fear a depression. They will be among the first to suffer its consequences, just as they were in the 1930s. The current interest in the Depression and the possibility of its recurrence, however, may reflect middle class memories and apprehensions even more than those of the working classes. After all, the media are mostly a middle class preserve.

Since the urban consensus seems to be that food costs too much, depression worries probably do not for most people who are subject to them include the fear that agricultural prices will collapse. . . . It is unemployment that is feared. The state-sponsored protections against its worst consequences are much better than they were forty-five years ago, but against this stands the much greater use of consumer credit at the present time. Many people, including many middle class people, would be severely embarrassed if they had to do without a couple of paycheques, UIC payouts notwithstanding.

The last Depression proved calamitous to many Canadians. Psychologically, however, it probably had its biggest effect on the urban middle classes. They were people who had no experience with economic hardship or believed firmly that they had left it behind. The Great Depression disabused them of such notions. Only a minority was unemployed for a long time, saw a business collapse, lost a home through mortgage foreclosure or tax sale, could not get started in a profession, or had to postpone marriage or children. (That a large part of that minority were young people takes on added significance today.) A smaller minority yet had to undergo the shame which came with having to go on relief. But the minority was large enough so that everyone knew people who had lost the precious "independence" which came with paid employment, or who, upon emerging from school, could not get it for a long time to begin with. In a society, furthermore, in which 30 percent of the population still lived on the farm while many others were first generation city dwellers, not a few middle class people knew very well the kinds of difficulties farmers were experiencing. Some, no doubt, knew farmers who lost everything through mortgage foreclosure.

The loss of the ability to provide for oneself and one's family was a most serious matter. Unemployment or failure in one's business tended to be equated with personal inadequacy, and not by the middle classes alone. Studies during the 1930s indicated that many of the unemployed blamed themselves for their misfortune.[21]

To the fear that one might be found wanting was added the fear that "foreigners" and Communists, not necessarily seen as being distinct, were plotting to take away one's property or destroy Canada's British institutions. But all these fears paled alongside the fear that one might have to ask for public relief. That was for many people almost the fear of hell itself. The pit was open; some were sliding in. Who was really safe? Middle class Canadians may have come to realize during the Depression, as never before, that the independence and security which they derived from their work were illusory, that their incomes were at the mercy of economic forces which they did not and could not control. Because the loss of the ability to pay one's way was also a loss of status and led almost invariably to a loss of self-respect—something which still seems to be true of middle class people in the 1970s[22]—the Depression brought about great psychological as well as material deprivation. The latter was spared most middle class Canadians. The former probably was not, for the fear could be as damaging as the fact. Both forms of deprivation must be recognized and understood in order to make sense of Canada's Depression legacy, of the anxiety and urgency which many Canadians and their governments feel when the economy falters and unemployment rises.

During World War II, with the economy booming, the government of William Lyon Mackenzie King committed itself to the increase of social welfare benefits and to the maintenance of full employment after the war. Humanitarian concern and party advantage both played a part in this. More important were widespread fears, recognized and shared by politicians and civil servants, of a renewed post-war depression. There was apprehension not only of high unemployment but also of social disorder. The troubles of 1918–1919 had not been forgotten. Evidence of growing left-wing sentiments among the people and among the soldiers overseas reinforced the belief that Canadians, especially young Canadians, would not quietly return to the depressed conditions of the 1930s. Prodded also by documents like the Report of the Advisory Committee on Reconstruction (1943), prepared by Leonard Marsh, and the White Paper on Employment and Income (1945), drafted by W.A. Mackintosh, the Liberals introduced policies which laid the basis for an incomplete welfare state,[23] and which have helped to keep unemployment since 1945 down to levels which even at their worst would have been welcomed in any year from 1930 to 1940. Measures were also taken to try to ensure stability in the grain trade, for example,[24] and, with the drought itself gradually fading in the memory, farmers in the West, while often unhappy, have not since the 1930s experienced anything like the disasters of those hungry years.

No New Jerusalem was created in postwar Canada. Inequalities of wealth and income were somewhat modified as a result of wartime taxation and the new social and economic policies. But inequalities have remained and since 1945 they have changed little. With a general rise in the standard of living since the end of the Thirties—this may now be halted and even reversed—poverty has been reduced in one sense. While perhaps half of the Canadian population could be classified as poor in 1931, approximately a fifth can be so described today. This is limited cause for self-congratulation at best, because the absolute number of the poor, around five million, has changed little in the last forty years. The relative deprivation felt by Canadians in the second to fifth quintiles of family incomes when they compare themselves with the upper fifth, moreover, may be as great as it ever was. Meanwhile urban and rural slums remain, and a good deal of the chronic dependence that Charlotte Whitton and Leonard Marsh warned against has become a fact.

Until recently, however, the Great Depression at least seemed to be safely behind us, even if it continued to affect the behaviour and attitudes of older Canadians. Now we are no longer sure. We are in a recession which some say can or will become a serious depression. Others disagree. From the nature of the discussion we infer that both sides in the argument consider a repetition of the Dirty Thirties, allowing for changes of circumstances which make the exact or near-exact recurrence of an historical event impossible, to be the worst thing that could happen. Even the current inflation or its acceleration are apparently less menacing. That judgements of this kind are made testifies to the magnitude of the deprivations that Canadians lived through, and to the anxieties that the Great Depression left behind.

1988 Postscript

An article using the world "present" in its title risks becoming obsolete as soon as it appears in print. However, the fear of an economic depression has continued to be with us into the late 1980s, though it has been stronger at some times than others. The recession early in this decade seemed to have the potential to become a serious depression. Such apprehensions faded as the American administration started to stimulate the economy by means of tax cuts and large budget deficits, and as the Wall Street stock market entered in 1982 on its five-year rise.

Fears of an economic slump receded in spite of the troubling weakness of several sectors of the economy. For example, the experience of farmers, notably those on the western plains, has come closer in the 1980s to that of the 1930s than I thought possible when I wrote this article in 1975. Agriculture has fallen victim to the "war against inflation," fought with considerable success by central bankers in recent years, as well as to increased production in many parts of the world. An apparently low rate of inflation has concealed serious declines in the prices of a number of commodities. One example is petroleum, currently in oversupply; this has had devastating consequences for the economy of Alberta. At the same time prices in manufacturing and service industries have tended to hold their own or have continued to rise. Moreover unemployment, at least in Canada, has remained since the 1970s at levels that would have been thought unacceptably high during most of the post-war period.

The stock market crash of "Black Monday," 19 October 1987, recalled to many minds the crash of October 1929 and raised the depression spectre in a particularly vivid way. The media nervously asked economists and historians: "Will there be a repetition of the 1930s?"

That the question should have been asked at that time and for that reason underlines the continued importance of middle-class sensibilities in the shaping both of our image of the Depression and our fears of its return. Significant parts of the world, and of Canada, have been depressed for several years, beset by low prices for the commodities they produce and the burden of debt that they incurred during the most recent inflation-linked period of growth. The debts are all the more burdensome because real interest rates are higher than at any time since the early 1930s. Unemployment troubles many parts of Canada and the world, with particularly harsh effects on young people. Newspaper articles occasionally draw attention to these problems. But it is only when some members of the urban middle classes get stung in a spectacular stock market collapse that fears of a new Great Depression return to the forefront of public consciousness.

The historian is not a prophet. History does not repeat itself. If we are heading into an economic depression it will be different in significant ways from the downturn of the early 1930s. Governments play a much larger role in the economies of their countries than they did at that time, and we must hope that they will not commit the blunders of policy of which their predecessors were guilty. If private investment and consumption falter, we may hope that public investment and consumption will grow as part of a consciously counter-cyclical strategy. Politicians and bureaucrats may avoid using the name of John Maynard Keynes, the British economist whose trenchant analysis of the 1930s Depression and proposals for preventing its recurrence constitute one of the high points in the history of economic thought. But even if they avoid his name, discredited in the eyes of the conservatives, who have in recent years guided the governments of the English-speaking world, they will probably borrow his proposals. This should forestall the disastrous declines in incomes and prices of the Great Depression.

We should not underestimate the dangers, however. The signs of weakness are many. A huge burden of debt, public and private, threatens to cripple the banking system of the western world while it undermines the economies of many of the developing nations, and not theirs alone. A "credit crunch," in which many would-be borrowers will not be able to obtain loans, and business and commerce will slow down drastically, is certainly possible. The huge trade imbalances within the industrialized world augur ill for the future. So does the near-chaos in the exchange rates of currencies during the past seventeen years, of which the recent weakness of the U.S. dollar is a startling example. It is even more menacing that no country is at present strong enough to stabilize the world economic system. The United States, which for a quarter century after the Second world War possessed that strength, now manifestly lacks it, but no other country has been able to take its place. This makes international co-operation essential. Unfortunately, that co-operation has in recent years proved very difficult to attain. Yet the price of failure could be high indeed.

The fears of a renewed Depression may be exaggerated, but they are far from groundless. They are more realistic now than in the mid-seventies when I wrote my article. It will require both planning and luck to prevent the recurrence of some of the disasters discussed in this book of essays.

Notes

1. L.C. Marsh, *Canadians In and Out of Work* (Toronto, 1940), 389-403. This study has been too long ignored by Canadian social scientists, many of whom seem to think that John Porter pioneered the study of social class in this country.

2. Ibid., 193-94. At 1930-31 prices, a minimum family income based on urban standards has been set at $1 040. See also: L.C. Marsh and others, *Health and Unemployment* (Toronto, 1938), chap. 20.

3. [Harry Hereford], "An Appreciation of the Relief Situation," 9 August 1935,

R.B. Bennett Papers, vol. 782, Public Archives of Canada (hereinafter PAC) Marsh, *Canadians In and Out of Work*, 367-68, citing H.M. Cassidy and Charlotte Whitton.

4. H.M. Cassidy, *Unemployment and Relief in Ontario, 1929–1932* (Toronto, [1932]), 45-46.

5. [C.M. Whitton], "Report Concerning Unemployment and Relief in Western Canada, June–August 1932," Bennett Papers, vol. 781, PAC.

6. "Summary: Montreal Relief Situation," Bennett Papers, vol. 782, PAC.

7. "Memorandum re: Unemployment Situation etc., Sydney, North Sydney, Sydney Mines, New Waterford, Dominion, Glace Bay, Louisbourg and Springhill, N.S.," August 1931, Bennett Papers, vol. 779, PAC. The number of family heads on relief suggests a total number of relief recipients of at least five thousand or close to a quarter of the population at Glace Bay.

8. Manitoba, "Application for Relief for Rural Municipalities or Unorganized Districts," H.R.C. Avison Papers, vol. 3, PAC.

9. "Report on Unemployment and Relief in Winnipeg," 1931, Bennett Papers, vol. 778, PAC.

10. R.K. F[inlayson], "Memorandum for the Prime Minister," 11 June 1934, Bennett Papers, vol. 782, PAC.

11. [C.M. Whitton], "The Challenge of Relief Control," March 1934, Bennett Papers, vol. 804, PAC.

12. Marsh, *Canadians In and Out of Work*, 371-72.

13. Canadian Council on Social Development, *Men on Relief* (Ottawa, 1971), cited in: *Toronto Daily Star*, 16 June 1971.

14. Canada, Royal Commission on Dominion–Provincial Relations, *Report*, Book 1, *Canada: 1867–1939* (Ottawa, 1940), 150.

15. H.B. Neatby, "The Saskatchewan Relief Commission, 1931–34," *Saskatchewan History* 3, no. 2 (Spring 1950): 52.

16. Hugh MacLennan, "What It Was Like to Be in Your Twenties in the Thirties," *The Great Depression: Essays & Memoirs from Canada & the United States*, ed. Victor Hoar (Toronto, 1969), 145.

17. League for Social Reconstruction, Research Committee, *Social Planning for Canada* (Toronto, 1935), 17; March, *Canadians In and Out of Work*, 494. The amounts cited are in current dollars, and thus overstate the decline, which in real income was significantly less.

18. Marsh, *Canadians In and Out of Work*, chap. 13. See also: Marsh, *Employment Research* (Toronto, 1935); L. Richter, ed., *Canada's Unemployment Problem* (Toronto, 1939).

19. Marsh, *Canadians In and Out of Work*, 304.

20. People earning less than $6 000 were least optimistic in answering both questions. Those earning over $10 000 were most optimistic. Someone like the *Toronto Star*'s Dennis Braithwaite, who periodically informs us what a useful event another Depression would be, will quarrel with my use of the word "optimistic" as well as the *Citizen*'s use of the word "fear."

21. See, for example: Philip Eisenberg and Paul F. Lazarsfeld, "The Psychological Effects of Unemployment," *Psychological Bulletin* 35, no. 6 (June 1938). This has a useful bibliography. See also: S.W. Ginsburg, "What Unemployment Does to People," *American Journal of Psychiatry* 99 (November 1942). Melitta Schmideberg, "Zum Verständnis massenpsychologischer Erscheinungen," *Imago: Zeitschrift für Anwendung der Psychoanalyse* 21 (1935): 448-50, tries to link male reactions to unemployment to masturbation fears. The effort is on the whole convincing, given attitudes to masturbation earlier in the century.

22. Douglas H. Powell and Paul F. Driscoll, "Middle-Class Professionals Face Unemployment," *Transaction: Social Science and Modern Society* 10, no. 2 (January–February 1973).

23. J.L. Granatstein, *Canada's War: The Politics of the Mackenzie King Government, 1939–1945* (Toronto, 1975), chap. 7.

24. See: D.A. MacGibbon, *The Canadian Grain Trade 1931–1951* (Toronto, 1952).

FURTHER READING

An indispensable bibliographical aid is *A Reader's Guide to Canadian History*, vol. 2, *Confederation to the Present*, edited by J.L. Granatstein and Paul Stevens. It should be referred to often, and especially for fields not covered here such as foreign relations, defence and immigration policy.

One excellent general survey of the inter-war years exists, *Canada 1922–1939: Decades of Discord*, by John Herd Thompson with Allen Seager. Michiel Horn's booklet, *The Great Depression of the 1930s in Canada*, offers a brief account; his book *The Dirty Thirties* is a collection of documents and readings that deals with business and social as well as political history. Compiled by Victor Hoar, *The Great Depression* is a useful collection of articles and memoirs. *The Dirty Thirties in Prairie Canada*, edited by Doug Francis and Herman Ganzevoort, contains essays on various aspects of the western experience. Several articles in another collection, *Building the Co-operative Commonwealth: Essays on the Democratic Socialist Tradition in Canada*, edited by William Brennan, also shed light on the Depression years.

A.E. Safarian's *The Canadian Economy in the Great Depression* is not easy to read, but it is essential to anyone trying to make sense of the economics of the period. Government finances of the era are discussed in the first volume of J.H. Perry's *Taxes, Tariffs, and Subsidies*. A more specialized account of tariffs is Richard N. Kottman's *Reciprocity and the North Atlantic Triangle 1932–1938*. Some superb primary sources for financial and economic history are readily accessible, the most important being the *Report* of the Royal Commission on Dominion–Provincial Relations. A number of the research studies done for the Commission are still useful, such as those by W.A. Mackintosh, *The Economic Background of Dominion–Provincial Relations*; H.C. Goldenberg, *Municipal Finance in Canada*; and F.A. Knox, *Dominion Monetary Policy (1929–1934)*. Not to be neglected is the *Report* of the Royal Commission on Price Spreads, and the reports of several government studies of the grain trade. Several scholarly books published during the Depression years are still important and interesting, including George Britnell's *The Wheat Economy*; L.C. Marsh's *Employment Research* and *Canadians In and Out of Work*; and two collections of essays, *The Canadian Economy and Its Problems*, edited by H.A. Innis and A.F.W. Plumptre; and *Canada's Unemployment Problem*, edited by L. Richter. Irving Brecher has explored *Monetary and Fiscal Thought and Policy in Canada 1919–1939*, and Douglas Owram sheds light on ideas about the Canadian state in his recent *The Government Generation*. The early pages of J.L. Granatstein's *The Ottawa Men* are also helpful. In *Maturing in Hard Times*, Robert B.

Bryce offers a valuable personal account of the Department of Finance in the Depression.

Good provincial histories that contain material on the Depression include Margaret Ormsby's *British Columbia*, John Archer's *Saskatchewan*, and W.L. Morton's *Manitoba*. Gerald Friesen's recent *The Canadian Prairies* provides a fine synthesis. Robert Rumilly's *Histoire de la province de Québec*, vols. 32 through 37, must be read critically. Ontario and the Atlantic provinces lack single volume histories that deal at much length with the Depression, although Joseph Schull's *Ontario Since 1867* is of some value.

H.B. Neatby's *The Politics of Chaos* offers a short overview of the politics of the 1930s; the two volumes that he has contributed to the biography of *William Lyon Mackenzie King* provide much valuable detail. Other books that shed light on politics include J.R.H. Wilbur's biography of H.H. Stevens, his booklet *The Bennett Administration*, and his documentary collection, *The Bennett New Deal*. There is as yet no good biography of R.B. Bennett, but a Ph.D. thesis completed for York University by Larry Glassford, "Canadian Conservatism in Crisis," deals with the Conservative Party during the Bennett years (1927–1938). Alvin Finkel's *Businessmen and Reform in the Thirties* casts a critical eye on business responses to the Bennett "New Deal" and related matters. Marc La Terreur's *Les Tribulations des conservateurs au Québec* and Andrée Lévesque's *Virage à gauche interdit* offer good insight into Quebec politics, as does H.F. Quinn's *The Union Nationale*. Conrad Black's *Duplessis* is rather too admiring in its view of the Quebec premier but needs to be consulted.

The Politics of Discontent, edited by Ramsay Cook, contains four articles on federal and provincial politics. Cook is also the author of *The Politics of John W. Dafoe and the Free Press*, which devotes a fair number of pages to the politics and economics of the 1930s. The CCF is ably discussed in Walter Young's *The Anatomy of a Party*. Gerald Caplan, in *The Dilemma of Canadian Socialism*, and J.T. Morley, in *Secular Socialists*, provide information on the Ontario CCF in the 1930s; Nelson Wiseman, in *Social Democracy in Manitoba*, does likewise for the CCF in that province. Seymour Martin Lipset's *Agrarian Socialism*, a study of the CCF in Saskatchewan, has good material on the 1930s. Its assessment of the party during those years, however, must be corrected by the insights of Peter Sinclair, notably in the *Canadian Historical Review* of December 1973. Dorothy Steeves, in her biography of Ernest Winch, *Compassionate Rebel*, offers a first-hand account of the history of the CCF in British Columbia. Kenneth McNaught has, in *A Prophet in Politics*, contributed a fine biography of the CCF's first national leader, J.S. Woodsworth. David Lewis's *The Good Fight* has several chapters of reminiscences about the CCF during the Depression years. Frank R. Scott's *A New Endeavour* is a selection from his political writings, almost a third of them from the 1930s. Michiel Horn's *The League for Social Reconstruction* deals with the CCF's "brain trust," of which both Lewis and Scott were founders.

Norman Penner's *The Left in Canada* is good on the Communist Party; more recently he has completed *Canadian Communism*. Ivan Avakumovic has contributed *The Communist Party in Canada*. Donald Avery's *"Dangerous Foreigners": European Immigrant Workers and Labour Radicalism in Canada 1896–1932* discusses the links between the party and immigrant workers as well as the hostility of many Canadians against both. *Yours in the Struggle*, the reminiscences of Communist Party leader Tim Buck as edited by William Beeching and Phyllis Clarke, is entertaining but not very reliable. Lita-Rose Betcherman's *The Little Band* is a lively account of the conflict between the CPC and the authorities in the late 1920s and early 1930s. Her book *The Swastika and the Maple Leaf* is better as a study of anti-semitism than as a history of Canadian fascism in the 1930s. Jonathan Wagner discusses National Socialism in Canada in *Brothers Beyond the Sea*.

John Irving's *The Social Credit Movement in Alberta* is still useful, although Alvin Finkel's recent work on this subject, as in the Summer 1986 issue of *Prairie Forum*, augurs well for the book he is preparing. Neil McKenty's *Mitchell Hepburn* illuminates the career of Ontario's maverick Liberal premier while telling us a good deal about Ontario during the Depression. No similar book exists for any Depression-era politician of the Atlantic provinces. Even Nova Scotia's Angus L. Macdonald still awaits a good biography. No doubt one reason for the relative lack of publications about the Maritimes during the Depression is that the region did not prosper during the 1920s to the degree that the rest of Canada did. The 1930s therefore did not constitute the startling contrast that they did in the west. Nevertheless times were hard, especially in Newfoundland. G.E. Panting provides a clear view of Newfoundland's economic and financial problems, leading to the loss of responsible government, in vol. 2 of *Documentary Problems in Canadian History*, edited by J.M. Bumsted. Also helpful are several chapters in S.J.R. Noel's *Politics in Newfoundland*.

In the form of books much less is available in social than in political history, and of business history there is less yet though there is some information in Michael Bliss's recent survey, *Northern Enterprise*. Among books dealing with individual business enterprises only William Kilbourn's *The Elements Combined*, a history of the Steel Company of Canada, has a really useful chapter on how the company fared during the Depression years. Volume 5 in the *Readings in Canadian Social History* series, edited by Michael Cross and Gregory Kealey, contains several articles that deal in part with the 1930s. The problems of education during the Depression have not received the attention they deserve, but several excellent university historians have given due attention to how these institutions fared during the 1930s, among them John Reid's *Mount Allison University*, vol. 2; Frederick W. Gibson's *Queen's University*, vol. 2; Charles M. Johnston's *McMaster University*, vol. 2; and Michael Hayden's *Seeking a Balance*, a history of the University of Saskatchewan.

One recent important book which straddles social, business and political history is *"No Fault of Their Own": Unemployment and the Canadian Welfare State 1914–1941* by James Struthers; it deals with unemployment as well as attitudes and policy towards it during the 1920s and 1930s. Dennis Guest's *The Emergence of Social Security in Canada* has a good chapter on the Depression. James Gray's *Men Against the Desert* is an excellent account of the Dustbowl. *The Wretched of Canada*, a somewhat overpowering selection of begging letters to R.B. Bennett edited by Linda M. Grayson and Michael Bliss, has a useful introduction. Stuart Jamieson's *Times of Trouble* has a long chapter on industrial conflict in the Depression. *On Strike*, edited by Irving Abella, contains three articles dealing with 1930s labour unrest; the early chapters of Abella's book *Nationalism, Communism, and Canadian Labour* are also helpful. Victor Howard's *"We Were the Salt of the Earth!"* is a lively history of the On-to-Ottawa Trek by relief camp strikers in 1935 and of the Regina Riot on Dominion Day of that year. Evelyn Dumas's *The Bitter Thirties in Quebec* tracks labour relations in that province.

Much of the work that has recently been done on the social history of the 1930s is available only in article form. Among the journals that should be consulted are *Acadiensis, Alberta History, Atlantis, BC Studies, Canadian Historical Review, Histoire sociale/Social History, Journal of Canadian Studies, Labour/Le Travail, Ontario History, Prairie Forum, Revue d'histoire de l'Amerique française, Saskatchewan History*, and *Urban History Review/Revue d'histoire urbaine*. The *Historical Papers* published annually by the Canadian Historical Association also constitute a fruitful source.

Several books of reminiscences and memoirs deserve to be mentioned. James Gray's *The Winter Years* is a splendidly evocative account of the Depression in the West and more particularly in Winnipeg. Ronald T. Liversedge has provided his *Recollections of the On-to-Ottawa Trek*; his editor, Victor Howard, has added a number of documents that shed further light on the relief camps and the Trek. Sydney Hutcheson's *Depression Stories* offer a spirited account of Depression life in the interior of British Columbia. Dorothy Livesay's *Right Hand, Left Hand* is also fascinating. The memoirs of Thérèse Casgrain, *A Woman in a Man's World* and even more those of Jean-Paul Desbiens ("Brother Anonymous"), *For Pity's Sake*, have chapters offering fine insight into Quebec during the Depression years. Barry Broadfoot's *Ten Lost Years*, a work of oral history, is interesting but flawed.

Mary Patricia Powell, "A Response to the Depression: The Local Council of Women of Vancouver," in *In Her Own Right: Selected Essays on Women's History in B.C.*, ed. Barbara Latham and Cathy Kess (Victoria, B.C.: Camosun College, 1980), 255-78. Reprinted by permission of the publisher.

John Herd Thompson and Allen Seager, "Workers, Growers and Monopolists: The 'Labour Problem' in the Alberta Beet Sugar Industry During the 1930s." Reprinted from *Labour/Le Travailleur* 3 (1978): 153-74, by permission of the editor. © Committee on Canadian Labour History.

T.J.D. Powell, "Northern Settlement, 1929-1935," *Saskatchewan History* 30, no. 3 (Autumn 1977): 81-98; Lorne A. Brown, "Unemployment Relief Camps in Saskatchewan, 1933-1936," *Saskatchewan History* 23, no. 3 (Autumn 1970): 81-104. Reprinted by permission of the Saskatchewan Archives Board and of the authors.

C. David Naylor, "Canada's First Doctors' Strike: Medical Relief in Winnipeg, 1932-4," *Canadian Historical Review* 67, no. 2 (1986): 151-80; James Struthers, "A Profession in Crisis: Charlotte Whitton and Canadian Social Work in the 1930s," *Canadian Historical Review* 62, no. 2 (1981): 169-85. Reprinted by permission of the authors and University of Toronto Press.

Dianne Dodd, "The Hamilton Birth Control Clinic of the 1930s," *Ontario History* 75, no. 1 (March 1983): 71-86. Reprinted by permission of the Ontario Historical Society.

Terry Copp, "Montreal's Municipal Government and the Crisis of the 1930s," in *The Usable Urban Past*, ed. Alan J. Artibise and Gilbert Stelter, Carleton Library Series, no. 119 (Macmillan for the Carleton Library, 1979), 112-29. Reprinted by permission of the author.

Wendy Johnston, "Keeping Children in School: The Response of the Montreal Catholic School Commission to the Depression of the 1930s," Canadian Historical Association, *Historical Papers* (1985): 193-217. Reprinted by permission of the author and the Canadian Historical Association.

Paul Axelrod, "Moulding the Middle Class: Student Life at Dalhousie University in the 1930s," *Acadiensis* 15, no. 1 (Autumn 1985): 84-122. Reprinted by permission of the journal.

John Taylor, "'Relief from Relief': The Cities' Answer to Depression Dependency," *Journal of Canadian Studies* 14, no. 1 (Spring 1979): 16-23; Michiel Horn, "The Great Depression: Past and Present," *Journal of Canadian Studies* 11, no. 1 (February 1976): 41-50. Reprinted by permission of the journal.

H. Blair Neatby, "The Liberal Way: Fiscal and Monetary Policy in the 1930s," in *The Great Depression: Essays and Memoirs from Canada and the United States* (Toronto: Copp Clark Ltd., 1969), 84-114. Reprinted with permission of the author.